The Greening of Trade Law

The Greening of Trade Law

International Trade Organizations and Environmental Issues

Edited by
Richard H. Steinberg

A Berkeley Roundtable on the International Economy (BRIE) Project

ROWMAN & LITTLEFIELD PUBLISHERS, INC.
Lanham • Boulder • New York • Oxford

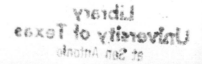

ROWMAN & LITTLEFIELD PUBLISHERS, INC.

Published in the United States of America
by Rowman & Littlefield Publishers, Inc.
4720 Boston Way, Lanham, Maryland 20706
www.rowmanlittlefield.com

12 Hid's Copse Road, Cumnor Hill, Oxford OX2 9JJ, England

British Library Cataloguing in Publication Information Available

Library of Congress Cataloging-in-Publication Data

The greening of trade law : international trade organizations and environmental issues / edited by Richard H. Steinberg.
    p.   cm.
   Includes bibliographical references and index.
   ISBN 0-7425-1045-X (cloth : alk. paper)—ISBN 0-7425-1046-8 (pbk. : alk. paper)
    1. Foreign trade regulation—Environmental aspects.   2. International trade—Environmental aspects.   3. Environmental law, International—Economic aspects.   4. Environmental protection—Economic aspects.   5. International agencies.   6. Non-governmental organizations.   I. Steinberg, Richard H., 1960–
   K3943 .G74   2001
   341.7′54—dc21   2001041688

Printed in the United States of America

♾ ™ The paper used in this publication meets the minimum requirements of American National Standard for Information Services—Permanence of Paper for Printed Library Materials, ANSI/NISO Z39.48-1992.

Contents

Acknowledgments

This book's origins are rooted in a series of conversations in the 1990–95 period on differences between the way various international trade organizations address environmental issues, on the explanations for those differences, and on the development of a U.S. strategy for handling trade-environment issues in international organizations. While working in the Office of the U.S. Trade Representative, I considered these questions as they were first unfolding in the U.S. public policy debate. In initial thinking about the questions, I benefited greatly from conversations with policymakers and dedicated civil servants who had a wealth of experience in trade, environmental, and agricultural policy, including Joshua Bolten, A. Jane Bradley, Ken Freiberg, Carla A. Hills, Julius Katz, Amelia Porges, and Chip Roh from the Office of the U.S. Trade Representative; Dick Crowder, Ann Veneman, and Clayton Yeutter from the Department of Agriculture; William Jordan and Stuart Nightingale from the Environmental Protection Agency; Marian Barell and Walter Batts from the Food and Drug Administration; and Catherine Copp from the Department of Health and Human Services. I was first exposed to European perspectives on the questions in memorable discussions with Helen Wallace, Frieder Roessler from the GATT secretariat, and European Commission negotiators Lars Hoelgaard and Jacques Vonthron.

In 1993, on joining the Berkeley Roundtable on the International Economy (BRIE), a University of California think tank, I drafted a paper that set forth my approach to these questions, and I received useful feedback from Jose Canela-Cacho, David Caron, Eileen Doherty, Lloyd Gruber, Robert Kagan, Steve Krasner, David Vogel, Lyuba Zarsky, and John Zysman. The essence of that analysis has endured to frame all my subsequent work on trade-environment issues, including a 1997 article on the subject that was published in the *American Journal of International Law* (*AJIL*) and my analysis in the concluding chapter of this volume.

The idea of organizing a collaborative research project on these questions emerged after a 1994 conference held at the East-West Center in Honolulu and organized by the Nautilus Institute for Security and Sustainable Development, a Berkeley-based think tank. That conference brought together academics from several disciplines, policymakers from several governments, business leaders from throughout Asia-Pacific, and environmental activists from several countries to analyze how trade-environment issues were being handled in the Asia-Pacific region. By the end of the conference, at least three things were clear: There were big differences in the way that trade-environment issues were being addressed in Asia-Pacific trade-related regimes—such as APEC, ASEAN, and NAFTA; there was great interest in understanding why; and radically different approaches to those questions resulted in analysts often talking past one another.

On the basis of those insights, Nautilus Institute Codirector Lyuba Zarsky and I (on behalf of BRIE) organized a collaborative project with Bruce Stokes, senior fellow and director of trade programs at the Council on Foreign Relations, and Stewart Hudson, vice president of the National Wildlife Federation (NWF), to explore how trade-environment issues were being addressed in different international trade organizations. Rodrigo Prudencio later assumed responsibility for coordinating NWF's involvement in the project. Two successive assistant U.S. trade representatives for the environment and natural resources, Chris Marcich and Jennifer Haverkamp, provided useful input on the project's design and suggestions for good participants. In 1996, The Pew Charitable Trusts awarded a generous grant to these four organizations to collaborate in research on how environmental rules were developing in different international trade organizations and to convene four national roundtable meetings to consider trade-environment rule development in the World Trade Organization, Asia-Pacific, the Americas, and the trans-Atlantic contexts, respectively. Those meetings were held in 1997 and 1998 in Washington, D.C., San Francisco, and Los Angeles. The logistics for these meetings were facilitated by Ann Mine, Noriko Katagari, and Marybeth Schubert from BRIE; Atziri Ibanez from the NWF; and Jason Hunter from the Nautilus Institute. Papers were commissioned from scholars and leaders of environmental NGOs for presentation at each meeting. Some of the contributions to this book grew out of the more than twenty-five papers presented at these meetings. The other contributions were collected to offer other geographic or theoretical perspectives.

During the course of developing and writing my contributions to the book, and editing it, I benefited greatly from the input of many of those mentioned previously as well as Jody Freeman, Kal Raustiala, reviewers of my *AJIL* article (Detlev Vagts and two anonymous referees), and several anonymous reviewers of the book manuscript. The dedicated research assistance of UCLA law students Lorenzo Alvarado, Sayema Hameed, and Michael Stransky was helpful and appreciated. Linda O'Connor, the de facto international law librarian at UCLA, provided invaluable assistance, finding hard-to-get foreign and international legal materials. Ellis Green, my secretary, always provided reliable and timely logistical and administrative support. And my wife, Diane H. Steinberg, provided constant moral support and intellectual input.

I also appreciate the hard work and patience of the editors and staff at Rowman & Littlefield. Executive Editor Susan McEachern and her assistant Matthew Hammon cheerfully provided useful input, editorial assistance, and good anonymous reviews. Assistant Managing Editor Janice Braunstein coordinated a smooth-running production process. And Bruce Owens's attention to detail during the copyediting process improved the manuscript.

Finally, I am indebted to BRIE Codirectors Michael Borrus, Stephen S. Cohen, and John Zysman, who backed the project in every way possible from the early days of its inception to its completion.

Richard H. Steinberg
Los Angeles, California
March 2001

1

Understanding Trade and the Environment: Conceptual Frameworks

Richard H. Steinberg

The so-called trade and the environment or trade-environment set of issues has been a hot topic of public policy and scholarly debate in the United States for more than a decade. Before the late 1980s, the U.S. government had recognized a potential link between trade and environmental protection,[1] and some environmental issues occasionally appeared on the U.S. government's trade policy agenda, usually in the context of disputes at the General Agreement on Tariffs and Trade (GATT)[2] as to whether particular trade-related actions were bona fide safety measures or disguised barriers to trade.[3] But trade-environment issues did not emerge as a priority of U.S. trade policy until 1988, when agribusiness leaders complained that sanitary and phytosanitary measures (particularly in Europe) were being used as thinly disguised barriers to several hundred million dollars of U.S. exports. The issues really heated up in the U.S. public policy debate in 1991, when environmentalists responded unfavorably to a dispute settlement decision and a draft negotiating text relating to the environment that emerged from the GATT.[4] Some trade negotiators and government officials hoped the issues would die, but they did not. On establishment of the World Trade Organization (WTO), the organizational successor to the GATT, the U.S. government and the European Commission demanded and succeeded in establishing a WTO Committee on Trade and the Environment (CTE). By the late 1990s, WTO members were attempting to implement several dispute settlement decisions that bear on the environment.[5] And, at the 1999 WTO ministerial meeting in Seattle, protesting environmentalists made it clear that the issues were not going to die anytime soon, while diplomats deadlocked over the extent to which environmental issues should be addressed in a new round of multilateral trade negotiations.[6]

Trade disputes and negotiations have increasingly engaged many powerful nongovernmental organizations (NGOs) in the United States, Europe, and elsewhere. Environmentalists and labor union leaders have been concerned that falling international trade barriers, as well as international trade organizations associated with free trade, are undermining environmental protection. They have argued that free trade and liberal investment rules are providing opportunities and incentives for investment to relocate in countries with lax environmental regulation, creating downward pressure on environmental regulations globally—what some have called a "race to the bottom."[7] They also have been concerned that the world's trade ministers have been negotiating new international rules and establishing new international processes that are degrading national environmental regulations in the name of free trade.

As NGOs embraced the issues, they became prominent in U.S. domestic politics. In the 1992 U.S. presidential election, candidate Bill Clinton accused President George Bush of ignoring the environment in trade negotiations. Trade-environment issues were among the most important in the 1993 debate over congressional approval of the North American Free Trade Agreement (NAFTA) and again in the 1994 debate over congressional approval of the GATT/WTO agreements. And, from 1995 through at least 2000, the U.S. Congress and the president were deadlocked over the extent to which the president's trade negotiating authority should include environmental issues.

As detailed in the chapters in this volume, trade and the environment issues have been important in other international trade fora as well. Members of the European Community (EC)—and now the European Union (EU)—have argued for over thirty years about the extent to which national environmental regulations should be harmonized in Brussels. Ministers from the NAFTA member states and NAFTA-related institutions continuously grapple with environmental measures and enforcement in the three North American countries. Heads of state from all the Western Hemisphere countries have met annually for six years to discuss the extent to which environmental issues should be addressed in negotiations for a Free Trade Area of the Americas (FTAA). Members of the Asia Pacific Economic Cooperation forum (APEC) debate the issues, and the International Organization for Standardization (ISO), which is dominated by business interests, has recently adopted its own approach that it purports will improve the environment.

Finally, in academia, public policy scholars, law school professors, political scientists, economists, business school professors, and environmental scientists debate the issues from varying perspectives. For example, employing a largely economic perspective, some scholars champion "regulatory competition"[8] and free trade. Other scholars focus instead on the need to remedy externalities and to avoid a potential "race toward the bottom" associated with regulatory competition as international economic integration deepens.[9] Some political scientists predict simply that the trade-environment issues are "spillovers" that will naturally find their way onto the trade negotiating agenda.[10] Other scholars argue that powerful, affluent countries will use their power to compel less powerful, poorer countries into raising their environmental standards.[11] Still others suggest that business interests dominate the trade agenda in affluent countries and that environmentalists are largely excluded from participation at the international level.[12]

This volume compares how each of the world's major international trade organizations addresses environmental issues. Understanding this range of behavior will help shed light on crucial questions of policy and theory. How are trade-environment issues being addressed in different geographic and historical contexts? Have trade-environment rules become more or less environment-friendly as economic integration has deepened in international fora? What meaningful roles, if any, may be played by NGOs in the process of trade-environment rule development? To what extent do the institutional rules and procedures of each international trade organization shape the development of trade-environment rules? The different analytical approaches employed in this volume will help shed light on why there are contested answers to these questions and why environmentalists, business leaders, government negotiators, and scholars often seem to be talking past one another. But, before examining the treatment of environmental issues in particular trade organizations, it will be useful to briefly distill the main trade-environment policies at stake and the primary analytical approaches used in the trade-environment debate.

THE MAIN TRADE-ENVIRONMENT POLICY ISSUES

What defines the set of trade-environment policy issues? There are, of course, many international environmental policy issues that are not usually considered part of the trade-environment debate—for example, the phaseout dates for specific ozone-depleting substances or policies bearing on nuclear dumping or acid rain. Moreover, there are some international policy issues—such as those bearing on food safety and animal welfare—that could be considered outside the realm of "environmental" policy but are nonetheless generally treated by policymakers as within the scope of trade-environment issues. While there have been many attempts to offer a clear definition of what should *logically* or does in fact fall within the scope of trade-environment issues, many such efforts have turned on the perspective of a particular discipline (e.g., legal, political, or environmental),[13] the perspective of a particular interest group (e.g., definitions offered by environmental NGOs versus those offered by business interests),[14] or perspectives from countries with different levels of economic development (e.g., developed versus developing countries).[15] Most definitions are therefore contested.

The scope of a particular public policy debate may be defined by the interests and perspectives of those individuals and societal groups engaging in it.[16] Therefore, the complete set of trade-environment issues may be defined inductively from empirical observation as an aggregation of every policy issue deemed a trade-environment issue by any individual or group engaging in political action and discourse—environmental NGOs, business interests, lawyers, economists, environmental scientists, or government officials, whether they are from developed or developing countries. The main trade-environment policy issues of the last decade may be classified into four categories, as described in the following sections.

Domestic Health, Safety, and Environmental Protection

International trade organizations grapple with the tension between free trade and the desire of national governments to maintain domestic health, safety, and environmental standards.[17] Environmentalists, consumer advocates, and labor unions often argue that liberalization increases the threat posed by imports to domestic health and safety standards, as imports with unsafe or dirty characteristics will face fewer trade barriers. To what extent may a country restrict imports for reasons related to protection of the environment within its territory?

Many who champion free trade are concerned that environmental regulations on international trade may be protectionist measures dressed up as "environmental" measures. Such measures may garner domestic political support from what Bruce Yandle and others have called "Baptist-bootlegger" coalitions of environmentalists and protectionists.[18] Trade-environment issues in the United States first attracted serious government attention in response to concerns over European trade measures that were supported by coalitions of protectionists and environmentalists. Specifically, the EC's Beef Hormones Directive,[19] which bans the European importation of beef from hormone-treated cattle, was perceived by the U.S. meat industry as a disguised barrier to trade. So was the EC's Third Country Meat Directive,[20] which bans the European importation of meat that was subject to a veterinary health inspection system that differs from Europe's.

While protectionists might have a hand in measures like these, most governments want to be able to ban the importation of goods embodying standards that do not meet their chosen level of domestic environmental protection. Most governments also want to be able to ban the importation of products embodying untested chemicals or genetically modified structures until they have finished scientific testing and analysis of the potential harm posed by those products to humans, animals, plants, and the environment. And most governments want to permit the eco-labeling of products so as to provide accurate and meaningful information to consumers about the potential environmental impacts of the products.

Extrajurisdictional Activity: Endangered Species, Foreign Pollution, and the "Race to the Bottom"

Many governments have expressed concern about activities affecting the environment that take place outside their jurisdiction.[21] For example, several U.S. statutes[22] and multilateral environmental agreements (MEAs) to which the United States is a signatory[23] are aimed at restoring populations of endangered or threatened species, or managing populations of other species, that inhabit territories outside the United States by means that affect the activities of persons who are not U.S. nationals. And some of those statutes and MEAs require parties to impose import restrictions or prohibitions on specified products—for example, those derived from some endangered species. Moreover, some U.S. environmentalists, labor unions, economists, and policy analysts are concerned about lax environmental standards in jurisdictions outside the United States, not only for moral reasons or because of associated externalities (e.g., resulting environmental degradation in the United States or in the global commons) but also because of fear that economic processes will combine with those lax standards to exert downward pressure on U.S. environmental standards.[24] Specifically, some environmentalists, economists, and policy analysts are concerned that goods will tend to be produced in and imported from countries imposing less stringent production and processing methods (PPMs) because ceteris paribus goods are less expensive to produce under such conditions; some fear that such a phenomenon could cause industrial flight to such countries and place downward pressure on the stringency of environmental rules worldwide—a "race to the bottom."[25] From that perspective, liberalization increases the probability that production will locate in poorer countries with less stringent environmental standards since liberalization means that goods produced there will face lowered barriers to their export into wealthier, greener countries.

At the same time, perhaps the most fundamental international legal and political principle—sovereignty—suggests that states have the exclusive right to control activities within their own jurisdiction.[26] This principle has been used to argue that a country may not restrict the importation of a product on the basis that it was made in a jurisdiction that requires less stringent PPMs.[27] Most developing country governments fear that affluent countries may use extrajurisdictional measures to effectively coerce them into raising their environmental standards to levels that will interfere with their economic development. Moreover, it has been suggested that compliance with some MEAs that require the imposition of trade restrictions might—under some circumstances—contravene the GATT.[28]

Transboundary Remediation

In the context of international trade negotiations or within international trade organizations, member states may agree to undertake or finance environmental cleanup projects, often in border areas or shared waterways but sometimes also across the entire territories of member states. Liberalization increases concerns about border-area environmental degradation as more people and goods travel through the border region and as trade creation combines with consideration of transportation costs to yield the establishment of more industries in border regions.

Trade-Environment Institutions

To varying degrees, international trade organizations create or modify existing institutions to perform functions relating to environmental issues. Various administrative, legislative, judicial, or advisory bodies may be granted legal competence to address, monitor, or adjudicate environmental issues, and various parties (e.g., member-state governments, political parties, NGOs, and scientific or technical advisers) may be granted standing to participate in those processes. Banks may be established to finance environment-related projects, such as remediation. As liberalization increases the salience of the foregoing trade-environment concerns, it also raises the question of whether institutions are constituted to perform appropriate functions. And, as these institutions begin to address environmental issues, questions are raised as to whether the institutions permit enough direct participation by interested NGOs and civil society more broadly.[29]

These four categories of trade-environment issues are not exhaustive. Some environmentalists worry that the rapid pace of trade liberalization may be undermining the principle of "sustainable development"[30] and facilitating a greater global scale of consumption, which will not be good for the environment.[31] Some focus on reducing tariffs on "green" products and technologies.[32] Some focus on reducing logging and fishing subsidies.[33] And some argue that intellectual property protection should be extended to indigenous species of plants and animals used in pharmaceutical products and that this is a trade-environment issue.[34] While there may be a seemingly endless list of trade-environment issues, the four issues described in the previous sections have persisted continuously at the heart of the trade-environment policy debate for the last decade.

THREE APPROACHES TO POLITICAL ANALYSIS OF THE DEVELOPMENT OF TRADE-ENVIRONMENT RULES IN INTERNATIONAL TRADE ORGANIZATIONS

The logic of the problem defined in each of the four previous sections suggests that as trade liberalization deepens in an international organization, the trade-environment debate will become more pronounced. Liberalization may increase the salience of the trade-environment policy concerns, but that relationship neither fully explains nor fully predicts how environmental rules will develop in trade organizations. Understanding that development requires a political-economic theory about how international law develops in international trade organizations.

Three approaches, each corresponding to a theory of international relations, have dominated the international trade-environment policy and scholarly debates: realism, liberalism, and institutionalism.[35] Efforts to distill the attributes of each theoretical approach, and drawing sharp lines between approaches, usually engenders criticism from those within one school or another, simply because the precise scope of each of these theories is contested. Theorists often like to claim as much turf as they can, subsuming a broad set of concepts and causal arguments within their favored theoretical approach so as to maximize its explanatory power. The scope of concepts and causal arguments subsumed within a single theory should be limited by several factors, including the need to maintain parsimony, internal consistency and coherence, and, some argue, consistency with the intellectual history of the approach. One result is an ongoing turf battle over what concepts, causal arguments, and approaches should be included in one theory or another.[36]

Nonetheless, a description of the approaches helps clarify the concepts, assumptions, and essential causal relationships used by those engaging in the trade-environment debate. Moreover, description of the three approaches elucidates both the essence and the nuances of particular trade-environment arguments, including those in this volume. While many analysts employ a combination of concepts and theoretical arguments so that their analyses do not fit easily into one of the theoretical traditions identified here, clear analyses tend to emphasize a causal argument that rests within one of the three theoretical traditions. And descriptions of these alternative approaches may facilitate improved communication among those engaging in the trade-environment debate.

Realist Arguments: The Primacy of State Power

Realist international relations theory (which is distinct from the early twentieth-century legal realism movement in the United States) offers explanations of and predictions about a broad range of international phenomena.[37] Realist theory of international law, which may be seen as part of realist international relations theory, emphasizes the role of state power in determining international law and international outcomes. States pursue their interests by bringing their power to bear on international negotiations.[38] The most powerful states get their way. For that reason, international law and international outcomes reflect the interests of powerful states. For the most hardened structural realists, international law is epiphenomenal: It does not independently explain international outcomes.[39] International law may have some independent explanatory value for more traditional, neoclassical realists,[40] but even these analysts are usually more interested in explaining how power and interests shape the development of international law than how international law independently affects outcomes. Hence, most realist explanations of international law focus on the distributive consequences of international negotiations—and how powerful states have advanced their interests.[41] Realist predictions center on the kind of international legal developments that may be expected as power disperses or concentrates in particular international organizational or historical contexts[42] or as the interests of powerful states change.[43] And realist prescriptions tend to focus on the kinds of legal-political maneuvers that states may use to advance their interests.[44]

Defining state "interests" presents a crucial challenge for realist analyses of international law development. Interests are generally exogenous to the realist model; structural realist theory assigns no interests to the state, except for survival and a few other basic interests that may be deduced from the power structure of the international system.[45] Some other theory, observation, or assumption about interests is necessary to supplement any "pure" realist analysis of the development of international law. One of the more common approaches is to join the realist international argument with a liberal domestic political model of national preference formation.[46] The result of that approach is a "two-level"[47] explanation of international law development: a domestic political story about how state interests are defined and an international story about how powerful states secure the adoption of international rules that reflect their interests. But even for those using that two-level approach, the international story is a realist one—a story about power.

Similarly, operationalizing state "power" poses another challenge to realists. Defining power has been a persistent problem for anyone interested in politics, but power is defined by many as the ability to get others to do what they otherwise would not do.[48] Measuring it is another problem. Some realists have evaluated state power in the aggregate, considering total military and economic might in order to classify countries as a "great power" or not.[49] But in a specific negotiating context, like trade negotiations, in which only some dimensions of power are likely to be brought to bear, the measure of power must be more tailored. In analyzing trade negotiations, many realists consider market size—the capacity to open or close a market—as a good proxy for power.[50] In this view, the United States and the EU— the world's two largest markets—have the greatest power in negotiations over international trade law.

Many of the chapters in this volume employ realist arguments at the heart of their explanations about the development of environmental rules in international trade organizations. In chapter 7, Sanford Gaines argues that environment rules in the FTAA should and will differ from those in the NAFTA because the United States has less power in the hemisphere than it did over Mexico in the NAFTA talks, U.S. interests in the hemispheric environment differ from its interests in the North American environment, and continuing post-NAFTA internal divisions in the United States will constrain its government negotiators in the FTAA environmental negotiations. Some other contributors use realist arguments centrally, but not exclusively, to explain the development of environmental rules in trade organizations. In chapter 5, Damien Geradin argues that the power and demands of the more affluent northern European countries go a long way in explaining why the EU's environmental rules are generally environment-friendly. In chapter 8, Lyuba Zarsky explains the lack of progress on environmental issues in APEC as due largely to wide differences in state interests and the dispersed structure of state power in the organization. And in the book's concluding chapter, Richard Steinberg argues that the environment-friendliness of rules in international trade organizations depends largely on the extent of northern power in the organization, as well as the extent of integration in the organization (since the salience of trade-environment issues in northern countries is directly related to the extent of integration) and the geographic scope of the organization (since the salience of environmental externalities and other environmental concerns dissipates as geographic scope increases). While two-level analyses are common to many of these explanations, in all of them the development of international trade-environment rules may be seen primarily as a story about the power and interests of the negotiating states.

Institutional Arguments: The Primacy of Institutional Rules and Processes

A second analytical approach emphasizes how institutional rules and processes generate outcomes. Many of these arguments take a rationalist form:[51] States are treated as rational, self-interested, egoistic agents. One insight of rationalist approaches is that without institutions, states find cheating to be attractive and cooperation difficult; institutions can reduce the attractiveness of cheating and increase the attractiveness of cooperation.[52] More broadly, these arguments assert that institutions can solve market failures, reduce transactions costs or information costs, and thereby solve cooperation problems.[53]

Other institutionalist arguments take a more sociological form. These arguments often suggest that human action is driven by a "logic of appropriateness" and identity; in this view, institutional rules, identities, and scripts shape roles, judgments, and purpose.[54] Arguments from this perspective offer perhaps the most dominant approach to explaining compliance with and the effectiveness of international law.[55]

While most institutionalist arguments focus on how institutional rules and processes affect behavior and outcomes, institutionalist arguments may also be used to help explain the development of rules. For example, for rationalist-institutionalists, the rules' facilitation of preferred cooperative outcomes may be seen as functions favored by the states that generate the rules.[56] And from the sociological perspective, rules and identities are regulative but are themselves shaped by social interaction and experience that must be understood in their institutional context.[57]

Most of the institutional arguments in this volume take rules and procedures as given and explore the opportunities, incentives, and roles they create for behavior by states, NGOs, and individuals. For example, in chapter 3, Gustavo Grunbaum shows that the WTO's substantive rules, dispute settlement procedures, and dispute settlement decisions have declared that four U.S. statutes, enacted as a result of pressure on Congress from U.S. Baptist-bootlegger (environmentalist-protectionist) coalitions, violate WTO rules. He contends that WTO institutions are functioning as a check on U.S. environmental statutes supported by such coalitions: International law is serving as a check on domestic politics. In chapter 5, in addition to realist arguments, Geradin shows that the EU's decision-making rules and regulatory techniques conceived by the European Commission have made it possible to achieve more environmental regulatory harmonization in Europe than otherwise could have taken place. For example, instead of complete harmonization of environmental regulations across Europe, derogations for particular EC member states and regulatory "floors" have been crucial techniques in a process of "approximating" European environmental regulations. And in chapter 6, Julie Soloway argues that in NAFTA both the national treatment rules and the regulatory techniques relating to the environment are resulting in greater economic efficiency in North America—Pareto improvement that otherwise would not occur.

Liberal Arguments: The Primacy of Nongovernmental and Transgovernmental Actors

A third tradition argues that nongovernmental and transgovernmental activity is key to understanding the development of the substantive rules of international organizations. For most liberals, politics must be understood from the "bottom up," with an array of domestic societal interests considered prior to or simultaneous with international politics. Domestic politics is a competition among individuals and organized interests with varying societal influence. The state is not an actor but a "transmission belt" that represents the interests of a subset of domestic society at the international level. This is not to say that the state is irrelevant to liberalism: Perhaps most important, for example, the structure of state institutions affects the process and outcome of domestic societal competition.[58] But liberal arguments (in contrast to some realist arguments)[59] do not usually treat the state as defining the national interest independent of a domestic competition among societal actors.[60]

There is a variety of liberal arguments about what happens at the international level. For some liberals, the state plays a central role at the international level. What some have called "structural liberalism" suggests a two-level analysis[61] of international outcomes, simultaneously considering stories at the domestic politics level and at the interstate level. For these analysts, the nature of interstate activity—the extent to which it is conflictual or cooperative—depends on underlying state preferences. To the extent that these structural liberal explanations of negotiation at the international level depend on relative state power, structural liberalism sees state power as a function of national will (i.e., not as a function of national capacity)—and national will depends mostly on domestic politics.[62] Hence, for structural liberals, states may be meaningful analytic entities at the international level, but domestic politics and the activity of nongovernmental and transgovernmental actors are key to understanding international outcomes.

For some other liberals, particularly those who adhere to what might be called "transnational liberalism," transnational actors participate directly and decisively in the development of international rules, with states playing a role of limited explanatory significance. For example, in some issue areas, interactions between transgovernmental actors, professionals from international organizations, and other transnational actors such as scientists will sometimes develop an authoritative transnational epistemic community, with shared norms about appropriate international rules and principles, shared causal beliefs, shared notions of validity and validation, and a common policy enterprise.[63] Neofunctionalists argue that as economic integration has deepened, societal interest groups have begun shifting their loyalties and focus of participation from national to transnational fora.[64] And some "soft" social construction theorists may be seen as liberals: Some of these theorists argue that transnational advocacy networks may effectively participate in international negotiations, shaping the normative and cognitive bases of the negotiating agenda, the development of legal rules, and increasing compliance with those rules.[65] In all these arguments, understanding the activity of nonstate actors (sometimes referred to as "civil society") and transgovernmental actors is central to understanding how international law develops: Interaction among nonstate and transgovernmental actors and direct participation by nonstate actors in international organizations and processes explain the development and content of international law.[66] These liberals often prescribe greater access for and direct participation by NGOs in international organizations. Some liberals suggest that such increased access and direct participation may result in a system of international law that is more complete and enjoys greater compliance than a more traditional, state-centric system.[67]

Several chapters in this volume contain liberal strains, although these liberal arguments are usually combined with realist or institutional factors to explain the development (or lack) of environmental rules in international organizations. For example, in chapter 2, James Cameron and Karen Campbell argue that the lack of transparency and few avenues for direct participation by nonstate actors in WTO activities have alienated many environmental NGOs into coalition with an NGO-led anti-globalization movement, forestalling any agreement in the CTE (and WTO more broadly) on trade-environment rules. In chapter 8, Lyuba Zarsky argues that ineffective transnational coordination of NGO activities and the exclusion of NGOs from direct participation in the APEC process help explain why APEC has made so little progress in developing environmental rules. And in chapter 9, Naomi Roht-Arriaza argues that the "procedural approach" to environmental standards setting, which is embodied in the ISO 14000 series, resulted from the direct participation of business-dominated standards-setting organizations in the ISO standards development process. For each of these authors, the actions, omissions, or exclusion of nonstate actors in international rule-making processes are central to understanding the development of trade-environment rules.

THE LOGIC OF COMPARING THE DEVELOPMENT OF TRADE-ENVIRONMENT RULES ACROSS INTERNATIONAL TRADE ORGANIZATIONS

These different theoretical approaches offer fundamentally different explanations, predictions, and prescriptions about the development of trade-environment rules and the effects of those developments. For example, realists predict that environmental rules are likely to develop more quickly in regional fora, such as the EU and NAFTA, where green affluent countries (such as Germany and the United States, respectively) have great market power; conversely, they predict slower development of environment-friendly rules in global organizations like the WTO, where the power of green affluent countries is more dispersed. Realists would prescribe linking trade openness to more stringent environmental rules in those regional organizations in order to advance an environmental agenda. In contrast, some liberals predict that the environmental agenda will be advanced in those trade organizations in which transnational advocacy networks can frame issues, provide relevant information and draft legal rules for policymakers, and help monitor corporate environmental practices and environmental degradation. These liberals often prescribe more direct "democratic" participation by NGOs in international trade negotiations and dispute settlement. Institutionalists offer still a different view, with some predicting that the environmentalist agenda in trade organizations will advance most effectively where trade organization secretariats learn regulatory techniques that account for variance in member-state regulatory styles and needs, and these institutionalists prescribe the use of those techniques.

By using these theoretical lenses to compare how trade-environment rules are developing in different international organizations and by empirical examination of the rules and their histories, we can better understand the extent to which trade organizations are addressing environmental issues, the contexts in which they are doing so, and the alternative approaches by which environmental issues are being addressed. Moreover, we can better understand various perspectives on trade-environment issues, why interlocutors on the topic often seem to be talking past each other, and rationales for the range of policy prescriptions being offered.

Consistent with those objectives, this volume evaluates the development of trade-environment rules across a broad scope of international trade organizations. For purposes of understanding the broad range of trade-environment issues and how they are playing out in different contexts, "international trade organizations" is defined broadly. For example, the cases considered in this volume include the EU, which began as a customs union but has evolved into something much more; negotiation of the FTAA, which has not yet been concluded and has few *formal* organizational attributes; and ISO, which is not typically considered a *trade* organization.

While the scope of trade organizations studied in this volume is broad, the list of cases studied is necessarily incomplete. This book covers all the world's trade organizations that have developed environment-friendly "hard law" (i.e., binding obligations) and covers the world's largest trade organizations,[68] but it cannot cover all the world's trade organizations. There has been a proliferation of regional trade organizations in the world; there are now more than fifty. Case studies of all international trade organizations would be both impractical and unnecessary for the purposes of this volume. Two main criteria were used for case selection. First, as this volume is intended partly for use by those interested in U.S. policy, the cases were selected to cover all the major trade organizations in or to which the United States is (or is negotiating to be) a member, party, or participant. Second, given that one of the volume's primary goals is to explain variation in the development of trade-environment rules in the world's trade organizations, a primary methodological requirement is to cover cases along a continuum of trade-environment rule development, ranging from organizations that have developed a broad and deep set of rules, norms, and institutions relating to trade-environment issues to those that have developed none (or almost none). Therefore, the EU is included: As seen through the case studies and the conclusion to this volume, among the world's trade organizations, the EU has developed the broadest and deepest rules and institutions relating to trade and the environment issues. At the other end of the spectrum, there are many trade organizations with weak trade-environment rule development;[69] for the purposes of this volume, APEC was chosen for study since it has weak trade-environment rule development and meets the first criterion (i.e., the United States is a member).

ORGANIZATION AND OVERVIEW OF THE BOOK

Part I examines trade-environment rules in the world's multilateral trade organization: the GATT/WTO system. Three chapters offer two essentially liberal arguments and one institutionalist approach. In chapter 2, Cameron and Campbell summarize WTO rules relating to the environment and then offer a fundamentally liberal explanation for the stalemate in WTO trade-environment discussions: The interest groups that are driving interstate negotiations at the WTO cannot agree—free trade–oriented business interests from both developed and developing countries are clashing with environmentalists and antiglobalization forces that perceive themselves as shut out of WTO processes. In chapter 3, Grunbaum offers an essentially institutionalist analysis of WTO dispute settlement cases against the United States relating to trade-environment: These rulings are serving as a check on the U.S. trade-environment legislative process. And in chapter 4, Shaffer offers a two-level intergovernmentalist account of the development of WTO trade-environment rules, which has a decidedly liberal slant on the slow development of trade-environment rules in the WTO: The United States and the EU, which are the most powerful *demandeurs* of such rule development, each suffer from internal political divisions and transatlantic differences that sap their will to act more decisively and cooperatively in Geneva.

Part II considers how trade-environment issues have been handled in some of the world's regional trade organizations: the EU, NAFTA, the nascent FTAA, and APEC.

Part III considers a single trade-related international organization in which the private sector formally drives negotiations and rule making: the ISO. The politics, legal competence, and outcomes on environmental issues in this organization differ from those of the other organizations considered in this volume.

The volume concludes in Part IV with comparison of the extent of environment-friendly rule development across international trade organizations. There is wide variance in the extent to which these trade organizations have adopted environment-friendly rules, ranging from those with stringent environmental rules and highly developed associated institutions (such as the EU) to those with no environmental rule development (such as APEC). What explains the differences? Trade-environment policies become more salient to environmentalists and labor unions with each round of deeper liberalization, so affluent states seek the development of green rules and institutions as part of deep liberalization packages. Moreover, since the concentration of trade-environment externalities (i.e., the environmental and political-economic externalities associated with divergence in environmental standards across countries) generally increase with geographic proximity, trade-environment linkages are more salient the smaller the geographic scope of a trade organization. But salience is only part of the story: Realism is needed to explain how the preferences of affluent states are translated into trade-environment rules. Green affluent countries have used their asymmetrical bargaining power and threats to exit an organization (or a negotiation) to drive the development of environment-friendly trade rules. Ceteris paribus, the more dispersed the concentration of affluent-country power in an organization, the slower the development of environment-friendly rules. In the WTO, where the power of affluent states is low and diminishing over time, environment-friendly rules have not developed extensively and are not likely to develop quickly in the future. This incapacity of affluent states to successfully negotiate the development of trade-environment rules in the WTO does not bode well for reestablishing in affluent countries a broad domestic consensus favoring deeper multilateral liberalization.

NOTES

1. For example, in November 1971, the U.S. government supported a consensus Decision of the GATT Council to Establish a Group on Environmental Measures and International Trade (available at <http://www.wto.org/english/tratope/hist1e.htm>, June 20, 2000).

2. General Agreement on Tariffs and Trade, October 30, 1947, Article XX(b), (g), TIAS No. 1700, 55 UNTS 187 (hereafter GATT).

3. For example, in the mid-1980s, the U.S. government consulted with the government of Japan, pursuant to GATT Article XXII, over Japanese restrictions on the importation of oranges, which had been banned or subject to long periods of quarantine, resulting in spoilage allegedly because of phytosanitary concerns. GATT Document L/6037. This dispute was joined with U.S. complaints over Japanese restrictions on beef imports, and the two disputes were settled in 1988. See Japanese-U.S. Exchange of Letters on Beef and Citrus, July 5, 1988, 27 I.L.M. 1539 (1988). See also Amelia Porges, "Japan: Beef & Citrus," in Thomas O. Bayard and Kimberly Ann Elliott, eds., *Reciprocity and Retaliation in U.S. Trade Policy* (Washington, D.C.: Institute for International Economics, 1994), 233. Similarly, in the late 1980s, the U.S. government held Article XXII consultations with the government of Korea and other

Asian governments over claims that apples of U.S. origin sprayed with alar posed health risks. See "Unfair Trade Practices: Policies of South Korea, Japan Lead List of Those Recommended for Super 301 Review," *International Trade Reporter* 7, no. 9 (Washington, D.C.: Bureau of National Affairs, February 28, 1990), 284, and "Agriculture: U.S. Grapefruit Sales to Korea, Taiwan, Diminish after Group Reports Alar Residues," *International Trade Reporter* 6, no. 30 (Washington, D.C.: Bureau of National Affairs, July 26, 1989), 982. See also "Thailand—Restrictions on Importation of and Internal Taxes on Cigarettes," Report of the Panel, GATT Document DS10/R, adopted on November 7, 1990, 37S/200.

4. Environmentalists reacted with alarm to two developments: (1) a dispute settlement decision ruling as GATT-inconsistent a U.S. statute restricting the importation of tuna from certain countries that did not require dolphin-friendly tuna-fishing methods and (2) leaked confidential drafts of the Agreement on the Application of Sanitary and Phytosanitary Measures (hereafter SPS Agreement), which was eventually concluded as part of the Uruguay Round agricultural negotiations. See "United States—Restrictions on Imports of Tuna," Report of the Panel, DS21/R (unadopted), dated September 9, 1991, 39S/155 (hereafter *Tuna I*), and Agreement on the Application of Sanitary and Phytosanitary Measures, April 15, 1994.

5. For example, "United States—Import Prohibition of Certain Shrimp and Shrimp Products, Report of the Appellate Body," WTO Document WT/DS58/AB/R, October 12, 1998, and World Trade Organization, European Communities—Measures concerning Meat and Meat Products (Hormones), WT/DS26/AB/R, WT/DS48/AB/R, January 16, 1998.

6. See Mark Felsenthal, Daniel Pruzin, and Gary G. Yerkey, "WTO Seattle Ministerial Fails: Talks to Resume at a Later Date," *International Trade Reporter* 16, no. 48: 1990.

7. Richard B. Stewart, "Pyramids of Sacrifice? Problems of Federalism in Mandating State Implementation of National Environmental Policy," *Yale Law Journal* 86, no. 6 (1977): 1196. See also Daniel C. Esty and Damien Geradin, "Regulatory Co-Opetition," in *Regulatory Competition and Economic Integration: Comparative Perspectives* (New York: Oxford University Press, 2001).

8. See, generally, Charles Tiebout, "A Pure Theory of Local Expenditures," *Journal of Political Economy* 64, no. 5 (1956): 416. For more recent and largely domestic arguments, see Richard L. Revesz, "Federalism and Regulation: Some Generalizations," in Esty and Geradin, *Regulatory Competition and Economic Integration,* and Roberta Romano, "Empowering Investors: A Market Approach to Securities Regulation," *Yale Law Journal* 107, no. 8 (1998): 2359.

9. See, for example, Dan Esty and Damien Geradin, "Regulatory Co-Opetition," in *Regulatory Competition and Economic Integration.*

10. On spillovers, generally, see Ernst Haas, *The Uniting of Europe* (London: Stevens & Sons, 1958).

11. Richard H. Steinberg, "Trade-Environment Negotiations in the EU, NAFTA, and WTO: Regional Trajectories of Rule Development," *American Journal of International Law* 91, no. 2 (April 1997): 231–67. See also David Vogel, *Trading Up* (Cambridge, Mass.: Harvard University Press, 1995).

12. See, for example, David Wirth, "Public Participation in International Processes: Environmental Case Studies at the National and International Levels," *Colorado Journal of International Environmental Law and Policy* 7, no. 1 (1996): 1.

13. C. Ford Runge makes this point clearly in *Freer Trade, Protected Environment: Bal-*

ancing Trade Liberalization and Environmental Interests (New York: Council on Foreign Relations Books, 1994), 9–33.

14. Daniel Esty makes this point most clearly in *Greening the GATT* (New York: Council on Foreign Relations Press, 1994).

15. Compare, for example, the express and implicit definition of trade-environment problems in Peider Konz, ed., *Trade, Environment and Sustainable Development: Views from Sub-Saharan Africa and Latin America* (Tokyo: United Nations University Institute of Advanced Studies, 2000), with those in Office of the U.S. Trade Representative, "Trade and the Environment," in *2000 Trade Policy Agenda and 1999 Annual Report of the President of the United States on the Trade Agreements Program* (Washington, D.C.: USTR, 1999).

16. Liberal theory takes this as a starting point for analysis.

17. For more discussion of this topic, see Runge, *Freer Trade, Protected Environment,* esp. 15–19.

18. Bruce Yandle, "Bootleggers and Baptists—The Education of a Regulatory Economist," *Regulation,* May/June 1983, 12; Elizabeth R. DeSombre, "Baptists and Bootleggers for the Environment: The Origins of U.S. Unilateral Sanctions," *Journal of Environment and Development* 4, no. 1 (winter 1995): 53–75.

19. Council Directive 96/22/EC of April 29, 1996, concerning the Prohibition on the Use in Stockfarming of Certain Substances Having a Hormonal or Thyrostatic Action, 1996 O.J. L125, 3. This directive supersedes and repeals previous directives governing the topic, including Council Directive 81/602/EEC, 1981 O.J. L 222, 7; Council Directive 88/146/EEC, 1988 O.J. L 70, 16; and Council Directive 88/299/EEC, 1988 O.J. L 128, 21.

20. Council Directive 72/462/EEC of December 12,1972, on Health and Veterinary Inspection Problems upon Importation of Bovine, Ovine, and Caprine Animals and Swine, Fresh Meat or Meat Products from Third Countries, 1972 O.J. L 302, 28, as last amended by Directive 97/79/EC of December 18, 1997, 1998 O.J. L 24, 31.

21. "Extrajurisdictional" may be contrasted to "extraterritorial." The latter relates to the right to prescribe law, enforce law, and adjudicate conflict outside the *territory* of a particular state, whereas the former relates to the right to prescribe law, enforce law, and adjudicate conflict outside the *jurisdiction* of a particular state. The distinction makes a difference to the extent that a state generally has jurisdiction over activities of its own nationals and vessels even if those activities take place outside its territory. See, generally, The Restatement (Third) of Foreign Relations Law of the United States, esp. secs. 400–33. For more discussion of this point, see GATT, "United States—Restrictions on Imports of Tuna, Report of the Panel," GATT Document DS29/R (June 1994) (*Tuna II*), and WTO, "Report of the WTO Committee on Trade and the Environment," November 14, 1996, GATT Document PRESS/TE 014, esp. para. 7.

22. See, for example, African Elephant Conservation Act, Title II of the Endangered Species Act Amendments of 1988, P.L. 100–478; Marine Mammal Protection Act, 16 U.S.C. Sec. 1361 ff.; Pelly Amendment to the Fisherman's Protective Act, P.L. 92–219 (1971); and Sec. 609 of P.L. 101–62 (1989) (generally prohibits imports of shrimp or shrimp products "which have been harvested with commercial fishing technology that may affect adversely such species of sea turtles" protected under the U.S. Endangered Species Act).

23. See, for example, Convention on International Trade in Endangered Species of Wild Flora and Fauna. The WTO secretariat has identified twenty multilateral environmental agreements with trade provisions. See WTO, "Report of the Committee on Trade and the Environment," WTO Document PRESS/TE 014, November 14, 1996, para. 8.

24. See Esty and Geradin, "Regulatory Co-Opetition."

25. For more discussion of the "race to the bottom" and the associated "industrial flight" hypothesis, see Richard Stewart, "Pyramids of Sacrifice?" and Esty, *Greening the GATT.* See also C. Leigh Anderson and Robert A. Kagan, "Adversarial Legalism, Transaction Costs, and the Industrial Flight Hypothesis," *BRIE Working Paper No. 93* (Berkeley, Calif.: Berkeley Roundtable on the International Economy, 1997).

26. "Sovereignty" may be a contested concept, but the asserted principle is well supported in international law discourse. See, for example, Ian Brownlie, *Principles of Public International Law* (Oxford: Oxford University Press, 1998). There is a countervailing principle that states should refrain from activities that cause environmental damage across their border. "Trail Smelter Case, *United States v. Canada,* Arbitral Tribunal, 1941," *United Nations Reports of International Arbitral Awards* 3 (1949): 1905. But that principle has not generally been relevant or applied to conflicts over PPMs.

27. For example, this argument was advanced in *Tuna I.*

28. This debate is detailed in chapter 3.

29. See, generally, Aseem Prakash and Jeffrey A. Hart, eds., *Globalization and Governance* (New York: Routledge, 1999).

30. World Commission on Environment and Development, *Our Common Future* (Oxford: Oxford University Press, 1987).

31. See Steve Charnovitz, "Free Trade, Fair Trade, Green Trade: Defogging the Debate," *Cornell International Law Journal* 27, no. 3 (1994): 459–525.

32. For example, in November 1999, the U.S. government proposed negotiating on the elimination of barriers to trade in so-called clean technologies. International Centre for Trade and Sustainable Development, "Environment," *BRIDGES Weekly Trade News Digest* 3, no. 46 (November 24, 1999): 8.

33. For example, in November 1999, the U.S. government proposed negotiating on the elimination of subsidies that promote overfishing. International Centre for Trade and Sustainable Development, "Environment," *BRIDGES Weekly Trade News Digest* 3, no. 46 (November 24, 1999): 8.

34. See, for example, WTO Committee on Trade and the Environment, Report of the Meeting held on 21–22 June 1995, WTO Document WT/CTE/M/3, para. 21, Statement of the Representative from India.

35. This list of theories is not exhaustive. Economists, positivists, naturalists, and hard constructivists may all offer their analyses of the problem. But these other approaches do not lie at the center of the international trade-environment debate.

36. For example, Andrew Moravcsik alludes to these turf battles in his effort to formulate a clear theory of liberalism. Andrew Moravcsik, "Taking Preferences Seriously: A Liberal Theory of International Politics," *International Organization* 51, no. 4 (autumn 1997): 513–54. And Moravcsik's efforts have, in turn, been accused of "the equivalent of an unfriendly takeover in the business world." Peter D. Feaver, Gunther Hellman, et al., "Correspondence: Brother, Can You Spare a Paradigm? (Or Was Anybody Ever a Realist?)," *International Security* 25, no. 1 (summer 2000): 165–93.

37. For an excellent recent retrospective on realism, see Robert Jervis, "Realism in the Study of World Politics," *International Organization* 52, no. 4 (autumn 1998): 971–91.

38. See Hans J. Morgenthau, "Positivism, Functionalism, and International Law," *American Journal of International Law* 34, no. 2 (1940): 260–84.

39. See, for example, Susan Strange, "Cave! Hic dragones: A Critique of Regime Analysis," in Stephen D. Krasner, ed., *International Regimes* (Ithaca, N.Y.: Cornell University Press, 1983). See also Stanley Hoffman, "International Law and the Control of Force," in Stanley Hoffman and Karl Deutsch, eds., *The Relevance of International Law* (Garden City, N.Y.: Anchor Books, 1971).

40. See, for example, Hans J. Morgenthau, *Politics among Nations* (New York: Alfred A. Knopf, 1978), esp. 277–334.

41. See, for example, Stephen D. Krasner, "Global Communications and National Power: Life on the Pareto Frontier," *World Politics* 43, no. 3 (1991): 336.

42. See, for example, Kenneth Waltz, *Theory of International Politics* (Palo Alto, Calif.: Addison-Wesley, 1978).

43. See, generally, Stephen D. Krasner, *Sovereignty: Organized Hypocrisy* (Princeton, N.J.: Princeton University Press, 1999).

44. See, for example, Steinberg, "Trade-Environment Negotiations . . .," 266–67, and "The Prospects for Partnership: Overcoming Obstacles to Transatlantic Trade Policy Cooperation in Asia," in Richard H. Steinberg and Bruce Stokes, eds., *Partners or Competitors? The Prospects for U.S.-European Cooperation on Asian Trade* (Boulder, Colo.: Rowman & Littlefield, 1999).

45. See Waltz, *Theory of International Politics.*

46. There are several useful analyses that combine liberal state preferences, or liberal preference formation, with a realist model of politics at the international level. See, for example, Andrew Moravcsik, "Negotiating the Single European Act," *International Organization* 45, no. 1 (winter 1991): 19. See also Moravcsik, "Taking Preferences Seriously."

47. Robert Putnam has argued that trade negotiators must simultaneously play two "games," one at the international bargaining table and one with the legislative branch. Robert Putnam, "Diplomacy and Domestic Politics: The Logic of Two-Level Games," *International Organization* 42, no. 3 (summer 1988): 427. Negotiations on trade-environment issues may be seen as part of such a two-level game.

48. Robert Keohane and Joseph Nye, *Power and Interdependence* (Boston: Little, Brown, 1977), 11.

49. See, for example, Waltz, *Theory of International Politics,* 97–99.

50. See Steinberg, "Trade-Environment Negotiations . . . ," 232–33, and "Great Power Management of the World Trading System: A Transatlantic Strategy for Liberal Multilateralism," *Law and Policy in International Business* 29, no. 2 (winter 1998): 216–19. See also Albert Hirschman, *National Power and the Structure of Foreign Trade* (Berkeley and Los Angeles: University of California Press, 1945).

51. Some who have called themselves "liberal institutionalists" are dropping the term "liberal" from the concept and are referring to it as "rationalist institutionalism." See, for example, Helen V. Milner, "Rationalizing Politics: The Emerging Synthesis of International, American, and Comparative Politics," *International Organization* 52, no. 4 (autumn 1998): 759–86, and Moravcsik, "Taking Preferences Seriously," esp. 537. The categories of "rationalist-institutionalism" and "liberalism" in this chapter will be kept as distinct as possible for purposes of analytic clarity.

52. See, for example, Arthur Stein, *Why Nations Cooperate: Circumstance and Choice in International Relations* (Ithaca, N.Y.: Cornell University Press, 1990).

53. Robert Keohane, "The Demand for International Regimes," in Krasner, ed., *Interna-*

tional Regimes, 141–71; Robert Keohane, *After Hegemony* (Princeton, N.J.: Princeton University Press, 1984); Moravcsik, "Taking Preferences Seriously."

54. James G. March and Johan P. Olsen, "The Institutional Dynamics of International Political Orders," *International Organization* 52, no. 4 (autumn 1998): 943–69, and Martha Finnemore, "Norms, Culture, and World Politics: Insights from Sociology's Institutionalism," *International Organization* 50, no. 2 (spring 1996): 325–47.

55. See, for example, Thomas Franck, "Legitimacy in the International System," *American Journal of International Law* 82, no. 4 (1988): 705–31; Oran Young, *Compliance with Public Authority: A Theory with International Implications* (Baltimore: The Johns Hopkins University Press, 1979); and Abram Chayes and Antonia Handler Chayes, *The New Sovereignty: Compliance with International Regulatory Agreements* (Cambridge, Mass.: Harvard University Press, 1995).

56. Keohane, *After Hegemony.* For a specific example in the international law context, see Ken Abbott, "Trust but Verify: The Production of Information in Arms Control Agreements," *Cornell International Law Journal* 26, no. 1 (1993): 1–58.

57. March and Simon, "The Institutional Dynamics of International Political Orders," 952. See, for example, Alexander Wendt, "Collective Identity Formation and the International State," *American Political Science Review* 88, no. 2 (1994): 384–96, and Martha Finnemore, *National Interests in International Society* (Ithaca, N.Y.: Cornell University Press, 1996).

58. See, for example, Kal Raustiala, "Domestic Institutions and Regulatory Cooperation: Comparative Responses to the Global Biodiversity Regime," *World Politics* 49, no. 4 (1997): 482.

59. For examples of realist arguments that do so, see Stephen Krasner, *Defending the National Interest* (Princeton, N.J.: Princeton University Press, 1978), and Stephen Krasner, "State Power and the Structure of International Trade," *World Politics* 28, no. 3 (1976): 317–47.

60. This description of liberal theory in international politics is influenced strongly by Andrew Moravcsik's recent, provocative, and clear reformulation in his "Taking Preferences Seriously."

61. Putnam, "Two-Level Games."

62. See, for example, Moravcsik, "Taking Preferences Seriously." See also, Jeffrey W. Legro and Andrew Moravcsik, "Is Anybody Still a Realist?" *International Security* 24, no. 2 (fall 1999): 5–55.

63. See Peter Haas, "Introduction: Epistemic Communities and International Policy Coordination," *International Organization* 46, no. 1 (winter 1992): 1, and "Banning Chlorofluorocarbons: Epistemic Community Efforts to Protect Stratospheric Ozone," *International Organization* 46, no. 1 (winter 1992): 187.

64. See Haas, *The Uniting of Europe,* and *Beyond the Nation-State* (Stanford, Calif.: Stanford University Press, 1964). See also Anne-Marie Burley and Walter Mattli, "Europe before the Court: A Political Theory of Legal Integration," *International Organization* 47, no. 1 (winter 1993): 41–77.

65. Katherine Sikkink, "Transnational Advocacy Networks and the Social Construction of Legal Rules," in *New Challenges for the Rule of Law* (Chicago: American Bar Foundation, 2000). On the compatibility of liberalism and "soft" social construction theory, see Alexander Wendt, "Anarchy Is What States Make of It," *International Organization* 46, no. 2 (spring 1992): 391.

66. Many of these analysts mix institutional theory into their arguments, and many of them have been considered "liberal institutionalists." See, for example, Joseph Grieco's treatment of neofunctionalism. Joseph Grieco, *Cooperation among Nations* (Ithaca, N.Y.: Cornell University Press, 1990).

67. See, for example, Richard Falk, "A New Paradigm for International Legal Studies: Prospects and Proposals," in Richard Falk, Friedrich Kratochwil, and Saul Mendelovitz, eds., *International Law: A Contemporary Perspective* (Boulder, Colo.: Westview Press, 1985). See also Robert Keohane, Anne-Marie Slaughter, and Andrew Moravcsik, "Legalized Dispute Resolution: Interstate and Transnational," *International Organization* 54, no. 3 (summer 2000): 457–88.

68. The size of a trade organization may be measured by the total trade—imports plus exports—between member states of the organization. By this measure, the world's largest trade organizations with "hard law" are the WTO, the EU, and NAFTA.

69. Several alternative cases of weak trade-environment rules development were considered but rejected. For example, studies of neither the Association of Southeast Asian Nations (ASEAN) Free Trade Area (AFTA) nor Latin America's Southern Cone Common Market (MERCOSUR) have been included in the book. Trade-environment issues have not been raised by the states that are members of the AFTA. And, while MERCOSUR has been considering a draft environmental protocol, Argentina has blocked its adoption, and the terms of the protocol are completely hortatory.

I

THE WORLD TRADE ORGANIZATION

2

A Reluctant Global Policymaker

James Cameron and Karen Campbell

The period since the Rio Summit in 1992 and the signing of the Uruguay Round Agreement in Marrakech in 1994 has seen unprecedented developments in both world trade and global environmental issues. The impact of the World Trade Organization (WTO) is being felt directly as the new foundation for international economics. Similarly, the evolution of global environmental issues such as global warming and the loss of biodiversity now occupy much time on the public agenda. Both of these issues present significant regulatory challenges for national governments and the international community, which inevitably interact and occasionally conflict. Increasingly, for good or ill, the international community has been looking to the WTO to act as the main mechanism to address both the interaction and the conflict of trade and environmental policy, in its capacity as a dispute resolution body and as a policymaker.

Despite this challenge, trade and environmental policy have always been regarded as separate disciplines or regimes,[1] their essential linkages often overlooked by policymakers. There has been little success to date in the many efforts to develop viable policy alternatives to integrate these policy realms. Indeed, not only did the 1999 WTO ministerial meeting in Seattle fail to launch a new trade round—as was reported widely—but the draft ministerial declaration that was being negotiated as a possible basis for a new round largely excluded environmental issues.[2] Yet, as globalization becomes more real, there is an even greater need to coordinate the often competing goals of trade liberalization and environmental protection.

This chapter examines the WTO's important role in the integration of these two policy areas. Given its central position in governing international economic relations, the WTO has inevitably had the role of global trade-environment policymaker foisted on it. Thus, there are many who look to the WTO to achieve some level of integration. While it has accepted this responsibility to some extent, notably through the decision to establish a Committee on Trade and the Environment (CTE),[3] WTO members continue to operate under a dominant trade paradigm. The prevalence of this paradigm is reflected in the rules and emerging jurisprudence of the WTO, indicating that the WTO itself, despite its position as inevitable global policymaker, remains one of the largest threats to the successful integration of these two policy realms. This challenge is further complicated by the emergence of yet another policy community, the antiglobalization community, which has the potential to drive a wedge between the trade and environmental communities, thereby further inhibiting the WTO's ability to achieve its integrative potential.

The first section of this chapter frames these issues for further discussion, placing them in a current political and theoretical context. The second section examines the rules that emerged out of the Uruguay Round and recent decisions of the Dispute Settlement Body (panels and the Appellate Body), which together form baseline trade and environment rules. The third section considers the substance of seven key trade-environment issues and how they have been addressed at the WTO to date. In this regard, the 1996 Report of the CTE[4] still stands out as the basis for definition and evaluation of these matters in the WTO. The issues include the role of nonstate actors, multilateral environmental agreements, the reform of Dispute Settlement Understanding (DSU), processes and production methods, eco-labeling, domestically prohibited goods, and market access. Recommendations to improve the functioning of the CTE and treatment of trade-environment issues at the WTO more generally are found throughout. This section will also comment on difficulties in using a new trade round as a means of integrating the policy dialogue. Conclusions and an assessment of the WTO's potential for success as a global policymaker are found in the final section.

THE CHALLENGE OF TRADE-ENVIRONMENT POLICYMAKING IN THE WTO

The evolution of a global public policy that effectively integrates trade liberalization and environmental protection is occurring slower than many in the environmental community had hoped. The institutional barriers posed by the WTO—a consensus-based organization with diverse membership, consisting of representatives largely from national trade ministries, and a traditional mandate of trade liberalization—have precluded substantial integration of environmental issues into trade rules since the Uruguay Round. Indeed, much of the pressure driving the trade-environment agenda comes not from the member states within the WTO but from the increasing contributions of nonstate actors concerned about the evolution of international trade and environmental policy.[5] This group of actors consists of broad coalitions of policymakers, advocates, and scientists, many of whom are united in their perception of causal ideas and prescriptive solutions for policy challenges.

At least three paths for the development of trade-environment rules at the WTO can be envisioned. First, realism suggests that powerful WTO members with an interest in environmental protection (such as the United States and the European Union [EU]) could coerce less powerful countries into accepting greener rules in the WTO.[6] Second, rationalist institutionalism could envision policy compromises between WTO members interested in greater environmental protection and those members less interested in it—or perhaps commercial concessions by greener countries in exchange for trade-environment policy concessions by countries less interested in environmental protection.[7] Third, some have hoped for the development of an epistemic consensus among WTO negotiators that would integrate trade and environment concerns into a coherent paradigm.[8] Such a paradigmatic consensus would differ subtly from the notion of "epistemic communities" in international policymaking; the epistemic consensus contemplated here would not require complete agreement on analytic, causal, or empirical underpinnings of trade-environment policies. However, it would entail a shared understanding among WTO negotiators of the consequences of unfettered liberalization on the environment as well as the consequences of strident global environmentalism on trade and sovereignty and a shared sense of an appropriate balance between the competing concerns.

The CTE has provided the main WTO forum in which one might have found evidence of trade-environment policy convergence—even though not all WTO founders intended such a result. The decision to establish the CTE at the GATT ministerial meeting in 1994 was welcomed by most of those concerned about the awkward relationship between trade policy and environment policy. It resulted indirectly from pressure mounted by environmental nongovernmental organizations in the United States and the EU, which were reflected in the positions of the EU and U.S. negotiators, who were determined to keep environment "on the table" after completion of the Uruguay Round. The decision directed the General Council of the WTO to establish a committee with the purpose of making "appropriate recommendations on whether any modifications of the provisions of the multilateral trading system are required" to ensure a positive interaction between trade and environment measures and policies. The CTE has been a key intergovernmental mechanism in the consideration of trade and environment issues.

The need for the CTE to live up to its potential for facilitating policy convergence on trade and the environment has never been as apparent as it is now, particularly given the failure to move forward. Disturbance of the trade agenda was evident with the collapse of the 1999 ministerial meeting through the riots in Seattle. Disturbance in negotiation of multilateral environmental agreements (MEAs) was made clear in evidence presented in 1999 to the British House of Commons Select Committee on Environment, indicating that concern about how a WTO panel would rule on an MEA trade measure has created an insecure position for MEAs. This issue has already inhibited the successful completion of some MEAs and contributed to the 1999 slowdown in negotiations in Cartagena over the Biosafety Protocol to the Convention on Biological Diversity.[9] Unless and until some ground rules are developed that will accommodate the objectives of both the multilateral trading regime and international environmental goals, progressive advances in both realms are likely to suffer.

International political theorists have long suggested that establishment of an institution containing competing perspectives (such as the CTE) is more likely to facilitate a cooperative solution to international problems than ad hoc international efforts.[10] But the CTE has not yet achieved its integrative potential. There are a number of reasons why the WTO has been unable to meaningfully advance this agenda. First, this institution, created to facilitate an integration of trade and environmental views and interests, was established within the WTO. Hence, the perspectives of the CTE's delegates still reflect primarily the WTO's dominant trade paradigm and the underlying commercial interests. Despite its stated objective of considering modifications to the multilateral trading system to accommodate environmental concerns, the CTE has been reluctant to make recommendations that would in any way be inconsistent with the GATT's core principles of nondiscrimination (most-favored nation and national treatment) and ongoing trade liberalization. Second, the CTE's composition may not be conducive to resolving the trade-environment challenges. Its delegates are largely midlevel bureaucrats from trade ministries—neither real decision makers nor necessarily experts on environmental issues. Moreover, political commitment to make WTO internal decision-making processes more transparent and accountable remains lacking. Until the WTO opens up its processes to more genuine and direct participation by environment ministries, nongovernmental organizations (NGOs), and intergovernmental organizations, and until it engages powerful political decision makers, it is unlikely to meet its integrative potential.

Nonetheless, the CTE has paradoxically fostered and invigorated a nascent community of those interested in trade-environment integration that does not generally operate within the WTO. This community has developed as a result of the energies of NGOs, philanthropic foundations, other funding agencies, and government delegates acting in their individual capacities. Since the CTE's formation, this community has generated a number of strategies and suggestions to address central issues facing the WTO.

With the WTO deadlock on trade-environment issues, reflected in both the CTE's 1996 report and the stalemate in Seattle, many environmentalists have been alienated from the WTO processes, and some of those have joined forces with another evolving community—the antiglobalization movement. The emergence of the antiglobalization movement, empowered by the defeat of the Multilateral Agreement on Investment at the Organization for Economic Cooperation and Development (OECD) in 1998 and encouraged by the events in Seattle, is driving a wedge between the trade and environmental communities.[11] Moreover, by polarizing the debate as between trade liberalization or environmental protection and other social justice concerns, the antiglobalization movement has the potential to hinder any steps toward trade-environment policy integration that may be on the horizon.

Given this backdrop, it is imperative that a new trade round—if it is launched—and other activity at the WTO deliver real solutions to the trade-environment dilemma. There is much good work already under way at the WTO—through the CTE, the Dispute Settlement Body, and the General Council. The High-Level Symposium on Trade and Environment, convened by the WTO in March 1999, is one example of the gradual recognition by the WTO of the need to develop some policy coherence.[12] If continuous efforts are not made, windows of opportunity to promote effective solutions to these issues may be lost.

BASELINE RULES FOR TRADE AND ENVIRONMENT IN THE WTO

When the GATT was concluded in 1947, environmental issues were not on the public agenda. The creation of the WTO in 1994 did little to substantially alter this situation, and baseline rules for the evaluation of environmental measures in the trade regime have evolved more as exceptions than as rules in the GATT. Trade-environment rules are not well articulated in the WTO. They are also less environment-friendly than those found in the NAFTA or the European Union, primarily because richer country power to affect trade-environmental solutions is weaker in the WTO. The challenge of reaching consensus among the diversity of WTO members is more acute than in regional trading blocs, where there is often greater commonality of interests.

This part will consider the baseline rules or guidelines that have evolved in the consideration of trade-related environmental measures. Some discussion of these rules will be continued in the "Seven Key Issues" section in this chapter. The rules can be divided into two categories, loosely modeled on those of common law jurisdictions: treaty rules, similar to statute law; and rules emerging from WTO jurisprudence, similar to case law.

Treaty Rules

The treaty rules guiding the consideration of trade and environment issues are found in Article XX of the GATT and in two related Uruguay Round Agreements: the Sanitary and Phytosanitary Standards (SPS) agreement and the Technical Barriers to Trade (TBT) agreement. These trade-environment rules are framed as exceptions to the general rules of nondiscrimination in the GATT—Articles I (most-favored nation) and III (national treatment)—and other articles of general application, such as Article XI (banning import prohibitions and quantitative restrictions). The key environmental exceptions to these general rules are paragraphs (b) and (g) of Article XX of GATT, which hold that deviations are acceptable in circumstances "necessary to protect human, animal or plant life or health" or in circumstances "relating to the conservation of exhaustible natural resources," respectively.[13] However, trade measures otherwise justified by these exceptions must not constitute "a means of arbitrary or unjustifiable discrimination"[14] or function as "a disguised restriction on international trade" in attempting to achieve the chosen level of environmental protection.[15] These latter two principles are also reflected in both the SPS and the TBT agreements.[16]

Both the SPS and the TBT agreements seek to avoid the use of environment-related standards as unnecessary obstacles to trade and to encourage the establishment of standards by international standardizing bodies. The SPS agreement establishes rules for addressing trade barriers related to agriculture and agricultural products; a key rule is that sanitary and phytosanitary measures are to be applied "only to the extent necessary to protect human, animal or plant life or health." The SPS agreement also promotes harmonization of standards based on the principles of risk assessment.[17] The TBT agreement contains objectives similar to those in the SPS agreement and ensures that technical standards and regulations not addressed by the SPS agreement are not used for protectionist purposes.[18] Under both agreements, countries may determine for themselves the level of risk appropriate to embody in their product standards, and such standards will be deemed GATT consistent if they conform to international standards or guidelines or if there is "sufficient scientific evidence" to warrant their continuation.[19] Countries may also provisionally prohibit imports of goods during the period under which national control, inspection, or approval procedures are under way.[20] This limited expression of the precautionary principle has been narrowly construed by the Appellate Body, and there remains some doubt as to whether Article 5.7 of the SPS agreement is a true expression of the precautionary principle at international law.

Thus, the basic GATT rules relating to trade related environmental measures are as follows:

- An environmental measure cannot conflict with the liberal trade principles in the GATT unless it is necessary for the protection of human, animal, or plant life or health or is related to the conservation of exhaustible natural resources.
- In addition, an environmental exception must not amount to arbitrary or unjustifiable discrimination or be more trade restrictive than is necessary.
- National standards for the protection of environment or health must be consistent with international standards or may be maintained by a national government if there is sufficient scientific evidence to warrant the standard.
- Provisional prohibition of imports is permissible during periods where national risk assessment procedures are under way to establish measures that may guard against an environmental or health-related effect.

Rules Based on Case Law

As with the treaty-based rules, there are few actual rules emerging from GATT and WTO jurisprudence regarding trade-environment issues. The guidelines that exist have evolved from a handful of GATT 1947 and WTO panel and Appellate Body rulings. The paucity of rules likely stems from the fact that more GATT jurisprudence has been devoted to narrowing the scope of the Article XX exceptions than to actually applying them. Rarely has a party to a GATT panel or Appellate Body proceeding successfully invoked Article XX to justify an environmental measure.[21]

Considerable GATT case law stems from the phrase "like product" found in Articles I and III, which has been read to suggest that countries may not distinguish between like products on the basis of their methods of production. This phrase was first interpreted in an environmental context in the highly publicized *Tuna/Dolphin* cases.[22] In the first *Tuna/Dolphin* decision, issued in 1991, a GATT panel held that that import restrictions may not be imposed on products solely because they have been made or obtained in an environmentally unsound manner outside the jurisdiction of the importing country. The effect was that any country's environmental regulations that restrict the importation of goods on the basis of their processes or production methods (PPMs) could not be applied extrajurisdictionally. Thus, many feared that this case could be read to establish a two-part rule for GATT/WTO members: Import restrictions had to be based on the characteristics of the imported good, not the PPMs used in producing the good, and countries could not apply their legislation extrajurisdictionally.

The recent ruling of the Appellate Body in the *Asbestos* case will undoubtedly have a significant impact on future assessments of like products under Article III.[23] While we are unable to undertake a fulsome review of this important ruling at this time, it is important to note that the Appellate Body has expanded the application of the criteria by which like product determinations will be made beyond a "market access" approach. In assessing whether chrysotile asbestos fibers are like polyvinyl alcohol fibers and cellulose and glass fibers, the Appellate Body held that health risks associated with a product, as well as consumer preferences, are relevant to a like product determination under Article III:4.[24] This is significant, as human health risks are increasingly being associated with environmental risks globally, and the broader scope for interpretation of Article III afforded by this ruling will undoubtedly influence the evolution of other domestic laws designed to protect human health, safety, and the environment.

The *Reformulated Gasoline* case was the first dispute referred to the Appellate Body under the WTO's DSU and marks the beginning of the Appellate Body's jurisprudence on environment and trade.[25] Many trade law scholars have praised the Appellate Body's decision for its emphasis on the chapeau of Article XX in any determination of the general exceptions and for showing how the reformulated gasoline rules of the United States were discriminatory. But the decision was just as notable for two other points. First, the Appellate Body confirmed that clean air is an exhaustible natural resource, expanding the scope of resources to include less tangible things such as air. Second, it noted that the WTO Agreement "is not to be read in clinical isolation from public international law," thus placing the WTO and its related agreements squarely within the ambit of public international law.[26] This latter point is critical because any examination of the linkages between the WTO and environmental protection must be framed on the assumption that the WTO is one organ in the body of public international law. The general perception of many WTO delegates and secretariat personnel had been that the GATT and the WTO function independently from public international law. Indeed, the CTE Report notes that "MEAs and the WTO both represent different bodies of international law."[27] Thus, the Appellate Body's statement clarifies that the GATT and its related agreements, while specialized, are not derived from a separate legal order and must be interpreted in light of general principles of public international law.

The *Beef Hormone* case is the first Appellate Body decision to apply the SPS agreement and has defined some specific standards for interpretation of the SPS agreement.[28] At stake, of course, has been the EU's directive banning the importation of hormone-treated beef. The European Commission produced laboratory studies showing potential adverse effects on humans of consuming such beef, but those studies were found to be based on unrealistic assumptions about the quantities and conditions of consumption and the qualities of the beef consumed. Hence, the decision clarifies that risk assessments to determine appropriate levels of environmental or health protection should be undertaken in the context of the real-world potential for adverse effects to human health, not just those effects identified in a laboratory setting. The Appellate Body also confirmed that, in such cases, deference should be given to the regulator in the member state's legal order, thus opening the door to a better integration of trade and environment policy.[29]

Finally, the *Shrimp/Turtle* ruling by the Appellate Body will undoubtedly have a significant impact on future trade-environment disputes in the WTO.[30] Four principles emerge from this case, two procedural and two substantive. First, and perhaps most significant, the Appellate Body confirmed that amicus curiae briefs prepared by individuals or interest groups can be submitted to a WTO panel, though the panel may choose to disregard them. Similarly, WTO members may expressly adopt the submissions in amicus curiae briefs by attaching them to their submissions in a WTO proceeding.[31] These principles have come under severe attack by more than eighteen developing countries, and at least one panel has since refused to consider amicus briefs. Second, the Appellate Body confirmed the two-tiered test for evaluating the consistency of an environmental measure under the Article XX exceptions. Panels must first evaluate whether the measure qualifies under one of the enumerated exceptions before considering whether a measure amounts to "arbitrary or unjustifiable discrimination" and a "disguised restriction on trade," as provided for in the chapeau.[32]

Substantively, the Appellate Body confirmed that the definition of the term "exhaustible natural resources" in Article XX is evolutionary and that it must be read in light of "contemporary concerns" about environmental protection. In this regard, the Appellate Body emphasized the reference in the preamble of the WTO Agreement to "the objective of sustainable development."[33] Fourth, the Appellate Body appears to have responded to concerns by the EU and United States about the extrajurisdictional application of domestic laws by recognizing their potential legitimacy. The Appellate Body decision focused on the fact that the procedures and process by which the U.S. measure was enacted, not the fact of the measure itself, was arbitrary and discriminatory.

Finally, the Appellate Body did not rule squarely on long-standing concerns about the application of MEAs within the WTO. The concern that it would be WTO inconsistent to comply with trade restrictions in many MEAs is one of the core issues in the trade-environment debate. In contrast to the *Tuna/Dolphin* cases, the *Shrimp/Turtle* Appellate Body decision did suggest that a member's environmental measure will not be deemed to fall outside the Article XX exceptions solely because it was aimed at extrajurisdictional activity, but the Appellate Body expressly refused to define the jurisdictional scope of the Article XX exceptions, and the holding did not eliminate all potential legal bases for challenging the WTO consistency of certain MEAs. Thus, it remains unclear whether the imposition of an import or export ban pursuant to an MEA against a WTO member that is not a signatory to the MEA would be GATT consistent.

In sum, the baseline rules in the WTO stemming from case law are as follows:

- Risks to human health are relevant to a "like product" determination under Articles I and III.
- Countries may in some circumstances (not yet fully defined) regulate trade to serve extrajurisdictional environmental objectives, provided that the regulation does not constitute "arbitrary or unjustifiable discrimination" or a "disguised restriction on international trade"—provisos applied broadly and strictly by the *Shrimp/Turtle* Appellate Body.
- The WTO is part of the body of public international law.
- Parties should keep in mind the objective of sustainable development contained in the WTO Agreement.
- "Exhaustible natural resources" in Article XX(g) has an expansive definition.
- Risk assessments under the SPS agreement should reflect real-world circumstances.
- Deference should be given to domestic regulators in determining levels of appropriate protection for SPS measures.
- Any individual or group can submit amicus curiae briefs to a panel or the Appellate Body that may or may not be adopted by parties to the dispute in their submission and may or may not be considered by the arbiter.

SEVEN KEY ISSUES: WTO STALEMATE AND THE NEXT ROUND

As discussed previously, the creation of the CTE at the conclusion of the Uruguay Round was greeted with optimism by those concerned about trade and environment issues, as it was taken as an indicator of a genuine desire to have greater clarity and measurable policy progress. Given the scope of its mandate and the resulting institutionalization of environmental issues in the WTO, the potential for the CTE to facilitate the evolution of an integrated approach to trade and environment issues was seen as significant. However, since the conclusion of the Uruguay Round, neither the CTE nor any other WTO institution (other than the Dispute Settlement Body [DSB]) has made substantial progress on trade-environment issues.

The CTE's only major report to date, tabled at the 1996 ministerial conference, continues to represent the state of play at the WTO. The 1996 Report can be viewed primarily as a summary of issues and differences among members, not an agenda for change. While the CTE has introduced an element of greater clarity in terms of issue definition, it has done little to bring about concrete action in ensuring a reconciliation or balance between trade and environment issues. The Report's basic conclusions were threefold: that no real modifications to the multilateral trading system are required, that some procedural modifications in terms of transparency and notification should be made, and that the work of the WTO in building a constructive policy relationship among trade, environment, and sustainable development should continue. This part will focus on differences on seven key issues, using the CTE's Report as a baseline for suggesting some possible changes.[34]

Role of Nonstate Actors

Perhaps one of the most dramatic and recent changes in international policymaking is the increased role of civil society. To date, many believe there has been insufficient scope for nonstate actors, such as NGOs, industry associations, and intergovernmental organizations (IGOs), to participate in the work of the WTO generally. The NGO frustration over that state of affairs was evident in the streets of Seattle during the 1999 WTO ministerial meeting. Item 10 of the CTE Report addresses the role of IGOs and NGOs in relation to the work of the WTO. Despite recognizing that WTO members have agreed "to improve public access to WTO documentation and to develop communication with NGOs,"[35] the Report's recommendations do little to give effect to this commitment.

Opening the deliberations of the WTO, including the CTE, to greater scrutiny and participation may be seen as good policy, as there is much that civil society can offer the WTO. The Appellate Body decision in the *Shrimp/Turtle* case suggested the acceptability of amicus curiae briefs in WTO disputes, whether or not adopted by the parties, indicating that the views of nonstate parties are indeed relevant to WTO disputes. At the *Shrimp/Turtle* panel level, the two amicus curiae briefs elaborated on both science and law in a novel way. A positive inference about their impact can be drawn from the fact that the conservation facts section in the Centre for International Environmental Law (CIEL) brief was adopted by the United States and therefore formally introduced before the Panel, while the experts who contributed evidence to the World Wildlife Fund (WWF) brief were called to the oral hearings of the Panel.[36]

Despite some arguments that the GATT and now WTO have functioned effectively in regulating international trade for the past fifty years, this initial purely trade-driven paradigm has been called into question. The mere existence of the CTE and the recent WTO High-Level Symposium on Trade and Environment suggest the interdisciplinary nature of global policy development. The CTE's initial failure to provide access to its documentation caused international attention to be focused on the inaccessibility of the WTO generally, and the NGO pressure for access to better information has resulted in the WTO improving access to all areas of its work, not simply trade and environment. In focusing attention on broader issues, many organizations reflecting different interests are now claiming benefits from the changes championed by environmental NGOs.

NGOs

The focus of the CTE's recommendations with respect to NGOs has been primarily on notification and communication in the WTO, which will not necessarily result in improved access and transparency. The CTE Report recommended that all remaining working documents prepared during its first two years of operations be derestricted and that the WTO secretariat "continue its interaction with NGOs that will contribute to the accuracy and richness of the public debate on trade and environment."[37] The CTE's recommendations with respect to NGO access, while minimal, are an indicator of progress on this issue. In this vein, the WTO secretariat recently has taken a number of steps to increase its interaction with NGOs. An NGO forum has been created on the WTO Web site, and the secretariat has proposed that regular briefings be held for NGOs and that a monthly list of documents received from NGOs be circulated to all members.

However, for meaningful progress on trade-environment issues to occur, it is imperative that in its continued work the WTO provide appropriate access to NGOs throughout its deliberations. One notable omission from the CTE Report is that, while it recommended that past documentation be derestricted, it made no reference to the derestriction of working papers for the ongoing deliberations concurrent with their discussion at the CTE or the WTO more broadly.[38] From the perspective of those favoring inclusiveness and transparency, current information, not simply previous documentation, should be derestricted and made available for public access and comment. The WTO's current policy of delaying the derestriction of documents until six months after circulation to WTO members seriously limits the value of these documents as public information and makes it harder for WTO members to explain clearly to domestic constituencies the rationale for national activities regarding the WTO. There appears to be no clear rationale for a rule that makes documents available to the public only after artificial delay.

Full access to documentation, perhaps best accomplished via the WTO Web site, would enable the quality of nonstate actor participation in the WTO to improve. Moreover, the burden in the WTO's policy on access to documentation should be shifted to provide unrestricted access to all documents unless there is a clear and convincing reason why they should not be. Increased transparency can only aid in a wider consideration of more complete information, issues, and potential solutions.

A similar concern also exists with regard to observer status at WTO and CTE meetings. While the WTO and CTE agreed to extend observer status on a permanent basis to IGOs that previously participated as observers on an ad hoc basis, this concession has not been extended to NGOs,[39] which were granted observer status at the 1996 ministerial conference in Singapore, a significant change to the status quo ante. Although there was not a great deal of activity for them to undertake in respect of arguments for change, their presence was generally perceived as largely constructive. The Singapore government's initiative in publicizing NGO activities at the ministerial conference was a notable gesture in favor of cooperation with nonstate actors.

Indeed, experience to date, in various fora, indicates that NGOs bring fresh perspectives and new information that ultimately enhance consideration of policy issues and help states resolve them. Both the WTO and the CTE are still in stages of relative institutional infancy, and there is much that NGOs can contribute to the effective operation and development of the WTO in terms of evaluating and commenting on the difficult issues it will be called on to consider. The experience of NGOs brings with it not only a frequently different perspective but also new information, hands-on expertise, the ability to represent interests not otherwise considered in state-to-state diplomacy, and a more immediate appreciation of issues of public concern. Instead of considering whether access should be granted, the WTO should consider drafting rules and conditions to facilitate such access. Ideas such as regular briefings during negotiations, opportunities for NGO experts to contribute views to delegations on matters of policy or on possible rule changes, and a place on the CTE agenda to hear arguments of representative NGOs could all be developed.

IGOs

Another important element of nonstate actor participation is the role of IGOs in the WTO. Experience to date indicates that enhanced institutional cooperation, particularly in the CTE, would be quite valuable. While IGOs have observer status in all relevant WTO committees, they cannot be heard in the CTE without the invitation of a country delegate.[40] Practice has so far not extended this courtesy, even though the committee could benefit from contributions by these organizations, in particular the UN Environment Program (UNEP) and the UN Conference on Trade and Development (UNCTAD). Unfortunately, attempts to bring UNEP and UNCTAD together on the trade, environment, and development policy nexus have not been altogether successful to date.[41] This raises larger questions about the effectiveness of international environmental institutions in addressing these important policy issues. The trade and environment debate has revealed the relative weakness of UNEP in the face of the WTO and the urgent need for a more coherent resonant voice for sustainable development at the global level. None of the world's IGOs currently play this integrative role. The system for the institutional management of global environment and development affairs is fractured. The WTO, despite flaws and its own financial worries, is not. While some would argue that the WTO is a trade and not an environmental forum, it nonetheless makes sense that the WTO facilitate integration with other IGOs. The preamble to the WTO Agreement recognizes the need for sustainable development, the Appellate Body has acknowledged this in its rulings, and WTO institutions should focus on this in their deliberations.

Multilateral Environmental Agreements and the WTO

The main issues concerning MEAs and the multilateral trading system are two-fold: reconciling trade-related environmental measures between the WTO and MEAs and the choice of a forum for the settlement of a trade-related environmental dispute. Although these are separate agenda items in the CTE, the overlap is such that the CTE Report presented its conclusions on these issues together. Overall, the Report's comments with respect to MEAs amount to little more than a recognition of the critical relationship between MEAs and the multilateral trading system, and their comments on this important issue are inconclusive and, at best, persuasive.

Concern about the failure, to date, to develop some means of reconciliation of trade-related environmental measures within the WTO is heightening. Trade measures are a proven effective means of achieving international environmental protection goals. The three major MEAs with trade measures have been successful: In the case of the Convention on International Trade in Endangered Species (CITES), no species listed in the appendices have become extinct since their listing; since the Basel Convention entered into force, the worst forms of hazardous waste dumping in developing countries have subsided; and evidence from some countries party to the Montreal Protocol makes clear that the trade provisions were a factor in persuading them to accede to the treaty.[42] That the issue of GATT consistency has inhibited the successful negotiation of certain MEAs is an indication of the urgency of this issue if efforts to improve the international environmental protection regime are to be effective.

Given the complexity of the issues, it is extremely disappointing that the CTE's only actual recommendation on these two key issues was "that the WTO Secretariat continue to play a constructive role through its cooperative efforts with Secretariats of MEAs and provide information to WTO Members on trade-related work in MEAs."[43] It would be useful for the WTO to take a more definitive approach to situations where a dispute looms regarding a trade-related environmental measure enacted pursuant to an MEA.

The deliberations of the CTE have provided little direction on this issue. The CTE Report states that where parties to an MEA agree to apply a specifically mandated trade measure, disputes over the application of such measures are unlikely to occur in the WTO.[44] Further, the Report recognizes that, to date, no parties have resorted to the WTO dispute settlement mechanism to undermine obligations accepted in becoming parties to an MEA and "considers [that] this will remain the case."[45] This is precarious reasoning for failing to make explicit recommendations on the reconciliation of disputes that arise in the context of both the WTO and an MEA. Furthermore, the Report's statement that, in the event of a dispute, parties should try to resolve the matter through the dispute settlement mechanism of the MEA falls conspicuously short of a recommendation even if we agree with its sense.[46]

Disputes will inevitably arise, playing trade-related environmental measures in MEAs off against the provisions of the WTO. Indeed, while the recent *Shrimp/Turtle* case did not directly invoke CITES, thus forcing a direct consideration of the relationship between MEAs and the WTO, it came perilously close.[47] The CTE's tactic of willing the issue to go away implies that they have, perhaps deliberately, failed to make a recommendation on an issue that will likely become contentious at some point. The gap left by the CTE means that the panels and the Appellate Body will need to address these issues on a case-by-case basis.

Despite not making an explicit recommendation, the language of the CTE Report clearly reflects a view that, in the event of a conflict, dispute settlement mechanisms in MEAs should take precedence over those in the WTO. It is unfortunate that the CTE failed to turn this view into a recommendation, particularly where the states involved in a dispute are parties to both the MEA and members of the WTO. As the British House of Commons Select Committee on World Trade and the Environment notes, "Successful negotiation and implementation of multilateral environmental agreements is a vital element in tackling global and transboundary environmental problems."[48] Undermining measures inspired by such agreements by making them subject to the potentially contrary policy goals of the WTO will frustrate MEAs and the pressing goals of global environmental protection generally. Further, if, as the CTE believes, it will be "the case" that no disputes regarding implementation of environmental measures under an MEA will be subject to the WTO dispute mechanism, then clearly providing that an MEA will prevail should be of little political consequence.

The reality is that cases are drawn to the WTO, and MEAs bear some responsibility for not developing their dispute settlement systems to offer a real alternative. Only the UN Law of the Sea Convention's dispute settlement mechanism has anything approaching the power and efficiency of the WTO. Thus, the WTO is likely to be the preferred option in the event that a complaining party goes forum shopping. It is not uncommon in international disputes for a complaining party to select a forum most likely to frame its case in a favorable light or provide the best remedy. Because of its comprehensive, quasi-judicial, and prompt nature, the DSU has become extremely popular as a means of resolving international disputes with a trade component. The issue is one of characterization: Should the dispute in question be framed as a trade dispute or as an environmental dispute? It is clear that trade disputes should be addressed by the WTO. However, in many cases the characterization of disputes over trade-related environmental measures will be very different and may warrant favoring the application of the relevant provisions of the MEA over those of the WTO. Yet often a complaining party will prefer the WTO forum over that of the MEA.

The international law of treaties provides general rules that could be interpreted such that, in some instances, MEA provisions will prevail over those of the WTO. Thus, recourse should be had to the principles of general international law and, more specifically, the Vienna Convention on the Law of Treaties, which establishes a set of rules and priority considerations for determining the competence of a forum to deal with a dispute, where such fora may overlap. An exploration of this complex issue is beyond the scope of this chapter, but some relevant factors include the existence of compatibility clauses in treaties, the issue of whether all parties to the dispute have ratified the treaties, and the primary subject matter of the dispute.[49] Perhaps the most important concern in this regard is political, as it is unclear whether a trade-related measure validly enacted pursuant to an MEA can withstand the scrutiny of the DSU.

The General Exceptions in Article XX contain ample protection against measures that could be viewed as arbitrary or unjustifiably discriminatory or as disguised restrictions on trade. That only two trade-related environmental measures have passed the test to benefit from the exceptions in Article XX is evidence of how rigorously this test has been applied to date. Indeed, the Appellate Body's ruling in the *Reformulated Gasoline* case and its 1998 ruling in the *Shrimp/Turtle* case further elaborate the Article XX test, giving greater credence and clarification to the chapeau in ensuring against abuse of the General Exceptions. In the *Reformulated Gasoline* case, the Appellate Body states that "it is important to underscore that the purpose and object of the introductory clauses of Article XX is generally the prevention of 'abuse of the exceptions.' "[50] The Appellate Body specifies further that "the provisions of the chapeau cannot logically refer to the same standard(s) by which a violation of a substantive rule has been determined to have occurred. To proceed down that path would be both to empty the chapeau of its contents and to deprive the exceptions in paragraphs (a) to (j) of meaning."[51] This two-tiered approach elaborated by the Appellate Body for Article XX (justification of the measure under the listed exceptions and further appraisal of the same measure under the chapeau) suggests that measures that could be perceived as abuses of the exceptions stand a minimal chance of passing the rigorous test for protection under Article XX.

The 2001 *Shrimp/Turtle* Panel,[52] which was convened to ascertain whether the United States was complying with the terms of the 1998 *Shrimp/Turtle* Appellate Body report, found that revised U.S. guidelines on application of its shrimp import ban and ongoing U.S. efforts to negotiate a multilateral agreement to conserve sea turtles were sufficient to except the import ban under Article XX. However, the Panel suggested that the U.S. import ban was being permitted only *provisionally* and would be found WTO inconsistent again if the United States were to cease "serious good faith efforts" to negotiate a multilateral agreement. This approach suggests that the WTO's DSB will sit in judgment of the seriousness of WTO members' efforts to negotiate MEAs, and the Panel offered little guidance about how panels would in the future evaluate whether "serious good faith efforts" were under way.

Thus, even where a measure may be found acceptable under one of the enumerated exceptions, it may nonetheless be found to be an abuse of the exceptions under the more stringent standard imposed by the chapeau. This effectively occurred in the *Reformulated Gasoline* case and also the 1998 *Shrimp/Turtle* case: The Appellate Body used the chapeau to find that the measure at issue was an abuse of the exceptions. While a measure enacted pursuant to an MEA may be accorded a broader scope within the exceptions, Appellate Body jurisprudence does not make this clear.

In our view, then, there is an explicit need to clarify how (e.g., according to what principles) specific provisions of MEAs or measures chosen by parties to implement obligations in MEAs will be considered in WTO dispute settlement. This clarification can easily be accomplished through simple amendment to Article XX of the GATT. Draft wording has been developed by the European Commission and was tabled on behalf of the EU and its member states before the CTE at its meeting in February 1996.[53] The need for articulated ground rules is clear—this is a view shared by such disparate interests as Greenpeace, the British House of Commons Select Committee on the Environment, and the U.S. Council for International Business. More recently, the British House of Commons Select Committee on the Environment advocated a separate agreement on MEAs that would exempt MEA trade measures from a WTO challenge.[54] No matter how difficult the present atmosphere for negotiation or how lacking the political will for a change of the rules, the addition of a subparagraph extending the exceptions to "measures taken pursuant to MEAs" would not, in our view, undermine the predictability and security of the trade regime.

Another option would be to adopt a political declaration setting out the basic assumption of compatibility where membership of the two agreements is the same, even where a nonparty to the MEA is affected. Ultimately, a political judgment must be made as to which route should be pursued.

Dispute Settlement Reform

The WTO's DSB is under pressure. Neither the CTE nor the WTO's 1999 Dispute Settlement Review has been able to effectively address outstanding concerns about the dispute settlement process in the WTO. While the CTE simply avoided the issue, the four-year review of the DSU became bogged down in disagreement despite a six-month deadline extension.[55]

Experience with the first years of the DSU leads to some interesting considerations about the future role of dispute settlement within the WTO. There is little doubt that dispute resolution is increasingly becoming a core function of the WTO and that more resources will be committed to balancing the interests of members in the context of disputes or potential disputes. This is not surprising, given the number and complexity of agreements administered by the WTO and the vast diversity of members' interests. In this context, the role of the Appellate Body will become more critical in interpreting these agreements and balancing interests of members such that it is conceivable that the focus of the WTO will shift away from panel proceedings and toward the work of the Appellate Body.

The DSU will become more integral to the functioning of the WTO, and it is essential that consideration be given to improving the WTO's ability to effectively adjudicate environment-related matters. It is notable that the CTE did not even explore potential mechanisms for improving the functioning of the Dispute Settlement Body in the context of trade and environment disputes. While environmental policy issues should be given adequate consideration in the context of trade disputes, a review of new approaches to dispute resolution is equally valuable for the resolution of disputes in other subject areas as well. The following four recommendations, all made before in some form or another, could enhance both trust and participation in WTO dispute resolution.

Appointment of Counsel to the Panel

The European Court of Justice model should inform the operation of the DSU. Specifically, consideration should be given to the appointment of an advocate-general or counsel to the Panel, whose role would be to supplement the work of the Panel. In the European Court of Justice, the advocate-general's function is similar to that of counsel to the Court. The advocate-general summarizes the submissions of the parties and makes recommendations as to where the Court should focus its efforts and to how the legal issues should be resolved. Notably, the scope of the advocate-general's authority is not limited to merely summarizing and presenting the submissions of the parties. He or she is also entitled to submit any other arguments that may be relevant to the Court's determination, and, in effect, almost becomes an expert on the issues involved in the dispute. More often than not, the advocate-general's preliminary opinion is followed by the Court in its ruling.

The advocate-general has a greater opportunity to become informed of the issues of the case and, where necessary, to incorporate additional legal arguments or the arguments of nonparties. In the context of the WTO, these factors would enhance the quality of information, analysis, and adjudication in panel proceedings. An advocate-general could act as an independent agent either to the Panel or, more ideally, to the Appellate Body, positioned to inform the adjudicator, in an evenhanded way, on relevant WTO and related law, including international law.

Establishment of a Right of Intervention

The 1998 *Shrimp/Turtle* Appellate Body Report provides that a panel may accept amicus curiae briefs under specified circumstances, but panels are not required to do so. Provision for the submission of amicus curiae briefs or nonstate interventions should be incorporated into the DSU. This right of intervention, at either the panel level or the Appellate Body, would allow an interested person or group to present evidence and argumentation to the Panel or Appellate Body—and would ensure their formal consideration. Initially, this right could be made available in the form of written briefs, on the basis of a sufficient interest test, and theoretically could be extended as full disputing party rights to persons or groups with a sufficient interest in the dispute. This concept is also compatible with the role of counsel to the panel.

As stated earlier, there is much that the NGO community can offer the WTO, in terms of both information and general policy direction, the *Shrimp/Turtle* dispute being a case in point. The expertise, knowledge, and insight of NGOs would clearly enhance decision making and adjudication of panels and the Appellate Body. Equally, most disputes that come before panels are disputes between states about access to markets. An established right of intervention would allow trade associations and NGOs to present their private interests distinct from the public interests of the state.

Provision for Increased Access to Information and Openness

Related to the notion of nonstate intervention is the extension of a general right to information regarding disputes. As mentioned earlier, access to all WTO documents should be unrestricted unless there is a clear and convincing reason why they should not be available. This right would include timely public access to submissions relating to disputes, official reports, digests of cases, and pending results. Panel hearings should also be made open to the public. The policy reasons for these recommendation are substantially the same as mentioned previously: Greater transparency will provide for more complete assessment and adjudication of the issues.

Advisory Opinions from the International Court of Justice

Finally, the panel or Appellate Body should have the power to seek advisory opinions from the International Court of Justice (ICJ) on matters of international law, as was intended by the drafters of the Havana Charter.[56] Situations, in particular those pertaining to environmental measures, will inevitably arise where WTO panels will not have the necessary expertise to adjudicate a highly specialized fact situation. Reference to an independent panel such as the ICJ would bolster the impartiality of the WTO in the resolution of environment-related disputes. In addition, such references to the ICJ could supplement an amendment to Article XX of the GATT, discussed earlier.[57]

Paradoxically, the previously discussed recommendations would have the effect of judicializing the WTO at a time when domestic courts and tribunals seem to be moving toward less adversarial methods of dispute resolution. However, changes such as those proposed will be essential to maintain the integrity and impartiality of the WTO dispute settlement system. The nature and diversity of interests in the multilateral trading system are such that clear legal approaches are the best way to protect against abuse of power and the impartial distribution of trade rights and obligations.

Processes and Production Methods

One of the thorniest issues in the trade-environment debate is that of processes and production methods (PPMs). Current GATT law presents a fundamental obstacle to the effective incorporation of environmental protection and sustainable development principles into its jurisprudence. Unless and until PPMs are recognized as a basis for distinguishing between otherwise "like products" under Articles I or III of the GATT, a whole category of environment-based trade measures will be subject to challenge.[58] While the recent ruling of the Appellate Body in the *Asbestos* case represents an important step toward this distinction, environmental law does not yet distinguish between products on the basis of how they are made. Either laws have to be harmonized (as in Europe), or, where markets are altered by environmental laws, distinctions based on PPMs should be accepted as being in the public interest. Determining what is or is not in the public interest is a matter of both politics and law, not simply one of applying technical trade rules (though fair and certain application of those rules is clearly in the public interest). The current accepted GATT definition of "like product" is based on the physical characteristics of the product. Such an assessment of physical characteristics permits determining that products are not "like products" where one is toxic (such as cement-based products containing asbestos) and another is not (such as cement-based products not containing asbestos).[59] However, current WTO doctrine does not permit considering the means by which a product is made to distinguish between products and to determine whether they are "like products." In many cases, these PPMs may have significant adverse environmental or health impacts, the *Tuna/Dolphin* and *Shrimp/Turtle* rulings being obvious examples.[60]

The issue of PPMs was reviewed previously in the context of measures relating to products. The main focus of the CTE's work was the trade implications of voluntary eco-labeling schemes, not the use of domestic product–related measures, which may have an extraterritorial effect. The CTE's failure to deal adequately with either PPMs or eco-labeling is evidenced by the fact that it failed to make any recommendations on either matter. On the basis of the discussion in the Report,[61] it appears that there is no political agreement on whether to tolerate PPM-based measures. Given that this issue has resulted in highly contentious Panel decisions in the past, this is an area where the CTE should have made definitive recommendations.

The WTO would benefit greatly from resolving this matter, and it should not be that difficult to develop a series of considerations for the evaluation of the nature and impact of PPMs as indirect barriers to trade. Effective approaches to dealing with the issue can be straightforward—if there are global or transboundary effects to a PPM, the best response will be international cooperation, the development of multilateral agreements, or harmonization. In most cases, PPMs are enacted for a legitimate environmental or health objective, such as the protection of species or endangered species (as in the *Tuna/Dolphin* and *Shrimp/Turtle* cases); or the protection of human health from potentially harmful food additives (as in the *Beef Hormone* case); or the protection of humans from exposure to cancer-causing materials such as asbestos (as in the *Asbestos* case).[62] An adverse trade ruling will not resolve these concerns; it will mean only that the parties must find new ways to deal with the issues. Thus, cooperation will always be the preferred approach. Where the effect of the PPM is local or domestic, the issue will be significantly less contentious, and the best response will be domestic regulation. It should not be presumed that states will regulate the local environmental effects of their domestic PPMs.

However, there are a host of PPMs, in a variety of sectors, such as those cited previously, that do cause transboundary or global effects, and there are real problems with the enforcement of domestic environmental law designed to deal with the local environmental effects of these PPMs. For these reasons, it is essential that some basic ground rules be drafted to guide environmental regulators in the exercise of their duties to protect the environment in a globalized economy. This issue warrants the negotiation of a specific MEA to address the international treatment of PPMs. At the same time, the issue of PPMs should initially be discussed in the context of existing MEAs. Of course, the MEA-WTO relationship should be resolved so as to enable MEAs to employ PPM-based measures even if they affect trade.

Another issue arises when PPMs so affect the product itself that an environmental or health issue crosses a border with a product. In that situation, Article XX already provides reasonable protection to the importing state, but it would be helpful if it were made absolutely clear that the environmental effects of traded goods or services were covered by Article XX.

Eco-Labeling

The CTE's failure to make recommendations about voluntary eco-labeling schemes suggests that no politically acceptable solutions have been proposed. This is disappointing given the scope of the CTE's consideration of the trade implications of such schemes. The CTE's comments on this topic reflect a desire to ensure transparency in the preparation, adoption, and application of such schemes and in ensuring fair access to foreign producers for such programs. But its only recommendation on this issue has been that WTO members follow the provisions of the TBT agreement and its Code of Good Practice.

There is clearly a need for more work to be undertaken on this matter and for development of a set of procedures and substantive principles. Eco-labeling schemes are an important way of increasing consumer awareness and altering production practices in the marketplace. Continued development of these schemes would serve consumers by providing more complete information and would enhance environmental protection to the extent that consumers value and act on that information.

While these schemes have the potential to create market distortions, including trade discrimination, that potential can be minimized or eliminated by the application of substantive rules and principles, such as those established for the Code of Good Practice. Increased transparency in the process by which eco-labeling criteria are established and guarantees of foreign participation in that process will reduce the chances of trade distortion and help avoid conflicts. However, eco-labeling is linked soundly to the PPMs issue because the labels usually contain information about PPMs. Thus, until the PPMs issue is resolved as well, it seems inevitable that eco-labeling conflicts will continue and find their way to WTO dispute settlement. Indeed, a challenge to the European Commission's Eco-label with its multicriteria life cycle approach is likely, and the DSB has been given no guidance from the CTE or from the WTO as a whole as to how it should settle disputes of this nature despite the increased use of such schemes. Clear guidance as to how the issue of eco-labeling should be addressed by panels and the Appellate Body would ensure the development of a consistent approach in this area.

Domestically Prohibited Goods

Item 7 of the CTE Report addresses still another WTO trade-environment issue: the problem of exports of domestically prohibited goods (DPGs). The export of DPGs is of primary concern to developing and least developed countries, and trade in potentially hazardous or harmful products is being addressed by a variety of different IGOs. As with most other trade-environment agenda items, the CTE's real contribution has been to acknowledge the importance of the issue and to recommend greater information sharing and more research. Specifically, the CTE has recommended greater cooperation with IGOs working on this issue and further research by the WTO secretariat.[63]

Further research and information sharing will contribute little to what developing countries perceive as a central problem: their inability to adequately protect themselves against exported hazardous DPGs. Several MEAs already establish rules to govern the shipment and disposal of DPGs, and there are a number of voluntary guidelines in place to ensure informed consent prior to disposal of such goods,[64] so the development of adequate international legal rules is not the problem. The real problem is that developing countries often do not have the resources to monitor their borders, leaving them unable to protect themselves against exported DPGs. Hence, the practical issue is one of financing to ensure that a prior informed consent (PIC) procedure could be implemented effectively. Thus, developing countries and environmentalists would like WTO efforts to focus on the development of positive complementary measures, such as financing mechanisms and capacity building. The recently concluded Rotterdam Convention on Hazardous Chemicals Trade, which is not yet in force, may assist developing countries in this regard. Of course, this convention is an MEA and should be treated as such in the WTO. From this perspective, the WTO's next steps on the issue of DPGs should be to work with other

IGOs to develop a system of financing for developing countries to identify and reject shipments of hazardous materials.

Market Access

As with other stalled trade-environment issues, the WTO has not made headway on the issue of restricted market access for exporting countries that has the effect of discouraging sustainable development. Protectionist measures such as tariff peaks, quotas, and domestic production subsidies often result in trade barriers that can have a negative effect on development and on the environment in exporting countries.[65] These measures are often applied to protect natural resource–based industries, such as coal production and forestry, causing both inefficiency and accelerated environmental degradation. Moreover, restricted market access often extends to environmental technology and other technical goods and services that could provide for the more sustainable use and management of natural resources.

As with other trade-environment issues, simple policy recommendations seem to elude the WTO. To ensure that restricted market access does not result in unnecessary environmental degradation, a systematic evaluation of trade barriers should be undertaken with a view to characterizing their environmental effects. In situations where trade barriers have the effect of prohibiting the flow of goods and services that can enhance environmental protection, the argument for removing such barriers becomes both economic and environmental. Both NGO and developing country access to relevant information and technology (which, in many cases, the private sector is becoming increasingly well positioned to provide) can assist in the development of creative solutions.

Expectations for advancing the trade-environment agenda were low going into the 1999 ministerial meeting to launch a new trade round, and they remain low. Those who have an established interest in integrating environment and trade policy are thinking through how to manage expectations given the reality of trade negotiation form and function. As negotiations over a new round have continued, analysis of what has to be done has fallen into three categories:

1. What can be inserted into the legally binding instrument that launches a round, which in turn will set up a new environmentally responsive negotiating agenda?
2. What can be done with the WTO's "built-in" agenda to deal with environment-related issues like reducing or eliminating environmentally damaging subsidies?
3. What parallel initiatives could be launched alongside a new round that would improve the negotiating atmosphere, compensate for, or offset the environmental effects of trade and provide real capacity-building resources for developing countries?

CONCLUSION

In the years since the conclusion of the Uruguay Round, the voices of environmentalists have been strong in repeatedly calling for a balance between the trade and environment agendas. There is a need for progressive reform of the WTO and its institutions to keep it dynamic, vital, and worthy of public trust. The overwhelming sense one has from assessing the WTO's work thus far is one of disappointment. In Marrakech, where the Uruguay Round agreements were signed, there was an explicit decision for the CTE to table concrete recommendations to ensure harmonious development of trade and environment policies. The CTE's 1996 Report merely characterized issues; there was little discussion of substantive issues other than recognizing the status quo. Progress on the real mandate of making recommendations regarding modifications to the multilateral trading system can be best described as glacial. The basic structure of the WTO remains unchanged; only the Appellate Body appears to be moving.

While the WTO has, de facto, brought together a range of views on trade-environment issues, the possibility that an integrated trade-environment regime will emerge with its encouragement is remote. The failure of the CTE to propose real policy solutions, in addition to its own limitations as an institution within the WTO, is evidence of this. Perhaps the WTO is still too closely connected in mind and spirit to the GATT—a purely trade-oriented organization. In the work leading to the 1996 Report, CTE delegates were uncomfortable at environment-related policymaking. Negotiation is understood, but all the training and experience is locked on to getting trade concessions. Policy planning for the avoidance of future conflicts is a different discipline. There is obviously much more work to do to properly integrate environment and trade policy.

The WTO secretariat has provided good analytical backup for trade-environment issues and has greatly facilitated the development of analysis of the various issues. We have learned a lot about the problems, and we have had serious proposals for solutions, but there has not been the political will to implement them. The CTE has provided new opportunities for NGOs to work together on these issues. It has spawned a number of informal trade, environment, and development networks or communities.[66] These networks have facilitated conferences, produced working papers, and participated in various fora, creating a dialogue between the principal players in the trade and environment debate from all sectors, allowing for a free flow of ideas that would not be possible in more formal arrangements. Many more initiatives are under way, and good work has been done by a variety of groups, including some excellent reports from the business community (e.g., the World Business Council for Sustainable Development Report on Trade and Environment). These new coalitions of interests may become more influential as the debate evolves, helping generate the political will necessary to advance all dimensions of the trade-environment agenda, as their focus tends to be more on what the WTO can do for the environment than merely seeing environmental concerns as a potential barrier to trade.[67] Indeed, the potential for win-win outcomes—in which economic and environmental objectives are both advanced—is real. Trade rules serving environmental and development objectives by removing perverse subsidies or superliberalizing environmental goods and services are such options.

These established NGO and trade policy networks have traveled some way down the path of considering progressive reform of the WTO. Let us hope that both these communities find a way to work cooperatively to integrate their respective objectives to ensure that our global institutions operate to maximize economic welfare and sustainable development.

There is deep skepticism about this integrative enterprise. The antiglobalization community is strong. They have demonstrated that they can move politicians and can communicate to global audiences. Ironically, the Internet, an instrument for globalization, is the main device for organizing opposition to the phenomenon. The media performs a similarly paradoxical function, acting as a force simultaneously for and against globalization.

In response to this skepticism, the WTO would prosper by securing constructive expertise and trust from nonstate actors and by establishing commitments on environment and development. Those objectives would be advanced by maximizing capacity building for developing countries to be genuine participants in the WTO, including the CTE. The CTE could be given a negotiating function in a new round. It might be given a supervisory role to ensure that environmental issues are integrated into the negotiating committees that are agreed to in the instruments that launch a round and govern the negotiations. The CTE could commission or collect environmental impact assessments of trade agreements and relate those assessments to the sustainable development objectives of the WTO and the new round.

This is all sensible policy, and it has the potential to advance both trade liberalization and environmental protection. Whether it satisfies the concerns of the antiglobalization movement is quite another matter.

NOTES

1. For a discussion of regime theory, see Andreas Hasenclever, Peter Mayer, and Volker Rittberger, *Theories of International Regimes* (Cambridge: Cambridge University Press, 1997), and Stephen Krasner, ed., *International Regimes* (Ithaca, N.Y.: Cornell University Press, 1983).

2. Draft Ministerial Text, December 1999 (on file with volume editor).

3. Decision to establish a Committee on Trade and the Environment, Marrakech, April 15, 1994.

4. Report of the Committee on Trade and Environment, WT/CTE/1, November 12, 1996.

5. See Wolfgang H. Reinecke, "Global Public Policy," *Foreign Affairs* 76, no. 127 (1997), and Abram Chayes and Antonia Handler Chayes, *The New Sovereignty: Compliance*

with International Regulatory Agreements (Cambridge, Mass.: Harvard University Press, 1995), 250–85.

6. For a discussion of realist regime theory, which suggests such uses of power, see Hasenclever, Mayer, and Rittberger; see also Krasner, ed.

7. For a general discussion of "contracting" between strong and weak states, see Stephen Krasner, *Sovereignty: Organized Hypocrisy* (Princeton, N.J.: Princeton University Press, 2000).

8. On epistemic communities generally, see Emmanuel Adler and Peter Haas, "Conclusion: Epistemic Communities, World Order, and the Creation of an Effective Research Program," *International Organization* 46, no. 367 (1992), and Oran R. Young, *International Governance: Protecting the Environment in a Stateless Society* (Ithaca, N.Y.: Cornell University Press, 1994).

9. For a review of the Biosafety Protocol negotiations breakdown, see "Concern about Trade Impacts Block Adoption of the Biosafety Protocol," *BRIDGES* 3, no. 2 (March 1999): 11, and *Earth Negotiations Bulletin* 9, no. 117 (February 26, 1999). In addition, "attempts to include trade provisions in the International Convention for the conservation of Atlantic Tuna, and in agreements to control driftnet fishing, were shelved because of their fear that they would be inconsistent with WTO rules; the same issue was raised in discussions in 1997 over the Kyoto Protocol and over the 'ban' amendment to the Basel Convention, in the 1998 negotiations over the Rotterdam Convention on prior informed consent and in 1999." See British House of Commons Select Committee Report on MEAs, Volume I Report and Proceedings of the Committee, July 21, 1999, para. 50. Despite this breakdown, the negotiations were restarted and concluded successfully in 2000.

10. This facilitative function would be performed regardless of which of the three paths (realism, liberalism, or epistemic communities) were followed. For an explanation of the value of institutions for solutions along the first two paths, see Robert Keohane, *After Hegemony* (Princeton, N.J.: Princeton University Press, 1984). For a theory suggesting the value of institutions along the third path, see Adler and Haas, 383.

11. The International Forum on Globalization has been seen as trying to do just that. See <http://www.ifg.org>.

12. For a summary and analysis of the meeting, see *BRIDGES, Special High-Level Symposium Issue* 3, no. 2 (March 1999).

13. GATT Articles XX(b) and (g). Article XX(g) continues on to state "if such measures are made effective in conjunction with restrictions on domestic production or consumption." It is worth noting that there is a slight variation in the way in which Article XX is articulated in the GATT and in its counterpart language in GATS. In the latter case, GATS Article 14 does not contain an exception in favor of the conservation of exhaustible natural resources. This may have implications in circumstances where there may be a crossover between services and environmental protection (such as regulations for guiding, in relation to protection of fisheries).

14. Article XX, chapeau.

15. Ibid.

16. See SPS agreement, Article 2.3, and TBT agreement, preamble. A footnote in the SPS agreement clarifies the meaning of this language: To successfully challenge an import restriction, the challenging party must show that another measure that would achieve the same level of protection is "reasonably available" and would be "significantly less restrictive to trade"; SPS agreement, footnote 3.

17. SPS agreement, Articles 2.2 and 3.

18. TBT agreement, Articles 2–4.

19. For example, SPS agreement, Articles 2.2 and 5.

20. SPS agreement, Article 5; TBT agreement, Articles 2–4.

21. As of 2001, there are two recent examples of successful applications of Article XX: the panel decision in "European Communities—Measures Affecting Asbestos and Asbestos-Containing Products, Report of the Panel," WT/DS135/R, and the ruling of a compliance panel in the ongoing *Shrimp-Turtle* dispute, discussed in *BRIDGES Weekly Trade News Digest* 5, no. 2 (June 19, 2001) (available at <http://www.ictsd.org>).

22. There are, in fact, two unadopted panel rulings in the *Tuna/Dolphin* dispute. See "United States—Restrictions on Imports of Tuna," *I.L.M.* 30, no. 1594 (1991), and "United States—Restrictions on Imports of Tuna," *I.L.M.* 33, no. 839 (1994).

23. "European Communities—Measures Affecting Asbestos and Asbestos-Containing Products," WT/DS135/AB/R, March 12, 2001.

24. Ibid., see paras. 110, 116, 121, and 122.

25. "United States—Standards for Reformulated and Conventional Gasoline," WT/DS2/AB/R, adopted May 20, 1996, reprinted in *I.T.L.R.* 1, no. 68 (1996).

26. *I.T.L.R.* 1, no. 68 (1996): 76.

27. CTE Report, para. 15.

28. WT/DS26/AB/R, WT/DS48/AB/R, January 5, 1998.

29. Ibid., para. 177.

30. "United States—Import Prohibitions on Certain Shrimp and Shrimp Products," Decision of the Appellate Body, WT/DS58/AB/R, October 12, 1998.

31. On the implications of this ruling, see James Cameron and Steven Orava, "Endangered Species Lose, but Has the World Trade Organization Spawned a New Breed of Lobbyist?" *London and Washington National Law Journal,* December 7, 1998.

32. In this instance, the Appellate Body was reversing the approach of the panel, which neglected to consider the listed exceptions in Article XX but based its determination under Article XX on the chapeau almost exclusively. For further discussion of this two-tiered approach, see Article XX discussion in note 13.

33. For a commentary on this and the implications of the ruling generally, see Gregory Shaffer, "*Shrimp/Turtle* Case Commentary," *American Journal of International Law* 93, no. 2 (April 1999): 507–14, and the Appellate Body decision, paras. 129–31.

34. This review of the CTE's 1996 Report is focused on areas of primary concern and does not purport to undertake a comprehensive review of each of the ten agenda items.

35. CTE Report, para. 214.

36. These briefs were prepared by the World Wildlife Fund (WWF), drafted by the Foundation for International Environmental Law and Development (FIELD) and by the Centre for International Environmental Law (CIEL) and the Centre for Marine Conservation.

37. CTE Report, paras. 216, 217.

38. In July 1996, the General Council adopted Procedures for the Circulation and Derestriction of WTO Documents.

39. See CTE Report, para. 217.

40. In July 1996, the General Council adopted Guidelines for Observer Status for International Intergovernmental Organizations in the WTO.

41. The recent High-Level Symposia reflect some effort on the part of the WTO to work with these other institutions; however, the fact that two independent meetings were held—one for trade and environment and one for trade and development—was noted by many with some regret. See "WTO Holds First-Ever High-Level Meetings on Sustainable Development but Environment and Trade Agendas Still Don't Mesh," *BRIDGES Weekly Trade News Digest* 3, no. 11 (March 22, 1999) (available at <http://www.ictsd.org>). A new UNCTAD/UNEP capacity-building program on trade and environment in developing countries has just been launched, so the future may display better cooperation than the past.

42. Memorandum by Duncan Brack of the Royal Institute of International Affairs to the British House of Commons Select Committee on Trade and Environment, 1999 Report, para. 1.4, 113.

43. CTE Report, para. 175.

44. Ibid., para. 174(iv).

45. Ibid., para. 178.

46. Ibid.

47. While the U.S. environmental measure technically regulates shrimp trawling practices, it actually seeks to protect sea turtles, listed under Annex 1 of CITES.

48. British House of Commons Select Committee on the Environment, Fourth Report, *World Trade and the Environment,* vol. I, para. 187.

49. These briefly identified factors are drawn from Stephan Ohlhoff and Hannes Schloemann, "Rational Allocation of Disputes and 'Constitutionalisation': Forum Choice as an Issue of Competence," in James Cameron and Karen Campbell, eds., *Dispute Resolution in the WTO* (London: Cameron May, 1998), 302. See also James Cameron and Jonathon Robinson, "The Use of Trade Provisions in International Environmental Agreements and their Compatibility with the GATT," *Y.I.E.L.* 2 (1991).

50. WT/DS2/AB/R, 22.

51. Ibid., 23.

52. "United States—Import Prohibition of Certain Shrimp and Shrimp Products, Recourse to Article 21.5 by Malaysia, Report to the Panel," WTO Document WT/DS58/RW, June 15, 2001, 100.

53. The proposal contains the following two options for amending Article XX: (1) Add an additional paragraph (k) with an Understanding to be agreed between WTO members (draft Understanding was included as Annex A to the proposal). Paragraph (k) to read: (k) taken pursuant to a MEA complying with the provisions of the Understanding on the relationship between MEA-based measures and the WTO rules. (2) Amend paragraph (b) to read: (b) necessary to protect human, animal, plant life or health or the environment; and measures taken pursuant to Multilateral Environmental Agreements complying with the provisions of the "Understanding on the relationship between MEA-based trade measures and the WTO rules" (Annex A).

54. British House of Commons Select Committee on Environment, 1999 Report, para. 55.

55. See "Dispute Settlement Review May Fizzle Out," *BRIDGES Weekly Trade News Digest* 3, no. 30 (August 2, 1999) (available at <http://www.ictsd.org>).

56. The Havana Charter for an International Trade Organization was drafted between 1946 and 1948 but never entered into force.

57. For a more detailed discussion of possible reforms to the WTO dispute settlement

process, see James Cameron and Zen Makuch, *Sustainable Development and Integrated Dispute Settlement in GATT 1994* (Gland, Switzerland: World Wildlife Fund, 1994). It might also be possible to set up a means for obtaining a scientific opinion, for example, on SPS and standards for health or environmental protection. Perhaps an advisory opinion from an IGO might assist in settling science-based disputes.

58. This chapter was written largely before the release of the Panel and Appellate Body decisions on asbestos, WT/DS.135R and WT/DS135/AB/R, respectively.

59. See, for example, "European Communities—Measures Affecting Asbestos and Asbestos-Containing Products, Report of the Appellate Body," WTO Document WT/DS135/AB/R.

60. Again, the Appellate Body's ruling in the *Shrimp/Turtle* dispute may offer principles on which this issue can be resolved favorably.

61. CTE Report, see paras. 61–73.

62. "United States—Measures concerning Meat and Meat Products (Hormones)," Report of the Panel, WT/DS26/R, August 18, 1997; Report of the Appellate Body, WT/DS26/AB/R, January 5, 1998.

63. Ibid., paras. 201 and 203, respectively.

64. The Basel Convention on the Transboundary Movements of Hazardous Waste has provisions governing the shipment of hazardous waste. In 1985, the FAO established an International Code of Conduct on the Distribution and Use of Pesticides; in 1987, UNEP promulgated the London Guidelines for the Exchange of Information on Chemicals in International Trade. Since 1989, FAO and UNEP have implemented a Joint Program for the Operation of a Prior Informed Consent Procedure for Certain Hazardous Chemicals in International Trade. In 1998, negotiations concluded and the FAO/UNEP Joint Program became the Rotterdam convention and was opened for signature. For a review, see *Earth Negotiations Bulletin* 15, no. 20 (July 19, 1999).

65. For a useful discussion of market access, see *Expert Panel on Trade and Sustainable Development: Report of First Meeting* (Gland, Switzerland: World Wildlife Fund, October 1996).

66. Examples of these networks include the Global Trade and Environment Study (GETS), the Policy Dialogue on Trade and the Environment (operated through the Consensus Building Institute), the Experts Panel on Trade and Sustainable Development (organized through WWF International), the International Centre for Trade and Sustainable Development (ICTSD), the International Institute for Sustainable Development (IISD), the World Conservation Union (IUCN), and the Third World Network, all of which are making good contributions to the trade, environment, and development debate.

67. Using the WTO to remove environmentally harmful subsidies is one example where both communities would benefit.

3

Dispute Settlement and U.S. Environmental Laws

Gustavo Grunbaum

Since the early 1990s, dispute settlement panels of the General Agreement on Tariffs and Trade (GATT) and the World Trade Organization (WTO) have repeatedly deemed particular U.S. environmental laws to be inconsistent with international trade law.[1] Four separate U.S. environmental laws have been challenged as being inconsistent with international obligations of the United States in either GATT or WTO dispute settlement proceedings. At least one element of each of these laws or regulations, adopted by the United States either to protect endangered species or to promote clean air, was declared to be inconsistent with U.S. treaty obligations and therefore illegal under international law.

It is shown in this chapter that all four of the U.S. environmental laws evaluated by GATT/WTO panels are the product, at least in part, of a convergence of interests between industry and environmental groups. These groups, voicing the interests of diverse constituencies, formed an effective lobby that has been called a "Baptist-bootlegger" coalition.[2] The success, increasing importance, and mechanics of Baptist-bootlegger coalitions of environmental nongovernmental organizations (ENGOs) and industry in promoting U.S. environmental laws that also act as import restrictions have been documented by other commentators.[3]

This chapter examines the four U.S. environmental laws that have been adjudicated in the GATT or WTO, considers the domestic politics of their enactment, analyzes the GATT/WTO legal decisions that pertain to them, and evaluates the extent to which the U.S. government has committed itself to complying with each applicable GATT/WTO decision. The four U.S. laws in question are (1) the import ban provisions of the Marine Mammal Protection Act (MMPA),[4] ruled to be inconsistent with GATT by two separate Dispute Panels; (2) the provision of the Energy and Conservation Act that calls for separating automobiles into domestic and import fleets in determining a manufacturer's average fuel economy (CAFE standard);[5] (3) an Environmental Protection Agency (EPA) reformulated gas regulation (Gas Rule),[6] promulgated under the authority of a Clean Air Act provision,[7] that treated foreign refiners and domestic refiners differently; and (4) the shrimp import ban provisions passed by Congress in 1989 to protect endangered sea turtles (Section 609).[8] In examining each case, I first discuss the development of the unique Baptist-bootlegger coalition in support of the particular law. The level of cooperation between the interest groups varied greatly, from submitting comments jointly (in the case of the Gas Rule) to being no more congenial to each other than the namesake Baptists and bootleggers may have been to each other in promoting Prohibition (in the case of the CAFE Standard). But in each case, actions or omissions by a de facto coalition of ENGOs and business interests supported enactment of the law at issue. I then discuss the legal analysis of and decision reached on each law by the GATT/WTO dispute settlement system. Finally, I examine the U.S. response to each GATT/WTO decision.

The chapter concludes by analyzing the implications of these WTO decisions for the WTO and for future efforts of U.S. Baptist-bootlegger coalitions to enact new environmental laws. The analysis suggests the likelihood that U.S. environmental laws challenged at the WTO will have been enacted with support of a Baptist-bootlegger coalition and that the WTO dispute settlement system will act as a check on laws supported by such a coalition. It further suggests that great care must be taken in crafting U.S. environmental legislation intended to garner support from environmentalists and business.

MMPA AND THE GATT TUNA/DOLPHIN DECISIONS

Congruence of Interests in Support of the MMPA

The MMPA, as well as the U.S. regulatory scheme it mandated, had undergone significant and gradual change in the nearly two decades between its adoption on October 21, 1972,[9] and its being first declared GATT inconsistent on August 16, 1991. One notable feature of the evolution of the MMPA provisions governing yellowfin tuna harvesting and importation is the continuing convergence of interests between the U.S. tuna fleet and the ENGOs concerned with promoting dolphin protection.

Prior to the MMPA's initial passage in 1972, comprehensive hearings were called to discuss a number of proposed bills that would eventually result in the MMPA.[10] At those hearings, the American tuna fleet, represented by the American Tunaboat

Association (ATA), opposed all proposed legislation aimed at regulating the industry for purposes of increasing marine mammal protection, including the use of trade restrictions as an enforcement measure.[11] A cynic might argue, not without support, that the U.S. tuna industry opposed import restrictions because it wanted to preserve the option of reflagging its ships to circumvent U.S. regulations.[12] Unlike the tuna industry, the ENGOs were on record promoting tuna import bans as a means of protecting dolphins from the beginning of the MMPA's history. In 1972, the Sierra Club suggested that Congress should pass legislation making it "unlawful to import into the United States any fish . . . if such fish was caught in a manner determined by the Secretary [of Commerce] to be injurious to marine mammals."[13] The final version of the MMPA gave this suggestion virtually full effect in Section 101(a)(2).[14] The original act did not, however, instruct the Commerce Department on how to determine whether an exporting country's fishing methods were "injurious to marine mammals."

In July 1984, Congress passed Public Law 98-364, significantly modifying the MMPA's effects on foreign fleets by strengthening the documentation requirements imposed on foreign fleets by the act.[15] Specifically, the amendment required the governments of nations seeking to export yellowfin tuna harvested with purse seine nets in the eastern tropical Pacific Ocean (ETP) to "provide documentary evidence that . . . the government of the harvesting nation has adopted a regulatory program governing the incidental taking of marine mammals in the course of such harvesting that is comparable to that of the United States."[16] At the hearings that preceded this amendment, the U.S. tuna industry, represented by the ATA and the United States Tuna Foundation (USTF),[17] advocated extending direct application of U.S. standards to foreign fleets harvesting tuna for the U.S. market. While neither industry group requested an import ban in their prepared statements,[18] the ATA did complain of the unfairness of applying MMPA standards solely on the United States fleet,[19] and the USTF suggested that "some sort of import tax on foreign can product coming in would certainly help," though the tuna industry did not explicitly ask Congress to impose any particular restriction on the importation of tuna.[20] The ENGOs continued to press for application of U.S.-comparable standards to foreign fleets by means of import restrictions.[21]

One noteworthy element of the 1984 debate about the MMPA was the extent to which the ENGOs and the tuna industry acknowledged the congruity of their interests and the extent to which Congress recognized this congruity. While the two groups still disagreed on many details, including their level of commitment to promoting import bans, in the words of Senator Bob Packwood, chairman of the Senate Finance Committee, "the differences between the tuna industry and the environmental groups have narrowed significantly. There have been good-faith efforts on both sides, an example of parties finally realizing they are going to have [to] live together and work together and so they have worked out reasonable relationships."[22]

Public Law 100-711, passed on November 23, 1988, further amended the MMPA in two significant ways.[23] First, Section 101(a)(2)(B) was clarified to make explicit Congress' intent that the secretary of commerce heed specific requirements in determining whether a country employing purse-seine nets in harvesting yellow-fin tuna in the ETP complied with U.S. standards.[24] Second, the 1988 amendments added an intermediary nation import ban provision: The secretary of commerce could now ban the import of tuna from an intermediary nation if it could not

> certify and provide reasonable proof . . . that it has acted to prohibit the importation of such tuna and tuna products from any nation from which direct import to the United States of such tuna and tuna products is barred under this section within sixty days following the effective date of such ban.[25]

This was added "in order to prevent embargoed nations from circumventing U.S. restrictions, thus weakening the effectiveness of U.S. law."[26]

The tuna industry's position on import restrictions in 1988 was neither aggressive nor united. The USTF, while not opposing the use of import restrictions for protecting dolphins, did not actively support this approach.[27] The ATA, on the other hand, simply reaffirmed its support for the 1984 import restrictions and opposed any new amendments to the MMPA.[28] The ENGOs continued to view import restrictions as an effective restraint on the dolphin-harmful practices of foreign fleets.[29]

The net result of the 1988 reauthorization effort was that Congress put into place further import restrictions that were either supported or not opposed by the components of what was referred to as a "working group of commercial fishing interests and the environmental community."[30] The ENGOs scored a victory through the bolstering of the mandates on the Department of Commerce in implementing the import restrictions, and the canning element of the tuna industry, which had the most to lose in the form of reduced supply and higher prices, could find some solace in the "intermediary nation" provisions: Their foreign competitors would not be able to sell dolphin-unsafe tuna within the U.S. market either.

In 1992, Congress passed two more laws that amended the MMPA's import provisions.[31] Hearings held at that time evidence a high level of agreement and cooperation on the parts of the ENGOs and industry on the issue of tuna import restrictions, especially in their reactions to proposals advanced by the administration of George H. W. Bush.[32] Richard Atchison, executive director of the ATA, described a part of the administration's proposal, which would in part impose a five-year moratorium on purse seine harvesting on the domestic fleet beginning on March 1, 1994, as "contain[ing] a glaring double-standard" that would discriminate against the domestic fleet in favor of foreign fleets.[33] He warned that such a tack would further hamper the U.S. tuna industry, already heavily burdened by MMPA restrictions.[34] ENGO representatives echoed these concerns. Traci Romine of Greenpeace warned against achieving the goal of switching to environmentally sound fishing techniques "at the expense of [U.S.] communities and workers,"[35] and John Fitzgerald of the Defenders of Wildlife condemned the administration's proposal as an undoing of the commendable progress that had been achieved in the area of improving dolphin protection[36] and questioned the fairness of the proposal.[37] Both ENGOs and the ATA, however, endorsed one aspect of the administration's proposal: the call for the adoption of a multilateral approach to protect the dolphins.[38] In short, the legislative process leading up to the 1992 amendments to the MMPA reflected renewed vitality of the Baptist-bootlegger coalition that had evolved between the tuna industry and the ENGOs for the purpose of guiding congressional policy on the issue of dolphin mortality.[39]

GATT Decisions

On August 16, 1991, a GATT dispute settlement panel decided in favor of some claims by Mexico that certain aspects of the MMPA laws were contrary to Article XI:1 of the GATT and were not justified by the Article XX exceptions of GATT.[40] This case, known as *Tuna I*, was the first of two GATT challenges to the MMPA. Mexico had challenged three provisions of U.S. law: Two of the provisions were trade provisions contained in Section 101 of the MMPA,[41] and the third was a tuna-labeling restriction contained in the Dolphin Protection Consumer Information Act (DPCIA).[42] The GATT Panel ruled that the trade restrictions were GATT inconsistent while the labeling provisions of the DPCIA were valid restrictions on trade.[43]

Mexico's primary argument was that the import ban provisions violated Article XI, constituting a quantitative restriction "made effective through quotas, import or export licenses or other measures" to limit the importation of Mexican product.[44] The United States countered that the MMPA import restrictions should be more appropriately tested against Article III because they were "laws, regulations and requirements affecting [the] internal sale [or] offering for sale" that were administered no less favorably on Mexican product than on domestic product.[45] The United States also argued that even if the restrictions were inconsistent with certain GATT articles, the general exceptions contained in Article XX salvaged them.[46]

The GATT Panel accepted the Mexican argument that the MMPA restrictions were "quantitative restrictions on importation" and therefore outlawed under Article XI and not "internal regulations enforced at the time or point of importation," which would have been permitted by Article III.4.[47] The Panel noted that the "United States [had] not present[ed] to the Panel any arguments to support a different legal conclusion regarding Article XI"[48] that bans "prohibitions or restrictions . . . whether made effective through quotas, import or export licenses or other measures . . . on the importation of any product of the territory of any contracting party."[49]

More important, the Panel dismissed the attempt by the United States to shield the MMPA provisions behind Article XX by holding that Article XX was not intended to justify actions aimed at extraterritorial environmental goals. The Panel focused on the intention of the drafters of Article XX and concluded that Article XX(b) was intended to excuse measures that protected animal life within the jurisdiction of the importing country and that Article XX(g) excused measures "primarily aimed at rendering effective restrictions on production or consumption within [a contracting nation's] jurisdiction."[50] The Panel also found that even if Article XX were to read to have the extraterritorial effect the United States argued for, the MMPA failed to qualify for exemption under Article XX on other grounds. The provisions were not "necessary to protect human, animal or plant life or health" and were therefore not excused under Article XX(b) because the United States had failed to meet the "necessary" standard laid out by the Panel: The United States had not demonstrated that it had "exhausted all options reasonably available to pursue its dolphin protection objectives through measures consistent with the [GATT]."[51] The Article XX(g) defense also failed because the MMPA provisions were not "primarily aimed" at the conservation of exhaustible natural resources, as the MMPA limitations on trade were based "on such unpredictable conditions [that they] could not be regarded as being aimed primarily at the conservation of dolphins."[52] The Panel applied the same logic in evaluating both the direct import ban of Section 101(a)(2) and the "intermediate nation" import ban and came to the same conclusion.[53]

The U.S. government blocked adoption of this *Tuna I* Panel report by the GATT General Council. And Mexico, which had begun negotiating the North American Free Trade Agreement (NAFTA) with the United States, did not press the matter.

But on May 20, 1994, a second GATT dispute settlement panel issued a decision (*Tuna II*) on a challenge of the MMPA trade restrictions—this time by the European Economic Community (EEC).[54] Though the request for consultations that eventually led to this decision was made in March 1992, months before the previously noted 1992 amendments (which were made in the fall), the Panel agreed to consider these new provisions of the MMPA.[55] The changes to the act did not appear to influence the *Tuna II* Panel; its analysis largely mirrored the *Tuna I* analysis[56] and likewise concluded that both the "primary nation" and the "intermediary nation" embargoes "did not meet the requirements of . . . Article III, were contrary to Article XI:1, and were not covered by the exceptions in Article XX(b), (g) or (d) of the [GATT]."[57]

The Panel also clarified the issue of the "territorial" or "jurisdictional" scope of Article XX. The Panel concluded that while Article XX(g) was not intended to "apply only to policies related to the conservation of exhaustible natural resources located within the territory of the contracting party invoking the provision," it was not intended "to permit contracting parties to take trade measures so as to force other contracting parties to change their policies within their jurisdictions."[58] Similarly, Article XX(b) did not excuse the primary or intermediary bans under the MMPA because they "were taken . . . to force other countries to change their policies with respect to persons and things within their own jurisdiction."[59] The dividing line between environmental measures excused by Article XX and those not excused, therefore, was not whether the effect of the measure was extraterritorial with respect to the country invoking Article XX but whether the measure would infringe on the policymaking jurisdiction of other contracting parties and therefore be extrajurisdictional. For example, the Panel pointed out that under international law, it is permissible for a nation to prescribe laws that apply to its own nationals and ships, even if those nationals or ships are located outside its territory. Therefore, the Panel concluded that Article XX could be invoked for extraterritorial but not extrajurisdictional purposes. The Panel concluded by recommending that "the Contracting Parties request the United States to bring the above measures into conformity with its obligations under the [GATT]."[60]

U.S. Compliance

Neither of the *Tuna I* nor the *Tuna II* decision had a binding effect on the United States because the United States could, and did, block the Panel decisions from being adopted by the GATT Council. Under the GATT dispute settlement framework, a Panel decision would be adopted and become GATT law only if it were approved by a consensus of the GATT Council, which had one representative of each of the contracting parties; therefore, any contracting party, including the losing party, could block passage of a GATT Panel decision.[61] In the period immediately following the Panel's decisions, the United States disregarded those decisions and continued enforcing the MMPA. For example, in 1994, despite the GATT Panel's decisions, the United States imposed embargoes of the importation of tuna on at least eight nations.[62]

In July 1997, however, motivated in part by a desire to prevent the MMPA from being rechallenged by Mexico and the EEC before the WTO, Congress passed the International Dolphin Conservation Program Act, which amended the MMPA by exempting nations in compliance with the International Dolphin Conservation Program from the import restrictions of the MMPA.[63] The International Dolphin Conservation Program essentially requires the tuna fleets of countries that had executed the 1995 Declaration of Panama to refrain from using tuna harvesting methods that injure or kill dolphins. Twelve countries are parties to the Declaration of Panama, including the United States, Mexico, and several other countries subject to MMPA trade restrictions.[64]

While domestic political support for the International Dolphin Program Conservation Act was strong, there were dissenters in Congress who felt that "the international trade dispute between Mexico and the United States over dolphin protection [was] the driving force behind the legislation" and that the legislation "weaken[ed] U.S. environmental protection and consumer information standards."[65] The International Dolphin Conservation Program also garnered mixed reviews from conservation groups. Though the program and the legislation were embraced by such groups as Greenpeace, the World Wildlife Fund, the Environmental Defense Fund, the National Wildlife Federation, and the Center for Marine Conservation,[66] a number of other environmental and consumer groups, including Earth Island Institute and the Humane Society, opposed the legislation as failing adequately to protect dolphins.[67]

Despite the mixed support the legislation received from the ENGOs that were so instrumental in passing the MMPA, the International Dolphin Conservation Program Act passed the House by an overwhelming margin.[68] The United States had pursued the negotiation of a multilateral treaty to pursue its dolphin protection objectives as advised by the *Tuna II* Panel.

THE CAFE REGULATION AND THE GATT DECISION

The Coalition behind the CAFE Provisions of the Energy Policy and Conservation Act

The Energy Policy and Conservation Act of 1975 imposed fuel efficiency standards on automobile manufacturers' fleets sold in the United States. Under the act, automobile manufacturers were subject to fines if the fuel efficiency of their fleets (measured by CAFE) did not meet certain standards. Section 503(b)(1) of the act required the EPA to consider separately the CAFEs of a car manufacturer's imported fleet and the manufacturer's domestically produced fleet.[69] This aspect of the act was challenged by the European Community (EC) as inconsistent with GATT.

In the thirteen months prior to passage of the Energy Policy and Conservation Act on December 22, 1975, a number of hearings were held on the issues of the energy crisis and the potential for conservation through automobile fuel efficiency standards.[70] These hearings took place during a very volatile period for the nation in general and for the special interests represented at the hearings in particular. The Arab oil embargo and the development of a national energy policy to reduce dependence on foreign energy sources were of critical concern to the automobile industry.[71] The Clean Air Act had recently been passed, drawing the ire of the automobile industry while at the same time heartening environmental and consumer groups in their opposition to the policies of that industry.[72]

At the same time, the automotive industry was in dire economic straits with severe implications for the entire American economy; the decrease in automobile sales experienced from 1973 to 1974 was estimated to have resulted in 600,000 lost jobs throughout the economy.[73] Foreign automobile imports were making sizable inroads into the domestic market, and the impact on labor was of great national concern.[74] Against this background, it is no surprise that a congruence of positions among ENGOs, labor unions, and the affected industry on the issue of fuel economy improvements never developed to the extent it did among the interest groups that supported the MMPA.

The domestic automobile industry's position on the issue of mandatory fuel economy standards was that they were a bad idea and that market forces would result in improved fuel efficiency.[75] The industry argued that it needed to be able to maintain its ability to serve the needs of a public that liked a wide range of cars, including large "gas guzzlers."[76] A serious concern of industry was that mandatory fuel economy improvements would impact its ability to produce large, expensive cars.[77] The automobile industry's desire to preserve this market was understandable in light of two facts. First, despite a growing public awareness of the desirability of fuel efficiency, the market for small cars had shrunk drastically in 1974–75[78] after a record year for small car sales in 1973–74.[79] Second, the market for large cars was where the industry generated most of its profits.[80] Even if mandatory fuel efficiency gains did not foreclose the option of producing larger cars, the automobile industry was very concerned that Congress would give small cars, both domestic and foreign produced, a selling advantage over large, domestically produced cars.

The position of the Public Interest Research Group (PIRG), a stand-in for ENGOs and consumer groups led by Ralph Nader, and of the United Auto Workers (UAW) on mandatory fuel efficiency improvements was the same: They favored them.[81] Nader's group viewed these mandatory fuel efficiency improvements as a means to improve on what he categorized as the automobile industry's reprehensible safety, competition, and innovation record.[82] Labor, on the other hand, viewed the industry's emphasis on large cars and lack of attention on fuel economy as a failed marketing strategy that was in large part to blame for the crisis in the automotive industry that was costing so many UAW members their jobs.[83] The industry disagreed and argued that any attempt to mandate fuel efficiencies would cost U.S. jobs by favoring small, mostly foreign cars over large, domestic ones.[84]

The Energy Policy and Conservation Act that was finally passed in December 1975 struck a compromise between the positions espoused by the domestic automobile industry and the other interested parties. While mandatory fuel economy standards were adopted, as PIRG and the UAW had advocated, the automobile industry could find some consolation in the fact that their large-car market share was afforded some protection. By mandating that fuel economy standards for U.S. producers would be established fleetwide for all cars "domestically" produced, Section 503 of the act effectively allowed smaller cars to subsidize the fuel inefficiency of larger cars.[85] More important from a protectionist perspective, the act did not give foreign producers the same opportunity—their fuel economy was based solely on the characteristics of the fleet of relatively large cars they actually exported to the United States, which could not be averaged with the characteristics of the smaller cars they produced in the United States or abroad.[86]

While publicly visible Baptist-bootlegger cooperation did not develop between industry and ENGOs or labor, the legislative process had produced a de facto Baptist-bootlegger coalition by creating a legislative compromise that offered something to the automobile industry, labor, and environmentalists.

The GATT Panel Decision

On October 11, 1994, a GATT dispute settlement panel handed down its decision on a challenge of three U.S. taxes on automobiles brought by the EC.[87] Three separate taxes on automobiles were challenged: a luxury tax, a "gas guzzler" tax, and a tax triggered by failure to meet the CAFE standard. The Panel ruled that the first two taxes were GATT consistent, while the CAFE regulation contravened the GATT.[88]

The specific CAFE regulation that the EC objected to was an EPA regulation governing the calculation of the average fuel economy of an automobile manufacturer's total fleet.[89] The CAFE regulation was alleged to be inconsistent with GATT on two grounds. First, it provided for a separate accounting of average fuel economy for import and domestic fleets, and, second, it provided for the calculation of a CAFE for a manufacturer's entire production line.[90] The EC argued that both elements of the CAFE regulation violated Article III:2 of the GATT, which prohibits the imposition of taxes or other charges on imported products in excess of those imposed on like domestic products. The EC argued that the fact that 99.99 percent of the CAFE penalties imposed between 1980 and 1992 fell on European cars was evidence that their products were subject to taxes that U.S. products were not.[91] The EC also argued that both aspects of the CAFE standard violated Article III:4 of the GATT, which required "treatment no less favorable than that accorded to like products of national origin in respect of all laws, regulations and requirements."[92] The EC also argued that the separate foreign fleet accounting provision of the CAFE regulation violated Article III:5 of the GATT, which prohibits the application of internal quantitative restrictions "so as to afford protection for domestic production."[93] Lastly, the EC argued that Article XX exemptions did not serve to remedy any GATT inconsistencies of the CAFE regulation and that the regulation should be denounced as a "disguised restriction on trade."[94]

The position of the United States as to the Article III claims was that the CAFE regulations imposed civil penalties, not taxes, for failure to comply with U.S. domestic law and that these penalties applied equally to domestic and imported fleets.[95] The United States also argued that while it was not necessary to shield the CAFE regulations behind Article XX, the exemption articulated in Article XX(g) applied in that the CAFE regulations were necessary to conserve an "exhaustible natural resource," fuel, and that the restrictions on foreign fleets were made "in conjunction with restrictions on domestic production and consumption."[96]

The GATT Dispute Panel first had to determine whether the CAFE regulation should be considered to fall within the category of "internal taxes or other internal charges," governed by Article III:2, or within the category of "law, regulations and requirements," subject to Article III:4. The Panel found that the Article III:4 characterization was the more appropriate one in light of its view that the "ordinary meaning of the terms used in the regulation" suggested that the regulation was a requirement enforced by penalties, not a tax.[97] The Panel went on to find that both aspects of the CAFE regulation outlined previously violated Article III:4. The separate averaging of foreign-produced fleets that were exported to the United States provided foreign manufacturers "less favourable conditions of competition" because it did not allow foreign manufacturers that exported large cars to the United States to increase the fuel economies of their fleets by including their smaller domestic fleets, while U.S. producers had that luxury.[98] The determination of a CAFE for an entire fleet was viewed as possibly resulting in "less favorable" treatment because it regulated cars on the basis of their ownership or control and therefore did not "relate to cars as products."[99] Lastly, the GATT Panel found Article XX(g) to be inapplicable because while the "CAFE scheme as a whole" might have been "primarily aimed at the conservation of natural resources," the specific measures of separate foreign fleet accounting and fleet averaging did not meet this standard.[100] The Panel did not find it necessary, in light of its Article III:4 findings, to consider the Article III:5 claim.[101]

U.S. Compliance

As with the *Tuna I* and *Tuna II* decisions, the United States was not technically under an international obligation to change its laws to conform with the *CAFE* Panel decision: The GATT Panel's decision was never adopted by the Council, so it was never formalized. The failure of the United States to act to address the *CAFE* Panel's decision may be explained by the fact that the United States chose simply to overlook the negative aspects of the decision. The Panel's decision was proclaimed by President Clinton as evidence that GATT was not a threat to U.S. environmental law and was generally heralded as a victory for the United States, a view the EC did not share.[102] The United States did, however, amend the provisions of the U.S. Code governing the calculation of corporate average fuel economy as part of the North America Free Trade Agreement Implementation Act.[103] The changes to this section of the code essentially opened up the classification of "domestic" vehicles to include vehicles manufactured largely in Mexico and Canada.

THE REFORMULATED GAS RULE

The Coalition in Favor of the Reformulated Gas Rule

Unlike the other environmental laws declared to be GATT inconsistent, the Gas Rule was not a congressional product; it was the result of an executive agency rule-making procedure. The EPA had decided to use the process known as "negotiated rule making" in developing the reformulated gas rule,[104] as authorized under the Clean Air Act.[105] This process entails convening a negotiating committee consisting of representatives from the EPA and all affected interests and generally including other government agencies, states, localities, industry, consumers, and environmental groups.[106] In the view of the EPA, this process was a means of "developing rules that are acceptable to all interests that will be significantly affected by the rules" and therefore "far less likely to be challenged in court."[107] Since the process aims at building a consensus between ENGOs and industry, "negotiated rule-making" provides a fertile breeding ground for the formation of Baptist-bootlegger coalitions, and its success is in large part measured by its ability to generate such a coalition.[108] In this particular rule making, among the Baptists and bootleggers that made up the negotiating committee were the National Petroleum Refiners Association, the American Independent Refiners Association, the Society of Independent Gasoline Marketers of America, the American Lung Association, the Sierra Club, and the Natural Resources Defense Council.[109]

The Gas Rule that was eventually challenged was a result of the Clean Air Act mandate to the EPA to determine 1990 gasoline quality in order to gauge future improvements in gas quality. The EPA established "statutory baselines" reflecting average domestic 1990 gasoline quality.[110] Individual domestic refineries were given the option of choosing among three methods to calculate individual refinery baselines that were used to track improvement. Importers, on the other hand, were offered no such choice: They had to calculate their baselines using a prescribed method; if the data required by this method were not available, the foreign refiner would be assigned the statutory baseline. If an importer was also a foreign refiner, it could qualify for domestic refinery treatment if it imported at least 75 percent of its foreign output into the United States. It was this disparate treatment that prompted Venezuela and Brazil to seek redress before a WTO dispute settlement panel.

The process that eventually resulted in the Gas Rule, a small part of which was later found to be inconsistent with GATT 1994, was long and complex. The negotiating committee was convened by the EPA for the first time on March 14, 1991.[111] On August 16, 1991, the diverse interests represented in the negotiating committee reached consensus on an outline of the underlying principles and signed the Agreement in Principle.[112] The EPA, working from this agreement and extensive public comment, issued a Final Rule, the Gas Rule, in February 1994, almost three years after the negotiated rule-making process had begun.[113] While the fairly technical and narrow issue (the process by which foreign refineries' baselines would be calculated) that led Venezuela to challenge the reformulated gas rule was not explicitly addressed by the negotiating committee,[114] the differential treatment of foreign refiners and the GATT 1994 implications of such treatment were discussed at a number of EPA-sponsored meetings prior to the release of the February 1994 Final Rule, and comments on the issue were solicited in the February 1993 Notice of Proposed Rule-making (NPRM).[115] Following these meetings and comments, the EPA attempted to justify the disparate treatment on concerns about its ability to verify foreign refiners' baselines and its statutory authority to audit and inspect foreign refineries.[116] Yet it was generally recognized at the time that the Gas Rule would be protectionist in structure and effect.

The Gas Rule was issued in February 1994. Less than three months after its issuance, the EPA proposed modifying the Final Rule to provide for similar treatment of domestic and foreign refineries.[117] This change in policy was credited by its opponents to pressure imposed by the State Department on behalf of Venezuela. The opposition to this proposed rule, known as the Venezuela Rule, was intense and manifested itself in two different fora. First, interested parties voiced their opinions directly to the EPA in the form of comments submitted to the EPA pursuant to the comment period following the NPRM for the Venezuela Rule. Second, hearings were held in Congress to evaluate the Venezuela Rule.[118] The statements submitted by ENGOs and industry in these fora, as well as Congress' legislative reaction to the Venezuela Rule (an appropriations rider preventing its implementation), sent out a simple and loud message: A strong Baptist-bootlegger coalition opposed the proposed rule.[119]

Perhaps some of the most telling evidence of the strength of the Baptist-bootlegger coalition was a set of comments submitted to the EPA docket on May 23, 1994, in opposition to the Venezuela Rule; it was submitted jointly by the Center for International Environmental Law, the Independent Refiners Coalition, the Defenders of Wildlife, and the Sierra Club.[120] The nature of this Baptist-bootlegger coalition was not lost on its constituent members.[121] In addition to this set of joint comments, diverse ENGO and industry representatives submitted extensive comments condemning the Venezuela Rule.[122] As a result of the intense backlash against the Venezuela Rule, the Gas Rule was adopted by the EPA.

The WTO Panel and Appellate Body Reports

In January 1995, the WTO came into existence, and Venezuela and Brazil almost immediately filed a dispute settlement challenge to the U.S. Gas Rule. On January 17, 1996, the WTO's first dispute panel report was issued in the *Gas Rule* case.[123] Venezuela and Brazil had raised two principal arguments against the Gas Rule. First, they argued that the Gas Rule was inconsistent with Articles I and III of the GATT in that it failed to provide most-favored-nation treatment and national treatment, respectively. The Panel concluded that domestic and imported gasoline were "like" products and that, because under the Gas Rule "imported gasoline was effectively prevented from benefiting from as favorable sales condition as were afforded domestic gasoline by an individual baseline tied to the producer of a product, imported gasoline was treated less favorably than domestic gasoline," constituting a violation of Article III:4 obligations.[124] The Panel did not find it necessary, in light of its conclusion regarding Article III:4, to examine the rule's consistency with Article III:1 or I:1.[125]

Second, Venezuela and Brazil argued that the Gas Rule was not justified by Article XX(b), (d), or (g). The Panel concluded that the rule did not fall under Article XX(b) in that it was not "necessary" for the protection of human, animal, or plant life or health: The United States had not met its burden of showing "that there was no other measure consistent, or less inconsistent, with Article III:4 reasonably available to enforce foreign refiner baselines."[126] Article XX(d), which permits measures "necessary to secure compliance with laws or regulations which are not inconsistent with the provisions of [GATT 1994]," did not serve to excuse the rule because, in the view of the Panel, the baseline establishment methods set forth in the rule were not an enforcement mechanism "secur[ing] compliance" with the baseline system; they were simply rules for determining baselines. Lastly, Article XX(g) failed to provide protection in the Panel's view because there was "no direct connection between less favourable treatment of imported gasoline . . . and the U.S. objective of improving air quality;"[127] the Gas Rule could not therefore be said to be "primarily aimed at the conservation of natural resources."[128]

The WTO Appellate Body disagreed with key parts of the Panel's legal analysis but also decided that the Gas Rule was GATT inconsistent. The Appellate Body agreed that the EPA's baseline establishment rules contravened GATT Article III but rejected the Panel's "direct connection" test under Article XX(g) and decided that the baseline establishment rules fell within the terms of Article XX(g). Nonetheless, the Appellate Body concluded that the baseline establishment rules constituted "unjustifiable discrimination" and a "disguised restriction on international trade," thereby failing to meet the requirement of the chapeau of Article XX.[129]

U.S. Compliance

The United States responded relatively quickly to the adoption by the WTO Dispute Settlement Body of the Appellate Body's report. In August 1997, motivated by the "U.S. commitment to comply with its obligations under the World Trade Organization agreement," the EPA issued a final rule revising the Gas Rule so that foreign refineries would be subjected to the same baseline calculation methodologies as domestic refineries.[130]

RESTRICTIONS ON THE IMPORT OF SHRIMP

Coalition in Support of the Shrimp Import Ban

On November 21, 1989, Congress passed Public Law 101-162, which provided in Section 609 that "the importation of shrimp or products from shrimp which have been harvested with commercial fishing technology which may adversely affect . . . species of sea turtles [the conservation of which is the subject of Department of Commerce regulations] shall be prohibited not later than May 1, 1991."[131] Similar to the MMPA, individual nations could avoid application of the import ban by being certified as having a regulatory program governing the incidental taking of such sea turtles comparable to the U.S. program.[132]

Prior to passage of Public Law 101-162, a congressional hearing was held on the reauthorization of the Endangered Species Act (ESA), which touched on the issue of how to protect sea turtles from incidental taking by shrimpers.[133] At this hearing, the essential element of a successful Baptist-bootlegger coalition—consensus on the part of the interested ENGOs and industry groups in their support of an import ban—was apparent. At the hearing, a number of shrimping associations voiced their approval of an import ban to further the goal of protecting endangered turtle species[134] and alluded to the working relationship they had established with the environmental movement.[135]

At the ESA hearing, the U.S. shrimp industry endorsed an import ban on shrimp from nations that did not adopt measures comparable to those of the United States in protecting sea turtles at the ESA hearings, but the much thornier issue for industry was what exactly the U.S. measures should be. In the years prior to the passage of Public Law 101-162, U.S. shrimpers found themselves under increasing regulatory pressure to use turtle excluder devices (TEDs) in their shrimp nets in order to protect sea turtles.[136] In July 1989, after years of promoting the use of TEDs to protect sea turtles, the Department of Commerce responded to the shrimpers' increasingly vehement resistance to these efforts by suspending enforcement of a regulation requiring U.S. shrimpers to use TEDs.[137] Conservationists were predictably disappointed by the Department of Commerce's reversal of position.[138]

In the hearings held by Congress to address the situation posed by the shrimpers' resistance to the TED regulations, the ENGOs and the shrimping industry made it clear to Congress that the two camps shared common ground in their support for import restrictions.[139] Michael Bean, chairman of the Wildlife Program of the Environmental Defense Fund, stated that while his and the other ENGOs he represented (the National Wildlife Federation, the National Audubon Society, and the Center for Marine Conservation) did not agree with U.S. shrimping associations on the fundamental issue of whether U.S. shrimpers should be required to use TEDs,[140] they were "very sensitive to the concerns of the shrimpers with foreign competitors."[141] "That [was] part of the reason why . . . the four organizations [he represented] submitted a petition to the Secretaries of Interior and Commerce requesting those Secretaries to . . . . empower [the president] to embargo shrimp . . . imports from those nations diminishing the effectiveness of CITES" and other treaties.[142]

The Concerned Shrimpers of America and the Louisiana Shrimp Association testified that their industry was in financial straits, in large part because "imports continue[d] to oversupply the U.S. markets," causing prices to drop.[143] In the view of these groups, "a control of imports from countries . . . that have not imposed conservation measures on sea turtles" was necessary to stimulate a recovery of their industry.[144] Although the executive branch had been authorized by Congress to restrict shrimp imports from countries that failed to meet certain conservation standards, it was not until a true Baptist-bootlegger coalition (whose members included the Earth Island Institute, the Sierra Club, and the Georgia Fisherman's Association) successfully sued the federal government that such an import ban was adopted.[145]

Treatment by the WTO

Shortly after the import ban was announced, India and several other nations threatened to fight the embargo at the WTO.[146] A WTO dispute settlement panel was established on February 25, 1997, to consider a complaint filed by India, Malaysia, Pakistan, and Thailand.[147] The arguments made by the complainants in their submissions to the dispute settlement panel and by the United States in its submissions to the Panel largely mirror the arguments made in the context of the MMPA disputes.[148] The complainants argued that the U.S. shrimp import ban violated U.S. obligations under GATT Articles I:1, XI:1, and XIII: and therefore represented a prima facie case of nullification and impairment of their trade benefits within the meaning of Article XXIII:1(a) of the GATT and that Article XX(b) and (g) did not justify the import ban.[149] Moreover, the complaints relied on the language of *Tuna I* and *Tuna II* in formulating their arguments.[150] The primary arguments of the United States were that the import ban was justified pursuant to Article XX(b) and (g) of the GATT.[151]

On May 15, 1998, the *Shrimp* Panel issued its report, which, as expected, found that Section 609 was inconsistent with the U.S. obligations under Article XI:1 of GATT and that Article XX did not excuse the violation.[152] The Panel relied on the logic of the holding in *Tuna I* and an "admission" by the United States to find that Section 609, as applied, amounted to "prohibitions or restrictions" on the importation of the product from the territory of another GATT 1994 signatory and therefore violated Article XI:1.[153] Following the example set by other dispute settlement panels, the *Shrimp* Panel did not address other alleged violations of the U.S. treaty obligation and proceeded to consider the U.S. defense under Article XX.

The Panel began its consideration of Article XX by analyzing whether Section 609 satisfied the conditions contained in the chapeau of Article XX. The United States would have to demonstrate that the Section 609 measures were "not applied in a manner that would constitute a means of arbitrary or unjustifiable discrimination between countries where the same conditions prevail" before the potential exception afforded by either Article XX(b) or Article XX(g) would be considered.

The United States argued that conditioning access of foreign shrimp to its market was carefully and justifiably tied to the particular conditions of each country and that each country using the same shrimp harvesting techniques was treated equally. The Panel disagreed and found that, in the context of analyzing Section 609, "countries where the same conditions prevail" corresponded to countries "seeking to export to the United States wild shrimp retrieved mechanically from waters where sea turtles and shrimp occur concurrently."[154] Because Section 609 discriminated among countries that the Panel had decided had the same prevailing conditions, the issue became whether such discrimination was "arbitrary" or "unjustified."

The *Shrimp* Panel relied on numerous previous Panel decisions, as well as the principle of *pacta sunt servanda,* to conclude that Section 609 constituted "unjustifiable" discrimination among WTO members. Section 609, as applied, allowed the United States to condition access to its market on the adoption by other countries of conservation measures that the United States itself, as sole arbiter, considered comparable to its own conservation measures. In the view of the Panel, if the chapeau of Article XX were to be in interpreted in such a way as to "allow a Member to adopt measures conditioning access to its market for a given product upon the adoption by the exporting Members of certain policies, including conservation policies, GATT 1994 and the WTO Agreement could no longer serve as a multilateral framework for trade among Members as security and predictability of trade relations under those agreements would be threatened."[155]

The Panel's analysis was evolutionary and represented a departure from previous GATT and WTO dispute settlement decisions because the Panel did not focus on the issue of the extrajurisdictional application of U.S. law. Section 609 was not excepted under Article XX, not because it represented an attempt by the United States to prescribe law beyond its jurisdiction and not because it infringed on the sovereignty of other members but because it represented a threat to the WTO multilateral trading system itself.[156] Having concluded that Section 609 represented "unjustified" discrimination among member countries facing the same prevailing conditions and therefore was outside the realm of measures permissible under the chapeau of Article XX, the Panel found it unnecessary to examine Articles XX(b) and XX(g).

The United States appealed the *Shrimp* Panel's decision, and on October 12, 1998, the Appellate Body of the WTO issued its report.[157] The Appellate Body's decision was a mixed blessing for the United States. On the one hand, it held that the Panel had erred in its interpretation of the chapeau of Article XX and that the Panel should have reached the issue of whether Section 609 was justified by any of the exceptions set forth in the subsections of Article XX. On the other hand, the body held that while Section 609 fell within the scope of Article XX(g), it was still in violation of the chapeau of Article XX.

According to the *Shrimp* Appellate Body, the Panel committed a number of errors in focusing on chapeau of Article XX without first determining whether the "design" of Section 609, as opposed to its application, conformed with any of the subparagraphs of Article XX.[158] The Panel mixed up the order in which a measure is to be evaluated; the proper approach, spelled out in the *Gas* Panel decision, is to engage in "first, provisional justification by reasons of characterization of the measure under XX(g); [and] second, [in] further appraisal of the same measure under the introductory clauses of Article XX."[159]

The *Shrimp* Appellate Body then proceeded to evaluate Section 609 for purposes of determining whether it fell under the scope of Article XX(g) and held that it did. This conclusion was based on three separate findings of the *Shrimp* Appellate Body. First, Section 609 was concerned with the "conservation of exhaustible natural resources," sea turtles. The fact that all seven recognized species of sea turtles are listed under Appendix I of CITES provided strong support for this finding.[160] Second, Section 609 was a measure "relating to the conservation" of such exhaustible natural resources. This conclusion rested on the Appellate Body's finding that the means of Section 609 were "reasonably related" to the ends of the policy objective of protection and conservation of sea turtles.[161] Third, Section 609 was "made effective in conjunction with restrictions on domestic production or consumption"; the restrictions imposed on and enforced against U.S. domestic shrimp harvesters showed that the U.S. approach to the issue was "even-handed."[162]

Having concluded that Section 609 did in fact fall under Article XX(g), the Appellate Body then considered whether Section 609 violated the requirements imposed by the chapeau of Article XX.[163] In the view of the Appellate Body, its job in interpreting the chapeau was "the delicate one of locating and marking out a line of equilibrium between the right of a Member to invoke an exception under Article XX and the rights of the other Members under varying substantive provisions . . . of GATT 1994, so that neither of the competing interests will cancel out the other and thereby distort and nullify the balance of rights and obligations constructed by the Members themselves in that Agreement."[164] The Appellate Body then went on to find that for a number of reasons—including Section 609's "intended and coercive effect on the specific policy decisions" of other members, the fact that the United States has pursued relevant bilateral and multilateral treaty negotiations with some members and not with others, and differing periods for putting into operation the requirement for use of TEDs in different countries—Section 609 represented both "unjustified" and "arbitrary" discrimination among members and therefore was not within the scope of measure permitted by Article XX.

Arguably more significant than the ruling itself, however, was what the Appellate Body Report suggests about the evolution of WTO/GATT jurisprudence on the issue of "extrajurisdictionality." The Appellate Body explicitly sidestepped the issue of "whether there is an implied jurisdictional limitation in Article XX(g)."[165] The Appellate Body found that "there is sufficient nexus between the migratory and endangered species involved and the United States for purposes of Article XX(g)," evidently basing that conclusion on the fact that all the sea turtle species covered by Section 609 were known to occur in waters over which the United States had jurisdiction.[166] While the *Shrimp* Appellate Body left the door open for future WTO decision-making bodies to find that under different circumstances a "jurisdictional limitation" may be found in Article XX(g), the *Shrimp* Appellate Body's decision represents an expansion in the applicability of Article XX(g). It was an implicit and subtle rejection of the bright-line rules regarding "extraterritoriality" or "extrajurisdictionality" espoused in *Tuna I* and *Tuna II,* respectively. Under the reasoning in the *Shrimp* Appellate Body Report, a member's conservation measure will not be deemed to fall outside the scope of Article XX(g) just because it seeks to conserve resources located outside its jurisdiction or aims to change policy outside its jurisdiction.

This doctrinal shift may exaggerate, however, the practical significance of the Appellate Body Report for unilateral measures aimed at extrajurisdictional activity. While the report suggests that extrajurisdictionality does not automatically destroy an Article XX(g) defense, the Appellate Body's decision used the chapeau to set conditions for approval of unilateral measures aimed at extrajurisdictional activity (described previously), and those conditions will prove very hard to meet. Thus, in practice, unilateral measures aimed at extrajurisdictional activity will likely continue to meet with skeptical reviews in Geneva.

U.S. Compliance

In early 1999, the parties to the shrimp dispute announced that they had agreed to a thirteen-month time line for implementation of the *Shrimp* Appellate Body's decision, a time line that started on issuance of the *Shrimp* Appellate Body Report.[167] This agreement suggested the continuing intent of the United States to comply with WTO dispute panel decisions. In March 1999, the State Department announced several steps being taken to implement the recommendations of the Dispute Settlement Body (DSB), including issuance of revised State Department guidelines, efforts to negotiate an agreement with the governments of the Indian Ocean region on the protection of sea turtles, and renewed offers of technical training in sea turtle conservation measures.[168]

On October 23, 2000, the government of Malaysia requested that the DSB establish a panel to examine whether the United States had implemented the recommendations and rulings of the DSB. In June 2001, a dispute settlement panel decided that the U.S. statute, as implemented by the revised State Department guidelines and as applied to date, was justified under GATT Article XX as long as the United States continued to engage in "ongoing serious good faith efforts to reach a multilateral agreement" to conserve sea turtles.[169]

CONCLUSION

The impact of the GATT and WTO decisions on the United States has at times been subtle. While the panel decisions reviewed here and issued under the GATT framework did not have binding, legal effect on the United States because they were never adopted by the GATT Council, they had direct political and indirect economic impacts.[170] The WTO dispute settlement framework established by the Uruguay Round, on the other hand, is more legalistic than the GATT's framework, with a binding enforcement provision: It legitimizes the unilateral withdrawal of trade concessions as retaliation for noncompliance with Panel reports.[171] While the actual withdrawal of concessions is generally viewed as an ineffective sanction, in that it often hurts the imposing nation as well as the transgressing nation,[172] the threat to withdraw concessions often succeeds in catalyzing compliance with GATT/WTO rules.

The U.S. government understandably likes the WTO dispute settlement system when the United States prevails in a dispute. But when the United States loses, there is often organized and vocal opposition to compliance. Congressional leaders on both the left and the right have voiced their concerns over alleged sovereignty implications of the WTO's influence.[173] Legislative responses to the perceived threat of WTO hegemony have varied. For example, as part of the Uruguay Round implementation exercise, Senator Bob Dole proposed (and President Clinton supported) establishment of a U.S. commission that could have passed judgment on WTO decisions: If the WTO handed down what the commission deemed to be three "wrong" decisions, the United States would then consider withdrawal from the WTO.[174] The alternative bills to establish such a commission never made it through Congress, but the substantial support it received suggests an omnipresent U.S. concern about WTO dispute settlement. From a theoretical perspective—a crude, simple version of realism—one might expect the United States to adopt a cavalier attitude toward the WTO, accepting its decisions when it suits the United States and ignoring them when they do not. The U.S. government could also choose not to comply with a particular decision and instead pay "compensation" for its noncompliance.

As the previous discussion illustrates, however, the United States continues to take the position that it is legally bound to comply with WTO dispute settlement decisions and continues to commit itself to compliance. The executive branch's commitment to the WTO has been unwavering, under both Republican and Democratic administrations. In the context of the trade disputes examined here, the executive branch has already demonstrated that it is willing to change regulations in order to abide with WTO findings.[175] It is not certain that the United States will forever continue to comply with WTO findings adverse to its position in any given dispute. But the evidence suggests that the United States is committed to using and advancing the legitimacy of the WTO as a mechanism to resolve trade disputes.[176] In short, the WTO, with its promise of opening foreign markets to the United States and its formal approach to dispute resolution, is likely to continue to receive the commitment and attention of the United States. The United States is already the WTO Dispute Settlement Body's most active participant as both complainant and respondent.[177]

All four U.S. environmental laws challenged at the GATT/WTO have been held (at least in the form they took when initially challenged) in contravention of U.S. international obligations, and all four laws resulted from Baptist-bootlegger coalitions. The implication is not that all U.S. environmental statutes resulting from such coalitions will be held WTO inconsistent. But this pattern and WTO legal doctrine suggest that U.S. environmental statutes supported by such coalitions are likely to be scrutinized closely by the WTO dispute settlement system.

Under a binding WTO dispute settlement system and U.S. government commitment to it, U.S. environmental legislation intended to garner support from a Baptist-bootlegger coalition will need to be crafted with great care and close attention to the rules of world trade. This new "check" on U.S. law, and its feedback onto the political process in Washington, also suggests the desirability of WTO doctrine on trade-environment issues that develops quickly and clearly. Bright-line rules will help interest groups, legislators, and executive branch policymakers craft viable environmental laws. In contrast, lack of clarity in WTO trade-environment legal doctrine—exemplified by the Shrimp/Turtle Appellate Body Report's explicit decision to not define the jurisdictional scope of Article XX(g) exception and its use of an ad hoc list of factors to determine the WTO legality of the measure in question—will tend to undermine continued U.S. political support for the WTO system. Uncertainty about whether a proposed U.S. environmental measure will pass muster in Geneva will frustrate Washington policymakers and interest groups. And uncertainty about WTO doctrine creates the potential for politically unstable cycles of interaction between the U.S. legislative process and WTO dispute settlement.

NOTES

1. See General Agreement on Tariffs and Trade (GATT) Dispute Resolution Panel Report on United States Restriction on Imports of Tuna, August 16, 1991, reprinted in 30 I.L.M. 1594 (1991) (hereinafter *Tuna/Dolphin I*); GATT Dispute Resolution Panel Report on United States Restrictions on Imports of Tuna, May 20, 1994, reprinted in 33 I.L.M. 839 (1994) (hereinafter *Tuna/Dolphin II*); GATT Dispute Panel Report on United States Taxes on Automobiles, October 11, 1994, reprinted in 30 I.L.M. 1397 (1994) (hereinafter *CAFE Panel*); World Trade Organization Dispute Resolution Panel Report on United States Regulation of Reformulated Gas, January 17, 1996 (hereinafter *Gas Panel*); World Trade Organization Dispute Resolution Report: United States—Import Prohibition of Certain Shrimp and Shrimp Products, May 15, 1998 (hereinafter *Shrimp Panel*); World Trade Organization Report of the Appellate Body: United States—Import Prohibition of Certain Shrimp and Shrimp Products, October 12, 1998 (hereinafter *Shrimp Appellate Report*).

2. This term was first popularized by Bruce Yandle, former executive director of the Federal Trade Commission, in describing cooperative efforts by industry and either labor or environmental groups in seeking regulation; they reminded him of alliances forged between bootleggers and Baptists, both of whom favored Sunday closing laws for bars and liquor stores, though for very different reasons. Bruce Yandle, "Bootleggers and Baptists: The Education of a Regulatory Economist," *Regulation,* May/June 1983, 12; Elizabeth R. DeSombre, "Baptists and Bootleggers for the Environment: The Origins of United States Unilateral Sanctions," *Journal of Environment & Development* 4 (winter 1995): 53; David Vogel, *Trading Up: Consumer and Environmental Regulation in a Global Economy* (Cambridge, Mass.: Harvard University Press, 1995), 196.

3. See DeSombre, "Baptists and Bootleggers for the Environment," 56–67 (discussing thirteen pieces of U.S. legislation authorizing unilateral trade sanction "that in almost all cases . . . is supported by an alliance of industry and environmentalists"); Vogel, Trading Up, 196–217 (generally discussing legislative power of these coalitions in United States); Richard B. Stewart, "Environmental Regulation and International Competitiveness," *Yale Law Journal* 102, nos. 2039, 2041 (1993). Michael P. Leidy and Bernard M. Hoekman, " 'Cleaning Up' while Cleaning Up: Pollution Abatement, Interest Groups and Contingent Trade Policies," *Public Choice* 78, no. 241 (1994). "There may be a confluence of interests among import-competing polluters, environmental interests, labor groups, and even foreign exporter, all favoring an inefficient regulatory package. And this support derives in part from the heightened expectation of trade restrictions likely to accompany the inefficient environmental regime" (ibid., 242).

4. 16 U.S.C.A. 1371 (a).

5. 15 U.S.C.A. 2003(b)(1) (West 1982), repealed and recodified at 49 U.S.C. 32904(b)(2) by Public Law 272, sec. 7(b), 108 Stat. 1379 (1994).

6. 40 C.F.R. 80.41.

7. 42 U.S.C. 7545(k).

8. Public Law 101-162, 103 Stat. 988 (codified at 16 U.S.C. 1537).

9. Marine Mammal Protection Act, Pub. L. 92-522, 86 Stat. 1027, 1972 U.S.C.C.A.N. 1202.

10. *Marine Mammals: Hearings before the Subcommittee on Fisheries and Wildlife Conservation of the Committee on Merchant Marine and Fisheries,* 92nd Cong., 1st sess. (1971) (hereinafter 1971 Hearings); *Ocean Mammal Protection: Hearings before the Subcommittee on Oceans and Atmosphere of the Committee on Commerce,* 92nd Cong., 2nd sess. (1972), 484–86 (hereinafter 1972 Hearings).

11. 1972 Hearings, 484 (statement of August Felando, general manager of the ATA). The ATA was comprised exclusively of tuna fishing vessel owners (ibid., 475).

12. "Denial of the use of efficient purse seine gear for the U.S. fleet would destroy this fishery as we know it today. Rather than return to bait fishing or go out of business U.S. operators would simply transfer to foreign flags and operate beyond the controls imposed" (1972 Hearings, 482).

13. Ibid., 271 (statement of Robert Hughes, Sierra Club).

14. Marine Mammal Protection Act, Public Law 92-522, sec. 101(a)(2), 86 Stat. 1027, 1972 U.S.C.C.A.N. 1202, 1206 (codified at 16 U.S.C.A. 1371[a][2]).

15. Public Law 98-364, sec. 101, 98 Stat. 440 (1984) (codified as awarded at 16 U.S.C. sec. 1371(a)(2)).

16. Ibid., sec. 101(a).

17. While the ATA represented exclusively tuna-fishing vessel owners, the United States Tuna Foundation (USTF) represented a broader spectrum of the tuna industry, including importers and canners.

18. See *Marine Mammal Protection Act Reauthorization: Hearings before the Subcommittee on Fisheries and Wildlife Conservation of the Committee on Merchant Marine and Fisheries,* 98th Cong., 2nd sess. (1984) (hereinafter 1984 House Hearings); *Marine Mammal Protection Act Reauthorization: Hearing before the National Ocean Policy Study of the Committee on Commerce, Science and Transportation,* 98th Cong., 2nd sess. (1984) (hereinafter 1984 Senate Hearings).

19. 1998 Senate Hearings, 39–41 (statement of Mr. Felando, president of the ATA).

20. Ibid., 43 (testimony of Mr. Burney, general counsel of the USTF).

21. "We agree with the U.S. tuna industry that the current regulatory scheme allowing importation of foreign caught tuna based upon a mere recital of consistency with U.S. standards places the U.S. fleet at a competitive disadvantage. . . . We believe that access to American markets is no less important that access to American waters and that it would be appropriate to require foreign flag vessels seeking to export tuna to the U.S. to . . . document their compliance with U.S. standards" (ibid., 48, statement of Robert Eisenbud, special counsel, Environmental Defense Fund, on behalf of a coalition of ENGOs).

22. Ibid., 42.

23. Marine Mammal Protection Act Amendments, Public Law 100-711, sec. 4(a)(2)(B), 1988 U.S.C.C.A.N (102 Stat.) 4755, 4765 (1988).

24. Ibid., sec. 4(a).

25. Ibid., sec. 4(a)(3).

26. H.R. Rep. 970, 100th Cong., 2nd sess. (1988), 30, reprinted in 1988 U.S.C.C.A.N. 6154, 6171.

27. "We have a serious problem with foreign mortality, and it is easy to bash the foreign fleets and say stop them, do not allow any more fish to come in from those countries. The real way to address the issue, however, is to get these countries to adopt U.S. techniques and

our technology" (*Marine Mammal Protection Act Reauthorization, Hearings before the National Ocean Policy Study of the Senate Committee on Commerce, Science, and Transportation,* 100th Cong. [1988], 131 [hereinafter 1988 Hearings]).

28. Ibid., 146 (statement of Mr. Felando).

29. See ibid., 104–5 (statement of Lesley Scheele).

30. 1988 Hearings, 9.

31. International Dolphin Conservation Act of 1992, Public Law 102-523, 1992 U.S.C. C.A.N. (106 Stat.) 3425; High Seas Driftnet Fisheries Enforcement Act, Public Law 102-582, 1992 U.S.C.C.A.N. (106 Stat.) 4900.

32. *Review of the Administration's Proposal to Promote Dolphin Protection: Hearing before the Subcommittee on Fisheries and Wildlife Conservation and the Environment of the Committee on Merchant Marine and Fisheries,* 102nd Cong., 2nd sess. (1992), 9 (hereinafter 1992 Hearings).

33. Ibid., 92.

34. "Less than ten years ago there were 12 tuna canneries in the United States and its possessions. Today there are only six remaining. Ten years ago the United States' tuna fleet was comprised of 107 vessels. Today there are only 54. We estimate that . . . we have lost over 30,000 jobs in this industry and over a billion dollars of gross revenue. . . . A major factor in the loss of a large of this industry pioneered by Americans is attributable to foreign . . . canneries and tuna boats avoiding well intentioned but costly environmental regulations" (ibid., 90; see generally ibid., 89–93).

35. Ibid., 28–29.

36. Ibid., 30.

37. "You asked whether the effect of the Administration's proposal would be to harm the U.S. tuna industry or American consumer. I am afraid it would. In good faith reliance upon [MMPA] standards, the U.S. tuna industry has by and large attempted to go dolphin-safe. . . . To undercut those efforts by passing this proposal would be to say to our own industry and our consumers, 'We set standards. We expect you to live by them. Then we are going to change them as soon as they are inconvenient for someone else' " (ibid., 31).

38. "The Administration should instead adopt an international, cooperative approach" (ibid., 91, statement of Richard Atchison); "What is needed is a multilateral agreement" (ibid., 28, statement of Traci Romine).

39. The collaborative efforts of these groups extended beyond their presenting similar messages at the congressional hearing. After the hearing, these groups participated in a mediated meeting called by congressional leaders intended "to ascertain ways to improve the Administration's proposal and find common areas on which to base similar legislation" (H.R. Rep. 746[I], 102nd Cong., 2nd sess. [1992], 13, reprinted in 1992 U.S.C.C.A.N. 2919, 2926).

40. *Tuna/Dolphin I*, para. 7.1(b), 1623. The GATT panel's analysis of these particular articles is discussed below. The dispute panel decision was never adopted by the parties and therefore did not bind the United States. The WTO's treatment of dispute resolution panel decisions makes this result unlikely in the future (see Young, 402).

41. 16 U.S.C.A. sec. 1371.

42. 16 U.S.C. sec. 1685.

43. *Tuna/Dolphin I*, paras. 7.1–7.3, 1623.

44. See *Tuna/Dolphin I*, paras. 3.1, 5.18, 1601, 1618. Mexico had also argued that the

trade restriction violated Article XIII of the GATT because they "established discriminatory specific for a specific geographical area," the ETP (ibid., para. 3.1[a], 1601). The Panel dismissed this argument as superfluous in light of the finding of Article XI incompatibility (ibid., para. 5.19, 1618).

45. See *Tuna/Dolphin I*, paras. 3.6, 5.9, 1601, 1617.

46. See *Tuna/Dolphin I*, paras. 3.6, 3.27–3.54, 1601, 1605–10.

47. Ibid., para. 5.8, 1617.

48. Ibid., para. 5.18, 1618.

49. Ibid., para. 5.18, 1618.

50. Ibid., paras. 5.26, 5.30, 1620, 1621.

51. Ibid., paras. 5.23, 5.28, 1619, 1620.

52. Ibid., para. 5.33, 1621. The "primarily aimed" requirement had come from an earlier GATT Panel decision, the *Canadian Salmon Case*, that "found that a measure could only be considered to have been taken 'in conjunction with production restrictions' " if it were primarily aimed at rendering effective those restrictions (ibid., para. 5.31, 1621–22).

53. Ibid., para. 5.38, 1621. Upon the Panel's finding that the primary nation embargo was GATT inconsistent, the U.S. argument that the intermediate nation ban was "necessary to secure compliance with laws or regulations which are not inconsistent with the provisions of this Agreement" and therefore excused under Article XX(d) collapsed in a heap (ibid., paras. 5.39, 5.40, 1622).

54. *Tuna/Dolphin II*.

55. Ibid., para. 1.4, 844.

56. Ibid., paras. 5.1–5.43, 886–8988.

57. Ibid., para. 6.1, 899.

58. Ibid., paras. 5.20, 5.26.

59. Ibid., para. 5.37.

60. Ibid., para. 6.1.

61. G. Richard Shell, "Trade Legalism and International Relations Theory: An Analysis of the World Trade Organization," *Duke Law Journal* 44, no. 829 (1995): 841–42.

62. H.R. Rep. 74 (Part I), 105th Cong., 14, reprinted in 1997 U.S.C.C.A.N. 1628, 1632.

63. Public Law 105-42, sec. 4, 111 Stat. 1122, 1123 (1997); see Brad Knickerbocker, "Dolphin-Safe Standard Revised for Tuna Fishers," *Christian Science Monitor,* July 31, 1997, 3.

64. H.R. Rep. 74 (Part I), 105th Cong., 14, reprinted in 1997 U.S.C.C.A.N. 1628, 1632.

65. Ibid., 63, 66, reprinted in 1997 U.S.C.C.A.N. 1628, 1652, 1655.

66. See Knickerbocker, "Dolphin-Safe Standard Revised for Tuna Fishers," 3.

67. Testimony of Jeffrey R. Pike, coordinator, Dolphin Safe/Fair Trade Campaign, Federal Document Clearing House Congressional Testimony, April 9, 1997, available in LEXIS, News File.

68. H.R. Rep. 74 (Part II), 105th Cong., 3, reprinted in 1997 U.S.C.C.A.N. 1657, 1659.

69. Public Law 94-163, sec. 503(b), 1975 U.S.C.C.A.N. (89 Stat.) 871 (codified at 15 U.S.C. 2003[b]).

70. *Energy Conservation Working Paper: Hearings before the Senate Committee on Com-*

merce, 93rd Cong., 2nd sess. (1974) (hereinafter 1974 Senate Hearings); *Energy Conservation and Oil Policy: Hearings before the Subcommittee on Energy and Power of the House Committee on Interstate and Foreign Commerce,* 94th Cong., 1st sess. (1975) (hereinafter Foreign Commerce Hearings); *The Energy Crisis and Proposed Solutions: Panel Discussions before the House Committee on Ways and Means,* 94th Cong., 1st sess. (1975) (hereinafter Ways and Means Hearings); *Automobile Fuel Economy and Research and Development, Hearings before the Senate Committee on Commerce,* 94th Cong., 1st sess. (1975) (hereinafter 1975 Senate Hearings).

71. See Ways and Means Hearings, 1453 (statement of Dr. Henry L. Duncombe, Jr., vice president and chief economist, General Motors Corporation).

72. See 1974 Senate Hearings, 158–61 (testimony of Fred G. Secrest, executive vice president, Ford Motor Company); 1975 Senate Hearings, 95 (testimony of Ralph Nader).

73. Ways and Means Hearings, 1451–52 (testimony of Dr. Duncombe).

74. The issue was significant enough to merit its own congressional hearing, *Impact of Motor Vehicle Imports on Employment in the United States: Hearings before the Subcommittee on Labor Standards of the House Committee on Education and Labor,* 94th Cong., 1st sess. (1975). Of particular concern were the over 200,000 cars produced by U.S. automobile manufacturers abroad and imported into the United States (ibid., 81–82).

75. "We believe strongly that to achieve fuel economy improvements the disciplines of competitive market forces are far superior to a legislative mandate. . . . In short, fuel economy is an essential attribute in the marketing of a new car" (1974 Senate Hearings, 184–85, testimony of Dr. Duncombe). See also ibid., 158–60 (testimony of Fred Secrest). "I would suggest that mandating fuel economy by standards in a law could inhibit technological innovation and create cost penalties similar to the Clean Air Act experience" (ibid., 159).

76. "There are businesses that require a somewhat larger car. . . . All that I am saying here is that unless we can produce a mix of cars that reflects the varieties of needs in the marketplace, we will not be successful" (ibid., 181, testimony of Dr. Duncombe).

77. "There is a certain segment of the public that has enjoyed the characteristics that come along with some of the higher weight. . . . Those are the kinds of things we will have to forgo and it is those kinds of cars on which we will make the greatest weight reduction in the name of improved fuel economy" (Foreign Commerce Hearings, 1515, statement of Frederick W. Bowditch, General Motors Corporation).

78. Brock Yates, *The Decline & Fall of the American Automobile Industry* (New York: Empire Books, 1983), 136. The 1976–77 sales year represented another dip in small car sales (ibid.).

79. See 1975 Senate Hearings, 97 (statement of Mr. Ditlow). This increase in small car sales was viewed to be an aberration by the automobile industry (ibid.).

80. Jeffrey Allen Hunker, *Structural Change in the U.S. Automobile Industry* (Lexington, Mass.: Lexington Books, 1983), 45.

81. See Foreign Commerce Hearings, 1512–14 (statement of Clarence Ditlow, PIRG); 1975 Senate Hearings, 195–97 (statement of Leonard Woodcock, president, UAW).

82. See generally 1975 Senate Hearings, 85–97 (statement of Ralph Nader).

83. "For too many years the UAW has pointed out that the Big Three auto companies have followed a marketing strategy based on cars that are too large, too expensive and that use too much fuel" (ibid., 195, statement of Mr. Woodcock). "The auto industry—and its employees, including UAW members—is suffering great economic difficulty. To some extent that is due to the industry's lack of attention to fuel economy" (ibid., 199).

84. See Foreign Commerce Hearings, 1484 (testimony of Mr. Bowditch, General Motors Corporation).

85. Public Law 94-163, sec. 503(b)(1)(A), 1975 U.S.C.C.A.N. (89 Stat.) 871, 906.

86. Ibid., sec. 503(b)(1)(B).

87. GATT Dispute Settlement Panel Report on the United States Taxes on Automobile, October 11, 1994, reprinted in 33 I.L.M. 1397 (1994) (hereinafter CAFE Panel).

88. Ibid., 1457.

89. 40 C.F.R. sec. 600.

90. The analysis that follows is gleaned from the text of the decision, *supra* note 1, and Mr. Charnovitz's analysis, *infra* note 102.

91. *CAFE Panel*, para. 3.220, 1429.

92. Ibid., paras. 3.226–3.299, 1430–40.

93. Ibid., 1440–41.

94. Ibid., 1441–45.

95. Ibid., 1430.

96. Ibid., 1441–43.

97. Ibid., 1453. The Panel noted that the language of the CAFE regulation first defined what was "unlawful conduct" and then provided civil penalties for any such violation (ibid., citing 15 U.S.C. secs. 2007, 2008[b][1][A]).

98. Ibid., 1454.

99. Ibid., 1454–55.

100. Ibid., 1455–56.

101. Ibid., 1457.

102. See Steve Charnovitz, "The GATT Panel Decision on Automobile Taxes," *International Environment Report* (BNA) no. 22 (November 2, 1994), 921. The European Commission described the U.S. interpretation to be a promulgation of "disinformation" (ibid.). See, for example, Vogel, 133 ("The [CAFE Rule] GATT dispute panel ruled in favor of the United States.").

103. Public Law 103–272, sec. 1(e), July 5, 1994, 108 Stat. 1062, and amended by Public Law 103–429, sec. 6(36), October 31, 1994, 108 Stat. 4380.

104. "Notice of Proposed Rulemaking," *Federal Register* 56, no. 31 (1991): 176.

105. 42 U.S.C. sec. 7545(k).

106. "Notice of Proposed Rulemaking."

107. Ibid.

108. For a more general discussion of the virtues and limitations of negotiated rule making, see Lawrence Susskind and Gerard McMahon, "The Theory and Practice of Negotiated Rulemaking," *Yale Journal on Regulation* 3 (1985), 133.

109. "Notice of Proposed Rulemaking."

110. The following description of the Gas Rule is based on the WTO Panel's description of the rule (see *Gas Panel*, paras. 2.5–2.8, 3–4) and on the description contained in an EPA's "Notice of Proposed Rulemaking" (see *Federal Register* 59 [May 3, 1994]: 22800, 22806).

111. Ibid.

112. "Supplemental Notice of Proposed Rulemaking," *Federal Register* 57 (April 16, 1992): 13416.

113. "Final Rule," *Federal Register* 59 (February 16, 1994): 7716. In addition to the original NPRM, the EPA had issued a supplemental NPRM (*Federal Register* 57 [April 16, 1992]:

13416) and a second NPRM (*Federal Register* 58 [February 26, 1993]: 11722) before issuing the final rule.

114. Telephone interview with George E. Lawrence, EPA, March 15, 1996.

115. See *Federal Register* 58 (February 26, 1993): 11758.

116. See *Federal Register* 59 (February 16, 1994): 7785–88.

117. *Federal Register* 59 (May 3, 1994): 22800.

118. Oversight of the Reformulated Gasoline Rule: Hearing before the Senate Committee on Environment and Public Works, 103rd Cong., 2nd sess. (1994); *Reformulated Gasoline: Hearing before the Subcommittee on Oversight and Investigations of the House Committee on Energy and Commerce,* 103rd Cong., 2nd sess. (1994) (hereinafter House Gas Hearing).

119. The pertinent Appropriations Act, passed on September 28, 1994, barred the EPA from expending any funds "to sign, promulgate, implement or enforce the requirement proposed as 'Regulation of Fuels and Fuel Additives: Individual Foreign Refinery Baseline Requirements for Reformulated Gasoline" (Public Law 103–327, 108 Stat. 2322 [1994]).

120. Center for International Environmental Law, Independent Refiners Coalition, Defenders of Wildlife and the Sierra Club, *Testimony before the Senate Committee on Environment and Public Works, Hearing on Importation of Reformulated Gasoline* (1994) (hereinafter Gas Comment I). These comments appear in the EPA docket as well as on the record of the Senate hearing.

121. "The EPA's Proposed Rule so directly conflicts with the environmental, labor, and economic interests of the United States that it has forged this somewhat unique coalition of organizations now before you" (ibid., 1).

122. See, for example, "Independent Fuel Terminal Operators Association Comments," June 23, 1994, 1, 4 (opposing the Venezuela Rule on the grounds that it would reduce competition in the gasoline market) (on file with author); letter from G. William Fick, vice president of the National Petroleum Refiners Association, to Mary Nichols, assistant administrator, EPA, June 23, 1994, 1) (arguing on behalf of the NPRA and the American Petroleum Institute that the Venezuela Rule is "unenforceable and would undermine the competitiveness of the domestic refining industry") (on file with author); Public Citizen Litigation Group, "Comments on Proposed Individual Foreign Refinery Baseline Requirements for Reformulated Gasoline," June 23, 1994 (arguing on the behalf of a number of ENGOs against the Venezuela Rule) (on file with author).

123. "World Trade Organization Dispute Resolution Final Report: United States Reformulated Gasoline Rule," January 17, 1996 (hereinafter *Gas Panel*) (on file with author).

124. *Gas Panel*, 36.

125. Ibid., 37.

126. Ibid., 41.

127. Ibid., 46.

128. Ibid., 45.

129. "United States—Standards for Reformulated and Conventional Gasoline," AB-1996-1, WTO Appellate Body Report, WT/DS2/AB/R, April 22, 1996, 23–32.

130. "Regulation of Fuels and Fuel Additives," Federal Register 62, no. 45 (August 28, 1997): 533; see "U.S. Agrees to Ease Rules on Imported Gas," *Orange County Register,* June 20, 1996, C4; Stuart S. Malawer, "WTO, a Quiet Success," *Legal Times,* September 8, 1997, S42.

131. Public Law 101–162, sec. 609(b)(1), 103 Stat. 988, 1038 (1989).

132. Ibid., sec. 609(b)(2).

133. *Endangered Species Act Reauthorization: Hearings on H.R. 1467 before the Subcommittee on Fisheries and Wildlife Conservation and the Environment of the House Committee on Merchant Marine and Fisheries,* 100th Cong., 100–1 (1987) (hereinafter ESA Hearing).

134. The Texas Shrimp Association submitted testimony that it was willing to cooperate "to establish a regime for economic sanctions against those countries not meeting internationally recognized standards for the protection of sea turtles" and proposed an amendment to the ESA, modeled after the MMPA, requiring a ban on the importation of shrimp from countries that fail to protect sea turtles from incidental takings by shrimpers in a manner comparable to the United States (EPA Hearing, 357–59). The Texas Shrimp and Sea Turtle Survival Coalition, a group of shrimp producers, similarly suggested that in order to protect sea turtles, legislation would need to provide for "embargoes on imports from the fisheries of nations not implementing comprehensive protective measures" (ibid., 366).

135. Ibid., 76 (testimony of Ralph Rayburn, executive director of the Texas Shrimp Association).

136. For a concise summary of the history of the TED regulations, see *Sea Turtle Conservation and the Shrimp Industry: Hearings before the Subcommittee on Fisheries and Wildlife Conservation and the Environment of the House Committee on Merchant Marine and Fisheries,* 100th Cong., 2d sess. (1990), 153–55 (hereinafter TED Hearing).

137. See Jeffrey Good and Patty Curtin, "Shrimpers Raise Stakes in Debate over TEDs," *St. Petersburg Times,* July 30, 1989, 1B.

138. See, for example, Michael Moline, "Conservationists Vow to Close Shrimp Fishery," United Press International, August 2, 1989, available in LEXIS, News Library.

139. TED Hearing.

140. TED Hearing, 17 ("The Concerned Shrimpers of America has been the principal antagonist of TED regulations.").

141. Ibid., 16–18.

142. Ibid., 18.

143. Ibid., 58.

144. Ibid.

145. See *Earth Island Institute v. Christopher,* 913 F.Supp. 559 (Court of International Trade, December 29, 1995); "Shrimp: State Dept. Issues Guidelines on US Import Ban," May 6, 1996, available in LEXIS, Greenwire File, News Library.

146. "Shrimp: State Dept. Issues Guidelines on US Import Ban," May 6, 1994, available in LEXIS, Greenwire File, News Library.

147. "United States—Import Prohibition on Certain Shrimp and Shrimp Product," First Submission of the United States, June 9, 1997, 2 (on file with author) (hereinafter U.S. Submission).

148. See U.S. Submission; "United States—Import Prohibition of Certain Shrimp and Shrimp Products," First Submission of India, May 20, 1997 (on file with author); "United States—Import Prohibition of Certain Shrimp and Shrimp Products," First Submission of Pakistan, May 20, 1997 (on file with author); "United States—Import Prohibition of Certain Shrimp and Shrimp Products," First Submission of Thailand, May 20, 1997 (on file with author).

149. See Thailand Submission, 8–31.

150. Ibid., secs. 48, 52,13, 15.

151. U.S. Submission, 73–92.

152. "World Trade Organization Dispute Resolution Report: United States—Import Prohibition of Certain Shrimp and Shrimp Products," May 15, 1998 (hereinafter *Shrimp Panel*).

153. In response to a question posed by the Panel, the United States responded in part that "with respect to countries not certified under Section 609, Section 609 amounts to a restriction on the importation of shrimp within the meaning of Article XI:1 of GATT 1994" (ibid., para. 7.15).

154. Ibid., para. 7.33.

155. Ibid., para. 7.45.

156. Ibid., para. 7.51.

157. "World Trade Organization Report of the Appellate Body: United States—Import Prohibition of Certain Shrimp and Shrimp Products," October 12, 1998 (hereinafter *Shrimp Appellate Report*).

158. Ibid., paras. 114–24.

159. Ibid., para. 118.

160. Ibid., paras. 125–34.

161. Ibid., 135–42.

162. Ibid., paras. 143–45.

163. The Appellate Body did not consider Section 609 in light of Article XX(b). Having found that Section 609 was provisionally justified under Article XX(g), there was no need to consider Article XX(b). Whether Section 609 would be deemed to be WTO/GATT consistent would depend on whether it satisfied the conditions set forth in the chapeau, a condition that would apply in equal force regardless of which subparagraph of Article XX provisionally justified Section 609.

164. *Shrimp Appellate Report,* para. 159.

165. Ibid., para. 133.

166. Ibid.

167. See Agence France Presse, "Parties in WTO Shrimp Turtle Case Settle on 13 Month Compliance Period," February 1, 1999.

168. Office of the United States Trade Representative, "Notice, WTO Dispute Settlement Proceeding Regarding Section 609 of Public Law 101-162 Relating to the Protection of Sea Turtles in Shrimp Trawl Fishing Operations," *Federal Register* 65 (November 15, 2000): 69118-03.

169. "Report of the Panel, United States—Import Prohibition of Certain Shrimp and Shrimp Products, Recourse to Article 21.5 by Malaysia," June 15, 2001, WTO Document WT/DS58/RW.

169. "Report of the Panel, United States—Import Prohibition of Certain Shrimp and Shrimp Products, Recourse to Article 21.5 by Malaysia," June 15, 2001, WTO Document WT/DS58/RW.

170. For example, the Tuna-Dolphin dispute panel decision greatly influenced the negotiations, both domestic and international, that resulted in the passage of NAFTA. David Vogel, 14.

171. Michael K. Young, "Dispute Resolution in the Uruguay Round: Lawyers Triumph over Diplomats," *International Lawyer* 29 (1995): 408. For an in-depth analysis of the legalistic aspects of WTO, see the previously cited article as well as G. Richard Shell, "Trade Legalism and International Relations Theory: An Analysis of the World Trade Organization," *Duke Law Journal* 44 (1995): 829.

172. Young, "Dispute Resolution in the Uruguay Round," 389.

173. See, for example, "Left-Right Coalition Comes Together to Defend U.S. Sovereignty in Trade Issues," Congressional Press Releases, September 18, 1997, available in LEXIS, News Library; Shell, 831, n. 4. "It is going to be on every other law that this Congress has passed that the [WTO] is going to try to subvert and undermine the laws that this Congress passed for the well-being and benefit of this country. . . . We should do the legislatively responsible thing to reverse our participation in the [WTO]" (*Congressional Record* 142 H876 (daily ed., January 25, 1996) (statement of Representative Coburn).

174. John Maggs, "The 'Sore Loser' Commission," *Journal of Commerce,* May 16, 1996, 6A.

175. "U.S. Agrees to Ease Rules on Imported Gas," *Orange County Register,* June 20, 1996, C4; Malawer, "WTO, a Quiet Success."

176. See Malawer, "WTO, a Quiet Success."

177. See ibid.; see also David Stoelting, "International Courts Flourish in the 1990s," *New York Law Journal,* August 4, 1997, S2.

4

The Nexus of Law and Politics: The WTO's Committee on Trade and Environment

Gregory C. Shaffer

This chapter examines how the World Trade Organization (WTO) has addressed trade and environment issues through the creation of a specialized Committee on Trade and Environment (CTE), treating the CTE as a site to assess central concerns of governance—that is, who governs—in a globalizing economy. Northern environmental interest groups and many northern academics criticize the CTE for failing to propose substantive changes to WTO law in order to grant more deference to national environmental priorities.[1] This chapter, through its focus on the positions and roles of state and nonstate actors, provides a better foundation to assess the accountability of the WTO's handling of trade-environment matters. The chapter assesses the representativeness of national trade ministries before the CTE, evaluates the impact of a sophisticated WTO international secretariat in framing debates and shaping knowledge about alternatives, and considers the role of commercial interests and transnational environmental advocacy groups pressing for their conflicting goals. Understanding the CTE is important for three primary reasons. First, many WTO critics challenge the legitimacy of WTO *judicial* decisions involving U.S. laws that impose trade restrictions on account of foreign environmental practices. The CTE discussions highlight how most countries (and their constituencies) believe panels *should* apply WTO rules to these cases. It is simply disingenuous to challenge the legitimacy and democratic accountability of WTO judicial decisions without recognizing how representatives in the WTO's *political* body (the CTE) believed that the rules should be interpreted and/or modified. In examining the respective roles and positions of state delegates, the WTO secretariat, and northern and southern business and other civil groups, this chapter provides a better understanding of who lies behind the WTO rules that dispute settlement panels ultimately must interpret.

Second, analysis of the CTE is important for understanding policymaking in the WTO as a whole. This inquiry provides a window for understanding how WTO negotiations work in practice and, in particular, why trade-environment discussions are sometimes more polarized within the WTO than in other fora. In this connection, this chapter assesses the impact of trade-environment discussions within the CTE on discussions over the "transparency" of WTO deliberations as well as on negotiations outside the WTO.

Third, this chapter has significant implications for understanding the law and politics of trade-environment linkages addressed in other international fora. Many environmental groups and trade policymakers, including the outgoing WTO director-general, Renato Ruggiero, have called for the creation of a World Environment Organization.[2] This chapter permits a better assessment of the prospects and limits of negotiations in such alternative institutions.

FRAMEWORKS FOR ANALYZING THE WTO'S TREATMENT OF TRADE AND ENVIRONMENT MATTERS

This chapter applies three "ideal types" as alternative frames of analysis[3] to respond to normative critiques of the WTO's treatment of trade and environment matters. The three examined perspectives are as follows:

1. An *intergovernmental perspective,* which holds that the creation of the WTO's CTE represents an attempt by states to bring the trade and environment debate into an organization that is state dominated. Under a *two-level intergovernmental model,* this first perspective incorporates portions of the latter two, maintaining that national positions are shaped by national political processes involving competition among business and other stakeholder interests attempting to influence government as well as competition among governmental actors attempting to respond to and shape constituent demands.
2. A *supranational technocratic perspective,* which appraises the WTO's handling of trade and environment matters as a cooptation (or capture) of policymaking by a technocratic network of trade policymakers having a *free trade* policy orientation; the network is composed of national trade officials working with the WTO secretariat, in turn supported by large private transnational businesses, all acting within the structure of the WTO trade regime.
3. A *stakeholder/civil society perspective,* which views the creation of the CTE as a response to ongoing systematic pressure from nongovernmental advocacy groups before international and domestic fora to change the rules and norms of the world trading system.

Scholars taking an intergovernmental approach view international organizations as formed and controlled entirely or predominantly by states to further state interests. From a structural realist perspective, international institutions reflect the interests of the most powerful states and do not constrain their operations.[4] Rational institutionalists, on the other hand, maintain that even powerful states often rationally agree to constraints imposed on them by international institutions in order to further national goals.[5] In their view, states create international institutions to reduce the transaction and information costs of negotiating and monitoring agreements, thereby helping ensure that reciprocally beneficial bargains are sustained.

A variant of intergovernmental theory broadens this analysis by focusing on a two-level game that combines competition between domestic private interests, leading to the formation of national positions, with competition between states that promote those interests internationally.[6] National positions are first formed through domestic political processes, often involving conflicts among competing interest groups. These national positions are then defended by state representatives in bilateral and multilateral "intergovernmental" negotiations. This two-level approach also admits a reversal of images in which intergovernmental negotiators may shape competition among domestic political actors through employing such strategies as offering side payments to domestic groups, targeting threats or concessions at foreign groups to modify foreign positions, linking issues to rally support of key domestic and foreign constituencies, or manipulating information about domestic political constraints or an agreement's terms. In other words, a two-level game can work in both directions, with domestic constituencies shaping state positions and state representatives attempting to manipulate domestic preferences advocated in domestic fora. Two-level intergovernmental analysis thereby combines the domestic and international arenas into a single bargaining model.

A competing perspective on international relations maintains that networks of midlevel national technocratic officials may be able to shape international policy through working within supranational regimes, such as the WTO, in a manner at least partly independent of national political processes. Keohane and Nye, for example, define "transgovernmental" relations "as sites of direct interaction among subunits of different governments that are not controlled by the policies of the cabinets or chief executives of those governments," at least with respect to the details of negotiated outcomes.[7] In other words, relatively autonomous networks of lower-level governmental representatives can work with members of international secretariats in specific policy areas to determine policy outcomes. To the extent that international civil servants at the WTO play the predominant role in a WTO policymaking network, such network would likely have a *free trade* orientation. Viewing trade-environment policymaking within the WTO as that of a technocratic network forging policy through the agency of a supranational organization lies at the center of normative debates over the legitimacy, accountability, and democratic representativeness of WTO decision making.

Finally, theorists taking a civil society, or stakeholder, approach depict nongovernmental actors as playing a central and increasingly direct role in international arena, independent of state representatives. Some nonstate theorists focus on how international market liberalization processes favor and reflect the power of transnational corporations that dominate policymaking nationally and internationally.[8] Many others, however, focus on the role of nonbusiness actors in constructing knowledge, setting agendas, and transforming perceptions of alternative outcomes through their interactions with policymakers at the national and international levels.[9] These theorists often focus precisely on the issue of environmental policymaking. Some go so far as to declare that transnational environmental activists not only "constructively" shape outcomes but also directly determine policy outcomes through transnational coordination within what they term "world civic politics," or a "world polity."[10]

Although the civil society approach has a positive, descriptive aspect, in the context of debates over the WTO, it is most commonly used in a normative sense. Most northern environmental activists advocate the adoption of a stakeholder model precisely because the model is *not* operational within the WTO or its CTE. Criticizing the WTO as unrepresentative and dominated by commercial concerns, they advocate an alternative pursuant to which "stakeholders" other than business interests play a greater role in international policy formation.[11] These advocates, however, often fail to differentiate which stakeholders would likely benefit were the model actually implemented, especially in light of which stakeholders already actively monitor CTE developments and lobby state representatives in defining their positions within the WTO Committee.

These three frameworks focus on the roles of different players in determining political outcomes. This chapter tests the relative ability of these frameworks to explain the outcome of negotiations over trade-environment matters within the WTO through its CTE. This study assesses the explanatory power of these three frameworks in helping us understand (1) why the CTE was formed, (2) what accounts for its agenda, (3) what explains the current status of CTE discussions, and (4) what external developments the CTE internal process has catalyzed.

WHY WAS THE CTE FORMED?

The CTE was formed pursuant to a Ministerial Declaration annexed to the Marrakesh Agreement establishing the WTO in April 1994. The process, however, was started over two years earlier, for the committee developed out of a working group first convened in November 1991 under the name Working Group on Environmental Measures and International Trade (or EMIT).[12]

There is a certain amount of debate about why the EMIT group was finally convened and the committee formed in the 1990s. Many assume that they were primarily the result of pressure from U.S. environmental groups, who harnessed U.S. negotiating power to achieve their ends. The assumption is understandable given the largely contemporaneous signature of the 1993 environmental side agreement to the North American Free Trade Agreement (NAFTA),[13] the importance of environmental issues in U.S. domestic debates over NAFTA's ratification, and the formation within the Organization for Economic Cooperation and Development (OECD) of an analogous "Joint Session of the Trade and Environment Committees."[14] Moreover, most developing countries opposed the EMIT group's convening and the CTE's formation precisely because they feared the group could serve to justify U.S. and European unilateral trade measures against developing country imports, resulting in "green protectionism." In the GATT Council meetings leading up to the EMIT group's convening, the Thai representative (on behalf of the ASEAN [Association of Southeast Asian Nations] group) asserted that "for GATT to address environmental protection problems as a general trade policy issue was inappropriate,"[15] the Moroccan delegate questioned whether the GATT had the "competence to legislate on this subject,"[16] and the Egyptian delegate concurred that GATT "was not the forum to deal with this matter."[17] They did not want to be pressured into signing an environmental side agreement analogous to NAFTA's.

However, the full explanation for the CTE's formation is twofold, involving both an effort to assuage northern environmental constituencies and an effort to subject environmental regulatory developments to greater GATT scrutiny and control. First, it is true that environmental groups within powerful states (principally the United States and the European Community [EC]) pressured those states to enact environmental measures that led to trade conflicts. The most famous of these measures in GATT history was the U.S. ban on tuna imports from Mexico in response to fishing methods used by Mexican tuna boats that killed dolphins trapped in their nets. Mexico reacted to the U.S. ban by filing a GATT complaint, giving rise to a GATT dispute settlement panel finding that the U.S. ban was contrary to GATT rules.[18] This trade conflict, known as the tuna-dolphin dispute, generated more commentary and publicity than any other dispute in GATT history. Suddenly, the GATT became a symbol for groups that had no interest whatsoever in trade issues other than the impact of trade rules on nontrade initiatives. Because environmental groups believed that GATT rules constrained their ability to achieve environmental goals, they lambasted, and at times demonized, the GATT system for failing to accommodate their desired policies.[19] The United States and the EC did not want environmentalist challenges to jeopardize the conclusion of the Uruguay Round of trade negotiations. They reacted to these challenges to trade policy by supporting the formation within GATT of the EMIT group, followed by the creation of a formal committee within the new and expanded WTO structure: the CTE.[20]

Second, however, trading interests in all states, including those same powerful states, were concerned with the proliferation of environmental measures, evidenced by new national labeling and packaging requirements, the 1991 tuna-dolphin case, and the upcoming 1992 UN Conference on Environment and Development, the largest international conference ever held. The first nations to formally call for the convening of the EMIT group were not the United States and the EC but members of the European Free Trade Association (EFTA), a grouping of northern European countries that were not EC members.[21] These northern European countries, despite their "green" reputations, demanded the EMIT group's convening to defend their trade interests, not only to promote environmental goals. As an EFTA representative stated before the GATT Council, GATT needed to confront "the rising tide of environmental measures and international environmental agreements . . . not least because many . . . used trade measures to realize their objectives."[22] The EFTA countries fretted about foreign environment-related measures impeding their exports, not about GATT's need to accommodate more of them.

Trading interests throughout the world, including in the United States and Europe, shared EFTA's concerns. Even in the context of the contemporaneous tuna-dolphin dispute, the U.S. representative maintained, "Contracting parties should not let the important principles of GATT be trampled upon by governments trying to protect the environment they deemed appropriate."[23] In respect of international environmental negotiations, the EC representative argued that "the sooner the GATT was involved in the design stages of environmental policies, therefore, the easier it would be to bring in a moderating influence from the trade policy point of view."[24] In the second tuna-dolphin case, the EC challenged a U.S. secondary ban on tuna imports imposed on environmental grounds.[25] The United States likewise threatened to challenge an EC directive that would have banned imports of U.S. fur products on account of U.S. trapping methods.[26]

In short, states convened the EMIT group and formed the CTE in large part because, in reaction to domestic producer complaints, they perceived that environmental measures increasingly threatened their trading interests. As traditional trade barriers such as tariffs and quotas steadily declined, U.S. and European environmental regulations proliferated. Environmental and other behind-the-border domestic regulatory policies correspondingly became the object of battle between governmental trade authorities.[27] Both trade and environmental factors were important to the CTE's formation. Yet it was the forces of trade competition, in reaction to the perception of environmental groups' growing success in promoting environmental regulation in national and other international fora, that are most important in explaining why environmental issues were brought to the GATT and the WTO.

WHAT ACCOUNTS FOR THE CTE AGENDA?

In considering how to frame the group's and committee's mandates, GATT contracting parties (and WTO members) had to consider that all environmental measures have economic effects and that all trade measures have environmental ones. Developing countries, in particular, persistently pointed out that the GATT was a "trade" organization, not an environmental one. In response to demands by developing countries, the member governments defined the trade and environment linkage in a manner that focused primarily on the trade impacts of environmental measures, not on the environmental impacts of trade rules. Governments, and particularly the trade bureaucracies within governments, see the WTO as a "dollars and cents organization,"[28] with rules and a dispute settlement system that affect their economic interests. States have relegated concerns over the environmental impacts of trade largely to other international institutions with fewer detailed rules and less judicialized enforcement regimes, such as the UN Environmental Program (UNEP) and single-issue international environmental organizations created under UNEP's and others' auspices.

The EMIT group's mandate was "to examine upon request any specific matters relevant to the *trade policy aspects* of measures to control pollution and protect human environment" (emphasis added),[29] not the environmental policy aspects of measures to liberalize and regulate trade. This general mandate was broken down by the EMIT group into three issues: "(a) trade provisions contained in existing *multilateral environmental agreements* . . . vis-à-vis GATT principles and provisions; (b) multilateral *transparency of national environmental regulations* likely to have trade effects; and (c) trade effects of new *packaging and labelling requirements* aimed at protecting the environment" (emphasis added).[30] While each of these issues permitted countries to assert environmental interests, countries focused the agenda on the adverse trade impacts of certain environmental measures.[31]

Although the initial push for the CTE's formation came from developed countries, developing countries agreed to its formation, provided the CTE's agenda reflected their development concerns as well.[32] This was part of their quid pro quo for agreeing to the CTE's formation as part of an overall package concluding the Uruguay Round and creating the WTO, which involved over twenty distinct agreements and numerous side "understandings," "decisions," and "declarations." The CTE's agenda was expanded to incorporate a package of ten items balancing concerns of developed and developing countries. The entire agenda is set forth in table 4.1, together with an indication of whether developed or developing countries were primarily interested in the item and noting the number of interventions of the most active developed and developing countries through 1998. Though the ten items have been formally retained, they were subsequently recategorized in 1997 into two central clusters, also identified in table 4.1: a cluster involving "market access" issues and a cluster involving "linkages between the multilateral environment and trade agendas."[33]

Market Access Issues of Concern to All

Countries' positions on the four items known as the "market access cluster"—items 2, 3, 4, and 6—challenge the conventional notion of a clean North-South split on trade-environment matters. Developing countries have been increasingly outward looking, demanding greater access to U.S. and European markets. They have been correspondingly less focused on preserving domestic import substitution

Table 4.1 The CTE Agenda and State Participation[a]

Item Number	Item Cluster and Relative State Interest	Most Active States[b] (Papers)	No. States/ Secretariat
Item 1. Trade Measures for Environmental Purposes *The relationship between the provisions of the multilateral trading system and trade measures for environmental purposes including those pursuant to multilateral environmental agreements*	Links between environment and trade agendas: U.S. and EC interest	EC, New Zealand (2 each)	State: 14 Secretariat: 26
Item 2. Trade-environment Catchall *The relationship between environmental policies relevant to trade and environmental measures with significant trade effects and the provisions of the multilateral trading system*	Market access cluster: discussion not focused	U.S. (2), Canada, India, Sweden (1 each)	State: 5 Secretariat: 1
Item 3. Eco-labeling, Packaging and Environmental Taxes *The relationship between the provisions of the multilateral trading system and (a) charges and taxes for environmental purposes and (b) requirements for environmental purposes relating to products including standards and technical regulations, packaging, labeling, and recycling*	Market access cluster: of great interest to all	U.S. (5) Canada (4) EC (3) Egypt, India, among others	State: 17 Secretariat: 9
Item 4. Making Environmental Measures Transparent *The provisions of the multilateral system with respect to the transparency of trade measures used for environmental purposes and environmental measures and requirements that have significant trade effects*	Market access cluster: of interest to all; result in substantive development: a new WTO database	Hong Kong (1)	State: 1 Secretariat: 8
Item 5. Dispute Settlement *The relationship between dispute settlement mechanisms in the multilateral trading system and those found in multilateral environmental agreements*	Links between environment and trade agendas: collapsed into item 1	Chile (1)	State: 1 Secretariat: 1

Item	Description	Interested states	Papers submitted
Item 6. Market Access and the Environmental Benefits of Removing Trade Distortions *The effect of environmental measures on market access, especially in relation to developing countries, in particular to the least developed among them, and environmental benefits of removing trade restrictions and distortions*	Market access cluster: of great interest to all, particularly the U.S. and Cairns Group[c]	EC (3), U.S. (2), Japan (2), Argentina, Australia, Brazil, India, Korea, among others	State: 17[d] Secretariat: 7
Item 7. Restricting Exports of Domestically Prohibited Goods (DPGs) *The issue of the export of domestically prohibited goods*	Links between environment and trade agendas: African interest	Nigeria (3)	State: 3 Secretariat: 4
Item 8. TRIPS *The relevant provisions of the Agreement on Trade-Related Aspects of Intellectual Property Rights*	Links between environment and trade agendas: India's interest	India (4), Australia, Korea (1 each)	State: 6 Secretariat: 3
Item 9. GATS *The work program envisaged in the Decision on Trade in Services and the Environment*	Links between environment and trade agendas: little discussed	U.S. and India (1 each)	State: 2 Secretariat: 2
Item 10. Relations with Intergovernmental Organizations and NGOs *Input to the relevant bodies in respect of appropriate arrangements for relations with intergovernmental and nongovernmental organizations referred to in Article V of the WTO*	Links between environment and trade agendas: U.S. and EC interest; debate moved to Council	U.S. (1)	State: 1 Secretariat: 2

[a]This represents the author's best count of papers submitted, based on data through December 31, 1998. The calculations in columns 3 and 4 are approximate, as (1) some items overlapped or were collapsed into each other; (2) states at times addressed more than one item in a single paper; (3) multiple states sometimes submitted a paper collectively, and (4) some Anon-papers were found, but others were not. The calculations include submissions before the EMIT Working Group on its three agenda items, which were revised slightly to become items 1, 2, and 3 of the CTE agenda, as well as all ten items addressed by the Preparatory Committee to the CTE during the eight-and-a-half-month period between signature of the Uruguay Round Agreements and formation of the WTO.

[b]The term "most active states" refers to those states submitting the greatest number of written submissions to the Committee on Trade and Environment. As for the most active states in terms of spoken interjections reported in the minutes of meetings, see infra note 33 and accompanying text.

[c]Cairns Group consists of a group of fourteen predominantly agricultural exporting countries, formed in Cairns Australia early in the Uruguay Round of trade negotiations, that includes developed and developing countries. The original members were Argentina, Australia, Brazil, Canada, Chile, Fiji, Hungary, Indonesia, Malaysia, the Philippines, New Zealand, Thailand, and Uruguay. See John Croome, *Reshaping the World Trading System: A History of the Uruguay Round* (Geneva: WTO 1995), pp. 30–31.

[d]States made nine further submissions on this market access item in 1999 in anticipation of a new round of trade negotiations. In contrast, only one state submitted a separate paper on one of the other nine items.

policies, which helps explain the decline of southern solidarity over trade policy.[34] This policy shift has facilitated the formation of North-South coalitions, as well as South-South conflicts, over specific trade matters.

The key market access issue was item 6, which broadly covers "the effect of environmental measures on market access . . . and environmental benefits of removing trade restrictions and distortions." The purported environmental benefits of eliminating politically sensitive agricultural, fishery, energy, and other subsidies generated extensive CTE debate. Agricultural exporting nations, including the United States, Australia, New Zealand, Argentina, Chile, Brazil, and even India, joined forces in the CTE to employ environmental rationale to challenge the EC, Japan, and Korea for protecting their agricultural sectors.[35] The issue of "packaging, labeling, and recycling" requirements (item 3) also resulted in North-South coalitions and pitted northern governments against each other, witnessed by ongoing disputes involving Canada and the United States against EC labeling of wood products and EFTA's early challenge to EC packaging and labeling requirements.

States attempted to harness the efforts of nonstate actors to support their negotiating positions. In 1997, the World Wildlife Fund (WWF) sponsored a symposium in Geneva on the detriments of subsidies to the fishing industry. This spurred the WTO secretariat assigned to the CTE to prepare its most ambitious analytical paper, a seventy-eight-page working paper prepared in two parts assessing the detrimental environmental affects of agricultural, fishing, energy, and other subsidies.[36] The focus on market access in item 6 permitted states (such as the Cairns Group) to harness trade liberal and environmental nongovernmental organization (NGO) support to advance their interests.[37] Yet though the framing may have temporarily aligned certain nonstate actors from the trade and environment communities, states continued to clash, in particular the United States and Europe, over their agricultural trading interests.

Environmental Issues of Primary Concern to the United States and the EC

The purportedly "environmental" items of primary interest to the United States and Europe were not surprisingly of primary interest to U.S. and European NGOs. These items examined, respectively, the existing environmental exceptions in GATT (item 1), in GATS (item 9), and their adjudication before WTO panels (item 5) as well as relations between the WTO and NGOs (item 10). Of these items, only item 1, concerning "the relationship between [WTO rules] and trade measures for environmental purposes," generated considerable debate, as it implicated current GATT rules around which the controversial tuna-dolphin dispute turned. Developing countries, supported by their respective trade, development, and environment constituencies, together with smaller developed countries, nonetheless successfully opposed U.S. and European proposals that could accommodate certain environmental measures.[38]

Environmental Issues of Primary Concern to Developing Countries

The two agenda items of primary interest to only developing countries similarly enabled them to adopt environmental arguments to restrict trade: item 7, concerning "the export of domestically prohibited goods," or DPGs (i.e., goods not permitted to be sold in developed countries), and item 8, concerning "the relevant provisions of the Agreement on Trade-Related Aspects of Intellectual Property Rights" (TRIPS) in relation to sustainable development objectives. Not surprisingly, these two items were opposed by northern business groups and advocated most fervently by southern environmental and developmental NGOs.[39]

Although the CTE focused primarily on the impact of environmental measures on state trading interests, states adopted environmental arguments where state trading interests could benefit. While most developing countries initially opposed the EMIT group's convening because environmental issues fell outside the WTO's "competence," they did not hesitate to wield environmental arguments to limit other countries' exports after the CTE was formed. African states, led by Nigeria, asserted that the WTO should restrict the export of waste materials and domestically prohibited goods to protect the African environment and African health.[40] India pressed for changes in the TRIPS Agreement to limit patent rights, create "farmer rights," and recognize "indigenous knowledge" in order to promote sustainable development.[41] India knew that these changes would economically benefit its farmers vis-à-vis U.S. and European agribusiness and pharmaceutical concerns. Yet when it came to calls for amending intellectual property rules, the United States and Europe switched stances on the issue of competence. In defense of U.S. biotechnology, agribusiness, and pharmaceutical interests, the United States responded, "The WTO was not an environmental organization and it lacked the competence to insert MEA [multilateral environmental agreement] goals in WTO Agreements."[42] The EC also took a clear bottom line: "The TRIPS Agreement should not be weakened by anything which might transpire in the CTE."[43]

What mattered in CTE debates was not the consistency of states' arguments concerning the WTO's competence to address environmental issues but rather the specific state objectives at stake. The sub-Saharan African countries' position on DPG and waste trade contradicted a host of developing country arguments, including those concerning the GATT illegality of extraterritorial regulation, the inappropriateness of holding developing countries to developed country standards, and GATT's limited competence on environmental policy matters. India likewise capitalized on environmental arguments to promote its economic interests in respect of TRIPS but upheld GATT's limited competence under item 1. States argued about the WTO's limited competence only when they believed that environmental arguments prejudiced their economic interests. States made dollars and cents of the trade-environment linkage before this "dollars and cents" organization.

WHAT EXPLAINS THE CURRENT STATUS
OF THE CTE PROCESS?

The CTE presented a forty-seven-page report to the first WTO ministerial meeting in November 1996 after a grueling negotiating process, culminating in a thirty-six-hour marathon session where the concluding portion of the report was negotiated line by line. Despite the intensity of the negotiation, none of the conclusions proposed any substantive legal changes to GATT rules but rather called for "further work" on all ten agenda items.[44]

It was not as if state representatives had not fully explored the issues. By December 1996, when the CTE delivered its Report, the WTO trade and environment body (in its various mutations) had met thirty-two times over multiple days, in addition to informal consultations among members. The minutes of the formal meetings alone, in their summarized form, total around 1,000 pages.[45] States submitted over fifty written proposals and observations.[46] In addition, at the member states' request, the WTO secretariat assigned to the CTE (the CTE secretariat) prepared over thirty working papers providing background information and analysis on the ten agenda items, which in turn cited numerous other studies from the World Bank, the OECD, the UN Conference on Trade and Development (UNCTAD), and other intergovernmental organizations.

Exhausted by a process that led to such a meager outcome, the CTE members significantly reduced the CTE's working schedule since 1996, meeting only three times per year from 1997 through 2000 and tailoring the meetings toward a study of the various issues more than a negotiation of outcomes. Although at the beckoning of the United States and the EC a "WTO high level symposium on trade and the environment" brought together representatives from around the world in March 1999 in an attempt to spur negotiation over trade-environment matters, it too resulted in no substantive developments.[47] At the third WTO ministerial meeting in December 1999, the United States and the EC again demanded negotiation of environmental issues, but again no consensus could be reached.

The intensity of the negotiations over the 1996 CTE Report may seem ironic given that it gave rise to no procedural or substantive changes in WTO rules or practices. Yet the line-by-line negotiation of the Report's language mattered because, as one state delegate noted, it was negotiated in an institution where "words have consequences."[48] Words have "consequences" in the WTO because of the economic impact of decisions rendered by its binding dispute settlement process.[49] Potential disputes with real economic impacts tend to polarize the discussion of complex trade-environment issues. In addition, the CTE Report was negotiated in the context of ongoing U.S. and EC parallel demands that the WTO address labor standards. Since WTO-authorized trade restrictions based on labor standards would even more severely prejudice developing country trading interests, the words of the CTE Report mattered.

National representatives justifiably feared that the Report could, in fact, be used against them in subsequent disputes implicating domestic economic and political interests. In the WTO's first major trade-environment dispute following the CTE Report—the shrimp-turtle dispute—the claimants (Thailand, Malaysia, India, and Pakistan), the respondent (the United States), and three third-party participants (Australia, Nigeria, and Singapore) each referred to different paragraphs from the CTE Report in support of their positions.[50] The dispute settlement panel likewise cited the Report both in its findings and in its "Concluding Remarks,"[51] as did the Appellate Body in reversing certain panel findings while still concluding that the U.S. import ban was "not justified" under GATT Article XX, the GATT exception clause.[52] By nonetheless applying Article XX in a manner more accommodating to U.S. trade restrictions than the earlier GATT tuna-dolphin reports, the Appellate Body affected developing countries' trading interests. In fact, the Thai shrimping industry had annually exported almost a billion dollars of shrimp and shrimp products to the United States in the years immediately preceding the ban, constituting over 50 percent of Thailand's total exports of these products.[53]

THE PREDOMINANT ROLE OF STATES: A TWO-LEVEL APPROACH AS THE STARTING POINT

The WTO is a state-dominated institution, and not surprisingly states played the dominant role in shaping the CTE agenda. Only states are formal members of the WTO, permitted to vote on WTO matters, and file claims under WTO rules. Moreover, only states may attend, speak, and submit papers to the CTE and other WTO committee meetings.[54] As the director of the Trade and Environment division of the WTO secretariat confirms, "The [CTE] process was driven by proposals from individual WTO members."[55] In total, states submitted over fifty documents to the CTE and its predecessors through December 1996, setting forth their national experiences, observations, and positions in respect of the CTE's ten agenda items. These supplemented their numerous statements at committee meetings. Yet a complete understanding of the CTE's difficulties requires understanding intrastate as well as interstate conflicts.

Intrastate Conflicts

The reason the CTE has been stalemated over its ten-point agenda is not solely because of a lack of consensus among states. Progress in the CTE has also been hampered by a lack of consensus within states. In the United States, for example, the Clinton administration was hampered in forming a clear position on the permissibility of trade restrictions on environmental grounds because of conflicts between powerful business constituents on the one hand and environmental constituents on the other.[56] One WTO secretariat representative criticized the United States for bringing to the WTO what it is "incapable of solving at the national level," calling this "madness."[57] Yet it was not madness for U.S. government representatives. They could appease domestic constituents by appearing to address issues in the WTO and letting other countries block changes to WTO rules that could affect U.S. business interests. They could use the CTE as a foil to avoid taking clear positions that would disaffect politically powerful constituencies. In any case, it was certainly not worth the Clinton administration's risk of exposing itself domestically were its position ultimately rejected by other WTO members.

CTE secretariat members were similarly never clear about the EC's position on the WTO legitimacy of private eco-labeling regimes (discussed under item 3), that is, eco-label regimes developed by the private sector, often in conjunction with environmental NGOs, without government involvement.[58] Divisions among EC business and environmental/consumer interests impeded the EC's ability to clarify its position.[59] These internal EC stakeholder divisions were reflected in divisions between the EC directorates responsible for trade and environmental policy. The environmental directorate argued that the EC should refrain from agreeing that private eco-labeling regimes are subject to WTO rules because they could then more easily be challenged before WTO panels.[60] The EC did not expend political capital within the WTO on eco-labeling and other environmental issues, in particular where it could thereby be pressed to trade off EC agricultural interests as part of a package deal.

State Power

States are not equal players within the WTO. In the hundreds of pages of minutes of CTE and EMIT group meetings, only twenty-two states (out of the WTO's then 134 members) spoke more than six times on the different items in the CTE's agenda.[61] The most active states were the United States, the EC, and Canada, in that order. India and Mexico were particularly active among developing countries, reflecting India's large population, relatively large gross national product, and its leading role among developing countries and Mexico's relative size and relevant experience with trade and environment negotiations under NAFTA. Smaller developing countries remain at a distinct disadvantage, for their bureaucracies are less experienced with the details of international trade rules, and often, given scarce resources, they have only one (or in many cases, no) representative in Geneva to follow all WTO matters. More powerful WTO members, such as the United States and the EC, thus drive WTO agendas.

Divisions between Powerful States

Divisions within and between powerful states helped block proposals that could adversely affect developing countries' trading interests. Divisions *within* the United States and the EC over controversial CTE items, such as item 1 (concerning trade measures for environmental purposes) and item 3 (concerning eco-labeling and related national regulations), hampered their taking a more aggressive role. Divisions *between* the United States and the EC over these matters impeded them from presenting a united, coherent negotiating package. The United States wished to leave item 1 for resolution by WTO dispute settlement panels, while the EC sought a politically negotiated clarification of GATT Article XX. The United States challenged EC eco-labeling schemes (most recently those concerning genetically modified seeds and food) and supported the CAIRNS Group's challenge of EC agricultural subsidies as detrimental to the environment. Because of these intra- and intertransatlantic divisions, the United States and the EC could not offer developing countries sufficient side payments to agree to changes in WTO rules advocated by U.S. and EC environmental groups. From a realist perspective, these divisions over trade-environment policy within and between the WTO's most powerful members explain why WTO rules have not changed.

FREE TRADE CAPTURE: DEBUNKING THE MYTH

Some critics of the WTO as a trade-biased institution imply that it is the WTO secretariat that defines the WTO's outlook. Yet since only states are entitled to speak and vote within the WTO, a more subtle analysis of free trade influences must focus on the role of state delegates, influenced by national commercial interests, assisted by the secretariat working within the WTO institutional context. In assessing free trade ideas and interests advanced within the CTE, one must start with states' representatives themselves, who largely came from state trade and foreign ministries.

Role of State Trade Bureaucracies

While it is true that states primarily (although not exclusively) framed the CTE debate in terms of a debate over trade, the actual role of free trade advocates in such framing was limited. The domestic political salience of most trade-environment issues addressed within the CTE, the trade and environmental slants actually adopted by state delegates, as well as the outcome of the debates (in particular item 6) all undermine the simplistic critique that the WTO and CTE have not accommodated environmental measures because they are trade-dominated institutions. While trade delegates played a predominant role in CTE debates, they received their instructions from home capitals, which, in countries with more developed bureaucratic systems, typically involved intraagency debates. Trade representatives did not even play the dominant role in determining and representing national positions on some agenda items. For example, representatives from the agricultural ministries of the United States, the EC, Japan, Korea, Canada, Australia, and New Zealand all attended CTE meetings and typically delivered their country's position maintaining or denying that liberalization of agricultural trade would benefit the environment (item 6).[62] The outcome in CTE debates on this issue was not a laissez-faire one.

National delegates advanced issues that were politically salient in their home countries, as a two-level approach would predict. Canada focused on challenging EC eco-label regimes for wood products because the wood products sector is of great importance to Canada. Argentina, Australia, Brazil, and New Zealand focused on attacking agricultural subsidies because this item was of great interest to their most vocal constituents on CTE matters, their agricultural export sector. Conversely, Japanese, Korean, and EC negotiators, recalling the large demonstrations in their cities in protest against the WTO agricultural agreement at the end of the Uruguay Round, were not about to permit the CTE to recommend further liberalization of agricultural trade. Similarly, farmers in India engaged in demonstrations against the TRIPS Agreement, and, not surprisingly, Indian negotiators correspondingly raised environmental arguments in support of an amendment of the TRIPS Agreement, even though they had earlier maintained that the WTO was not competent to discuss environmental matters.

Developing countries with a less developed governmental infrastructure were less likely to develop interagency processes to determine positions. However, especially where developing countries had more structured, experienced civil services (such as in Brazil, India, and Mexico), clear guidelines were typically established in national capitals.[63] For example, the United States, suspecting that Mexico's intransigence on U.S. demands in the CTE did not reflect Mexico's national position, complained to high officials in Mexico's central administration who quickly confirmed that these were indeed Mexico's positions.[64] When India's delegates opposed northern environmental demands for amending GATT Article XX to permit greater use of unilateral trade restrictions for environmental ends, India was not reflecting a commitment to free trade ideology. In fact, India is known for having one of the most protected economies in the WTO.[65]

In short, state delegates were careful to advance (if on the offensive) and not compromise (if on the defensive) their national positions within the CTE for future WTO negotiations over agriculture, intellectual property rights, technical standards, and all other matters. If anything, state representatives were not predominantly free traders but rather mercantilists.[66] Instead of promoting free trade regardless of their domestic producer interests, they attempted to expand their countries' exports and limit competition from imports.

Role of Business Interests

Large transnational businesses in the United States and Europe certainly organized to help shape the debate of trade and environment issues within the CTE and other fora. They operated through long-standing associations, such as the International Chamber of Commerce (ICC),[67] the United States Council on International Business, and Europe's UNICE, and relatively new ones, such as the World Business Council for Sustainable Development (WBCSD)[68] and the Transatlantic Business Dialogue (TABD).[69] These associations generally have greater access to state trade representatives than other nonstate actors because of their importance to domestic economies as well as to domestic elections. They thus can work more discretely than other nonstate actors. Businesses obtain information on what transpires in the WTO through consultants and trade association representatives, many of whom are based in Geneva[70] and many of whom were formerly in leading positions in international and national trade organizations. For example, Arthur Dunkel, the former director-general of GATT, became the chair of the ICC's Commission on International Trade and Investment Policy, which follows the CTE and other WTO committees.[71] Paula Stern, former chair of the U.S. International Trade Commission, became the TABD's trade consultant and was designated a member of President Clinton's Advisory Committee on Trade Policy and Negotiations.[72] Personal relations with key figures in government and intergovernmental organizations provide businesses with access unavailable to others.

Yet commercial interests are not always free trade oriented and, in any case, do not always prevail in domestic policy debates. Agricultural interests in the EC, Japan, and Korea, for example, certainly oppose the elimination of agricultural trade subsidies and tariff barriers on environmental or any other grounds. Developing country exporting interests are often more supportive of WTO trade liberalization initiatives than nonexporting interests.[73] Moreover, business interests do not always prevail, as witnessed by the collapse of negotiations for a Multilateral Agreement on Investment and the failure of the Clinton administration to obtain fast-track negotiating authority.

Role of the WTO Secretariat

Opponents of liberalization, on both the left and the right, typically critique the WTO for encroaching on national sovereignty, as if the WTO were an undemocratic autonomous actor with a single voice, independent of its member states. The WTO has become reified by its critics into an insidious agent of globalization of commerce and culture that infiltrates national borders and wreaks local havoc. At the WTO's sesquicentennial anniversary in 1998, protestors spray-painted Geneva walls with "WTO—World Terrorist Organization."[74]

Northern environmental activists are particularly upset by WTO judicial decisions in trade-environment disputes, which have held that U.S. laws enacted to address foreign environmental harms violated WTO rules. One of the purposes of the CTE was to attempt to provide guidance from a WTO political body to WTO judicial panels that hear these disputes. This section assesses the role of the WTO secretariat in that political process.

The WTO employs approximately 500 professional civil servants whose role is to provide assistance to the WTO's member states on request. This secretariat consists predominantly of trade economists and trade lawyers. Of the six secretariat members assigned to the CTE in 1998, four were neoclassical economists, and two were international trade lawyers, one formerly a member of a national trade ministry. WTO secretariat members thus potentially could be viewed as an epistemic community having "shared normative beliefs" (in free trade theory), "shared causal beliefs" (in how trade liberalization creates wealth), "shared notions of validity" (in applying neoclassical economic methodology), and "a common policy enterprise" (to facilitate government negotiations toward trade liberalization).[75] On the basis of their expertise, impartial reputation, inside information and close contacts with trade diplomats, secretariat members could, at least at the margins, help shape knowledge, frame issues, identify interests, facilitate coalition building, and thereby affect outcomes.

The capacity for the secretariat's proclivities to affect outcomes, however, depends on what the secretariat actually does and whether WTO members treat the secretariat as authoritative. The members of the CTE secretariat perform primarily five functions: the organization of meetings and recording of minutes; research on trade and environment issues; liaison with international organizations addressing these issues; public relations, especially vis-à-vis NGOs; and mediation between states. The primary means through which the secretariat can potentially influence outcomes are through its research, its liaison with other international organizations, and its mediation services.

States expect secretariat members to keep abreast of studies of trade and environment issues, particularly those conducted by other international organizations. In distributing information to all state delegates, the secretariat helps create a common base of understanding to defend the WTO from challenge by transnational environmental NGOs. On the request of states, the secretariat researches and prepares papers on specific issues. Through October 30, 1998, the CTE secretariat provided delegates with sixty-nine papers, totaling almost 1,000 pages. [76] Secretariat submissions addressed the environmental benefits of trade liberalization as well as the "economic and trade implications" of specific environmental instruments, such as packaging requirements,[77] eco-labeling schemes,[78] and eco-taxes and charges,[79] among other matters. The CTE secretariat relied to a large extent on research conducted by other international organizations, such as the OECD, the United Nations Conference on Trade and Development (UNCTAD), and the World Bank.[80]

The CTE secretariat also acts as a liaison with international environmental organizations to help states' delegates to the WTO monitor international developments. At the instruction of state delegates, members of the CTE secretariat observe meetings of, periodically address, submit papers to, and correspond with these environmental organizations and then report back to the CTE on developments within them. The secretariat thereby helps states quell potential conflicts between environmental measures proposed in these fora and WTO rules and principles. The secretariat's oversight also helps state delegates intervene by instructing their domestic colleagues of WTO constraints and thereby protect the states' WTO rights.

Finally, the secretariat provides mediation services when states negotiate over trade and environment issues. The secretariat's mediation services were central to the 1996 CTE Report. As confirmed by the former Canadian delegate to the CTE,

"The role of the Secretariat in the informal drafting process of October 31–November 1 reflects the professionalism and skill of the Secretariat in developing the basis for a consensus text."[81]

Nonetheless, within the CTE, secretariat members operate under the instructions of states and are under the watchful eyes of state delegates. The secretariat is by no means authoritative. States were not used by it as agents to enforce WTO trade liberalization norms. On the contrary, because of the consequential nature of WTO decision making, states keep the WTO secretariat on a "tighter leash."[82] Rather, the WTO secretariat was used as an agent by states to monitor international environmental negotiations in order to protect state trading interests. Ultimately, the CTE negotiations were dominated by states with conflicting interests.

ROLES OF OTHER STAKEHOLDERS: ENVIRONMENTAL AND DEVELOPMENTAL NGOS

Different interests have attempted to advance their goals through the institutionalization of trade and environment issues within the WTO, as suggested by the stakeholder and free trade capture (or supranational technocratic) and stakeholder perspectives. Northern environmental groups, in particular, are frustrated by the failure of the WTO's CTE to recommend any changes in WTO rules. They are especially frustrated regarding the issue most important to them, item 1 concerning the use of trade measures to enforce international environmental agreements and advance environmental goals through unilateral state action. Because of the stalemate within the CTE, they advocate a stakeholder model under which they would play a greater role in CTE deliberations. Not all NGOs, however, have advocated the adoption of a stakeholder model. The model has been advocated primarily by environmental groups in the United States and Europe, not the South, because southern NGOs recognize northern NGOs' advantage. Just as all states are not equal, all NGOs are not equal. Northern NGOs have more funding, are located closer to WTO offices in Geneva,[83] are more likely to finance international networks,[84] and have greater indirect access to information from their state representatives;[85] NGOs from the South have less access in part because southern governments themselves have difficulty monitoring all developments in the WTO (including in the CTE). In fact, one London-based environmental NGO, the Foundation for International Law and Development (FIELD), even negotiated a deal with a developing country, Sierra Leone, to represent it before the CTE. Beset by civil war, Sierra Leone did not have the resources or the priority to represent its "stakeholder" interests before the CTE.

Information comes at a price. Northern environmental NGOs, such as Greenpeace and the WWF, have multi-million-dollar budgets that they target to address environmental matters.[86] They can channel more resources toward CTE negotiations than most WTO members—harnessing the media to attempt to shape perceptions of problems and desired outcomes. Northern NGOs publish glossy magazines, circulate statements and pamphlets,[87] coordinate lobbying campaigns, call press conferences,[88] take out full-page adds in major publications such as the *New York Times,* and, more recently, submit amicus briefs to WTO dispute settlement panels.[89] NGOs such as the WWF proactively fund major symposia held within the United Nations to which they invite state delegates and representatives of the WTO and other international organizations.[90] The WWF has even created a parallel CTE, which it calls the Expert Group on Trade and the Environment, consisting of trade and environment specialists from developed and developing countries.[91] Nongovernmental organizations from the United States and Europe are already relatively powerful in affecting WTO agendas and outcomes precisely because they can work with and through the WTO's most powerful states.

In their information campaigns, northern NGOs do not represent a "global civil society" perspective. They have a specifically northern one and often, even more specifically, an Anglo-Saxon one.[92] Their representatives were raised and educated in the North. Almost all their funding comes from contributors from the North. They obtain their financing by focusing on issues that strike the northern public's imagination, in particular animal rights issues—a motivating force for their demand for changes in WTO rules under item 1. Southern states and southern NGOs thus distrust their demands for greater WTO transparency. Southern interests are wary that greater WTO transparency will merely permit northern NGOs, defending northern interests, to better exploit the media to pressure state delegates, the WTO secretariat, and WTO dispute settlement panelists to take their views into account and thereby advance northern ends.[93] Southern delegates precisely fear these aspects of the stakeholder model.

THE TWO-LEVEL APPROACH REDUX: FREE TRADERS, STAKEHOLDERS, AND STATE POSITIONS

It is certainly true that the views of U.S. and European NGOs on trade and environment matters conflict with those of most states, although in particular of southern states. It is also true that this is, in part, because business and economic concerns hold a privileged position in defining state interests. Yet what is often ignored in critiques of state-based WTO models is that NGO stakeholders' strongest defenders in the WTO on trade and environment matters are typically their own national representatives. On the issue of transparency, southern environmental and developmental NGOs largely support their national representatives in keeping the WTO process closed to private observers, while northern governments, lobbied by northern environmental NGOs, demand greater participatory rights for NGOs.[94] This is an easy issue for northern governments because northern business groups also adopt the "stakeholder" language to support northern environmental groups' demands for more transparency and private participation. In the words of the International Chamber of Commerce, the WTO must become more "transparent and open to all stakeholders—and in particular to the international business community—so that the stakeholders may be informed and involved in an effective manner."[95]

Similarly, on the issue of the relationship between GATT rules and environmental protection measures, although northern business interests may critique their own national representatives for going slightly too far, they nonetheless support an amendment of Article XX to accommodate some environmental measures, unlike southern NGOs. The International Chamber of Commerce, for example "proposed a way to make unilateral actions to protect an endangered species, such as the shrimp embargo, compatible with international rules."[96] Northern business groups were willing to compromise with northern environmental NGOs because they feared disputes over Asian sea turtles could derail trade liberalization negotiations over electronic commerce, financial services, insurance services, telecommunications, and other high-rent sectors. Northern business interests are not so much directly threatened by WTO decisions involving GATT Article XX, such as the tuna-dolphin or shrimp-turtle disputes, as they are indirectly threatened because these decisions rally environmental groups to generally oppose trade and investment liberalization initiatives.

Southern environmental NGOs, on the other hand, understand that Article XX is invoked primarily by northern states to restrict imports from the South and not vice versa. The Indian NGO Centre for Science and the Environment, in terms not so different than India's representative, "characterized the use of trade measures in MEAs [multilateral environmental agreements] as an inequitable lever available only to stronger countries."[97] These NGOs, while they may focus on environmental concerns in the South, also have a "southern" perspective and are concerned by U.S. and EC coercion affecting southern development. While environmental NGOs severely criticize their national governments at the national level, at the international level their champions are typically their own governments.[98]

SPILLOVER EFFECTS OF THE CTE PROCESS

The most enduring results of the WTO's CTE process are not the rather banal CTE reports or the interminable debates over the CTE's ten-point agenda. Rather, the importance of the CTE process lies primarily in its enhancement of the *transparency of WTO decision making*, and its facilitation of inter- and intrastate *coordination of trade-environment policy*, albeit primarily in advancing state commercial interests. The first legacy is partially in line with the predictions of a civil society/stakeholder approach. The second is partially in line with those of a supranational technocratic one. Yet in each case, state interests continue to predominate.

THE CTE AS A LABORATORY FOR INCREASED WTO TRANSPARENCY

The CTE process served as a laboratory for opening up WTO internal processes to the public. The WTO secretariat assigned to the CTE was the first to create a section of the WTO Web site providing relatively timely and detailed reporting of a WTO committee's deliberations. The CTE secretariat published the results of CTE meetings well before the minutes of the meeting were made public.[99] It worked with states toward expeditiously making all CTE submissions publicly available— whether proposals by states or analyses of the CTE secretariat. The CTE secretariat organized the first WTO symposium to which NGOs were invited to interact with the WTO secretariat and those state delegates who chose to attend. Few state delegates attended the first two symposia, one held following the second tuna-dolphin decision and the other in the midst of negotiation of the CTE 1996 Report.[100] Yet with the formal Report behind them, by the fourth symposium (held in 1998), state delegates and NGOs were asking and responding to each other's questions.[101] Gradually, even NGOs confirm that state delegates have become more comfortable engaging with them in such public fora, in large part because developing countries' fear of being isolated was assuaged.[102] In line with the predictions of the two-level approach, divisions among states were reflected largely in divisions among NGOs from those states.

More significant, the transparency issue migrated from the CTE to the WTO General Council. Following his participation in the fourth CTE-NGO symposium, Director-General Ruggiero publicly announced in July 1998 "a plan for enhanced cooperation with Non-governmental Organizations."[103] The plan included "regular briefings for NGOs on the work of WTO committees and working groups"; the circulation to state delegations of "a list of documents, position papers and newsletters submitted by NGOs"; and "a special section of the WTO Website . . . devoted to NGOs issues." The subsequent director-general, Michael Moore, confirmed that he would continue to promote greater openness.[104] These initiatives, first tested in the CTE, are being slowly promoted throughout the WTO system.

THE CTE AS A MECHANISM FOR OVERSEEING ENVIRONMENTAL POLICY

The CTE process has also made environmental issues more transparent for trade officials and trading interests. In line with rationalist institutionalist theory, states have used the CTE process to reduce information-gathering, monitoring, and coordination costs and thereby enhance state policy coordination.[105] States used the CTE to monitor and subject developments in international environmental fora to greater oversight. They used the WTO secretariat assigned to the CTE as agents to attend meetings of international environmental fora and to report on developments. The secretariat has prepared over twenty papers on such developments, including papers concerning the Rio Conference (under EMIT), the Commission on Sustainable Development, the Montreal Protocol on the Ozone Layer, the Kyoto Conference on Climate Change, the Basel Convention on the Control of Transboundary Movements of Wastes, the Convention on International Trade in Endangered Species of

Wild Flora and Fauna (CITES), the Food and Agricultural Organization (FAO), the International Tropical Timber Organization, and the Convention on Biodiversity.[106] Little now takes place in environmental fora without taking account of the WTO.[107] State trade delegates were able to use the CTE to more effectively ensure that trading interests and trading rules were understood and considered in international environmental fora.

States hoped to manage the trade impacts of domestic environmental measures at an early stage before disputes flare. By obtaining higher-quality information from the CTE secretariat, state representatives at the WTO could better defend WTO principles and rules at home in public and interagency debates. The secretariat prepared and cited numerous studies for state delegates showing that trade rules and environmental protection goals are mutually compatible. Drawing from these findings, the Australian delegate argued that "the CTE report should reject perceptions that a conflict existed between objectives of trade liberalization and environmental protection."[108] As the Egyptian delegate concluded, the CTE's 1996 Report was in good measure a public relations document, "a political statement largely to address the environmental community."[109] As the Canadian delegate confirmed, "The WTO Secretariat helps us manage the interface of the public and the WTO" on trade and environment matters.[110]

At first glance, this would appear to confirm the predictions of a supranational technocratic perspective. However, this attempt to "GATT the greens" has been primarily an effort by states through the WTO's agency, not by an independent WTO acting on its own. Moreover, the "GATTing" has been far from successful. Responding to internal domestic pressures, states continue to adopt environmental measures having extraterritorial trade effects, as witnessed by the WTO shrimp-turtle dispute. They also continue to adopt new environmental agreements with trade-restrictive provisions, as witnessed by the Cartagena Protocol on Biosafety.[111] Contrary to the predictions of a supranational technocratic model of governance, in the politically charged area of trade-environment policy, states' positions continue to reflect differing domestic constituency values, priorities, and interests.

The struggle over trade, environmental, and developmental goals nonetheless continues. State officials have used the CTE to help defend the WTO system in domestic debates. Yet northern environmental and other groups, disaffected with global economic processes, continue to target their disdain on the WTO. Although the CTE process has facilitated policy coordination within governments and among intergovernmental organizations, it has not defused entrenched grassroots opposition in the United States and Europe to economic globalization processes, symbolized—and thereby creating a target for attack—in the WTO.

CONCLUSION

The WTO is often critiqued by NGOs as if it were an undemocratic force independent of states. Yet the explanation for the stalemate within the WTO's CTE lies in conflicts within and between states, not in independent action of the WTO. In fact, from the standpoint of the pluralist representation of domestic political interests, the views of northern and southern NGOs on the CTE's agenda have been *most* closely aligned with those advanced by their own governments. The WTO's CTE has served as a conduit for states responding to domestic pressures.

The WTO secretariat did not block changes to WTO rules. Ultimately, WTO rule changes desired by northern environmental NGOs were blocked because northern NGOs either failed to win domestic policy debates or were unable to convince national representatives to offer sufficient side payments to gain developing country support of desired changes in WTO rules. Where there were divisions among powerful domestic constituencies, governments—including the most powerful—avoided taking a clear proactive stance within the CTE. Since establishment of the WTO, the United States and the EC have been simply unable or unwilling to adopt any of the strategies suggested by two-level intergovernmental bargaining theorists—from targeting threats or concessions, linking issues, manipulating information, or offering side payments—to induce developing countries to agree to amend WTO rules in a manner that developing countries justifiably believed would adversely affect their economic interests. Were U.S. and European environmental interest groups able to convince their own national representatives to prioritize environmental issues, WTO rules, rightly or wrongly, would also more likely be changed. Northern environmental groups have been simply unsuccessful in harnessing U.S. and EC clout to attain their aims.

In answer to this chapter's initial question, *the two-level perspective* best explains how trade and environment issues have been addressed to date within the WTO. Although the WTO institutional context creates a framework in which negotiations occur, and although the WTO secretariat can play a role as a broker within that framework, the WTO is not an institution controlled by a free trade ideological elite that is independent of states. Rather, state representatives closely defended their constituencies' interests within the CTE. Trade-environment issues are high-profile items reported in the news media and heavily lobbied in U.S., European, and other capitals precisely because of their potential environmental and economic impacts. While state delegates may attempt to manipulate domestic processes to enhance their policymaking discretion, they still must respond to domestic pressures. The more issues become politicized, the less discretion state delegates have. From both constructivist and instrumentalist perspectives, U.S. and European environmental groups failed to sufficiently shape the CTE's agenda, frame its treatment of the issues, or influence the outcome of CTE debates to accomplish their goals.

NOTES

This research was supported by a grant from the National Science Foundation Law and Social Science Program as well as support from the University of Wisconsin graduate school research competition and the University of Wisconsin World Affairs and the Global Economy (WAGE) Initiative. An early version of this chapter was presented at the annual meeting of the American Society of International Law in Washington, D.C., March 27, 1999. Thanks go to Sonia Brown, Matthew Kim-Miller, and Michael Mosser for valuable research assistance.

1. See, for example, Steve Charnovitz, "A Critical Guide to the WTO's Report on Trade and Environment," *Arizona Journal of International & Comparative Law* 14 (1997): 341, 342 (stating "hopes were dashed. When the CTE issued its report in November 1996, it became clear that two years of inter-governmental deliberations had yielded little output."); World Wide Fund for Nature (WWF), "Introduction to the WTO Committee on Trade and Environment: Is It Serious?" (maintaining that the CTE is not serious about "making appropriate recommendations on whether any modifications of WTO rules" are required to accommodate environment policies) (available at <http://www.panda.org/resources/publications/sustainability/wto/intro.htm>, visited October 31, 1999).

2. See Daniel Pruzin, "WTO Chief Outlines Plans for Increased Transparency," *International Trade Rep.* (BNA) (July 22, 1998): 1263.

3. These models are more fully developed in Mark Pollack and Gregory Shaffer, "Transatlantic Governance in Historical and Theoretical Perspective," in Mark Pollack and Gregory Shaffer, eds., *Transatlantic Governance in a Global Economy* (Lanham, Md.: Rowman & Littlefield, 2001), 3–43, and Gregory Shaffer, "The World Trade Organization under Challenge: Democracy and the Law and Politics of the WTO's Treatment of Trade and Environment Matters," *Harvard Environmental Law Review* 25 (2001): 1.

4. See, for example, the articles in Robert Keohane, ed., *Neorealism and Its Critics* (New York, N.Y.: Columbia University Press, 1986), in particular the chapters by Kenneth Waltz; see also Robert Gilpin, *The Political Economy of International Relations* (Princeton, N.J.: Princeton University Press, 1987).

5. See, for example, Robert Keohane, *After Hegemony: Cooperation and Discord in the World Political Economy* (Princeton, N.J.: Princeton University Press, 1984); Stephen Krasner, ed., *International Regimes* (Ithaca, N.Y.: Cornell University Press, 1983); and Ken Abbot, "Modern International Relations Theory: A Prospectus for International Lawyers," *Yale Journal of International Law* 14 (1989): 335.

6. See, for example, Robert Putman, "Diplomacy and Domestic Politics: The Logic of Two-Level Games, *International Organization* 42 (1988): 427; Peter B. Evans et al., eds., *Double-Edged Diplomacy: International Bargaining and Domestic Politics* (Berkeley, Calif.: University of California Press, 1993); and Andrew Moravcsik, "Preferences and Power in the European Community: A Liberal Intergovernmentalist Approach," *Journal of Common Market Studies* 31 (1993): 473, 483 ("Groups articulate preferences; governments aggregate them.").

7. Robert O. Keohane and Joseph S. Nye, "Transgovernmental Relations and International Organizations," *World Politics* 27 (1994): 39, 45.

8. See, for example, Susan Strange, *The Retreat of the State: The Diffusion of Power in the World Economy* (New York, N.Y.: Cambridge University Press, 1996); P. Chatterjee and Matthias Finger, *The Earth Brokers: Power, Politics and World Development* (London: Routledge, 1994); David C. Korten, *When Corporations Rule the World* (London: Earthscan, 1995); and Richard Barnett and John Cavanagh, *Global Dreams: Imperial Corporations and the New World Order* (New York, N.Y.: Simon & Schuster, 1994).

9. See, for example, Margaret Keck and Katherine Sikkink, *Activists beyond Borders: Advocacy Networks in International Politics* (Ithaca, N.Y.: Cornell University Press, 1998);

Thomas Risse-Kappen, "Introduction to Bringing Transnational Relations Back," in Thomas Risse-Kappen, ed., *Bringing Transnational Relations Back In: Non-State Actors, Domestic Structures, and International Institutions* (Cambridge: Cambridge University Press, 1995), 3–33; Martha Finnemore, *National Interests in International Society* (Ithaca, N.Y.: Cornell University Press, 1996); and John Boli and George M. Thomas, eds., *Constructing World Culture: International Nongovernmental Organizations since 1875* (Stanford, Calif.: Stanford University Press, 1999). The focus on how nonstate actors shape (or "construct") norms that thereby affect policy outcomes is often referred to as "constructivism." For an analytical account of "constructivism" in international relations theory, see John Ruggie, "What Makes the World Hang Together? Neo-Utilitarianism and the Social Constructivist Challenge," *International Organization* 52 (autumn 1998): 855.

10. See, for example, Paul Wapner, *Environmental Activism and World Civic Politics* (Albany, N.Y.: State University of New York Press, 1996), and Boli and Thomas, eds., *Constructing World Culture*.

11. An example of an attempt to create a stakeholder community bringing together northern and southern environmental and developmental NGOs is the International Centre for Trade and Sustainable Development (ICTSD), based in Geneva, Switzerland.

12. The convening of the EMIT Group was first raised in a Uruguay Round negotiating meeting in December 1990, but the first EMIT group meeting was not held until November 1991. See the proposal to convene the EMIT group, submitted by member countries of the European Free Trade Association, in "Statement on Trade and the Environment," MTN.-TNC/W/47, December 3, 1990. See EMIT, "Report of the Meeting of the Group on Environmental Measures and International Trade," TRE/1, December 17, 1991 (the minutes of the first EMIT group meeting).

13. See North American Agreement on Environmental Cooperation (Environmental Side Agreement, September 13, 1993), 32 I.L.M. 1480.

14. In 1991, the members of the Organization of Economic Cooperation and Development (OECD) also agreed to form an OECD Joint Session of the Trade and Environment Committees, which, as the CTE, continued to periodically meet through 2000. See Robert Youngman and Dale Andrew, "Trade and Environment in the OECD," in *Sustainable Development: OECD Policy Approaches for the 21st Century* 77 (Paris: Organization for Economic Cooperation and Development, 1997).

15. GATT Council, "Minutes of Meeting: Held in the Centre William Rappard on 6 February 1991," C/M/247, February 6, 1991, 22 (hereinafter February 1991 Council Meeting). ASEAN (Association of Southeast Asian Nations) typically designated one member to speak for the association within the EMIT working group and the CTE. The members of ASEAN within the WTO are Brunei, Indonesia, Malaysia, the Philippines, Singapore, and Thailand.

16. Ibid., 25.

17. GATT Council, "Minutes of Meeting Held in the Centre William Rappard on 12 March 1991," C/M/248, April 3, 1991, 18 (hereinafter March 1991 Council Meeting).

18. For an overview of the tuna-dolphin dispute, see Joel Trachtmann, "Decision: GATT Dispute Settlement," *American Journal of International Law* 86 (1992): 142.

19. See Nancy Dunne, "Fears over 'Gattzilla the Trade Monster,' " *Financial Times*, January 30, 1992, I3.

20. See U.S. and EC statements, in February Council Meeting, 24–26, and March Council Meeting, 17–22.

21. The EFTA consisted of European counties that were not members of the EC and at the time consisted of Norway, Sweden, Finland, Iceland, Austria, Switzerland, and Liechtenstein. Since 1991, Sweden, Finland, and Austria have joined the EC, and Switzerland has left EFTA on account of a treaty signed between EFTA and the EC establishing a European Economic Area (or EAA).

22. February 1991 Council Meeting, 20.

23. GATT Council, "Minutes of Meeting: Held in the Centre William Rappard on 29–30 May 1991," C/M/250, June 28, 1991, 14 (hereinafter May 1991 Council Meeting).

24. Ibid., 19.

25. That is, the United States also banned tuna imports from European countries that did not themselves ban imports of Mexican tuna on account of Mexican tuna-fishing methods.

26. For an overview, see Andre Nollkaemper, "The Legality of Moral Crusades Disguised in Trade Laws: An Analysis of the EC 'Ban' on Furs from Animals Taken by Leghold Traps," *Journal of Environmental Law* 8 (1996): 237.

27. See, for example, David Vogel, *Barriers or Benefits, Regulation in International Trade* (Washington, D.C.: Brookings Institution Press, 1997).

28. Interview with Andrew Griffith, formerly Canadian representative to the CTE, in Geneva, Switzerland, June 1997.

29. Group on Environmental Measures and International Trade, TRE/2, December 17, 1991. The preamble to the decision establishing a Committee on Trade and Environment provides that the Committee's competence "is limited to trade policies and those trade-related aspects of environmental policies which may result in significant trade effects for its members." See Trade and Environment, "Decision of April 14, 1994," MTN/TNC/45(MIN).

30. See TRE/1, 1.

31. Report by the Chairman of the Group on Environmental Measures and International Trade Presented to the Contracting Parties at Their Forty Ninth Session," GATT B.I.S.D. (40th Suppl.) (L/7402) (1995) para. 9, 75 (concerning the work of the EMIT in 1993 and referring to its focus on "trade-related aspects of environment policies").

32. The EMIT group's terms of reference explicitly provided that the group shall be "taking into account the particular problems of developing countries."

33. See table 4.1. The clustering was done in order to provide greater substantive focus to discussions. See "The WTO Committee on Trade and Environment Establishes Its Work Programme and Schedule of Meetings for 1997," *Trade and Environment Bulletin,* no. 17, PRESS/TE017, March 26, 1997 (available at <http://www.wto.org/wto/environ/te17.htm>).

34. See, for example, Alejandro Jara, "Bargaining Strategies of Developing Countries in the Uruguay Round," in Diana Tussie and David Glover, eds., *The Developing Countries in World Trade: Policies and Bargaining Strategies* (Boulder, Co.: Lynne Rienner, 1993), 11, 27 ("Coalitions seem to better serve their purpose when built around well-defined interests of like-minded countries, whether developed or developing."); Diana Tussie, "Bargaining at a Crossroads: Argentina," in Tussie and Glover, eds., *The Developing Countries in World Trade,* 119, 135 ("Before the Uruguay Round, Argentina, like most developing countries, had concentrated its trade diplomacy on the defense of import substitution, applying its skills mainly to securing import protection. . . . But gradually Argentine interests focused on issues of market access."); Rajiv Kumar, "The Walk away from Leadership," in Tussie and Glover,

eds., *The Developing Countries in World Trade,* 155, 165, 168 ("India's position in the multi-lateral trade negotiations will henceforth be more unambiguously inspired by clearly defined national interests" and not by "classical North-South positions.").

35. See presentation of state positions in "WTO Committee on Trade and Environment Welcomes Information Session with MEA Secretariats, Discusses Items Related to the Link-ages between the Multilateral Environment and Trade Agendas, Services and the Environ-ment, Relations with NGOs and IGOs, and Adopts 1997 Report," *Trade and Environment Bulletin,* no. 21, PRESS/TE021, December 19, 1997 (available at <http://www.wto.org/wto/environ/te021.htm>).

36. CTE, "Environmental Benefits of Removing Trade Restrictions and Distortions: Note by the Secretariat," WT/CTE/W/67, November 7, 1997, para. 5.

37. For example, the Argentine representative to the CTE, Hector Torres, was viewed by environmentalists as a potential environmental ally. Argentina's primary interest was in item 6. It aimed to use the CTE to pressure the EC, in particular, to reduce its agricultural subsid-ies and other barriers to market access for Argentina's agricultural products. In exchange, Argentina appeared more willing than other developing countries to accommodate NGO de-mands on items 1 and 10.

38. However, the U.S. and EC positions on the need for Article XX to better accommo-date environmental goals were largely accepted by the WTO Appellate Body through its sub-sequent interpretation of Article XX. For an overview of the WTO shrimp-turtle dispute, see Gregory Shaffer, "United States Import Prohibition of Certain Shrimp and Shrimp Prod-ucts," *American Journal of International Law* 93 (April 1999): 507.

39. See discussion in notes 41 and 43, and accompanying text.

40. Egypt, for example, argued that "commercial interests should not prevail over the protection of human, animal or plant life or health." CTE, "Report of the Meeting Held on 16 February 1995," WT/CTE/M/1, March 6, 1995, para. 5. The United States countered that these issues were more appropriately addressed by other international environmental fora. See CTE, "Report of the Meeting Held on 14 December 1995," WT/CTE/M/6, January 17, 1996, para. 32 (where the United States maintains that other organizations "had the competence and expertise" to address these items, unlike the CTE).

41. See CTE 1996 Report, paras. 133, 137, 139.

42. CTE, "Report of the Meeting Held on 11–13 September 1996," WT/CTE/M/12, October 21, 1996, para. 39.

43. EC comments quoted in "WTO Trade and Environment Committee Continues Discussing Proposals on Recommendations for the Singapore Ministerial Meeting and the Post-Singapore Work Programme," *Trade and Environment Bulletin,* no. 13, PRESS/TE 013, September 1996, 7 (available at <http://www.wto.org/wto/environ/te013.htm>).

44. At the conclusion of the 1996 WTO Ministerial Conference held in Singapore, the ministers issued a "Singapore Ministerial Declaration," paragraph 16 of which briefly sum-marized the work of the CTE, noting that "further work needs to be undertaken on all items of its agenda." Singapore Ministerial Declaration, WT/MIN(96)/DEC, December 11, 1996 (available at <http://www.wto.org/wto/archives/wtodec.htm> and 36 I.L.M. 218 [1997]).

45. In internal WTO terminology, there are "formal" and "informal" meetings. The most difficult negotiations, however, take place in "informal" ones, for which there are no minutes. When the delegates negotiated the language of the final CTE 1996 Report, they went into "closed" sessions (i.e., held "informal" meetings). Insiders confirm that, if busy,

delegates may attend only the "informal" meetings since those are the ones that "count." Interview with U.S. and Canadian delegates in Geneva, Switzerland, June 1997.

46. The precise number is difficult to calculate because many nonpapers are not available from WTO archives.

47. The EC's call for a "high level trade and environment meeting . . . to break the log jam" is cited in European Commission, "The Rt Hon. Sir Leon Brittan QC Vice-President of the European Commission Solving the Trade and Environment Conundrum," Bellerive GLOBE International Conference, Geneva, Switzerland, March 23, 1998, RAPID, March 23, 1998. Excluded from Brittan's list were the CTE issues of greatest interest to developing countries, including reduced agricultural and fishery subsidies and a revision of the TRIPS Agreement.

48. Interview with Chiedhu Osakwe, former Nigerian delegate to the CTE, in Geneva, Switzerland, June 1997. Osakwe was contrasting discussions among states within the WTO compared to those same discussions within UN bodies. Osakwe is now a member of the WTO secretariat assigned to the Trade and Development Section.

49. Within the first five years of the WTO, members filed 182 claims (as determined by number of formal consultations requested—the first step of the process) before its dispute settlement body, and WTO panels rendered twenty-five decisions that have been adopted by the WTO. Most of the filed claims, as well as claims never formally filed, were settled within the shadow of the WTO's dispute settlement system. See "Overview of the State-of-Play of WTO Disputes" (available at <http://www.wto.org/wto/dispute/bulletin.htm#Toc 464983829>).

50. See "Report of the Panel, United States—Import Prohibition of Certain Shrimp and Shrimp Products," WT/DS58/R, May 15, 1998, paras. 4.16, 4.53, 4.71 (summarizing third-party participants' observations) (hereinafter Shrimp-Turtle Panel Report).

51. See Shrimp-Turtle Panel Report, para. 7.50 (in findings) and para. 9.1 (in concluding remarks).

52. See "Report of the Appellate Body, United States—Import Prohibition of Certain Shrimp and Shrimp Products, WT/DS58/AB/R, October 12, 1998, paras. 154–55 and para. 168 (noting the CTE's affirmation of the importance of "multilateral solutions" in the context of its critique of the United States failure to engage in "serious, across-the-board negotiations," para. 167) (hereinafter Shrimp-Turtle Appellate Report).

53. See Fisheries of the United States, 1997 (Shrimp Imports by Country of Origin), U.S. Department of Commerce, National Oceanic and Atmospheric Administration (on file). See also "Executive Summary," 1 Bridges (April 1997).

54. The only exception to this rule is where states, by consensus, invite representatives of other international organizations to observe and sometimes present overviews of such organizations' work programs.

55. Interview with Richard Eglin, former Director of the Trade and Environment Division of the WTO, in Geneva, Switz. (June 15, 2000).

56. See, for example, "Administration Unclear on Policy for WTO Environment Committee," *Inside U.S. Trade,* January 26, 1996, 19.

57. Interview with a high-level official of the WTO secretariat in Geneva, Switzerland, June 1997.

58. Interview with a member of the CTE secretariat in Geneva, Switzerland, June 1998.

59. EC businesses, for example, under UNICE (Union des Confederations de l'Industrie

et des Employeurs d'Europe), argued that all eco-labels, including "voluntary" labels (i.e., those developed voluntarily by private groups), should be governed by the WTO Agreement on Technical Barriers to Trade. See "UNICE Position on Eco-Labelling for the WTO Discussion on Trade and Environment," July 22, 1996 (obtained by author from UNICE). EC environmental groups, fearing the constraints of TBT rules, argued otherwise.

60. Confirmed in interview with EC representative in Geneva, Switzerland, June 1998. As a CTE secretariat representative stated, "The Canadian Pulp and Paper Association has a file ready against EC eco-labeling schemes." Interview in Geneva, June 1998.

61. The OECD members so participating were Australia, Canada, the EC (collectively representing all member states), Japan, Mexico, New Zealand, Norway, South Korea, Sweden, Switzerland, and the United States. The only non-OECD members on this list were Argentina, ASEAN (as a group), Brazil, Chile, Egypt, Hong Kong, India, Morocco, Nigeria, Sierra Leone, and Venezuela. This is based on an approximate count of interventions found in the minutes of CTE meetings.

62. Confirmed in interviews with each of their Geneva-based representatives to the CTE in Geneva, Switzerland, June 1997 and June 1998.

63. Confirmed in interviews with representatives from Brazil in Geneva, Switzerland, June 1998.

64. Interview with Ricardo Barba, deputy permanent representative to the WTO from Mexico, in Geneva, Switzerland, June 1997.

65. See, for example, OECD, "Trade, Employment and Labor Standards" (1996), 139–40 (classifying India as having a restrictive trade regime).

66. As one developing country delegate states, "We are all a bunch of haggling merchants here." As merchants, when delegates use environmental arguments, they use them to advance their trading interests. Interview in Geneva, Switzerland, June 2000.

67. The members of the ICC consist of sixty-three national committees as well as individual companies from countries where a national committee has yet to be formed. The U.S. Council for International Business is the U.S. national member of the ICC. See the ICC's Web site at <http://www.iccwbo.org/iccww>.

68. The Geneva-based WBCSD consists of approximately 120 member corporations from around the world. The WBCSD reports that it "is expanding its network of national BCSDs to have a presence in every developing region of the world." See WBCSD, *Signals of Change: Business Progress towards Sustainable Development* (Switzerland: World Business Council for Sustainable Development 1996), 47.

69. A U.S. Department of Commerce official maintains that " 'virtually every' market-opening initiative undertaken by the United States and the EU in the past couple of years has been suggested by the TABD." Gary G. Yerkey "U.S., EU Business Leaders to Urge Further Easing of Impediments to Trade," *International Trade Rep.* (BNA) 14, no. 44: 1909 (Nov. 5, 1997).

70. The ICC and WBCSD have offices in Geneva. The International Council on Mining and the Environment (ICME) has hired as a consultant the husband of the WTO Appellate Body Secretariat division leader.

71. The ICC's Commission also "formulates recommendations on post-Uruguay Round trade policy issues for the 1990s including: trade and the environment, trade and competition, trade and investment, trade and labour standards." See ICC Policy Statement, "Trade Measures for Environmental Purposes," Document 103/187 Rev. and Document 210/535 Rev., October 24, 1996, 1.

72. Stern engages in what she terms "entrepreneurial diplomacy," whereby corporations take a leading entrepreneurial role in defining the agenda and the terms of trade negotiations. See, for example, Jeff Gerth, "Autos Are Focus of Pioneering Talks on World Standards," *New York Times,* January 9, 1998, D-1.

73. Interview with Ricardo Melendez, currently director of the International Center for Trade and Sustainable Development (ICTSD), based in Geneva, Switzerland, and formerly delegate for Columbia to the CTE, Geneva, June 1998.

74. They overturned and burned vehicles and ransacked such globalization symbols as a Burger King and a McDonald's outlet. It was reported to be the most violence Geneva had experienced in decades.

75. These attributes of epistemic communities are set forth in Peter Haas's work, which notes that epistemic communities "have (1) a shared set of normative and principled beliefs . . .; (2) shared causal beliefs . . .; (3) shared notions of validity . . .; and (4) a common policy enterprise." See Peter Haas, "Introduction: Epistemic Communities and International Policy Coordination," *International Organization* 46 (1992): 1–35 (Haas defines an "epistemic community" as "a network of professionals with recognized expertise and competence in a particular domain and an authoritative claim to policy relevant knowledge within that domain or issue-area," 3).

76. A count of 983 pages includes some annexes of new environmental agreements or proposed drafts of agreements. A list of all papers provided by the CTE secretariat on the agenda items through the November 1996 Singapore ministerial meeting is included in Annex IV to the CTE 1996 Report. These can be obtained through the document search option of the WTO's Web site. The most important CTE matters in terms of secretariat output were item 1 (twenty papers), item 3 (nine papers), and item 6 (five papers). Most of the secretariat's papers relevant to item 1 concerned developments in different international environmental fora.

77. See EMIT, Agenda Item 2: Multilateral Transparency of National Environmental Regulations Likely to Have Trade Effects: Note by the Secretariat," TRE/W/10, March 17, 1993.

78. EMIT, "Agenda Item 3: Packaging and Labelling Requirements: Note by the Secretariat," TRE/W/12, June 14, 1993.

79. CTE, "Taxes and Charges for Environmental Purposes—Border Tax Adjustment: Note by the Secretariat," WT/CTE/W/47, May 2, 1997, 1.

80. The most widely cited organizations in CTE papers were the OECD, UNCTAD, the World Bank, the FAO, and UNEP. For example, in a detailed 1997 report by the secretariat on the "Environmental Benefits of Removing Trade Restrictions and Distortions," the secretariat cites over fifteen international organizations, the predominant ones being the OECD (thirty-two cites), UNCTAD (thirty-two cites), the FAO (thirty-one cites), and the World Bank (twenty-nine cites). See "Environmental Benefits of Removing Trade Restrictions and Distortions: Note by the Secretariat," WT/CTE/W/67, and its addendum, WT/CTE/W/67/Add.1, March 13, 1998 (the count comprises the report and its addendum).

81. Andrew Griffith, Market Access and Environmental Protection: A Negotiator's Point of View (Ottawa: Dept. of Foreign Affairs and International Trade, 1997), 22–23.

82. Interview with a WTO secretariat member in Geneva, Switzerland, June 1997 (who also confirmed that "Parties oversee the secretariat when they feel affected by it").

83. Geographically, U.S. and European NGOs are located closer to Geneva, reducing their transportation costs and inconvenience.

84. WWF International, for example, has at least twenty national affiliates.

85. NGOs are represented, for example, on the U.S. administration's Trade and Advisory Committee. U.S. and EC trade representatives periodically meet with NGOs on trade-environment issues before WTO meetings.

86. Greenpeace's total income for 1998 was U.S.$125,297,000. See Greenpeace, *Greenpeace 1998 Annual Report,* June 16, 1999 (available at <http://www.greenpeace.org/report98/index.html>). The World Wildlife Fund had a 1998 total income of U.S.$53,450,000. See World Wildlife Fund, *Annual Report 1998* (available at <http://www.-panda.org/wwf/Report98/accounts.html>).

87. See, for example, "The GATT Trade and Environment Work Programmes: A Joint NGO Statement," signed on March 3, 1994, in Gland, Switzerland (WWF International's headquarters), and signed by WWF International and twenty WWF national affiliates, by Greenpeace International and ten Greenpeace national affiliates, and twenty-nine other NGOs.

88. See, for example, Michael Battye, "Environmental Groups Blast World Trade Body," *Reuter European Community Report,* December 8, 1996.

89. See discussion in Shaffer, Shrimp-Turtle, supra note 38.

90. The WWF-UNEP conference on fisheries, held in June 1997 at the United Nations in Geneva, Switzerland, was funded primarily by the WWF. It brought together state delegates to the CTE, representatives of the CTE secretariat, and representatives of other international organizations (including of the UN Environmental Program, the UN Development Program, the Food and Agricultural Organization, and the OECD).

91. The group meets a few times per year and issues periodic reports that the WWF then distributes to the CTE secretariat and state delegates to the CTE as well as any other interested party. See, for example, Expert Panel on Trade and Sustainable Development, 2nd meeting, Cairo, February 16–18, 1997, WWF EPTSD Secretariat Report, 1.

92. Environmental NGOs are typically located (or headquartered) in Anglo-Saxon countries. The four environmental NGOs that most actively followed and commented on CTE developments were WWF International (based in Gland, Switzerland, near Geneva), the Center for International and Environmental Law (CIEL) (based in Washington, D.C.), the Foundation for International and Environmental Law and Development (FIELD) (based in London, England), and the International Institute for Sustainable Development (IISD) (based in Winnipeg, Canada). Though WWF International is based in Switzerland, it has affiliates throughout the world, the most important being WWF (USA).

93. As a former representative from UNCTAD confirmed, "developing countries are concerned about the weighting of the transparency process, that it will be northern-dominated, that it will be biased in that it will predominantly present the views of northern interests." Interview with Veena Jha in Geneva, Switzerland, June 11, 1997.

94. Southern NGOs are more concerned about how the U.S. drives the WTO agenda, working behind the scenes with the EC, Canada, and other developed countries to place developing countries always on the defensive, having to react to U.S. initiatives, such as over intellectual property rights, liberalization of service sectors, and, more recently, electronic commerce. Confirmed in discussions with Pradeep Mehta, secretary-general, Consumer Unity & Trust Society (CUTS) (Jaipur, India), and Roberto Bissio, executive director, Instituto del Tercer Mundo (Montivideo, Uruguay), at UNCTAD conference on relations with NGOs in Geneva, Switzerland, in June 1998.

95. ICC, Commission on International Trade and Investment Policy, and the Commission on Environment, "Trade Measures for Environmental Purposes," October 24, 1996, para. 3 (available at <http://www.iccwbo.org/home/statements_rules/statements/1996/trade_measures.asp>).

96. See Abraham Katz, "Trade and Environment: Let's Talk," *Journal of Commerce,* April 29, 1998. Katz refers to an ICC paper, "Trade Measures for Environmental Purposes," Document 103/187 Rev. and Document 210/535 Rev., October 24, 1996.

97. 1997 NGO Symposium Transcript, comments of Sunita Narain, representative of the Indian NGO Centre for Science and Environment, on the issue "Multilateral Environmental Agreements and the WTO."

98. For example, in respect of the shrimp-turtle dispute between India and the United States, the Center for Science and Environment (CSE), an Indian environmental NGO, critiques the Indian government for not insisting "that all trawlers catching shrimp must use a turtle excluder device." As it says, "Trust the government of India and its arms like the ministry of environment and forests to sit idle while the turtle massacre goes on. . . . The government of India is probably the most hypocritical government of the Earth." Yet in the same publication, the CSE confirms that it "has consistently opposed the use of trade sanctions to conserve the global environment because of the simple reason that only economically powerful nations can impose effective trade sanctions against less economically powerful nations." Anil Agarwal, "Turtles Shrimp and a Ban," *Down to Earth,* June 15, 1998. See also "Trade Control Is Not a Fair Instrument," *Down to Earth* 7(2), August 15, 1992, 4 (referring to how "trade and human rights are being used today as sticks to beat the South").

99. These are available from the WTO's Web site. More recent bulletins now provide direct hyperlinks to unrestricted and derestricted state and secretariat submissions to CTE meetings.

100. The first NGO symposium is discussed briefly in "WTO Symposium on Trade, Environment and Sustainable Development," prepared by Chad Carpenter and Aaron Cosbey of IISD, May 27, 1997 (hereinafter 1997 NGO Symposium Transcript). For an overview of the second Trade and Environment NGO Symposium, see "Report of the WTO Informal Session with Non-Governmental Organizations (NGOs) on Trade and Environment," *Trade and Environment Bulletin,* no. 16, PRESS/TE016, November 28, 1996 (hereinafter 1996 NGO Symposium) (available at <www.wto.org/wto/environ/te016.htm>).

101. An overview of the third NGO symposium (in 1997) is compiled in the 1997 NGO Symposium Transcript. The fourth NGO trade and environment symposium was again larger. Attendees included more than sixty state delegates and over 150 representatives from environment and development NGOs, business associations, and research and academic institutes. The meeting's symbolic significance was punctuated by the participation of high-level figures, including the director-general of the WTO (Renato Ruggiero), the secretary-general of UNCTAD (Rubens Ricupero), the executive director of UNEP (Klaus Topfer), and the director of the Bureau of Development Policy of UNDP (Eimi Wantanabe). For an overview of the fourth NGO symposium, see International Institute for Sustainable Development, "Report of the World Trade Organization Symposium of Non-Governmental Organizations on Trade, Environment and Sustainable Development," March 17–18, 1998 (hereinafter 1998 NGO Symposium) (available at <http://www.iisd.ca/linkages/sd/wtosymp/sdvol12-no1e.html>). A fifth NGO symposium was held in Geneva, Switzerland, in March 1999 in conjunction with the High Level Symposium on Trade and Environment and the High Level

Symposium on Trade and Development. Full documentation of these symposia may be obtained from the WTO's Web site at <http://www.wto.org/wto/hlms/highlevel.htm>.

102. A Canadian environmental NGO, the International Institute for Sustainable Development (IISD), concluded about the 1998 exchange that participants felt that "this symposium had witnessed more sophisticated commentary than previous sessions" and that "most came away with a greater understanding, though perhaps not sympathy, for the positions of their traditional 'opponents,' " 1998 NGO Symposium, 2, 17.

103. WTO, "Ruggiero Announces Enhanced WTO Plan for Cooperation with NGOs," PRESS/107, July 17, 1998 (available at <www.wto.org/wto/new/press107.htm>).

104. See, for example, "Moore Sees Least-Developed Nations, Transparency as WTO Challenges," *Inside U.S. Trade,* October 1, 1999, 23 (citing Moore's statement that "if we are not inclusive, we cannot expect public support").

105. As the Austrian representative stated within the EMIT group, "[MEAs] were not fixed but were evolving over time, and this evolution had to be closely monitored. This could be done in two ways: by continuous contact between the Secretariat of GATT and the respective Secretariats of the various MEAs and by inviting the Secretariats of these MEAs to attend the Group's meetings as observers." EMIT, "Report of the Meeting Held on 9–10 July 1992," TRE/6, August 18, 1992, para. 193.

106. Many of these reports are cited in the annex to the CTE 1996 Report. They may also be downloaded from the WTO's Web site.

107. The CTE chairman's "Summary of Activities of the CTE 1995" notes receipt of "requests for information and advice from MEAs" (secretariats responsible for multilateral environmental agreements), 2.

108. See *Trade and Environment Bulletin,* no. 10, 4, and no. 13, 4.

109. See "Report of the Meetings Held on 30 October and 6–8 November 1996," para. 26.

110. Interview with Andrew Griffith, Canadian delegate to the CTE, in Geneva, Switzerland, June 1997.

111. See discussion of the results of the negotiation of the Cartagena Protocol on Biosafety, which arguably conflicts with the WTO Agreement on Sanitary and Phytosanitary Measures, in Mark Pollack and Gregory Shaffer, "Genetically Modified Organisms: The Next Transatlantic Trade War?" *Washington Quarterly* 23 (October 1991): 41.

II

REGIONAL ORGANIZATIONS

5

The European Community: Environmental Issues in an Integrated Market

Damien Geradin

The European Community (hereafter the EC) is perhaps the most sophisticated and successful example of trade and economic integration between independent states.[1] The EC Treaty (hereafter the Treaty), which was adopted in 1957, has as its essential objective the creation of a common market based on the free movement of goods, services, capital, and persons as well as the establishment of undistorted conditions of competition among its contracting parties (hereafter the member states).[2] The vision of the Treaty framers was that liberalized trade among previously hostile countries was the most effective tool to bring about peace and prosperity in Europe. Hence, for the last four decades, the activity of EC institutions (Council of Ministers, Commission, European Parliament, and European Court of Justice) has focused on developing the conditions necessary to ensure the establishment of a free, undistorted market among an increasingly large number of European states.[3]

In parallel with this movement toward trade liberalization, member states have developed increasingly sophisticated policies to protect the environment. These policies have led to the adoption of various kinds of environmental laws. Environmental legislation may regulate the characteristics of products or the production methods by which they are made. The objective of many environmental laws is to internalize the costs of environmental degradation into the prices consumers pay and thereby create an incentive for producers to reduce air, water, and soil pollution. Environmental legislation also comprises waste management and disposal regimes as well as programs to ensure the conservation of natural resources (minerals, vegetation, and wildlife).

Though trade liberalization and environmental protection policies pursue different goals, they are increasingly intersecting and may even conflict. There are indeed circumstances where member states' environmental policies have the effect of restricting and/or distorting intra-EC trade. In this regard, it is useful to distinguish between two areas of environmental regulation: product standards and process standards.[4] As will be seen through this chapter, these areas of regulations generally raise different trade issues and require separate treatment:

1. Product standards regulate the (environmental) characteristics of products offered for sale on a given member state market.[5] Although they do not specifically regulate intra-EC trade, such standards may be used as an instrument of protectionism when their effect is to discriminate between domestic and imported products. In addition, in the absence of discrimination, inconsistent product standards impede intra-EC trade since they deny manufacturers the ability to realize economies of scale in production and distribution and generally create market fragmentation.[6]

2. Process standards (also often referred to as process and production methods [PPM] standards) do not regulate the characteristics of the products themselves but the production methods used in the manufacture of products.[7] Although inconsistent process standards do not impede intra-EC trade, they may affect the conditions of competition.[8] Other things being equal, companies operating in jurisdictions with lax environmental rules will face lower compliance costs and, hence, be able to bring their goods to market at lower costs than those operating in high-standard jurisdictions.[9] This economic advantage may result in increased sales, market share, and profitability. In some circumstances, inconsistent process standards may induce industries located in high-standard jurisdictions to relocate to low-standard jurisdictions to preserve their competitive position.[10] This industrial migration will result in lost jobs, reduced investment, and downward pressure on wages in high-standard jurisdictions.

As I have argued elsewhere,[11] the various kinds of tension that may arise between trade liberalization in the areas of product and process standards can generally be dealt with through two complementary institutional responses. First, the EC can set common environmental standards for all member states in order to avoid the trade restrictions/distortions that may be generated by inconsistent member state (product/process) regulations. Second, in the absence of harmonized legislation, the Court of Justice of the EC can use the free trade provisions in the Treaty in order to invalidate member state environmental measures impeding trade in an unacceptable manner.[12] In this study, I will concentrate on the first of these responses. Indeed, while the Court of Justice has had to deal with few trade-environment cases,[13] the harmonization activity of the EC legislature has been extremely intense and has led to the adoption of a very substantial amount of legislation. Moreover, this harmonization process represents an original feature of the EC system that, so far, has not been replicated in other regional or global trade agreements, such as the North American Free Trade Agreement (NAFTA), Asia Pacific Economic Cooperation Forum (APEC), and the World Trade Organization (WTO).[14]

This chapter is divided into three parts. The first part discusses the powers of the EC to take action in the environmental field as well as the instruments (regulations and directives) used by the EC in the context of such an action. It also discusses the political dynamics of environmental protection in Europe as well as the impact of such dynamics on EC environmental action. The second part examines the trade-environment conflicts arising in the areas of product and process standards. As will be seen, the tension between trade and environmental protection takes different forms, depending on which of these areas of environmental regulation is concerned, and, hence, it has generated different responses from the EC. Finally, the third part discusses the extent to which the EC's experience of harmonization of environmental standards provides a useful reference to deal with the trade-environment issues in other regional or global trade agreements, such as NAFTA and the WTO.

INSTITUTIONAL AND POLITICAL FRAMEWORK FOR THE HARMONIZATION OF ENVIRONMENTAL STANDARDS IN THE EC

The institutional framework for the harmonization of environmental standards in the EC has been considerably modified and strengthened by the successive amendments that were made to the Treaty since the mid-1980s. The use of the current framework may be understood only in the context of EC politics. As will be seen, member states do not share the same degree of commitment to environmental protection. In particular, there is an important divide between northern member states (which are generally very committed to the environment) and southern member states (which are generally not very committed to environmental protection). Hence, EC environmental measures usually take the form of compromises between the northern and southern member states' competing positions.

THE INSTITUTIONAL FRAMEWORK

This section examines the place given to environmental protection in the EC Treaty, the powers of the EC to take environmental measures, and the legislative instruments and patterns of EC intervention in the environmental field.

Powers of the Community to Take Action in the Environmental Field

Like the U.S. Constitution, the EC Treaty is based on a system of attributed, enumerated powers.[15] The essential feature of such a system is that the EC can act only when it has been expressly given the power to do so by a provision of the Treaty.

With respect to the question of the existence of one or several legal bases for EC action in the environmental field, a distinction can usefully be drawn among four distinct phases: (1) the Treaty of Rome (1957); (2) the Single European Act (1986); (3) the Treaty on European Union, also known as the Maastricht Treaty (1992); and (4) the Treaty of Amsterdam, which was signed in July 1997 and entered into force in the spring of 1999. As will be seen in this chapter, the various amendments made by the Single European Act and the Treaty on European Union have considerably strengthened the status of environmental protection in the EC Treaty. While the Treaty of Amsterdam falls short of the environmentalists' expectations,[16] it confirms the central role played by environmental protection in the EC legal order.

As will be seen shortly, the increasingly central place occupied by environmental protection in the EC reflects the EC institutions' belief that in order to create a single, integrated market, it is necessary to harmonize member state environmental product and process regulations.[17] It also reflects the fact environmental protection per se, that is, independently of its connection with the internal market, is also perceived by the EC institutions, member states, and citizens as a central goal of European integration.[18]

The Treaty of Rome

When it was signed in 1957, the Treaty establishing the EC did not contain any provision relating to environmental protection. This omission can be explained by the fact that, in the years during which the Treaty of Rome was being drawn up, environmental protection was considered to be of secondary importance. However, against a background of increasing prosperity, it was soon felt by many that economic expansion should also result in improvements to the quality of life, including a better environment. In the absence of a specific Treaty provision for the implementation of an environmental policy, two provisions originally created for economic purposes, Articles 100 and 235, were employed as the legal basis for initial EC environmental legislation.[19] In fact, these two articles provided the legal framework for an extensive body of substantive environmental rules covering air, water, and noise quality; the management of waste and hazardous substances; and the protection of fauna and flora.[20]

Article 100 provides for the harmonization of national laws that affect the functioning of the common market. The view that environmental protection can be based on Article 100 has been implicitly acknowledged by the European Court of Justice.[21] However, this article provides only an incomplete basis for environmental action. Indeed, a clear economic nexus with the functioning of the common market is necessary for the use of this provision as a legal basis for EC action in the environmental field.[22] Environmental measures in the pre–Single European Act period were also sometimes based on Article 235 of the Treaty, which empowers the Council to take action that "should prove necessary to attain, in the course of the operation of the common market, one objective of the Community." If the wording of Article 235 requires that its use is linked with the operation of the common market, the link required apparently does not need to be as close as that required by Article 100. A flexible interpretation of Article 235 thus permitted the EC to take environmental action in matters not directly related to the harmonization of national rules having an influence on the common market.[23] In a pragmatic approach, action taken by the EC has often been based on both Article 100 and Article 235.[24]

As will be seen shortly, an important difference between Article 100 and Article 235 is that the latter does not limit EC action to the issuance of directives but permits action by any other legal instrument listed in Article 189 of the Treaty, including regulations directly applicable in all member states.[25] A common characteristic is, however, that, in both cases, decision making required unanimity on the part of the member states of the Council and not a simple or qualified majority. This had the effect of making the decision-making process cumbersome. Indeed, as will be seen shortly, a rule of unanimous consent considerably impedes the negotiation and adoption of environmental standards, as the opposition of one member state can paralyze the entire decision-making process. It also provides for the lowest-common-denominator approach and, hence, the adoption of suboptimal environmental standards.

The fundamental inconvenience created by the rigidity of the decision-making process, combined with the lack of a proper legal basis for environmental action, motivated the amendments to the EC Treaty by the Single European Act.

The Single European Act

The inadequate legal foundation of EC action in the environmental field was rectified by the Single European Act, which introduced two categories of provisions capable of constituting a legal basis for EC action in this area.[26]

First, the environment per se, that is, independently of its connection with the internal market, was made the subject of a special Title of the Treaty (Title VII, including Articles 130R, 130S, and 130T). Article 130R specified the objectives of EC environmental policy and the principles such a policy must observe. Article 130S(1) provided that environmental action could be taken by the Council unanimously on a proposal from the Commission and after a consultation with the European Parliament. Following Article 130S(3), the Council could also unanimously decide to take action by a qualified majority. Finally, Article 130T provided that the environmental protection measures adopted under Article 130S shall not preclude any member state from maintaining or introducing more stringent domestic measures as long as they are not incompatible with other articles of the Treaty.

Second, concern for environmental protection was also present in the chapter devoted to the internal market. Article 100A(1) granted the Council, acting by a qualified majority on a proposal from the Commission in cooperation with the European Parliament, the power to adopt measures for the approximation of national laws to achieve the internal market, including measures related to environmental protection. Article 100A(4) also allows a member state to derogate from (i.e., to apply stricter domestic standards than) an EC environmental measure that was adopted by a qualified majority vote "on grounds of major needs . . . related to environmental protection."[27]

In practice, Article 100A has had a significant impact on EC environmental protection policy.[28] What makes Article 100A a powerful instrument for environmental action is that, unlike Article 130S, proposals brought under Article 100A may be adopted by a qualified majority of the Council. This facilitates the decision-making process and allows the EC to take faster steps in its environmental action.

The Treaty on European Union

The Treaty on European Union introduced important amendments with regard to the competence of the EC and the member states to take environmental action.[29]

First, Article 130S(1) of the Treaty on European Union provides that environmental action is to be taken by the Council acting in accordance with the cooperation procedure provided for in Article 189(B) of the Treaty.[30] This constitutes a very important step forward since it means that qualified majority in the Council becomes the norm for environmental matters. However, by way of derogation from Article 130S(1), Article 130S(2) of the Treaty on European Union provides that a certain number of measures must still be decided unanimously by the Council: (1) provisions primarily of a fiscal nature; (2) measures concerning town and country planning, land use with the exception of waste management, and measures of a general nature and management of water resources; and (3) measures significantly affecting a member state's choice between energy sources and the general structure of its energy supply.[31] In addition to the procedures mentioned in the first two paragraphs of Article 130S, Article 130S(3) states that "general action programmes setting out priority objectives to be attained" must be adopted following the procedure contained in Article 189B, that is, the codecision procedure that is especially applied in the context of Article 100A.

Second, Article 100A of the Treaty on European Union provides that, when the Council adopts measures for the approximation of national laws to complete the internal market, it has to act in accordance with the procedure referred to in Article 189B. Article 189B reinforces the powers of the Parliament in the decision-making process. It introduces a codecision procedure that places the Parliament and the Council as equal partners in the legislative process. Under the procedure of codecision, the Parliament also possesses a veto "by an absolute majority of its component members" over the legislative proposals to which it remains opposed. As will be seen shortly, the use of this codecision procedure should advance the environmental cause since the European Parliament has generally been in favor of the adoption of strict environmental legislation.[32]

Third, Article 3(B)(2) introduces the principle of subsidiarity in the Treaty.[33] Pursuant to this principle, in the areas that do not fall within its exclusive jurisdiction, the EC shall take action "only if and in so far as the objectives of the proposed action cannot be sufficiently achieved by the Member States and can, therefore, by reason of the scale and effects of the proposed action, be better achieved by the Community." This principle is generally seen as a safeguard against excessive EC intervention in the increasing number of fields where the EC has the power to take action, among which figures environmental protection.[34] However, because of the obscure language used in Article 3B, it has led to difficulties of interpretation. [35]

In its communication to the Council and the European Parliament of October 27, 1992, the Commission described the principle of subsidiarity as involving a "test of comparative efficiency between Community action and that of the Member States."[36] This interpretation was also endorsed by the European Council in its conclusions adopted at the Edinburgh meeting of December 11, 1992, where it defined the principle of subsidiarity as "the principle that the Community should only take action where an objective can be better attained at the level of the Community than at the level of the individual Member States."[37] The Council enunciated three guidelines that should be used in examining whether an EC action fulfills the requirements of subsidiarity:

—the issue under consideration has transnational aspects which cannot be satisfactorily regulated by action by the Member States; and/or
—actions by the Member States alone or lack of Community action would conflict with the requirements of the Treaty (such as the need to correct distortions of competition or avoid disguised restrictions on trade or strengthen economic or social cohesion) or would otherwise significantly damage Member States' interests; and/or
—the Council must be satisfied that action at Community level would produce clear benefits by reason of its scale and effects compared with action at the level of the Member States.

Placed in an environmental context, these guidelines seem to allow the EC to take a wide range of environmental actions.[38] The first guideline can safely be used to justify the need for EC action when such an action aims at regulating pollution spillovers, such as pollution of international rivers, transboundary air pollution, and the pollution caused by cross-border transfers of waste.[39] Pollution spillovers involve transnational aspects that, according to the first guideline, "cannot be satisfactorily regulated by action by Member States."[40] The second guideline also justifies the need for EC action when inconsistent national environmental regulations are likely to create barriers to intra-EC trade or distortions of competition between member states (economic spillovers). The need for EC action in the form of harmonization of environmental *product* and *process* standards cannot be doubted, although, as will be seen shortly, the nature and extent of such actions may be debated.

Finally, Article 3(B)(3) of the Treaty states that EC action "shall not go beyond what is necessary to achieve the objectives of the Treaty" (principle of proportionality). In its conclusions to its Edinburgh meeting, the European Council interpreted this provision as requiring that EC action should not affect member states' residual powers more than is necessary in order for the EC to be able to act effectively toward the achievement of its objective. In this regard, the Council declared that "Community measures should leave as much scope for national action as possible, consistent with securing the aim of the measure and observing the requirement of the Treaty" and that "where appropriate and subject to the need for proper enforcement, Community measures should provide Member States with alternative ways to achieve the objectives of the measures." The European Council also indicated that the EC "should legislate only to the extent necessary," and when a legislative intervention is necessary "directives should be preferred to regulation and framework directives rather than detailed directives." Finally, the Council marked its preference for the setting of minimum standards, leaving member states free to adopt stricter national measures.

It was expected that this principle of proportionality would have a significant influence on the development of EC environmental law, working in favor of less regulatory density in EC environmental legislation and, as far as possible, the adoption of nonuniform rather than uniform solutions.

The Treaty of Amsterdam

As has been seen in the preceding sections, the status of environmental protection in the Treaty has been considerably strengthened by the successive amendments made by the Single European Act and the Treaty on European Union.

Most commentators, however, consider that several reforms are still to be made in order to improve the effectiveness of the EC environmental policy. First, the decision-making process for the adoption of environmental measures should be simplified. The existence of two different legal basis for environmental action (Articles 100A and 130S) has generated bitter conflicts among EC institutions, which have impeded EC action.[41] The existence of three different decision-making procedures in Article 130S and the maintenance of unanimity voting for certain environmental matters also adds to the confusion. Second, data show that EC environmental legislation is often poorly implemented and enforced in the member states.[42] As will be discussed in greater detail shortly,[43] a number of member states, particularly southern ones, have failed to adopt the necessary procedures to ensure that, once transposed into national law, EC environmental directives are effectively enforced by their administrative authorities. While the EC has adopted a large number of environmental directives, a significant number of these directives have failed to ensure better protection of the environment. Finally, other reforms, such as greater transparency in the decision-making process and greater integration of environmental considerations in the implementation of other EC policies (e.g., transport, agriculture, and regional policy) are also often considered to be necessary by EC environmental experts.

The 1996–97 Inter-Governmental Conference (IGC), which was convened to revise the Treaty in order to reach a higher stage of European integration, appeared to be an excellent opportunity to address the various weaknesses outlined in the preceding paragraph.[44] Unfortunately, the Treaty of Amsterdam, which is the end result of these negotiations, failed to address these weaknesses convincingly.[45] In fact, the Treaty of Amsterdam does not significantly simplify the decision-making process in relation to environmental matters. The only significant progress made in the decision-making process is the extension of the codecision procedure to (almost) all environmental matters. This extension has strengthened the role of the European Parliament.[46] Moreover, this Treaty offered no solution to the problem of the enforcement of EC environmental directives by the member states.

By contrast, the Treaty contains provisions designed to ensure a greater integration of environmental protection requirements into the implementation of other EC policies[47] and a greater access for natural or legal persons to the documents prepared by EC institutions.[48] Though the introduction of these provisions in the Treaty was welcome, it should be noted that their content is rather loose, and it remains to be seen whether they will have any effect in practice. The Treaty also revised the safeguard clause contained in Article 100A(4), which, under certain circumstances, allows member states to apply stricter standards than EC harmonized standards. As will be seen shortly, the revised version of this provision is, however, likely to create considerable difficulty of interpretation and application.[49]

Finally, on a point of detail, it should be noted that the Amsterdam Treaty proceeds to a complete renumbering of the provisions of the Treaty. The numerous amendments brought in the Treaty of Rome by the Single European Act and the Treaty on European Union had indeed rendered Treaty numbering complex and confusing. As a result, the environmental provisions discussed previously now hold new numbers. For instance, Articles 3(B), 100, 100A, and 130S have become Articles 5, 94, 95, and 175, respectively.

In sum, the Treaty of Amsterdam aimed at consolidating the improvements resulting from the Single European Act and the Treaty on European Union instead of bringing about any fundamental change in the institutional framework for EC environmental action.

LEGISLATIVE INSTRUMENTS AND PATTERNS OF COMMUNITY INTERVENTION IN THE ENVIRONMENTAL FIELD

The EC has two kinds of legislative measures at its disposal for action in the environmental field: regulations and directives. These instruments must not be confused.

Article 189, paragraph 2 (new Article 250, paragraph 2), provides that a regulation has "general application."[50] As interpreted by the Court of Justice, this means that "it is applicable . . . to objectively determined situations and involves legal consequences for categories of persons viewed in a general and abstract manner."[51] It is also binding in every respect, that is, not only as to the results it intends to achieve but also as to the methods necessary to achieve that result. Finally, a regulation is directly applicable in all member states and has the force of law in their territories without the need of transformation or confirmation by their legislature.[52] By contrast, a directive has binding force only in relation to the result that can be achieved for each member state to which it is addressed but leaves the member states free to use the forms and methods of implementation.[53] Moreover, a directive can impose obligations only to the member states. A directive must therefore be incorporated into national law in order to have legal effect in the domestic legal order of the member states.

The directive is by far the most popular instrument for EC action in the environmental field. In the period prior to adoption of the Single European Act, the frequent recourse to directives could be explained by the fact that Article 100 (new Article 94), which was the main legal basis for environmental action, limited such action to the issuance of directives. The new legal bases introduced by the Single European Act, Articles 100A (new Article 95) and 130S (new Article 175), allow the EC legislature to use both directives and regulations in its environmental action. Despite this change, the directive is still the main legislative instrument in the environmental field. Reliance on this instrument can be explained by its flexibility. Directives are binding only "as to the results to be achieved," leaving national authorities "the choice of forms and methods." This increases the participation of the member states and gives them a chance to better fit EC requirements in their legal and administrative framework.

Although a literal interpretation of Article 189, paragraph 3 (new Article 250, paragraph 3), would reveal that directives should incorporate only broad policy goals implemented by the member states, in practice environmental directives vary considerably in the precision of their text. Rehbinder and Stewart distinguish three categories of directives.[54] First, some directives contain detailed substantive provisions. These "regulation-type" directives do not merely harmonize an area of environmental law but effectuate a complete unification of substantive law. This technique of comprehensive legislation has been used when the need for uniformity in the setting and implementation of environmental standards is essential, such as in the context of the regulation of EC-wide marketed products.[55] Other directives, even though containing some substantive requirements, leave the member states more discretion in the implementation process. This approach is usually followed when the regulated matters have no direct impact on trade and where, therefore, some divergences in the standards adopted by the member states is acceptable. An example is EC legislation setting environmental quality standards, such as the directives on the quality of drinking or bathing waters.[56] Finally, certain directives set out basic principles applicable only to a broad area of environmental protection. An example of such "framework directives" is Directive 75/442 on waste,[57] which lays down general obligations for waste management, including avoidance of waste arising and reuse of waste. To achieve these goals, Directive 75/442 requires member states to formulate waste disposal plants; establish permitting systems for waste disposal, treatment, and storage installations; and prevent the uncontrolled disposal of waste.

It may be argued, however, that, in order to comply with Article 3(C) (new Article 5[C]) of the Treaty (the principle proportionality) as interpreted by the European Council, the EC should refrain from adopting regulation-type directives. Instead, it should base its action on framework directives, leaving substantial discretion to the member states in the implementation.

The Political Framework

The objective of this section is to discuss the political dynamics of environmental protection in Europe as well as the impact of such dynamics on EC environmental action.

First, it is important to note that the degree of environmental consciousness varies considerably from one member state to another.[58] From a general standpoint, member states can be divided into three groups, depending on their commitment to the environment:

1. Several member states, including Austria, Denmark, Finland, Germany, Sweden, and the Netherlands (the northern Member States), have a strong commitment to environmental protection. These member states have developed sophisticated domestic environmental policies and are generally in favor of strong EC environmental action.
2. By contrast, member states such as Greece, Italy, Portugal, and Spain (the southern member states) are usually considered to have a weak commitment to environmental protection. These member states, which are concerned mainly with their economic development, have relatively unsophisticated domestic environmental policies and are not in favor of a strong intervention of the EC in the environmental field.[59]
3. Finally, some member states, such as Belgium, France, Ireland, Luxembourg, and the United Kingdom (the central Member States), have a moderate commitment to environmental protection. They have developed relatively sophisticated domestic policies and, in general, tend to support some degree of EC action in the environmental field.

Differences in the degree of environmental consciousness of member states can be perceived at the different levels of the EC lawmaking process. First, there are marked differences between member states at the level of the negotiation and adoption of EC environmental directives. While northern member states will generally push for the adoption of strict environmental standards, southern member states will not show the same commitment.[60] The differences between these member states can, however, be bridged through several strategies. First, as will be seen in the second part of this chapter, the EC legislature has often opted for flexible strategies of harmonization whereby different environmental requirements are imposed on the member states, depending on their environmental and economic situations. Second, Article 130S(5) (new Article 175[5]) of the EC Treaty authorizes the EC legislature to grant financial assistance from the Cohesion Fund to the member states that would be economically affected by an EC environmental measure.[61] Participation of less economically advanced member states can therefore be financially encouraged with EC funds.[62] Finally, there are circumstances where southern member states may be prepared to support environmental directives in order to gain political support from other member states in other areas of EC action.

Second, differences in the degree of commitment to the environment between member states can also be perceived at the level of implementation and enforcement of EC legislation.[63] While member states like Denmark and the Netherlands have elaborated mechanisms to ensure the implementation and enforcement of EC environmental directives,[64] southern member states have generally failed to ensure that such directives are properly implemented and enforced on their territory.[65] Failure to enforce EC environmental law may be due to various factors, such as lack of resources, administrative incompetence, or the priority given to economic development and investments by local authorities.

Before moving to the second part of this chapter, it is important to note that the preceding paragraphs proceed on the basis of generalizations. First, to consider environmental matters only from a North-South perspective is to ignore the important differences that exist between Greece, Spain, Portugal, and Italy.[66] Moreover, even among northern or central member states, disagreements may appear over certain environmental measures. For example, as will be seen shortly, member states hosting car manufacturers will be more concerned with the economic effect of the adoption of strict vehicle emission standards than the member states that do not have such an industry on their territory.[67] Hence, there may be circumstances where a member state generally committed to environmental protection may be strongly opposed to a particular environmental directive that affects its economic interests.

The North-South division outlined previously may also be more or less present and/or take different forms, depending on the areas of regulation concerned. As will be seen shortly, this division will usually be severe in the area of process standards. While northern member states seek adoption of strict EC process standards in order to ensure a level the playing field across the EC, southern member states will be concerned about the costs of such standards as well as their impact on their competitive position.[68] By contrast, northern and southern member states share a common interest in harmonization of environmental product standards, though they may disagree over the level of stringency of such standards.[69]

OVERVIEW OF EC HARMONIZATION IN THE AREAS
OF PRODUCT AND PROCESS STANDARDS

This part examines how, in the areas of product and process standards, the EC has concretely attempted to reconcile the competing interests of trade and environmental protection through its strategy of harmonization.[70]

Product Standards

Inconsistent member state product standards may fragment the market, increase transaction costs, and generate diseconomies of scale for all producers. For example, inconsistent noise emission standards for products impede intra-EC trade since they force producers to set up special production lines for each member state in which they wish to sell. The central means by which the EC has dealt with divergent product standards is through the adoption of EC legislation setting uniform standards for all member states. This technique of harmonization has been used to regulate the environmental characteristics of a large number of products, such as cars, fuels, chemicals, pesticides, noise-generating equipment, batteries and accumulators, and packaging.

In addition to the fact that it facilitates intra-EC trade, one advantage of harmonization of product standards is that it can be used to upgrade the level of environmental soundness of the products that are traded within the EC. Though nothing prevents the EC from adopting harmonization directives that further both free trade and environmental protection, some tension may nevertheless exist between these policy objectives.[71] While environmental protection requires the adoption of strict standards, all that is needed to satisfy the requirements of economic integration is that standards be uniform (or at least subject to a maximum requirement). Hence, there may be circumstances where member states may agree on harmonization directives that further economic integration but, because they contain standards that are too low, represent a setback for environmental protection.

The objective of this section is to examine whether environmental requirements have been at the core of EC regulation of products or whether such requirements have been merely ancillary to the economic objectives sought by such regulation. Another issue is to what extent the institutional changes brought about by the Single European Act and the Treaty on European Union have influenced the taking into account of environmental requirements into product standards harmonization. Although these issues are relevant to all areas of product regulation, their importance can perhaps be best illustrated by a short discussion of EC legislation in the area of motor vehicle exhaust emissions. The regulation of motor vehicle emissions is an area where enormous economic and environmental interests are at stake and where EC intervention has generated strong disagreements among member states. Moreover, as will be seen shortly, important lessons can be learned from the evolution of this area of regulation.

The involvement of the EC in the regulation of motor vehicle exhaust emissions started at the end of the 1960s, when it realized that the adoption of inconsistent exhaust emission limits by the member states was likely to fragment the EC car market. In order to avoid such a fragmentation, the EC adopted in 1970 a directive setting limits for emissions of carbon monoxide (CO) and unburned hydrocarbons (HC)[72] and in 1977 a directive setting limits for emissions of nitrogen oxides (NO$_x$).[73] The focus of these measures was clearly economic. Rather than imposing compulsory minimum emission limits, the EC opted for a strategy of optional harmonization whereby member states must ensure market access to vehicles that comply with EC standards but are free to allow on their territory the operation of vehicles that do not meet such standards.[74] The EC standards thus functioned as a ceiling rather than a floor: The only obligation that was required from the member states was not to adopt stricter standards than EC ones.[75]

In the beginning of the 1980s, the increasing concerns created by acid rain motivated the Commission to put forward proposals involving stricter emission limits. A number of member states, including Germany, Denmark, and the Netherlands, supported the Commission proposals for more stringent limits. These proposals were, however, strongly opposed by France, Italy, and the United Kingdom, which felt that these new limits would operate to the detriment of their car industries. These member states feared that small cars, which represented the major part of their production, would be rendered commercially unattractive if they had to be fitted with catalytic converters in order to comply with stricter emission requirements.[76]

In March 1985, the Council found a compromise solution, subject to the reservation of Denmark (the so-called Luxembourg compromise).[77] The main feature of that compromise was the decision to split the European car fleet into three major categories (small, medium, and large), according to their cubic capacity, making it possible to impose different emission limits for each category of vehicles. According to the compromise, only the limits for large cars would be stringent enough to require the use of catalytic converters. On the other hand, compliance with the limits imposed for small and medium cars could be ensured through the use of less expensive technologies, such as "lean-burn" engines.[78]

The conflict between member states over the scope and the level of stringency of the new emission limits appeared to be solved, and a directive reflecting the compromise should have been adopted in November 1985. Denmark, however, decided to maintain its objections because it considered that the new emission limits proposed in the compromise were not stringent enough. As a consequence, the unanimity required by Article 100 (new Article 94), the legal basis then proposed for the directive, could not be achieved.[79] The impasse reached as a result of the Danish objections was finally broken at a meeting of the Council on July 21, 1987, where the Council was for the first time able to use Article 100A (new Article 95), which required only voting at a qualified majority.[80] A directive based on the Luxembourg compromise was then formally adopted by the Council on December 3, 1987.[81]

The Luxembourg compromise provided that new stricter emission limits for vehicles below 1.4 liters would have to be fixed by the Council in 1987 on a proposal from the Commission.[82] A Commission proposal providing for such stricter limits was sent to the Council on February 10, 1988.[83] The Council reached a common position on this proposal at its meeting of November 24, 1988. The position incorporated the limit values that the Commission proposed for reducing emissions. Under the procedure of cooperation, the text of the directive still had to be communicated to the Parliament so that it could give its opinion. By an overwhelming majority, the Parliament rejected the common position in favor of stricter U.S. standards.[84] The Commission followed the opinion of the Parliament and strengthened its proposal accordingly.[85] At its meeting of June 8, 1989, the Council finally adopted emission limits equivalent to those existing at the same time in the United States.[86]

If the objective of ensuring free trade is still clearly present, Directive 89/458 was probably the first directive on car emissions to contain a strong environmental component. First, Directive 89/458 abandoned the strategy of optional harmonization for a strategy of total harmonization of exhaust emission limits.[87] Contrary to the prior directives, EC standards therefore represent not only a ceiling but also a floor below which no member state can go. Second, Directive 89/458 authorized member states to adopt tax incentives in order to encourage the sale of cars complying with the new stricter limits before the implementation dates set for such limits.[88] Finally, Directive 89/458 declared that, before the end of 1990, the Council should align the limit values for the emission of cars with an engine equal or superior to 1.4 liters to the standards adopted for small cars.[89] The Council adopted such limit values in Directive 91/441[90] and, together with the Parliament, lowered them in Directive 94/12.[91] Further reductions of vehicle emission limits were subsequently adopted in the framework of the so-called Auto-Oil program,[92] which was developed by the Commission in collaboration with the European oil and automobile industries.[93] Today, the EC vehicle emission standards are among the strictest in the world.

The evolution of EC legislation in the area of vehicle emission standards presents a number of important lessons that are generally applicable to other areas of product regulation. First, though economic objectives may induce member states to adopt measures that have a positive impact on the environment, economic integration and environmental protection do not always share common interests.[94] As already noted, while economic integration requires only that standards be uniform or at least contain a maximum requirement, environmental protection requires the adoption of compulsory minimum standards, set up at a high level of protection. Economic objectives may thus very well be pursued at the expense of environmental ones. For example, although the Luxembourg compromise avoided the fragmentation of the European car market, it offered little progress for environmental protection. Second, although Article 100A (new Article 95) was first used to break the Danish resistance to the adoption of lax emission limits, this provision has since permitted the adoption of much stricter emission limits. Because it permits isolating those member states opposed to environmental progress, the qualified majority voting system contained in this provision strongly favors the adoption of stricter environmental legislation.[95] Third, the evolution of car emissions legislation in the EC also illustrates the important role played by the Parliament in the area of environmental protection through the procedure of cooperation.[96] In this regard, the new procedure of codecision introduced in Article 100A (new Article 95) by the Treaty on European Union and now extended to Article 130S (new Article 175) by the Treaty of Amsterdam should generally favor the adoption of more stringent environmental product regulation.

The remaining part of this section deals with two important questions arising in the context of the product standards harmonization.

A first question is to what extent the "new approach" to harmonization of technical standards will have a significant impact on the harmonization of the environmental product standards.[97] The central characteristic of this new approach is that harmonization should be limited to the adoption of "essential requirements" necessary for ensuring the free movement throughout the EC of a particular product.[98] The task of drawing up on the basis of those essential requirements the detailed specifications for the particular product is left to European standards organizations, such as the Comité Européen de Normalisation (CEN).[99] If a product meets those specifications, it benefits from a presumption that it satisfies the EC's essential requirements and can move therefore freely throughout the EC. The principal advantage of the new approach is thus that it avoids the need for the EC to have recourse to extremely detailed directives that may require lengthy negotiations and result in the adoption of costly and inefficient regulation.

Prima facie, it seems that the new approach could be usefully applied to regulate the environmental characteristics of products capable of generating pollution.[100] For example, harmonization of noise emission limits for products is essentially a technical matter that could be regulated by standardization bodies.[101] The new approach seems also appropriate for the elaboration of common criteria for the life-cycle analysis and the recycling methods of products or parts of products, such as packaging.[102] On the other hand, it is not certain that member states will be ready to rely on the new approach, where the nature and the level of stringency of the standards adopted may have great economic implications, such as in the context of vehicle exhaust emissions or the composition of certain chemical substances.[103] When important economic interests are at stake, they may prefer to negotiate every single aspect of the matter at hand.

Another question of central importance is whether, once the EC has legislated, the member states are entitled to adopt stricter environmental standards than EC standards.[104] From a policy standpoint, the question of whether the member states should be able to do so, which generally relates to the doctrine of preemption,[105] is not always easy to answer. On the one hand, allowing member states to adopt more protective standards than EC standards seems desirable since it permits them to provide for particular local needs and to ensure a higher level of environmental protection on their territory. On the other hand, there may be circumstances where stricter member state standards may have the effect of reintroducing the kind of trade barriers that the EC attempted to remove by adopting uniform legislation.

In the area of product standards, this question is dealt with through Article 100A(4) of the Treaty (new Article 95), which was introduced in the Treaty in 1986 by the Single European Act. In its Single European Act version, Article 100A(4) provided the following:

> If, after the adoption of an harmonization measure by the Council acting by a qualified majority, a Member State deems it necessary to apply national provisions on grounds of major needs referred to in Article 36, or related to the protection of the environment or the working environment, it shall notify the Commission of these provisions.
>
> The Commission shall confirm the provisions involved after having verified that they are not means of arbitrary discrimination or a disguised restriction on trade between Member States.
>
> By way of derogation from the procedure laid down in Articles 169 and 170, the Commission or any Member State may bring the matter directly before the Court of Justice if it considers that another Member State is making improper use of the powers provided in this article.

This provision led to some difficulties of interpretation. In particular, it was not apparent from Article 100A(4) whether a member state could *introduce* new national provisions or whether it can only *maintain* provisions that were already in force before the EC measure of harmonization was adopted. Authors adopted diverging views on this issue. Kramer, for instance, argued that "the maintenance of existing stricter national measures is permitted in the case of majority decisions, but not the introduction of new measures of this nature."[106] On the other hand, Flynn considered that "Article 100A(4) by no means rules out the possibility of a Member State wishing to raise its standards after the adoption of a measure."[107]

Article 100A(4) was also strongly criticized by free traders on the ground that it allowed member states to maintain certain barriers to trade, even after the adoption of an EC measure of harmonization.[108] If member states were to use Article 100A(4), this could have very serious adverse effects on the establishment of the internal market. Now, fifteen years after the Single European Act, it appears that the fears expressed by those opposed to Article 100A(4) have failed to materialize. To date, Article 100A(4) has been used only by Germany and Denmark in the context of Directive 91/173 regarding dangerous substances.[109] In both cases, the Commission has allowed these member states to maintain stricter domestic standards for the use of pentachlorophenol (PCP).[110]

The Treaty of Amsterdam modifies the language and extends the scope of the antipreemption provision contained in Article 100A. Specifically, its relevant part, Article 95, provides the following:

> 4. If, after the adoption by the Council or by the Commission of a harmonization measure, a Member State deems it necessary to maintain national provisions on grounds

of major needs referred to in Article 36, or relating to the protection of the environment or the working environment, it shall notify the Commission of the envisaged provisions as well as the grounds for maintaining them.

5. Moreover, without prejudice to the previous paragraph, if, after the adoption by the Council or by the Commission of a harmonization measure, a Member State deems it necessary to introduce national provisions based on new scientific evidence relating to the protection of the environment or the working of the environment on grounds of a problem specific to that Member State arising after the adoption of the harmonizing measure, it shall notify the Commission of the envisaged provisions as well as the grounds for introducing them.

6. The Commission shall, within six months of the notifications as referred to in paragraphs 4 and 5, approve or reject the national provisions involved after having verified that they are a means of arbitrary discrimination or a disguised restriction on trade between Member States and that they shall not constitute an obstacle to the functioning of the internal market.

Article 95 confirms the right of the member states to *maintain* stricter national provisions than an EC measure of harmonization. More interestingly, Article 95(5) makes (at last) clear that, when a EC directive of harmonization has been adopted, member states retain the right to *adopt* stricter national standards. This provision is seen as an important victory for northern member states, which have always claimed the right to enact more stringent environmental standards than EC ones on their territory.[111] The freedom of member states to adopt more exacting national legislation is, however, constrained by several conditions. First, the legislation in question must be based on "new scientific evidence." Second, the legislation must be aimed at addressing "a problem specific to the Member State arising after the adoption of the harmonization measure." Finally, the member state adopting the stricter legislation must notify it to the European Commission, which, within six months, must approve or reject the national provisions "after having verified that they are not a means of arbitrary discrimination or a disguised restriction on trade between Member States and that they shall not constitute an obstacle to the functioning of the internal market" (Article 95[6]).

The first two conditions are particularly burdensome and likely to create difficulties of interpretation and application.[112] First, recent events, such as the British bovine spongiform encephalopathy (BSE) crisis or the EU/U.S. conflict on beef produced with hormones,[113] illustrate the uncertainties surrounding the concept of "scientific evidence" when it is used in the trade law context. In some circumstances, it could also be argued that the requirement that states adopting stricter standards provide "new scientific evidence" clashes with the precautionary principle, which is expressly mentioned in the Treaty as a principle of EC environmental policy.[114] Second, it is difficult to foresee what the Commission will consider to be a problem "specific to" a member state adopting more exacting requirements. For instance, will a Dutch measure prohibiting the sale of apples containing minor quantities of pesticide residues (assuming that the marketing of such apples is permitted by an

EC harmonization directive) be considered as attempting to deal with a specifically local problem? Probably not, unless the Dutch government is able to demonstrate that Dutch consumers eat much larger quantities of apples than other EC consumers and that, therefore, even minor quantities of pesticide residues in apples may potentially damage their health.

In sum, though Article 95(5) extends the scope of application of the antipreemption provision contained in the former Article 100A(4), the requirements that stricter national provisions be based "on new scientific evidence" and be aimed at addressing a specifically local problem impose serious limits on the ability of member states to choose higher levels of environmental protection than the levels chosen at EC level.

Process Standards

Harmonization of process standards in the EC has been justified by two main rationales. First, adoption of common process standards is seen as a way to address the various competitiveness concerns that may arise from differential environmental requirements across jurisdictions. Specifically, there is a perception in high-standard member states, such as Germany, that companies operating in low-standard member states benefit from an unfair competitive advantage because they face lower compliance costs and, other things being equal, are able to produce goods more cheaply. High-standard nations also fear that differences in the stringency of process standards could induce their heavy-polluting industries to relocate in low-standard jurisdictions, with resulting losses in jobs and investments. Harmonization of process standards by the EC has also been justified by the need to ensure that a minimum level of environmental protection is applied in all member states and to prevent certain types of transboundary pollution from occurring.

Although EC legislation harmonizing industrial processes can be justified on solid economic and environmental grounds, there are obstacles to the adoption of such legislation. Contrary to the case of product standards where member states share a common interest in harmonization in order to avoid market fragmentation, member states do not always share a common interest in harmonizing environmental processes.[115] On the one hand, harmonization will be clearly favored by the member states that have already adopted strict process standards on a domestic basis. On the other hand, member states applying less stringent process standards will usually oppose harmonization. In the absence of harmonization, their producers can continue to market their products in other member states even though their manufacturing processes have been less controlled than those of their competitors.

The difficulty of reaching agreement over harmonization of environmental process standards can be illustrated by the negotiations that led to the adoption of Directive 88/609 on the limitation of certain pollutants into the air from large combustion plants.[116] These negotiations started when, in December 1983, the Commission sent to the Council a proposal for substantial reductions in the emissions of SO_2

and NO_x from large combustion plants in order to curb the environmental damage caused by acid rain.[117] This proposal was strongly supported by Germany, which, following pressures from domestic environmental groups, had unilaterally adopted measures to reduce the emissions from its combustion plants. The Commission proposal required that the total emissions from existing plants with over fifty megawatts of thermal output be reduced by 60 percent in the case of SO_2 and 40 percent in the case of NO_x by 1995, compared with the reference period of 1980. The proposal also laid down mandatory uniform emission limits for new plants.

While the Commission proposal created few difficulties from a technological standpoint, it was nevertheless opposed by a number of member states.[118] In particular, Greece, Ireland, Portugal, and Spain were concerned that the required reductions in emissions would have a negative impact on their domestic industry and would generally impede their economic development.[119] The struggle between contending interests paralyzed the decision-making process, and it was only in June 1988, more than four and a half years after the initial Commission proposal, that the member states managed to agree on a common position. Directive 88/609 was eventually adopted on November 24, 1988.

The various compromises that were made to overcome the objections from individual member states complicated the structure of the directive and essentially provided for nonuniform emission reductions among member states. With regard to existing plants, Directive 88/609 requires overall reductions for SO_2 and NO_x and fixes implementation dates for such reductions.[120] However, different reduction targets are set for each member state, and a number of member states, including Greece, Ireland, and Portugal, are even authorized to increase their emissions.[121] To increase the flexibility of this control regime, member states have the discretion to allocate the permitted emissions among the various facilities within the territory.[122] With regard to new plants, Directive 88/609 also fixes emission limit values differentiated according to the size of the installations.[123] It also gave Spain a special authorization until 1999 to authorize the entry into service of additional combustion plants.[124]

It is subject to question whether the differentiated approach taken by Directive 88/609 is compatible with the requirements of a common market. Indeed, it may be argued this directive fails to create equal conditions of competition with respect to the operation of large combustion plants in Europe. On the other hand, one clear advantage of Directive 88/609 is that it takes into consideration the specific economic, energy, and environmental situations of each member state. Because of several enlargements, the EC is no longer composed of a small group of states with relatively homogeneous economic and ecological conditions. Differences among member states appear, however, to be increasingly taken into consideration by EC policymakers. For example, when the Dutch government took over the presidency of the European Union in January 1997, the Dutch environment minister indicated that one of her central objectives was to set up a "model for the reduction of CO_2 emissions featuring a burden-sharing formula appropriate for the specific situation in each Member State."[125] The Dutch minister added that such a model would "take into account the country's level of economic development, the type of industrial fabric and its energy needs, as well as population density."[126] The burden-sharing formula eventually adopted in 1998 by the Council of Ministers followed this line of thinking since, while it requires sharp emission reduction in the northern member states (e.g., Belgium and Germany), it allows southern member states to increase to maintain their emissions at existing levels or even to increase their emissions (e.g., Greece and Portugal).[127]

Another controversial issue with regard to the harmonization of environmental process standards relates to which regulatory technique is used for such harmonization.[128] The two main regulatory techniques that may be used for regulating industrial processes are environmental quality standards and effluent standards.[129] Environmental quality standards prescribe the level of pollution that must not be exceeded, without specifying any maximum level of discharge by a particular industry. By contrast, effluent standards specify the maximum allowable emissions of a substance into the atmosphere by industry. One of the advantages of environmental quality standards is that they create a "partnership" between the EC and the member states. The EC sets quality standards with reference to relatively objective criteria, such as what is needed to protect human health or public welfare. Then the member states are free to make determinations about how to limit pollution of individual sources to what is allowed under EC standards. However, as will be seen shortly, reliance on environmental quality standards is sometimes criticized— wrongly in my opinion—as being inequitable in that they give a competitive advantage to industries located in regions that are less polluted or that are better able to absorb pollution.

The most extensive discussion of environmental quality and effluent standards arose in the context of Directive 76/464 on pollution caused by certain dangerous substances discharged into the aquatic environment.[130] Directive 76/464 divides the dangerous substances into two categories: a "black list" of substances considered to be the most dangerous for the aquatic environment and a "gray list" covering substances that have a less harmful effect.[131] The point of contention in the proposal originally made by the Commission concerned the regime of control to be adopted with regard to black-list substances. The Commission proposed that effluent standards should be fixed in implementing directives for each substance on the list. All member states agreed on the proposed method, except the United Kingdom, which proposed instead that water quality standards be applied for the discharge of individual substances.[132] The United Kingdom wanted to exploit a natural locational advantage derived from its system of short, free-running rivers that permit water quality standards to be met in many locations even if the industry is granted generous emission limits.

Member states eventually reached a compromise whereby effluent standards would be the rule but a member state could, under strict conditions, opt for an alternative system of water quality standards.[133] The attitude taken by the United

Kingdom during the negotiations was nevertheless severely criticized as self-interested and contrary to the requirements of a common market because it prevented equalization of the conditions of competition in the industries concerned. It is suggested that this criticism is not entirely justified. Indeed, while the adoption of a pure system of effluent standards would have contributed to a level playing field, it would also have imposed a costly—and arguably unnecessary—regulatory burden on the regions of the EC with waters with a high absorptive capacity. Moreover, as Esty and I have argued elsewhere,[134] natural locational advantages are a legitimate form of comparative advantage that member states or regions should be free to enjoy.[135]

The controversy over which regulatory technique should be used for the EC harmonization of industrial processes reappeared with force in the context of the negotiations on the directive on integrated pollution prevention and control.[136] The objective of this directive, which contains the EC strategy for the regulation of industrial processes, is the prevention of industrial pollution at its source. In order to attain this objective, the system established by the directive operates a prior authorization procedure whereby industrial installations would apply to the competent authority in the appropriate member state for a permit to operate.[137] The conditions of the permit include emission limit values for the pollutant substances to be emitted from the installations authorized to operate.[138]

As in the case of Directive 76/464, there was a strong disagreement between member states on how these limit values should be set.[139] Certain northern member states argued these limit values should be fixed at the EC level on the basis of the "best available techniques" (i.e., technology-based effluent standards). In particular, German authorities insisted that common technologies be used in order to ensure a level playing field across the EC.[140] On the other hand, southern member states and the United Kingdom argued that these limit values had to be adopted at the member state level pursuant to more flexible EC environmental quality standards. The advantage that these member states saw in this approach was that, contrary to technology-based effluent standards, environmental quality standards would permit them to take into account their environmental circumstances and, hence, their natural locational advantages.

The common position reached by the Council in November 1995 attempted to reconcile these competing positions.[141] Pursuant to this common position, which was formally adopted by the Council and became binding law, the emission limit values included in the permits granted by the member states to controlled installations are to be "based on the best available techniques, without prescribing the use of any technique or specific technology, but taking into account the technical characteristics of the installation concerned, its geographical location and the local environmental conditions."[142] This provision has been strongly criticized by the European Parliament on the ground that it will lead to different levels of environmental protection in the EC.[143] In response to this criticism, former Environment Commissioner R. Bjerregaard made clear that the Commission would not allow permitting authorities to abuse the flexibility built in this provision by setting low standards designed to give local producers an unfair competitive advantage.[144] In this regard, the commissioner indicated that the Commission will not hesitate to propose to the Council uniform emission limit values if such authorities were tempted to deregulate the environment.

Finally, it should be noted that over the last few years, enthusiasm for the regulation of industrial processes has been tempered in EC circles by concern about the competitiveness of the EC industry. The failure to adopt a carbon tax provides a good illustration. In the absence of a similar effort by the United States and Japan, the EC found that such a tax would harm the competitive position of its producers on the EC and international markets.[145] Repeated calls by a number of industry lobbies to weaken the EC legislative framework in the area of waste[146] and biotechnology[147] and to rely increasingly on voluntary agreements instead of binding legislation[148] are also motivated by similar considerations. A possible solution to this problem would be to ensure some degree of harmonization or coordination of environmental process standards at a global level, though, as will be seen in the following discussion, such a strategy may be difficult to implement in practice.[149]

CONCLUSION: LESSONS OF THE EC HARMONIZATION EXPERIENCE FOR NAFTA AND THE WTO

To what extent may other regional or global trade agreements learn from the EC experience of dealing with trade-environment issues through regulatory harmonization?

The tension between trade and environmental protection policies has received a great deal of public attention and has generated an extremely hot political debate in the contexts of NAFTA and the WTO.[150] In particular, American environmental and consumer protection groups have argued that, because of the disciplines it implies, trade liberalization threatens U.S. environmental and food safety product standards.[151] Moreover, they argue that, by stimulating competition among nations applying different levels of pollution controls, trade agreements, such as NAFTA and the WTO, could trigger an environmentally destructive "race to the bottom."[152]

The main lesson that can be learned from the EC experience of harmonization is that trade liberalization and economic integration among European nations has led not to a decrease but to an increase in environmental protection.[153] European economic integration has not prevented northern member states, such as Germany, Denmark, and the Netherlands, to develop sophisticated pollution control strategies on a domestic basis. Moreover, through the EC harmonization process, such strategies have usually been extended to the southern member states, the environmental policies of which have been considerably strengthened by the participation of such countries in the EC.

This leads us to ask the following question: Why has the European experience of regulatory harmonization been so successful a response to trade-environment tensions? I believe that three factors have particularly contributed to the success of this harmonization process: (1) the existence of economically powerful, pro-environment member states that utilized the harmonization process to "export" their sophisticated environmental policies to other, less environmentally aware member states; (2) the improvements made to the EC decision-making process by the several amendments to the Treaty by the Single European Act and the Treaty on European Union; and (3) the flexibility of the harmonization directives adopted by EC institutions. Each of these factors will be examined here. In order to evaluate whether the EC experience of harmonization could be applied successfully in other contexts of economic integration, I will also examine the extent to which such factors can be found in other trade agreements, such as NAFTA and the WTO.

First, the presence of economically powerful, pro-environment member states has been a key factor in the success of EC regulatory harmonization.[154] As we have seen, northern member states, particularly Germany, have been anxious to "export" their strict pollution control requirements to other member states through the EC harmonization process. The main reason for this is that these countries perceive that, in the absence of similar requirements in the other member states, their domestic industry would suffer a competitive disadvantage. Rather than leading to a "race to the bottom," competitiveness concerns have therefore led to a "leveling up" whereby member states applying strict standards have generally managed to ensure that member states applying lax standards realign their standards on their own stricter standards. As pointed out by Richard Steinberg, economically powerful, pro-environment states are also dominant in NAFTA.[155] This explains why Mexico has had to upgrade its environmental policies in the last few years. Here again, as illustrated by the "pollution haven" provision in NAFTA (Article 1114)[156] and the enforcement provisions in the Environmental Side Agreement,[157] competitiveness concerns played an important role. By contrast, because of the very large number of WTO members among which figure a majority of developing countries, the richer, pro-environment states have been much less dominant in that organization.[158] This may help explain why, despite considerable diplomatic efforts on the part of industrialized states, the achievements of the WTO Committee on Trade and the Environment (CTE) have been so far very modest.[159]

The EC harmonization process has also been considerably facilitated by the presence of a sophisticated institutional infrastructure (Commission, Council of Ministers, Parliament, and, more recently, the European Environment Agency) as well as by the considerable improvements made to the legislative process by various Treaty amendments. As has been noted, the introduction of Article 100A (new Article 95) in the Treaty, which provides for a qualified majority voting procedure, has immensely facilitated the EC decision-making process and strengthened the "supranational" character of EC institutions.[160] In contrast to the EC Treaty, NAFTA does not create a set of institutions with broad legislative powers. The reason is that the creators of NAFTA did not pursue regulatory harmonization as a primary response to trade-environment tensions.[161] Some degree of regulatory convergence has, however, been realized through other tools, such as cooperative environment programs established by both the United States and Canada with Mexico, as well as by joint enforcement efforts.[162] The relative weakness of NAFTA's institutional framework and the absence of a harmonization program have thus been overcome by the considerable financial, technical, and administrative assistance offered to Mexico by its two trading partners.

The regulatory infrastructure of the WTO is even weaker that the one of NAFTA. The CTE provides a forum to discuss trade-related environmental matters but, as has been noted, has achieved only modest progress. Moreover, the presence of a large number of developing countries among the WTO members has prevented the wealthier, greener states from offering the kind of assistance that has been provided by the United States and Canada to Mexico. This makes the prospect for regulatory harmonization at the international level relatively bleak. Nevertheless, some degree of international harmonization of product standards is taking place under the auspices of standardization bodies, such as the International Organization for Standardization and Codex Alimentarius.[163] Because of the considerable differences in environmental and economic conditions between nations, international harmonization of environmental process standards is generally considered to be impossible, or at least extremely difficult,[164] to achieve.[165] Yet, over the last few years, the UN Environment Program (UNEP) has also stimulated the adoption of several multilateral environmental agreements, such as the Montreal Protocol,[166] the Basel Convention,[167] and the Climate Change Convention.[168] Though these agreements do not, strictly speaking, attempt to harmonize process standards, they encourage policy convergence by calling on contracting parties to adopt appropriate environmental pollution control strategies.

A third factor contributing to the success of the EC harmonization process is its flexibility. In the area of product standards, for instance, the EC is increasingly relying on the so-called new approach to technical harmonization. As we have seen, the central characteristic of the new approach is that harmonization should be limited to the adoption of "essential requirements."[169] The task of drawing up, on the basis of these essential requirements, the detailed specifications for the products in questions is left to European standardization organizations. The advantage of this approach is that it simplifies the decision-making process and, hence, lowers the costs of reaching agreement. It also permits some regulatory diversity while ensuring the free movement of goods across member states. Flexible solutions have also been used in the area of process standards. For instance, Directive 88/609 on pollution from large combustion plants provides for a multitier regulatory regime whereby the requirements imposed on the member states vary, depending on local environmental and economic circumstances.[170] A multitier regime has also been adopted to share the burden of CO_2 emissions reduction among EC member states.[171] Such a strategy of multitier harmonization, which echoes the principle of "common differentiated responsibility," which is at the center of Agenda 21,[172] could be increasingly used at the global level to induce developing countries to participate in multilateral environmental agreements.[173] The EC's new approach to technical harmonization could also provide a useful tool to facilitate harmonization of product standards at the global level.[174]

The examination of the factors that have contributed to the success of the EC harmonization process (i.e., leadership of pro-environment member states, development of an efficient legislative process, and adoption of flexible regulatory regimes), as well as the applicability of such factors to the NAFTA and WTO, leads us to the three following conclusions.

First, as a general rule, regulatory harmonization will be easier to achieve on a regional basis than on a multilateral one. As we have seen, the power or sphere of influence of richer, greener states in the context of regional trade agreements, which usually develop around a few economically powerful, pro-environment nations, is greater than in a global context, where the influence of such states is reduced by the participation of a large number of poor, pro-development nations. Regional agreements will generally therefore allow the richer states to export their strict environmental standards to the poorer, less environmentally aware states.

Second, it is not only because regulatory harmonization is easier to achieve in a regional context that it will necessarily take place in such a context. Contrary to the EC, NAFTA does not seek to harmonize the U.S., Canadian, and Mexican environmental standards through the adoption of a common regulatory regime. However, we have seen that some degree of environmental policy convergence between the three NAFTA contracting parties is taking place through other, less formal, means, such as the large financial, technical, and administrative assistance offered by the United States and Canada to Mexico.

Third, and conversely to the previous proposition, just because regulatory harmonization is more difficult to achieve at the multilateral level does not mean that it will never take place at such a level. The EC experience, however, teaches that comprehensive regulatory harmonization programs will take place at the multilateral level only if the three following conditions are met. First, global harmonization of environmental standards requires that a high degree of consensus exist among industrialized nations. Such a degree of consensus will usually be much easier to find in the context of product standards—where all industrialized nations have a common interest in creating a global product market unimpeded by regulatory barriers to trade—than with respect to environmental process standards where their economic and environmental interests may vary considerably. A second precondition for global environmental harmonization is that the international regulatory framework be strengthened. As we have seen, some harmonization of environmental product standards already takes place on an ad hoc basis or through private standardization organizations. It seems, however, that more systematic and comprehensive (i.e., also covering process standards harmonization) programs will require the creation of a proper international environmental legislature. Several authors have suggested that such a role should be played by a new Global Environmental Organization (GEO).[175] Finally, international environmental harmonization will take place only if it is sufficiently flexible to meet the interests of both industrialized and developing nations. In this regard, the EC experience shows the usefulness of multitier harmonization regimes whereby the requirements imposed on nations vary, depending on the local environmental and economic conditions.

NOTES

The research for this article was carried out thanks to a grant from the Poles d'Attraction Inter-Universitaire (PAI), a research program initiated by the Belgian State, Prime Minister's Office, Science Policy Programming.

1. The reason I refer to the European Community (the EC) instead of the European Union (the EU) is that, with respect to the matter at hand, the EC is the more precise term. Under the Treaty on European Union (also known as the Maastricht Treaty), the member states agreed to establish a European Union. The institutional framework for the EU is based on three pillars: the EC, the common and foreign security policy and cooperation in the fields of justice and home affairs. Since trade and environment policies are exclusively dealt with in the context of the first pillar, this chapter will refer to the EC, which represents the more relevant, more specific legal order.

2. See, generally, G. Bermann et al., *Cases and Materials on European Community Law* (St. Paul, Minn.: West Publishing Co., 1995), chaps. 9–25.

3. There are currently fifteen member states in the EC: Belgium, France, Germany, Italy, Luxembourg, the Netherlands (the six original member states that signed the Treaty of Rome in 1957); Denmark, Ireland, and the United Kingdom (which joined the EC in 1973); Greece (which joined the EC in 1981); Portugal and Spain (which joined the EC in 1986); and Austria, Finland, and Sweden (which joined in 1995). It is expected that additional states, particularly central and eastern European states, will join the EC in the future.

4. A tension between trade and environmental protection may also arise in the area of waste. For example, member states may restrict imports of waste in order to protect their environment against the environmental damage created by the disposal of such waste and/or to retain their waste disposal resources for local use (see, e.g., case C-2/90, *Commission v. Belgium* [1992] E.C.R. I-4431). Member states may also restrict exports of waste in order to protect their waste treatment undertakings against competitors from other member states (see, e.g., case 172/82, *Interhuiles* [1983] E.C.R. 555). Because of their specific character, the trade-environment issues arising in the area of waste will not be examined in this chapter. On these issues, however, see P. Von Wilmowsky, "Waste Disposal in the Internal Market: The State of Play after the ECJ's Ruling on the Walloon Import Ban," *Common Market Law Review* 30 (1993): 541.

5. Product standards "prescribe the physical or chemical properties of a product (e.g., lead additives in gasoline), the maximum permissible polluting emissions from a product during its use (e.g., automobile emissions, detergent biodegradability) and the rules for making up, packaging or presenting a product (e.g., prescribed conditions for the elimination of packaging material, product labeling)." Christopher Thomas and Greg A. Tereposky, "The Evolv-

ing Relationship between Trade and Environmental Regulation," *Journal of World Trade* 27 (1993): 35, 37.

6. This problem is clearly expressed by Advocate-General Van Gerven in its opinion in joined cases C-401/92 and C-402/92, *Boermans* (1994), E.C.R. I-2199, 2215 ("Product requirements by nature impede the access to the market of the Member State which laid them down, because they mean that a product lawfully manufactured and marketed in the Member State of origin must be adapted where it is imported into another Member State in order to suit the product requirements in force there, and therefore have the effect of requiring the product to satisfy the requirements of two different sets of legislation. . . . In view of the costs entailed by this where the product is imported, the producer has an additional burden imposed upon him, which almost certainly has the effect of impeding the imported product's access to the market or even, when the costs are prohibitive, of making access impossible.").

7. Process standards "include emission and effluent standards and other standards governing the production process." Thomas and Tereposky, "The Evolving Relationship between Trade and Environmental Regulation," 37.

8. See, for example, case C-300/89, *Commission v. Council* (1991), E.C.R. I-2867, 2901 ("provisions which are made necessary by considerations relating to the environment and health may be a burden upon the undertakings to which they apply and, if there is no harmonization of national provisions on the matter, competition may be appreciably distorted"). Generally on this issue, see D. Esty and D. Geradin, "Environmental Protection and International Competitiveness: A Conceptual Framework," *Journal of World Trade* 32 (1998): 5.

9. Most economists and trade theorists point out, however, that a series of sophisticated macroeconomic studies have failed to establish a link between the level of environmental regulation and the performance of companies in international product markets. See, for example, A. B. Jaffe et al., "Environmental Regulation and International Competitiveness: What Does the Evidence Tell Us?" *Journal of Economic Literature* 33 (1995): 132. More recent studies suggest, however, that the economics literature may have systematically underestimated pollution control costs because past analyses rely on mispecified data or use too narrow a definition of such costs. See R. B. Stewart, "Environmental Regulation and International Competitiveness," *Yale Law Journal* 102 (1994): 2039, 2063.

10. Most economic studies carried out on this issue failed to find a link between the stringency of environmental regulation and location decisions. Some empirical evidence suggests that there are circumstances where such shifts toward "pollution havens" take place. See Esty and Geradin, "Environmental Protection and International Competitiveness," 13.

11. See D. Geradin, "Trade and Environmental Protection: Community Harmonization and National Environmental Standards," in A. Barav and D. Wyatt, eds., *Yearbook of European Law*, vol. 13 (New York: Oxford University Press, 1994), 151.

12. In particular, Article 30 of the Treaty provides that all quantitative restrictions on imports and measures having equivalent effect shall be prohibited between member states. This provision has been interpreted broadly by the Court of Justice to include both discriminatory and nondiscriminatory measures affecting trade. See case 8/74, *Dassonville* (1974), E.C.R. 837. Generally on Article 30, see W. Wils, "The Search for the Rule of Article 30 EEC: Much Ado about Nothing," *European Law Review* 19 (1993): 475.

13. For a discussion of these cases as well as a comparison with relevant U.S. cases, see D. Geradin, "Free Trade and Environmental Protection in an Integrated Market: A Survey of the Case Law of the United States Supreme Court and the European Court of Justice," *Journal of Transnational Law & Policy* 2 (1993): 141.

14. See D. Esty and D. Geradin, "Market Access, Competitiveness and Harmonization: Dealing with Trade and Environment Issues in the European Community and NAFTA," *Harvard Environmental Law Review* 21 (1997): 265.

15. Article 3B(1) of the Treaty.

16. See chapter text accompanying notes 42 to 50.

17. See chapter text accompanying notes 28 and 29.

18. Ibid.

19. See G. Close, "Harmonization of Laws: Use and Abuse of Powers under the EC Treaty?" *European Law Review* 6 (1978): 461.

20. For an overview of these rules, see S. Johnson and G. Corcelle, *The Environmental Policy of the European Communities* (Boston: Graham & Trotman 1989).

21. See case 91/79, *Commission v. Italy* (1980), E.C.R. 1099, 1106, and case 92/79, *Commission v. Italy* (1980), E.C.R. 1115, 1122 (holding that Article 100 was a sufficient legal basis for the directive on the biodegradability of detergents and the sulfur content of liquid fuels, respectively).

22. The use of "economic provisions" by central/federal authorities to adopt environmental measures can be observed in other federal-type systems. For example, the U.S. Congress has relied on the "commerce clause" to adopt the vast majority of federal environmental laws. See J. Dwyer, "The Commerce Clause and the Limits of Congressional Authority to Regulate the Environment," *Environmental Law Report* 25 (August 1995): 10, 421. Economic provisions were also used by the Australian Commonwealth to regulate environmental matters. See J. Crawford, "The Constitution and the Environment," *Sidney Law Review* 13 (1991): 11.

23. See, for example, Council Directive 79/409 on the conservation of wild birds, O.J. 1979, L 103/1, and Council Decision 81/462 on the conclusion of the Convention on Long-Range Transboundary Air-Pollution, O.J. 1981, L 171/1.

24. See, for example, Council Directive 82/501 on the major accident hazards of certain industrial activities, O.J. 1982, L 230/1, and Council Directive 85/337 on the assessment of the effects of certain public and private projects on the environment, O.J. 1985, L 175/40.

25. See chapter text accompanying notes 47 to 54.

26. See, generally, D. Vandermeersch, "The Single European Act and the Environmental Policy of the European Community," *European Law Review* 12 (1987): 407, and L. Kramer, "The Single European Act and Environment Protection: Reflections on Several New Provisions in Community Law," *Common Market Law Review* 24 (1987): 659.

27. See chapter text accompanying notes 100 to 109.

28. P. Sands, "EC Environmental Legislation: The ECJ and Common-Interest Groups," *Modern Law Review* 53 (1990): 685.

29. See, generally, M. Hession and R. Macrory, "Maastricht and the Environmental Policy of the European Community: Legal Issues for a New Environmental Policy in Legal Issues of the Maastricht Treaty," in *Legal Issues of the Maastricht Treaty*, edited by David O'Keeffe and Patrick Twoney (New York: Chancery Law Publishing, 1993), 151, and D. Wilkinson, "Maastricht and the Environment: Implications for the EC's Environment Policy of the Treaty on European Union," *Journal of Environmental Law* 4 (1992): 221.

30. The new legislative procedures adopted pursuant to the TEU are not easily described because of their extreme sophistication and complexity. For a detailed analysis of these procedures, see A. Dashwood, "Community Legislative Procedures in the Era of the European Union," *European Law Review* 19 (1994): 343.

31. The second sentence of Article 130S(2) provides, nevertheless, that the Council may, unanimously, on a proposal from the Commission and after consulting the European Parliament, define those matters referred to in its first sentence on which decisions are to be taken at a qualified majority.

32. See chapter text accompanying note 97.

33. In fact, the principle of subsidiarity had already been introduced in the Treaty by 130R(4) of the Single European Act. However, this provision had never been applied in practice.

34. See N. Emiliou, "Subsidiarity: An Effective Barrier against 'the Enterprises of Ambition'?" *European Law Review* 17 (1992): 383.

35. For a discussion of subsidiarity in the environmental field, see Rudolf Steinberg, "The Subsidiarity Principle in European Environmental Law," in I. Pernice, ed., *Harmonization of Legislation in Federal Systems* (Baden-Baden: Nomos, 1996), 81.

36. Reprinted in *Agence Europe,* October 30, 1992.

37. Reprinted in *Agence Europe,* December 13–14, 1994.

38. See K. Lenaerts, "The Principle of Subsidiarity and the Environment in the European Union: Keeping the Balance of Federalism," *Fordham International Law Journal* 17 (1994): 846, and W. Wils, "Subsidiarity and EC Environmental Policy: Taking People's Concern Seriously," *Journal of Environmental Law* 6 (1994): 85, 88.

39. On the concept of spillovers and the various kinds of spillovers that may arise in the environmental context, see R. B. Stewart, "Environmental Law in the United States and the European Community: Spillovers, Cooperation, Rivalry, Institutions," *University of Chicago Legal Forum* (1992): 39, 45.

40. Moreover, in the (unlikely) event where both Community and member states appear to be equally able to deal with such spillovers, the third guideline still gives preference to Community action when such an action is more efficient than action undertaken at the level of the member states.

41. Indeed, while the Commission and the European Parliament were generally in favor of Article 100A, the Council of Ministers was in favor of Article 130S. This led to a great deal of litigation between these institutions. See case C-300/89, *Commission v. Council* (1991), E.C.R. I-2867; case C-155/91, *Commission v. Council* (1993), E.C.R. I-939; and case C-187/93, *Parliament v. Council* (1994), E.C.R. I-2857. Generally on these cases, see N. Emiliou, "Opening the Pandora's Box: The Legal Basis of Community Measures before the Court of Justice," *European Law Review* 19 (1994): 488.

42. See F. Gaskin, "The Implementation of EC Environmental Law," *Review of European Community & International Environmental Law* 2 (1992): 335. See also R. Macrory, "The Enforcement of Community Environmental Laws: Some Critical Issues," *Common Market Law Review* 29 (1992): 347.

43. See chapter text accompanying notes 64 to 66.

44. Generally on the IGC and its objectives, see Justus Lipsius, "The 1996 Intergovernmental Conference," *European Law Review* 20 (1995): 235.

45. For a detailed discussion of the amendments changes introduced by the Amsterdam Treaty, see S. Bär and A. Kraemer, "European Environmental Policy after Maastricht," *Journal of Environmental Law* 10 (1998): 315.

46. See, however, the exception contained in Article 175(2), which maintains unanimity voting for several environmental matters.

47. Article 3(c) of the Treaty of Amsterdam (new Article 6) provides that "environmental protection requirements must be integrated into the definition and implementation of Community policies and activities referred to in Article 3, in particular with a view to promoting sustainable development."

48. Article 191(A) of the Treaty of Amsterdam (new Article 255) provides that "1. Any citizen of the Union, and any natural or legal person residing of having its registered office in a Member State, shall have a right of access to European Parliament, Council and Commission documents, subject to the principles and the conditions to be defined in accordance with paragraphs 2 and 3. 2. General principles and limits on grounds of public and private interest governing this right of access to documents shall be determined by the Council, acting in accordance with the procedures referred to in Article 189b within two years of the entry into force of the Treaty. 3. Each institution referred to above shall elaborate in its own rules of procedures specific provisions regarding access to its documents."

49. See chapter text accompanying notes 112 to 115.

50. Article 189(2) of the Treaty.

51. Case 6/68, *Zuckerfabrik Watenstedt GmbH v. Council* (1968), E.C.R. 409, 415.

52. See Article 189(3) of the Treaty.

53. Ibid.

54. E. Rebhinder and R. B. Stewart, "Environmental Protection Policy" in *Integration through Law*, in Mauro Cappelletti et al., eds. (New York, N.Y.: Wade Gruyter, 1985).

55. See, for example, Council Directive 84/538 of September 17, 1984, on the approximation of the laws of the member states relating to the permissible sound power level of lawn mowers, O.J. 1984, L 300/71, and Council Directive 84/533 of September 17, 1984, on the approximation of the laws of the member states relating to the permissible sound power level of compressors, O.J. 1984, L 300/123.

56. Council Directive 75/440 of June 16, 1975, concerning the quality required of surface water intended for the abstraction of drinking water in the member states, O.J. 1975, L 194/00, amended in O.J. 1979, L 271/44, and Council Directive 76/160 of December 8, 1975, concerning the quality of bathing waters, O.J. 1976, L 31/1.

57. Council Directive 75/442 on waste, O.J. 1975, L 194/39, recently amended by Council Directive 91/156, O.J. 1991, L 78/32.

58. See, generally, R. Steinberg, "Trade-Environment Negotiations in the EU, NAFTA and WTO: Regional Trajectories of Rule Development," *American Journal of International Law* 91 (1996): 231, 260.

59. See G. Pridham and M. Cini, "Enforcing Environmental Standards in the European Union: Is There a Southern Problem?" in M. Faure et al., eds., *Environmental Standards in the European Union in an Interdisciplinary Framework* (Antwerpen: Maklu, 1994), 251, 261 ("[Italy, Greece, and Spain] will have, as a whole, been among the less activist of the Member States over EU environmental policy. . . . They have tended not to push for new European legislation or show a concern for maintaining high standards.").

60. The position of central member states considerably varies from one directive to another, depending on the economic and environmental interests at stake.

61. This fund was established by the Council in Regulation 1164/94, O.J. 1994, L 130/1. In conformity with the protocol on economic and social cohesion annexed to the TEU, the granting of financial assistance to member states from the Cohesion Fund is subject to two conditions: first, that they have a per capita gross national product (GNP) of less than

90 percent of the Community average (currently only Greece, Ireland, Portugal, and Spain fulfill that condition), and, second, that they have a program leading to the fulfillment of the conditions of economic convergence set out in Article 104(C) of the Treaty. For a discussion on these funds, see D. Wilkinson, "Using the European Union's Structural and Cohesion Funds for the Protection of the Environment," *Review of European Community & International Environmental Law* 3 (1994): 119.

62. Prior to the creation of the Cohesion Fund, the Community had already provided financial assistance for environmental protection projects to southern European countries through programs such as ENVIREG, which aimed at promoting regional socioeconomic development and environment (O.J. 1990, C 115/3), and MEDSPA, which funded actions designed to contribute to the protection of the environment in the Mediterranean basin (O.J. 1984, C 133/1).

63. See J. Meitzes, "The Inconsistent Implementation of the Environmental Laws of the European Community," *Environmental Law Report* 22 (August 1992): 10523.

64. For an overview of the Danish experience, see M. Moe, "Implementation and Enforcement in Federal System," *Ecology Law Quarterly* 20 (1993): 151.

65. See Pridham and Cini, "Enforcing Environmental Standards in the European Union."

66. For a discussion of these differences, see ibid.

67. See chapter text accompanying note 77.

68. See E. Rehbinder, "Regulatory Federalism: Environmental Protection in the European Community" in I. Pernice, ed., *Harmonization of Legislation in Federal Systems,* 61, 78.

69. See chapter text accompanying note 72.

70. This part draws on D. Geradin, *Trade and Environment: A Comparative Study of EC and U.S. Law* (New York, N.Y.: Cambridge University Press, 1997).

71. See also O. Lomas, "Environmental Protection, Economic Conflict and the European Community," *McGill Law Journal* 33 (1988): 506.

72. Council Directive 70/220 on the approximation of the laws of the member states relating to measures to be taken against air pollution by gases from positive-ignition engines of motor vehicles, O.J. 1970, L 76/1.

73. Council Directive 77/102, O.J. 1977, L 32/32.

74. Optional harmonization is the strategy generally used by the Community when it regulates the environmental characteristics of products. See, for example, the directives harmonizing noise emission limits for products, such as Council Directive 78/1015 on the approximation of the laws of the member states on the permissible sound level and exhaust system of motorcycles, O.J. 1978, L 349/21, and Council Directive 77/311 on the approximation of the laws of the member states relating to the driver-perceived noise level of wheeled agricultural or forestry tractors, O.J. 1977, L 105/1.

75. D. Vogel, "Environmental Protection and the Creation of the Single European Market" (paper presented at the 1992 annual meeting of the American Political Science Association, September 3–6, 1992), 64.

76. Lomas, "Environmental Protection, Economic Conflict and the European Community," 526.

77. See Johnson and Corcelle, *The Environmental Policy of the European Communities,* 128.

78. Lomas, "Environmental Protection, Economic Conflict and the European Community," 526.

79. See Johnson and Corcelle, *The Environmental Policy of the European Communities,* 129.

80. See Lomas, "Environmental Protection, Economic Conflict and the European Community," 531.

81. Council Directive 88/76 amending Directive 70/220, 1988 O.J., L 36/1.

82. See Article 4 of Council Directive 88/76.

83. O.J. 1988, C 56/9.

84. O.J. 1989, C 120.

85. O.J. 1989, C 134/8.

86. Council Directive 89/548 amending with regard to European emission standards for cars below 1.4 liters, Council Directive 70/220, O.J. 1989, L 226/1.

87. See Article 2 of Council Directive 89/458. The strategy of optional harmonization had been already partly abandoned in Council Directive 88/76. See Articles 3 and 4 of that directive.

88. Ibid., Article 3.

89. Ibid., Article 5.

90. Council Directive 91/441 amending Council Directive 70/220, O.J. 1991, L 242/1.

91. Council Directive 94/12 amending Council Directive 70/220, O.J. 1994, L 100/42.

92. See "Communication of the Commission on a Future Strategy for the Control of Atmospheric Emissions from Road Transport Taking into Account the Results from the Auto/ Oil Program," COM(96)248.

93. Council Directive 98/69, amending Council Directive 70/220, O.J. 1998, L 350/1.

94. See Lomas, "Environmental Protection, Economic Conflict and the European Community," 532.

95. In this context, one should welcome the generalization of this system of qualified majority voting to all environmental lawmaking procedures by Article 130S(1) (new Article 175[1]) of the Treaty on European Union. See, however, the exceptions contained in Article 130S(2) (new Article 175[2]).

96. The Parliament has traditionally been in favor of strong environmental measures. See K. Collins, "Plans and Prospects for the European Parliament in Shaping Future Environmental Policy," *European Environmental Law Review* 4 (1995): 74.

97. Generally on the New Approach, see J. Pelkmans, "The New Approach to Technical Harmonization and Standardization," *Journal of Common Market Studies* 25 (1986): 249.

98. The New Approach relies on the concept of "mutual recognition" according to which a product that is lawfully produced and marketed in one member state must be admitted in another member state except when the latter can refer to essential or mandatory requirements. See case 120/78, *Rewe Zentral AG v. Bundesmonopolverwaltung für Branntwei* (1978), E.C.R. 649. The harmonization of those essential requirements would therefore be necessary and sufficient to ensure the free movement of goods throughout the Community.

99. Generally on CEN, see S. Farr, *Harmonization of Technical Standards in the European Community* (Colorado Springs, Colo.: Wiley, 1992), 33.

100. For a good discussion of the role of standardization of bodies in the environmental field, see R. D. Hunter, "Standardization and the Environment," *International Environment Reporter* 16, March 10, 1993, 185.

101. See, for example, Council Directive 86/594 on airborne noise emitted by household appliances, O.J. 1986, L 344/24. This directive establishes the general principles on the publi-

cation of information on noise emitted by household equipment when a member state makes such information compulsory on its territory. It also defines the technical requirements needed to carry out checks on the noise levels declared by the manufacturers and importers. In that respect, Council Directive 86/594 considers that, in line with the new approach to technical harmonization, it is up to standardization organizations to set detailed harmonized standards in this area.

102. See, for example, Article 10 of Council Directive 94/62 on packaging and packaging waste, which expressly encourages the development of European standards with regard to these matters, O.J. 1994, L 365/14.

103. See, for example, Stewart, "Environmental Law in the United States and the European Community," 35.

104. See T. Joseph, "Preaching Heresy: Permitting Member States to Enforce Stricter Environmental Laws Than the European Community," *Yale Law Journal* 20 (1995): 277.

105. On the doctrine of preemption, see generally E. Cross, "Preemption of Member State Law in the European Community: A Framework for Analysis," *Common Market Law Review* 28 (1992): 447. See also S. Weatherill, "Beyond Preemption? Shared Competence and Constitutional Change in the European Community in Legal Issues of the Maastricht Treaty," in O'Keeffe and Twoney, supra note 29.

106. Kramer, "The Single European Act and Environment Protection," 681.

107. J. Flynn, "How Will Article 100A(4) Work? A Comparison with Article 93," *Common Market Law Review* 24 (1987): 689, 696.

108. See, in particular, P. Pescatore, "Some Critical Remarks on the Single European Act," *Common Market Law Review* 24 (1987): 689.

109. O.J. 1991, L 85/34.

110. In the case of Germany, the Commission decision to maintain stricter national measures was successfully challenged by the French government. The Court of Justice declared that this decision was void because the Commission failed to state clearly the reason of its decision. See case C-41/93, *France v. Commission* (1994), E.C.R. I-1829. Following this Court judgment, the Commission adopted a decision reauthorizing Germany to maintain its more restrictive rules on the use and sale of PCP on the basis of Article 100A(4). In order to comply with the judgment of the Court, this decision states in greater detail the reasons why stricter German rules can be justified by Article 100A(4). See Sloan and Carbonnel, "Exemptions from Harmonization Measures under Article 100A(4): The Second Authorization of the German Ban on PCP," *European Environmental Law Review* 4 (1995): 45.

111. See "Austria, Finland, Sweden Warn Commission of Legal Battle over Their Stricter Laws," *International Environment Reporter,* April 30, 1997, 415.

112. See Bär and Kraemer, "European Environmental Policy after Maastricht," 319 ff.

113. See S. Charmovitz, "The World Trade Organization, Meat Hormones and Food Safety," *International Trade Reporter* 14 (1997): 1781.

114. See Article 130R(2) (new Article 174[2]) of the Treaty.

115. See Rehbinder and Stewart, "Environmental Protection Policy in Integration through Law," 11.

116. O.J. 1988, L 336/1, amended by Council Directive 94/66, O.J. 1994, L 337/83.

117. O.J. 1983, C 49/1.

118. Interestingly enough, the United Kingdom was also opposed to the Commission proposal because it would have meant surrendering the competitive advantage arising from its

geographic location. Being an island exposed to Atlantic weather systems and westerly winds, the United Kingdom was able to disperse air pollution more easily than other member states and, hence, would preserve the integrity of its environment at a lesser cost for industry. The United Kingdom was therefore against any type of uniform reductions. See Lomas, "Environmental Protection, Economic Conflict and the European Community," 535.

119. See ibid., 522.

120. See Article 3 and Annexes I and II of the directive.

121. Ibid.

122. See Article 3.2.

123. See Article 4.

124. See Article 5.3.

125. See "CO_2 Heads List of Dutch Presidency's Priorities," *Europe Environment* 14 (January 1997): 7.

126. Ibid.

127. For an overview of the Community strategy in this field, see "Preparing for Implementation of the Kyoto Protocol, Communication of the Commission to the Council and Parliament," COM(1999)230, May 19, 1999.

128. See Rehbinder and Stewart, "Environmental Protection Policy in Integration through Law," 216.

129. A third, less frequently used strategy is for the Community to impose a limitation on total loading of emissions. See, for example, Council Directive 88/609 on the limitation of certain pollutants into the air from large combustion plants to regulate emissions from existing installations (discussed in the chapter text accompanying notes 117 to 125).

130. O.J. 1976, L 129/23.

131. See Lists I and II in the Annex of the directive.

132. Lomas, "Environmental Protection, Economic Conflict and the European Community," 516.

133. See Article 6 of the directive.

134. See Esty and Geradin, "Environmental Protection and International Competitiveness," 11.

135. For example, D. Vogel quotes a British official arguing against the adoption of technology-based uniform water effluent standards in Europe: "Italy economically benefits from the amount of sunshine that it receives every year. Why should not our industry be able to take a similar advantage of our long coastline . . . and rapidly flowing rivers?" D. Vogel, *National Styles of Regulation: Environmental Policy in Great Britain and the United States* (Ithaca, N.Y.: Cornell University Press, 1986), 103.

136. Council Directive 96/61 of September 24, 1996, on integrated pollution prevention and control, O.J. 1996, L 257/26.

137. See Articles 3 to 7 of the draft directive.

138. See Articles 8 and 9 of the draft directive.

139. See "Industrial Pollution: 'Philosophical' Problems Subsist on IPPC Directive," *Europe Environment,* March 7, 1995, 2.

140. For a discussion of the German position, see J. Schnutenhaus, "Integrated Prevention Pollution and Control: New German Initiatives in the European Environment Council," *European Environmental Law Review* 3 (1994): 323.

141. Common Position 9/96 adopted by the Council on November 27, 1995, with a view

to adopting Council Directive 9/96 concerning integrated pollution prevention control, O.J. 1996, C 87/8.

142. See Article 9.4 of the common position.

143. See "Parliament Approves IPPC Proposal, Sends Measure to Council for Final Action," *International Environmental Report,* May 29, 1996, 431.

144. See "Bjerregaard Defends Flexibility in IPPC Directive," *Environment Watch,* June 7, 1996, 13.

145. See "Finance Ministers Reject Latest Proposals on Carbon Tax to Curb Greenhouse Emissions," *International Environmental Report,* November 1, 1995, 817.

146. See "Business Targets Waste Laws in EU Deregulation Drive," *Environment Watch,* October 27, 1995, 3.

147. See "Commission Votes to Loosen Rules Governing Genetically Modified Organisms," *International Environmental Report,* December 13, 1995, 938.

148. See "Voluntary Accords Seen as Way to Protect the Environment while Remaining Competitive," *International Environmental Report,* July 26, 1995, 585.

149. See chapter text accompanying notes 164 to 168.

150. In the NAFTA context, see, for example, S. Charnovitz, "The North American Free Trade Agreement: Green Law or Green Spin?" *Law and Policy in International Business* 26 (1994): 1, and D. Esty, "Making Trade and Environmental Policies Work Together: Lessons from NAFTA," *Aussenwirtschaft* 49 (1994): 59. In the context of the WTO, see, for example, J. Jackson, "World Trade Rules and Environmental Policies: Congruence or Conflict?" *Washington and Lee Law Review* 49 (1992): 1227, and E. U. Petersmann, "International Trade and International Environmental Law," *Journal of World Trade* 16 (1993): 43.

151. See, for example, P. Goldman, "The Legal Effects of Trade Agreements on Domestic Health and Environmental Regulations," *Journal of Environmental Law and Litigation* 7 (1992): 11, and R. Nader, "Free Trade and the Decline of Democracy," in R. Nader et al., eds., *The Case against Free Trade* (San Francisco, Calif.: Earth Island Press, 1993).

152. The "race to the bottom" has been defined by Revesz as a "race from the desirable levels of environmental quality that states would pursue if they did not face competition for industry to the increasingly undesirable levels they choose in the face of such competition." R. Revesz, "Rehabilitating Interstate Competition: Rethinking the 'Race to the Bottom' Rationale for Federal Environmental Regulation," *New York University Law Review* 67 (1992): 1210. For a discussion of the "race to the bottom" in the context of international trade liberalization, see Esty and Geradin, "Environmental Protection and International Competitiveness," 273.

153. See Geradin, "Trade and Environmental Protection," 201.

154. This view is consistent with Steinberg, "Trade-Environment Negotiations in the EU, NAFTA and WTO," 259.

155. Ibid., 245.

156. Article 1114 of NAFTA provides that "the parties recognize that it is inappropriate to encourage investment by relaxing domestic health, safety or environmental measures. Accordingly, a Party should not waive or otherwise derogate from, or offer to waive or otherwise derogate from, such measures as an encouragement for the establishment, acquisition, expansion or retention in its territory of an investment of an investor. If a party considers that another Party has offered such an encouragement, it may request consultation with the other Party and the two Parties shall consult with a view to avoid any such encouragement."

For a discussion on this provision, see Esty and Geradin, "Environmental Protection and International Competitiveness," 314–15.

157. For a discussion on such provisions, see ibid., 315–16. See also R. Housman et al., "Enforcement of Environmental Laws under a Supplemental Agreement by the North Free Trade Agreement," *Georgetown International Environmental Law Review* 5 (1993): 593.

158. See Steinberg, "Trade-Environment Negotiations in the EU, NAFTA and WTO," 240–44.

159. The CTE succeeded to the GATT working group on Environmental Measures and International Trade (EMIT), which was established by decision of the General Council in November 1971 but did not become active until October 1991. Generally on the CTE, see G. Van Calster, "The World Trade Organization Committee on Trade and the Environment: Exploring the Challenges of the Greening of Free Trade," *European Environmental Law Review* 5 (1996): 14.

160. See chapter text accompanying note 29.

161. See J. Attick, "Environmental Standards within NAFTA: Difference by Design and Retreat from Harmonization," *Indiana Journal of Global Legal Studies* 3 (1995): 81, 85 ("NAFTA represents a sharp break from the European experience. Whereas the European Community treaty calls for 'approximation' of member state laws and regulations generally in order to bring an 'ever closer Union,' NAFTA institutionalizes sharp regulatory gradients, repudiating among other things, any pretense of universal harmonization."). See also F. Abbott, "Integration without Institutions: The NAFTA Mutation of the ERC Model and the Future of the GATT Regime," *American Journal of Comparative Law* 40 (1992): 917.

162. See Steinberg, "Trade Environment Negotiations in the EU, NAFTA, and WTO," 249–52.

163. For example, ISO's Committee TC 207 is actively working on international standards for eco-labeling. See "EU Member Unhappy at Draft ISO Ecolabel Standards," *Environment Watch,* April 5, 1996, 1.

164. See Richard B. Stewart, "Environmental Regulation and International Competitiveness," *Yale Law Journal* 102 (1993): 2039, 2099.

165. Some authors will also argue that harmonization of process standards is not desirable and that regulatory competition among nations is preferable. See, for example, A. Klevorick, "The Race to the Bottom in Federal System," *Yale Law & Policy Review and Yale Journal on Regulation, Symposium: Constructing a New Federalism* 14 (1996): 177. For reasons of space, I will not enter into this debate here.

166. Montreal Protocol on Substances That Deplete the Ozone Layer, reprinted in 26 I.L.M. 1541 (1987). Generally on the Montreal Protocol, see Richard Elliot Benedick, *Ozone Diplomacy* (Cambridge, Mass.: Harvard University Press, 1988).

167. Basel Convention on the Control of Transboundary Movements of Hazardous Wastes and Their Disposal, reprinted in 26 I.L.M. 567 (1987). Generally on the Basel Convention, see Lang, "The International Waste Regime," in W. Lang et al., eds., *Environmental Protection and International Law* (London: Graham & Trotman, 1991).

168. Framework Convention on Climate Change, reprinted in 31 I.L.M. 849 (1992).

169. See chapter text accompanying notes 98 to 103.

170. See chapter text accompanying note 122.

171. See chapter text accompanying notes 127 and 128.

172. Agenda 21 is reprinted and annotated in Stanley P. Johnson, ed., *The Earth Summit—The United Nations Conference on Environment and Development (UNCED)* (London: Graham & Trotman, 1993).

173. For an example of this approach, see Article 4 of the UN Framework Convention on Climate Change, which imposes different requirements on developed and developing countries. See Johnson, ed., *The Earth Summit,* 57.

174. See D. Geradin, "Trade and Environmental Protection in the Context of World Trade Rules: A View from the European Union," *European Foreign Affairs Review* 2 (1997): 33, 58–59.

175. See, for example, D. Esty, "The Case for a Global Environmental Organization," in P. Kenen, ed., *Managing the World Economy Fifty Years after Bretton Woods* (Washington, D.C.: Institute for International Economics, 1994), 287.

6

The North American Free Trade Agreement: Alternative Models of Managing Trade and the Environment

Julie A. Soloway

Environmental issues were a major concern in the debate leading up to the passage of the North American Free Trade Agreement (NAFTA), partly because of the fear that Mexico had considerably less stringent environmental enforcement than Canada and the United States. The environmental concerns about NAFTA revolved around three main interrelated issues. First, Mexican firms would gain an "unfair" competitive advantage vis-à-vis Canadian and U.S. firms because of lower environmental compliance costs. Second, Canadian and U.S. firms would be drawn to Mexico to capitalize on reduced environmental compliance costs in order to remain competitive; that is, Mexico would become a "pollution haven." Third, Canadian and U.S. firms would lobby their governments to lower domestic environmental standards in order to "level the playing field."[1] More generally, however, each of these issues can be characterized as a problem of managing the often significant variations in domestic regulation in the context of deepened economic integration across three distinct countries.

The response to these concerns led to a number of novel provisions in NAFTA that took account of the inextricable link between trade and the environment. They marked a sharp departure from NAFTA's predecessor, the Canada-U.S. Free Trade Agreement (FTA) and from the existing trade and environment provisions in the General Agreement on Tariffs and Trade (GATT) and the World Trade Organization (WTO).[2] The dominant legal model used to manage the trade and environment interface had historically been "national treatment"—the obligation not to discriminate against foreign goods, with specific exceptions. In other words, the national treatment model would permit countries the freedom to adopt their own environmental regulations and standards as they deem appropriate so long as they did so in a nondiscriminatory manner. Indeed, the national treatment principle forms the basis of more sophisticated formulations of managing the trade and domestic environmental regulation interface, such as the NAFTA and WTO rules governing sanitary and phytosanitary regulation. "Increasingly, however, the concept of national treatment has viewed itself as inadequate to manage trade frictions that are connected to regulatory diversity among nations."[3] Regulation that is not discriminatory on its face can still have significant trade-restricting effects.[4] Moreover, the nondiscriminatory application of environmental regulation does not speak to the actual stringency of that regulation. In response to the perceived inadequacies of the national treatment model, NAFTA also incorporated extensive harmonization provisions throughout its text.

The harmonization model extends much beyond its "crudest form" of rendering all laws and regulations identical. Leebron identifies four central categories of harmonization.[5] First is the more commonly understood notion of *rule harmonization,* which makes similar the "fairly specific rules that regulate the outcome, characteristics, or performance of economic goods, actors, transactions, institutions, and productive facilities."[6] This would include, for example, the identification of a specific environmental emission standard to be operative throughout the NAFTA region. It could also include the obligation to adhere to certain minimum international standards accompanied by the freedom to adopt higher standards. Second is *policy harmonization,* the rendering similar of general governmental policy objectives and guidelines rather than specific rules, for example, prescribing objectives for national ambient air standards and not specific limits for manufacturing plants. Such harmonization does not prescribe a specific means to an end but rather allows a government to retain broad discretion in how to meet the prescribed policy goal. Third is *process harmonization,* the adoption of "certain agreed principles that are intended to influence or constrain the factors that are taken into account in making policies and rules . . . [which can then] limit the structure or implementation of policies."[7] For example, NAFTA works to harmonize policy inputs by requiring that health or safety measures be based on "sound science and risk assessment." NAFTA also includes, throughout its text, the obligation to work toward the mutual recognition of procedures adopted by standard setting bodies (i.e., licensing and testing procedures) and/or the recognition of equivalency of standards between the parties. Fourth is *institutional harmonization,* the harmonization of either public or private institutions and institutional processes. Here Leebron explains "that if the aim is to harmonize decisional outcomes by various private and institutional actors, both the substantive criteria and decisional outcomes are implicated. Rules, policies, and principles will generally not be truly harmonized unless the procedures and institutions for implementing them are made similarly effective, and doing so may mean making them more similar."[8] For example, under the North American Agreement on Environmental Cooperation (NAAEC), the NAFTA parties are all similarly obliged to enforce their environmental laws, an obligation that can be reviewed by a trinational dispute settlement mechanism.

Harmonization is a tempting means by which to solve the trade and environment dilemma because of its efficacy: By removing the differences between domestic regulations in different countries, trade conflict ceases to exist. Differences in environmental regulation would no longer be a means by which to preclude market access. Goods would be able to move freely, which, according to trade theorists, should enhance both global and domestic welfare.

There are many other normative rationales for the harmonization model.[9] From an environmental perspective, foremost is the argument that harmonization of environmental regulation and standards will "level the playing field"; that is, producers in different jurisdictions will have to incur similar environmental compliance costs, thereby eliminating downward pressures on environmental standards as a means by which to gain competitive advantage. As well, harmonization may reduce jurisdictional interface costs and thus ease cross-border transactions, for example, in the case of telecommunications equipment or transportation of dangerous goods. Harmonization of pollution regulations may also reduce transborder externalities created by differences in environmental regulation. Harmonization of regulations can additionally facilitate trade by reducing multiple compliance costs and allow producers to achieve economies of scale in production and distribution when selling to multiple Jurisdictions

Despite these persuasive rationales, some authors have expressed skepticism about the broad-based use of harmonization as a welfare-enhancing policy tool. Leebron notes that there are costs associated with sameness, namely, that "differences between nations may also have value, and that harmonization can only be achieved at the cost of eliminating or reducing differences."[10] Rules are adopted in different countries according to differences in inter alia endowments, technology, or preferences.[11] More specifically, environmental regulations are adopted to reflect unique ecological conditions and challenges. Where regulation reflects such differences, it is likely that harmonization will result in welfare losses for citizens in at least one of the countries. Moreover, diversity and resulting races can lead to experimentation, innovation, and finding a more effective and efficient way to meet environmental goals. Trebilcock and Howse also raise serious questions about the desirability of widespread harmonization, viewing both the global and the domestic welfare implications of policy harmonization as "highly ambiguous" in many contexts.[12] They are not convinced that the costs of *not* harmonizing are sufficiently high that they warrant the widespread prescription of harmonization and are further concerned that harmonization may discount the importance of competitive governments. In general, they view the proposition that trade in all goods worldwide ought to be conducted on a level playing field as one that is at odds with the theory of comparative advantage, which is centrally predicated on nations exploiting their differences (not similarities) in international trade.[13] "Few international trade theorists believe any longer that comparative advantage is exclusively exogenously determined, but is significantly shaped by endogenous government polices, including health and safety regulation."[14] Exploiting differences in government policies is no less legitimate than exploiting differences in natural endowments and may indeed be desirable in certain circumstances. And they see the international institutions responsible for making these harmonization decisions as less than ideal. For example, trade dispute settlement panelists may lack the expertise necessary to arbitrate highly technical disputes. And the harmonizing institutions themselves (such as the Codex Alimentarius) may raise concerns about transparency and "democratic deficits."

Thus, each of the two models, national treatment and harmonization, seeks to resolve the trade and domestic regulation tension in different ways. Yet each model brings with it a unique set of costs and benefits in domestic and global welfare terms. NAFTA, in the operation of its rules and institutional regime, utilizes adaptations of both of these models to address the challenges posed by integrating environmental concerns into a trade regime. To some extent, the "greenness" of the NAFTA regime reflects the differences in the relative power and interests of the richer, greener *demandeur* United States vis-à-vis Mexico.[15] Yet the problem remains of how best to execute a green strategy in the context of deepened regional integration. In other words, what instruments will be most effective in balancing the various objectives of the parties?

The purpose of this chapter is to evaluate the effect of these alternative models on domestic and global welfare as they have been embedded in NAFTA and employed during the first six years of the NAFTA regime in formal operation. It will do so by first identifying the extent to which NAFTA's central environmental provisions have incorporated either harmonization or national treatment as a means to resolve the tension between trade and environmental differences and what the rationales were for those choices. Second, this chapter will evaluate these alternative models according to how they affect both domestic and global welfare. This calculus will not only contemplate the increases to domestic and global welfare that free trade is presumed to create but will also include an analysis of social welfare to the extent it is affected by a particular environmental standard or regulation.

Thus, the first section reviews the environmental provisions within the core NAFTA text, identifying the use of the various models and their operation in their first six years in order to make judgments about their welfare impacts. The second section examines the environmental side agreement to NAFTA—the NAAEC—and identifies its harmonization provisions, their operation, and the degree and form of their welfare effects. The third section does the same for the two NAFTA-inspired environmental institutions: the North American Development Bank (NADBank) and the Border Environmental Cooperation Commission (BECC). Finally, some conclusions are offered.

THE NAFTA TRADE RULES AND THEIR USE

NAFTA has incorporated a large number of often innovative environmental provisions throughout its text. These can be divided into six major categories: (1) the NAFTA preamble, (2) NAFTA's relationship with international environmental agreements, (3) sanitary and phytosanitary measures, (4) technical barriers to trade, (5) the pollution haven investment provision, and (6) the dispute resolution provisions. This section will review each of these six categories and examine how they have been utilized since NAFTA's inception.

NAFTA Preamble

The preamble to NAFTA contains three references to the environment, two of which are particularly innovative. Among the goals of the three countries are measures to ensure a "predictable and stable commercial framework." The preamble adds that these measures should be undertaken "in a manner consistent with environmental protection and conservation." Yet strikingly, the preamble also includes two parallel environmental commitments to the main trade-related commitments by adding as goals two proactive principles: first, the "promotion of sustainable development" and, second, the "strengthening of the development and enforcement of environmental laws and regulations" among the three parties. Although these provisions do not impose directly concrete or specific obligations on the parties, they are significant in that such extensive environmental language had not to date appeared in the text of a trade agreement in the Western Hemisphere.[16] Preambles are also gaining increased prominence in the adjudication of international legal disputes. The preamble further sets the tone of "increased sensitivity to the complex relationships in both policy domains."[17] The effect of these provisions is not tangible or readily measurable, although, by placing environmental considerations alongside the broader goals of trade liberalization and market access in the preambular commitments, the NAFTA parties harmonized the general context in which the rules of the trading game would be interpreted and, in the future, how they will evolve. The preambular commitments in NAFTA may function to constrain future interpretations of NAFTA. This is consistent with Leebron's third category of process harmonization outlined previously.

NAFTA's Relationship with International Environmental Agreements

The relationship between international trade agreements and multilateral environmental agreements (MEAs) has been the subject of exhaustive debate. It continues to remain a focus of work but an issue ambiguously resolved at the WTO. The problem is that international environmental agreements occasionally include trade sanctions as punishment for noncompliance, the legality of which is subject to a newly formulated and untested set of complex criteria under the WTO's jurisprudence.[18] Here NAFTA is clear. According to Article 103, NAFTA in general would take precedence over other international agreements. However, NAFTA specified an exception to this general rule. Article 104 states that NAFTA will not take precedence over the trade provisions of specific environmental/conservation agreements, including the Convention on International Trade in Endangered Species,[19] the Montreal Protocol on Ozone-Depleting Substances,[20] the Basel Convention on Transboundary Movements of Hazardous Wastes,[21] and two additional bilateral environmental cooperation agreements,[22] provided that the parties choose the least trade-inconsistent measure available.

The parties thus harmonized their recognition that the world's most important MEAs can legitimately incorporate trade measures as a means of enforcement. This commitment "facilitates transnational environmental regulation, allowing trade sanctions otherwise inconsistent with NAFTA to be a part of the compliance and enforcement regimes for international environmental norms."[23] By giving these international environmental agreements precedence over the NAFTA commitments, the parties have made a clear choice to place any welfare losses that emanate from restricted trade behind the competing priorities of environmental conservation. Whether or not these balance out in welfare terms is extremely difficult to measure. It would require asking how much trade is affected in fact through the existence, deterrent effect, and actual use of such sanctions, and some measurement of the degree to which welfare would be consequently reduced. It would also require some welfare measurements to be made about the value of an endangered species or the value of the earth's ozone layer. Valuation of public goods is difficult and impracticable. Howse and Trebilcock have, however, found that sanctions, under certain conditions, can increase welfare both globally and in the targeted country.[24]

Whatever the welfare effects may be, this provision may not have settled the issue of the relationship between MEAs and NAFTA. First, the exemption is limited to the enumerated agreements and excludes the UN Convention on Biological Diversity[25] and the UN Framework Convention on Climate Change.[26] Moreover, there will be difficulties in adding any future MEAs to the list, as expansion would require agreement by all three NAFTA parties. Audley notes that this "complicates the already difficult task of national MEA ratification by institutionalizing trading partner pressure on Congress."[27] A second problem is the interpretation of the "least inconsistent" test. The meaning of this term is similar to the GATT term "least trade restrictive" but at this time lacks its own jurisprudence, "leaving the interpretation of the term to future trade disputes to be resolved under NAFTA"[28] Third, it is not clear how these provisions will apply to the parties' obligations under GATT, as these obligations were in effect prior to NAFTA.[29] In such a case, the trade sanctions could be still considered to violate the GATT. This provision has not been the subject of interpretation to date.

Sanitary and Phytosanitary Standards

NAFTA Chapter 7 governs the application of sanitary and phytosanitary (SPS) standards. An SPS standard is any measure taken to protect human, animal, or plant life or health from the threat of disease, pests, contamination, or other dangers.[30] The SPS rules govern, for example, the types of pesticides that can be used on fresh fruit imported into a country or the inspection processes for imported meat products. Such issues, although seemingly benign, are often the subject of intense controversy—one country's allowable risk is another country's potential health disaster.[31]

During the NAFTA negotiations, there was substantial concern among the parties that SPS standards would be set at stringent or arbitrary levels so as to serve a protectionist purpose, at least in part. At the same time, environmental and consumer groups, particularly in the United States, wanted to maintain the ability to respond appropriately to health risks (from primarily Mexico) and not lose the freedom to set standards as it deemed appropriate.

To allay these fears, the NAFTA text developed a national treatment model, enhanced with elements of harmonization throughout. NAFTA articulates the freedom of parties to adopt such levels of protection as they see fit. Article 712(1) establishes the positive right of a party to adopt any SPS measure necessary for the protection of human, animal, or plant life or health, including measures more stringent than international standards. This is supported by Article 712(2), which states that notwithstanding any other provision, parties remain free to establish "appropriate levels of protection." This has been interpreted as a clear statement that NAFTA countries are not obliged to harmonize their standards.[32] Article 712 also states that SPS measures are to be "applied only to the extent necessary to achieve its appropriate level of protection" and that they may not be applied "with a view to, or with the effect of, creating a disguised restriction on trade between the parties." In general, consistent with the national treatment model, the provisions of NAFTA require that standards cannot create unnecessary obstacles, unjustifiably discriminate, or be used as a disguised restriction on trade. Ideally, they foster upward convergence of environmental protection while at the same time preserving each party's sovereignty by allowing them to adopt the level of protection that best suits the needs of the parties' local conditions and concerns. These provisions have not as yet been tested: There have been no dispute panels dealing with such issues under NAFTA. It is consequently unclear how these terms will be interpreted. For example, what would constitute a "necessary" as opposed to an unnecessary obstacle to trade? Jurisprudence of the GATT/WTO may provide some guidance, as the relevant legal provisions are quite similar. For example, the WTO Appellate Body recently affirmed an earlier WTO Panel decision that found the European Union (EU) ban on hormone-treated beef from the United States and Canada to be inconsistent with its obligations under the WTO.[33] In this case, the freedom of the EU to set its own SPS rules was curtailed by competing trade obligations under GATT/WTO rules.

NAFTA moves substantially beyond the national treatment model into the harmonization model in a number of ways. Harmonization is often necessary to provide a basis by which to actively facilitate trade between the NAFTA parties. The national treatment provisions, which treat like products alike, are really insufficient because parties would have to resort to costly and disruptive dispute settlement as a means to enforce their rights. Moreover, much of the harmonization provisions in Chapter 7 reflect the desire of the United States and Canada to bring Mexico up to a compatible level of SPS protection. This requires institutional harmonization in the form of trilateral institutional cooperation and capacity building at the micro-level rather than state-to-state dispute settlement.

NAFTA thus contains a number of provisions that encourage the harmonization of standards without lowering the level of protection, which can be classified as process harmonization. Specifically, NAFTA harmonizes the policy inputs to the adoption of an SPS measure in Article 712(3), which requires that SPS measures be based on scientific principles and risk assessment. Article 715 lists the factors that NAFTA countries must take into account when assessing risk and determining appropriate levels of protection. Like the WTO's SPS Agreement, parties are obligated to take international risk assessment methodologies into account along with other scientific considerations. Moreover, NAFTA Article 713 encourages NAFTA parties to use relevant international standards, guidelines, or recommendations as a basis for an SPS measure. A heavy premium is placed on international standards and standardizing organizations: If parties use the relevant international guidelines and recommendations as a basis for their SPS measures, other parties will not be able to challenge their provisions on the basis that they restrict trade. If they do not conform to such standards and adopt more stringent ones, they will be required to justify those decisions. Article 713(5) requires parties "to the greatest extent practicable" to participate in international standardizing organizations, such as the Codex Alimentarius Commission. Article 714 states that the parties shall, to the greatest extent practicable, pursue equivalence in their SPS measures, as long as levels of protection are not reduced.

Despite the formal maintenance of national autonomy, one commentator has actually noted that the "autonomy is highly restrictive in practice. By creating arduous processes to justify imposing environmental regulations more stringent than the international norms, the NAFTA negotiators opted to, in effect, encourage harmonization."[34] This process is best in evidence in the work of the many NAFTA committees, subcommittees, and working groups. These bodies have been charged with the overall implementation of the commitments in various areas throughout the NAFTA text, particularly in Chapter 7, where the agriculturally related committees and working groups have been active in pursuing a harmonization agenda.

The most notable of these groups is the Technical Working Group on Pesticides (TWGP), which was formed in direct response to concerns about the type and amount of pesticides on agricultural goods imported into the United States and Canada from Mexico. It has been found to be fulfilling its mandate "in a manner fully consistent with NAFTA's sustainable development goals."[35] The goal of the TWGP is "to develop a coordinated pesticides regulatory framework among NAFTA partners to address trade irritants, build national regulatory/scientific capacity, share the review burden, and coordinate scientific and regulatory decisions on pesticides."[36] The group has worked toward harmonizing specific trade irritants, such as maximum residue limits (MRLs). The TWGP has also been "developing a better understanding of each regulatory agency's assessment practices working to *harmonize* each country's procedures and requirements, and encouraging pesticide registrants (product owners) to make coordinated data submissions to the three NAFTA countries."[37] Technical subcommittees have been established in four areas: joint review of chemical pesticides, food residues, risk reduction, and regulatory capacity building. Each of these groups has been active. In some cases they have agreed on harmonization of specific measures. Concrete achievements include the harmonization of specific MRLs for seven pesticides used on potatoes, blueberries, preharvest oats, celery, lettuce, and canola; the harmonization of pesticide environmental fate and toxicology data requirements for registration; and the harmonization of worker and residential exposure guideline studies and policy issues.[38]

As well, the Committee on Sanitary and Phytosanitary Measures (SPS Committee) has met up to three times per year in an attempt to deal with policy harmonization issues and bilateral trade irritants such as the export of U.S. cherries to Mexico, the export of Mexican pork to the United States, and the export of Canadian Christmas trees to Mexico. Supporting the work of the SPS Committee are eight technical working groups that deal with a number of animal and plant health issues.[39]

There have been no formal disputes under NAFTA regarding SPS measures despite the fact that the complex technical issues dealt with in the SPS provisions provide a "fertile field for disputes among the NAFTA partners."[40] There was one dispute settlement panel under the FTA concerning SPS standards, illustrating some of the difficulties involved in litigating SPS issues. In this dispute, the Canadian government challenged a Puerto Rican regulation banning the import of ultra-high-temperature (UHT) processed milk from Quebec.[41] Despite a fourteen-year history of trouble-free exports to Puerto Rico, UHT milk from Quebec produced by Lactel Inc. was denied entry on the basis that it did not comply with the requisite health and safety standards. The Canadian government claimed that this newfound health and safety standard was a sham and more properly characterized as a restriction on trade and an outright violation of the FTA. The U.S. government claimed that it was free to set its own health and safety standards and that its obligations under the FTA did not diminish that freedom. Despite repeated attempts by the Canadian government at diplomatic and bureaucratic levels to be afforded an opportunity to demonstrate the equivalency of Quebec's milk sanitation standards, Puerto Rico continued to prohibit imports of Quebec UHT milk. In the fall of 1992, Canada submitted a formal request for dispute resolution pursuant to Chapter 18 of the FTA.

The FTA Panel offered mixed results. The Panel did not view the milk regulations as a disguised restriction on trade. It found that the obligation to pursue equivalency was of a "best efforts" nature only, which means that it was essentially a hortatory obligation. However, the Panel noted that the efforts among government officials to establish equivalency were unsatisfactory and that Canada's reasonably expected benefits under the FTA had been denied, although not by the fault of the United States. This essentially meant that it was reasonable for the Canadian regulations, after fourteen years of exports, to have been granted equivalency status. At the same time, however, the Panel did not find any wrongdoing on the part of the United States, nor did it find that the United States had acted in bad faith. This illustrates the reluctance of the Panel to find bad faith on the part of a government, even in the face of blatant discrimination. The Panel recommended that an equivalency study be undertaken within two months in order to allow UHT milk from Quebec to reenter the Puerto Rican market. It was not until late 1995, a full two years after the Panel report and four years after the imposition of the ban, that the equivalency study was completed and UHT milk from Quebec was permitted to enter the Puerto Rico market. Despite having achieved the desired result, this was a case of "too little, too late." Lactel had been denied market entry for three years, after which time it found it almost impossible to regain its market share and corresponding advantages. Thus, while this was a FTA case and not a NAFTA case, the outcome illustrates how the failure to strictly enforce national treatment provisions may lead to welfare losses with no corresponding welfare gain in terms of health or safety protection.

In fact, the welfare justification for stringent SPS rules in terms of plant protection can be ambiguous in some cases. Orden and Romano have recently found that even when there is a significant risk of pest infestation, the gains from trade may outweigh those potential health and safety welfare losses.[42] In the context of the eighty-two-year-long California ban on Mexican avocados and the subsequent partial lifting of the ban in 1997, they found that a welfare analysis of alternate scenarios reveal that even if there is a high risk of pest infestation, free trade will increase consumer surplus, lower producer surplus, and increase national welfare. For a partial lifting of the ban and limited imports, Orden and Romano found that consumer and net welfare gains from trade depend on the risk of pest infestation. Where the risk of pest infestation is high, consumer and net welfare gains are "relatively small and can be exceeded by the costs of pest infestation."[43] Where the risk of pest infestation is low, consumer surplus increases, and "the expected gains offset expected producer surplus losses and raise expected net welfare."[44]

Thus, the two models seem to have different rates of success in the context of SPS measures. To the extent that national treatment preserves the legitimate preferences of consumers, it is welfare enhancing. However, the rationale for harmonization has been primarily the facilitation of agricultural trade within North America and the upward harmonization of Mexican SPS standards, which increases consumer welfare by preserving the welfare gains of trade without sacrificing levels of protection. Here, harmonization has been pursued largely through the committees and working groups responsible for implementing the specific provisions of Chapter 7B. As the intergovernmental groups meet, discuss, and work through the various issues, they reach results that reflect the interests of all three parties. The records of these committees indicate that there has not been a downward harmonization of Canadian and U.S. standards toward Mexican standards but rather a trilateral "upward harmonization" process. Efforts at issue resolution, harmonization, and equivalence have been instituted as part of an ongoing process among the intergovernmental committees that regularly meet to review and discuss such issues. These institutional arrangements have generally been successful in securing market access among the parties and have helped foster higher standards in Mexico through education and technology assistance.[45] Thus, to the extent that such harmonization has facilitated trade and caused upward harmonization, it can be concluded that the work undertaken in the area of SPS measures has had largely welfare-enhancing effects in terms of both global (increased trade) and domestic welfare (lower pesticides and consumer surpluses).

There are, however, trade issues that resist resolution and remain especially problematic in the area of agriculture, as the SPS provisions are allegedly used more to protect domestic commercial interests rather than consumer health interests. For example, there are over thirty plant and animal health issues outstanding between the United States and Mexico that severely impede trade, resulting in harmful impacts on commercial agricultural interests.[46] There is further evidence that in many cases domestic interests have "captured" the process by which these regulations are made and that the parties have resisted reaching any sort of resolution of certain SPS issues in order that their constituencies benefit from decreased competition.[47] This violates both the spirit and the intent of the drafters of NAFTA: The preservation of the right to set environmental standards as a party sees fit in order to avoid a "race to the bottom" has become a tool by which parties can promote protectionist policies. The fact that there has not been any use of the panel process to deal with such matters points to areas requiring further institutional development.[48]

Technical Barriers to Trade

Standards-related measures, also referred to as "technical barriers to trade" (TBTs), are governed in much the same way as the SPS measures. Technical barriers to trade cover all human health, safety, and environmental standards not covered by the SPS rules. The NAFTA rules were developed concurrently with the WTO Technical Barriers to Trade Agreement during the Uruguay Round and are consequently quite similar.[49] They seek to provide a framework by which technical standards that unduly restrict trade can be separated from those that serve legitimate consumer and safety interests.

NAFTA's TBT rules are found in Chapter 9. Following the national treatment model, the right to establish measures "relating to safety, the protection of human, animal or plant life or health, the environment or consumers" is positively established in Article 904. Thus, NAFTA parties are free to establish the level of protection they deem appropriate to achieve a legitimate objective, which is defined to include sustainable development as well as the protection of human, animal, and plant life and health. They are not obliged to harmonize. This would allow countries to vary in their levels of allowable risk.[50] Parties are prevented from establishing standards that create an unnecessary obstacle to trade (Article 904[4]). But here NAFTA provides stronger protection for disparate standards than its Uruguay Round WTO counterpart, which states that whenever a technical regulation is created for a legitimate objective and is in accordance with relevant international standards, it "shall be rebutably presumed not to create an obstacle to trade."[51] This also represents a departure from the comparable FTA language, which used the term "legitimate domestic objective." This provision may have been added to permit extrajurisdictional protection measures, a subject of controversy under the GATT.[52]

The NAFTA TBT Code also differs from the Uruguay Round TBT Agreement in that it does not contain an express "least-trade-restrictive" requirement. Both the NAFTA TBT Code and the Uruguay Round TBT Agreement differ from the SPS disciplines in that they permit national regulations to be more stringent than international standards without requiring that those standards be justified by scientific evidence. Article 907 uses permissive language: A party "may" take into account available scientific evidence. Again, rule harmonization is strongly encouraged through the use of Article 905, which places a premium on the use of international standards by presuming them to be consistent with the obligations under this chapter.

There have been no dispute settlement panels to date that have considered a challenge to a technical measure that creates an allegedly undue restriction on trade. However, TBTs are a problematic issue on the international trade agenda, and there have been many such concerns that have been the subject of WTO dispute settlement since its inception in 1995. There is an extensive intergovernmental institutional framework supporting the work done in this area. There is thus a significant potential for both the rules and the institutions responsible for implementing those rules to have a strong harmonizing effect.

NAFTA created a ministerial-level Free Trade Commission (FTC), supported by a network of at least thirty-nine different committees, subcommittees, and working groups, many of which are actively involved in the harmonization of technical barriers to trade. Some of these groups have specific environmentally related mandates within the text of NAFTA itself. Others were given permissive mandates to take up environmental concerns if necessary. A recent review of the NAFTA institutions found mixed results across the range of bodies. While virtually all the groups with environmental mandates had begun to take action on the basis of those mandates and have "attained concrete achievements that may have far-reaching effects," other bodies have been less effective in mobilizing environmental mandates.[53] The review further found that there were no cases where "NAFTA's economic bodies have acted on the permissive environmental mandates assigned to them by NAFTA" and further found that "in some areas their mandatory environmental responsibilities, from a political if not a legal standpoint, remain unfulfilled."[54] These groups are critical in working out the "nuts and bolts" differences in various regulations and policies that may have profound environmental implications, such as those in the transportation and agriculture sectors. They work toward harmonization and mutual recognition of standards in order to support the free flow of goods, critical to the deep economic integration process under way in North America.

Concrete environmental accomplishments include a trilateral *Emergency Response Guidebook* for accidents involving dangerous substances, developed by one of the Land Transportation Standards subcommittees in order to reduce accidents with grave environmental consequences. Another related group, the Automotive Standards Council, seeks to harmonize standards applying to automotive products. Its work plan, which has been only partially acted on, provides for examination of vehicle emissions, fuel standards, and engines.

Much like the SPS rules of NAFTA, the TBT rules use a national treatment framework, supplemented by language that encourages rather than obliges the parties to harmonize. Thus, where parties are willing to undertake harmonization efforts, progress has been made in terms of trade facilitation and upward harmonization, which translates into welfare gains for consumers.

The Pollution Haven Provision

One of the prime concerns in the debate leading to the passage of NAFTA was the fear that Mexico would become a "pollution haven," that is, an area that would attract production and investment through a weak environmental regulatory structure. This concern was addressed through Article 1114(2), contained in the rules dealing with investment. It provides that it is "inappropriate to encourage investment by relaxing domestic health, safety or environmental measures." NAFTA rules also provide for a consultation process if one party believes that this provision has been violated. Although there have been concerns to date that environmental laws have not been adequately stringent or enforced in each of the parties' jurisdictions, none of these allegations to date has been linked to an intent to attract investment. It is possible that the existence of a pollution haven provision has served to discourage the relaxation and enforcement of environmental regulations to attract investment on the part of governments.

Despite its effectiveness as a deterrent, this provision will probably not have a strong effect on regulatory diversity.[55] First, the provision sets as a baseline the standards in place at the time of NAFTA's entry into force and accepts them as legitimate.[56] It thus does not contemplate an equalization of standards. Second, it will be difficult to establish that a particular change in regulation or enforcement occurred for the sole reason of encouraging investment.[57] Third, the language "should not" is "weaker than the obligatory language found in most parts of NAFTA. As was already seen in the *UHT Milk* case, any deviation from the strongest expression of obligation may be a basis for viewing a provision as merely a 'best efforts' commitment that is largely nonjusticiable."[58] However, there may be a small rule and process harmonization effect over time because as standards subsequently rise or converge, this provision prevents backslides in the levels of stringency; in other words, change can move only in an upward direction. In this way, Article 1114(2) promotes harmonization.

Dispute Resolution Provisions

NAFTA established a number of dispute settlement mechanisms that serve to enforce both the national treatment and the harmonization provisions throughout the NAFTA text. The creation of a trilateral institution to enforce treaty commitments fall into Leebron's fourth category of harmonization of institutional processes.

Chapter 20

NAFTA Chapter 20 provides for a state-to-state dispute settlement process in the event that any party believes that its rights under NAFTA have been affected. This process was developed to be more environmentally sensitive than its predecessor, Chapter 18 of the FTA. This was done largely in response to the public outcry surrounding the GATT Panel decision in the much publicized *Tuna-Dolphin* case.[59] That panel report (which was not adopted) found the U.S. ban on imports of Mexican tuna caught in a dolphin-unfriendly manner to be inconsistent with U.S. obligations under the GATT. It was against this backdrop that the NAFTA negotiators sought to find a trilateral dispute settlement process that would incorporate environmental sensitivities.[60]

Chapter 20 provides for a three-step process. It begins first with consultations "on any matter that could affect the NAFTA party's rights."[61] Failing resolution of the issue through consultations, a meeting of the three trade ministers (the FTC) can be requested within forty-five days to address the issue.[62] If progress is not made through such meetings, the aggrieved party can initiate proceedings to convene a dispute settlement panel.[63] However, Article 2018 requires parties to agree on a resolution of the issue "which normally shall conform with the determinations and recommendations of the panel." And parties may retaliate where a mutually satisfactory resolution has not been made.

NAFTA makes this process environmentally sensitive in three ways.[64] First, Article 723(6) provides that if an SPS provision is the subject of the dispute, the party challenging the provision bears the burden of establishing the inconsistency. Second, Articles 2014 and 2015 provide rules that allow expert scientific evidence to be considered on any issue that may affect environmental health or safety. This provision allows the Panel to be informed of, and take account of, the environmental implications of a decision. Third, parties to a dispute usually have a choice of forum between NAFTA and the GATT/WTO. NAFTA Article 2005 provides a mechanism by which parties can insist that panels hear the dispute under the environmentally sensitive NAFTA dispute settlement provisions if the dispute concerns the relationship between NAFTA Article 104 and an MEA or concerns an SPS/TBT measure that invokes environmental, health, and safety issues.

Chapter 20 dispute settlement has not been utilized to consider an environmental measure to date. The fact that this provision has not been utilized, however, does not necessarily lead to the conclusion that there are no issues under NAFTA ripe for resolution. In fact, the opposite is true. A review of the issues that were the subject of consultations among the parties, rather than those that reached formal dispute settlement panels, reveals a number of potential environmentally sensitive issues. These include U.S. standards for reformulated gasoline regulations, meat inspection procedures and standards, fish conservation, and recycled content in Canadian-procured U.S. government paper.[65] On the basis of this list, "it would seem clear that Canadian and American trade negotiators deal regularly with matters that raise environmental issues."[66] Thus, there has been an apparent underutilization of NAFTA Chapter 20, the state-to-state dispute settlement mechanism applicable to this issue area. A recent study by the author found that the reasons for this failure were as follows: (1) a lack of direct access on the part of nonstate actors to this dispute settlement mechanisms, unlike those elsewhere in NAFTA; (2) the rules of NAFTA that govern trade-restricting environmental regulation do not have "direct effect"—that is, they create no justiciable rights for affected nonstate actors; (3) the difficulty and unpredictability in the legal tests that discern valid environmental regulation from protectionist environmental regulation; and (4) the fact that the dispute settlement process remains essentially a political process.[67] In a world where governments have limited resources and trade disputes are resource intensive, a government may not be eager to take up the case of an exporter unless it meets some minimum threshold of economic significance or political salience. Such a case may also interfere with a sensitive political agenda with that trading partner that a government may not wish to put at risk for a comparatively minor trade irritant.

The Chapter 20 mechanism thus harmonizes the way in which disputes will be dealt with under NAFTA in an environmentally sensitive manner. An advantage of this type of mechanism is that it is flexible in balancing competing trade and environmental goals. "Judges or panelists do not usually apply trade disciplines strictly, but attempt to weigh trade liberalization objectives against other aims such as environmental protection."[68] Thus, where parties are uncomfortable agreeing to a harmonization model within the context of their substantive treaty commitments, dispute settlement rules can potentially add an environmental sensitivity to a given issue. However, Esty and Gerardin caution against an "exclusive reliance on courts or trade panels to unify markets and, simultaneously, to uphold environmental standards," as trade disputes can only correct a specific obstacle to trade, not prevent them from arising altogether.[69] Therefore, "ultimately, collective action in the form of harmonized product standards appears to be a surer and swifter strategy than selective invalidation of trade-restrictive environmental measures."[70]

Chapter 11

Chapter 11 establishes a dispute settlement mechanism that allows private investors or firms to challenge NAFTA governments directly for breach of investment
provisions, including the NAFTA requirement that host countries compensate investors from NAFTA countries for takings. There has been only one completed case
under Chapter 11 through 2000, although twelve cases had been initiated.[71] Chapter
11 has been the most contentious of the dispute settlement mechanisms, as it has
been used in ways that have been unanticipated by the NAFTA governments, such
as the challenge of a wide range of domestic regulations. Coinciding with the underutilization of Chapter 20 has been the increased use of Chapter 11. Where Chapter
20 failed to provide an effective means by which firms could gain or maintain market access, Chapter 11 is being used in novel ways to do the same. Chapter 11 is
doing what Chapter 20 does not do: It contains justiciable investment obligations
on which private parties (foreign investors) may initiate direct actions against
NAFTA governments. Private parties no longer have to wait for their governments
to decide to bring a challenge on the basis of considerations extraneous to the case at
hand. They may use the NAFTA provisions prohibiting regulatory takings without
compensation to achieve a similar goal.

The Chapter 11 investment provisions have recently become the focal point of
environment-related concern among government, business, and nongovernmental
organizations (NGOs).[72] In seven of the environment-related disputes initiated to
date under Chapter 11, investors have alleged that an environmental regulation or
policy enacted by the government has affected the rights of an investor in such a
way that it constituted a measure tantamount to expropriation—also known as a
"regulatory taking."[73] There is, however, a lack of determinacy in defining what
precisely constitutes a regulatory taking under international law. This lack of determinacy, coupled with a lack of transparency throughout the Chapter 11 process, has
fueled broad-based concern about the wisdom of the Chapter 11 process.[74] How
NAFTA's regulatory takings provisions will be interpreted has thus become a critical
issue where much is at stake. Too expansive a definition could impose potentially
huge financial obligations on governments, create disincentives to enact health and
safety regulation, and introduce multiple distortions and social inefficiencies. On
the other hand, too restrictive a definition would obliterate a key investment guarantee that serves to protect foreign investors and undermine significant domestic and
global welfare gains made possible by the creation of a North American liberalized
investment regime.

Concern over the issue of regulatory takings spilled over into the negotiations
within the Organization for Economic Development (OECD) on the Multilateral
Agreement on Investment (MAI) and was at least partially responsible for their demise. The expropriation provisions of Chapter 11 have formed a major component
of the anti-globalization critique—a debate by no means confined to the desirability
of trade and investment liberalization regimes.[75] Rather, these specific provisions

seem to have catalyzed concern across a range of issues fundamental to liberalized economic markets and institutions, that is, a questioning of the normative value of a capitalist economy, capital mobility in financial markets, deregulation of state enterprise, labor rights, and so on.[76] This concern has been accompanied by corresponding demands to reevaluate the globalization paradigm and its effects on social cohesion and integration. How NAFTA's expropriation provisions operate in practice therefore carry significant importance. It will affect the tenor of this debate and possibly the future of international economic institutions such as NAFTA and the WTO.[77] This is ironic when one considers the history of Chapter 11. As *The Economist* notes, "NAFTA's wide-ranging protection for investors was aimed mainly at Mexico, whose legal system Canadian and American negotiators did not trust.[78] Apparently no one imagined that the text might be wielded by crafty American firms in Canada."[79]

More specifically, NGOs are concerned that national sovereignty is being eroded as the capacity of governments to regulate in sensitive areas such as the environment is thwarted by private party challenges. Opponents of the Chapter 11 provisions believe that it will affect any "law or regulation that impedes or will impede an investor's right to make a profit, [arguing that any] environmental, health or workers' rights legislation that could threaten profits would be interpreted as 'expropriation.' "[80] Otherwise stated, NGOs believe that the Chapter 11 process de facto allows multinationals to set policy and law in ways hitherto unknown in North America. Business interests, on the other hand, have expressed a desire that there be a clear set of objective rules that provide foreign investment protection from the arbitrary actions of foreign governments as well as an effective dispute settlement mechanism in support of those objectives. And each of the NAFTA governments wants to ensure that it is able to regulate without the threat of ongoing lawsuits.

Under NAFTA, the "applicable rules of international law" govern the question of when a regulation becomes compensable to a foreign investor.[81] It is important to note that every regulation can alter the relative costs and opportunities of firms, whether domestic or foreign.[82] Under international law, the majority of takings cases deal with direct expropriation rather than the more subtle cases of expropriation through regulatory measures.[83] The evaluation of whether a particular regulation is indeed tantamount to expropriation lies in the takings jurisprudence in international law, largely informed by U.S. constitutional law.[84] On this issue, the international law jurisprudence provides little guidance, as "there does not . . . appear to be any universally agreed set of principles as to when one government action should fall into one category and another in the other."[85] Howse and Feldman warn that regulation construed to be expropriation "could make regulatory reform extremely costly, but is an interpretation of the meaning of expropriation quite common in the U.S. domestic takings jurisprudence."[86] In the United States, property rights are constitutionally entrenched, and a significant body of case law exists where government has been required to compensate those adversely affected by its regulation.[87] In Canada, however, where property rights are not constitutionally entrenched, the extent of judicial control over government action is far less stringent.[88]

To address these concerns, the governments of Canada, the United States, and Mexico are currently involved in negotiations and have established a number of working groups to research the implications of various interpretations of the regulatory takings provisions.[89] There have been no clear outcomes from these groups among the range of options under consideration. However, a number of civil society groups are calling for a complete removal of the expropriation provisions of NAFTA or blanket exclusions of particular categories of regulation (such as those relating to the environment) from the takings provisions.[90] In response to a consensus developing against these provisions, the Canadian government is pressing strongly for a tightly constrained interpretation of the regulatory takings rules so that it would be almost impossible to find any regulation as a taking.[91] Thus, the ability of governments to regulate would continue unfettered, and "measures tantamount to expropriation"—or regulatory takings—would cease to be grounds by which nonstate actors could challenge government measures.

By harmonizing the rights of nonstate actors to challenge environmental, health, and safety regulation, Chapter 11 has the potential to reduce domestic consumer welfare. Regulation that serves a broad public interest may be sacrificed to augment private investor welfare. Issues concerning environmental regulation would better be dealt with under the provisions of SPS or TBT rules in NAFTA, which would mean that the adjudication of environmental, health, and safety measures would be more appropriately undertaken in the context of the more environmentally sensitive Chapter 20 or the NAFTA institutional structure, as these rules were designed to balance the trade effects of a provision against the public interest concerns.

NAFTA'S ENVIRONMENTAL SIDE AGREEMENT

Probably the most significant achievement of NAFTA, from an environmental standpoint, was the creation of the North American Agreement on Environmental Cooperation (NAAEC), also referred to as NAFTA's environmental side agreement. Created at the urging of environmental groups in the United States, Canada, and Mexico, it is one of the world's most far-reaching environmental cooperation agreements linked to an international trade agreement. It has incorporated extensive harmonization provisions on many levels, but primarily through the creation of trinational institutional processes to manage regional environmental issues. The NAAEC provides an overarching trilateral structure for North American environmental governance that has demonstrated real signs of a strong regulatory harmonization effect. Kirton writes that the rules and institutions created by the NAAEC are "now beginning to have a real impact on environmental activities between and within the United States and Canada, and [are building] a strong rules-based regime that constrains the actions of member governments."[92] This harmonizing effect can be expected to extend beyond North America as trade regimes extend toward Latin America. Thus, the NAAEC will function to "deepe[n] its societal and governmental roots within the three countries, and broade[n] its environmental relevance beyond the North American community to the expanded partnership now being forged with Chile and prospective members of the Free Trade Agreement of the Americas (FTAA)."[93]

The rationale for this strong harmonizing effect can be traced "most broadly to the increasing intensity, severity, and scientific and public recognition of trilateral environmental interdependencies and problems in the North American region during the 1990s."[94] Although such issues were not linked to trade per se, it was believed among environmental nongovernmental organizations (ENGOs) that further trade and investment liberalization would exacerbate these issues.[95] Strong and focused ENGO pressure stalled the passage of NAFTA for two years (1992–94) in order to create the NAAEC to address a range environmental concerns, particularly the environmental regulatory capacity of the Mexican government. One of the most significant effects of NAFTA was the improvement in Mexico's administrative capacity in environmental matters made by the Salinas government at the time of the NAAEC negotiations.[96]

Objectives and Obligations

The NAAEC's preamble and objectives "recognize the interrelationship of the North American environment, express a commitment to the goals of sustainable development and emphasize public participation and transparency."[97] Out of the ten objectives listed in its preamble, nine relate to environmental objectives and one to trade objectives.[98] This reflects the degree to which the NAAEC is really an agreement about regional environmental cooperation rather than trade.[99]

The NAAEC lists a number of obligations relating to domestic environmental law and international cooperation. They do not direct the level of environmental protection that a country is required to set, as that remains under the exclusive jurisdiction of sovereign country. In fact, many of the obligations can be best described as "soft law," as they do not create hard and binding commitments for the parties. For example, in the case of a defined obligation regarding the export of pesticides, the parties are obligated only to "consider" prohibiting the export of pesticides or other toxic substances from its territory. Some of the obligations in the NAAEC are fairly vague, such as the requirement to "promote education in environmental matters." Other obligations are more concrete, such as those that require that parties provide for just and fair access to private remedies on the part of individuals where an environmental law has been allegedly violated and those requiring that parties effectively enforce their environmental laws. This latter provision, and the use of it by NGOs and the NAAEC institutions, has had a far-reaching impact, which will be discussed at greater length shortly. Generally, however, the obligations under NAAEC reflect respect for state sovereignty in the formation and implementation of domestic environmental law. Yet the NAAEC is unique in that it articulates "an interest by all parties not only in environmental policies that may affect them through transboundary impacts, but also in what would normally be considered the purely domestic environmental issues of another state."[100] Thus, while many of the more pure environmental obligations are indeed soft, the procedural obligations concerning openness, transparency, and the enforcement of existing environmental law are less so and are evidence of a powerful harmonization of policy objectives at work, especially when considered in the broader context of the NAAEC institutional arrangements. And although the harmonization language is tempered with substantial national autonomy, there remains a strong convergence effect.

The Commission for Environmental Cooperation

The NAAEC created an institutional structure to implement its objectives. The Commission for Environmental Cooperation (CEC) consists of a ministerial-level council as the governing body; a secretariat that provides technical, administrative, and operational support; and a Joint Public Advisory Committee (JPAC). The CEC's mission statement reads as follows:

> The CEC facilitates cooperation and public participation to foster conservation, protection and enhancement of the North American environment for the benefit of present and future generations, in the context of increasing economic, trade and social links between Canada, Mexico and the United States.

The council is the governing body of the CEC. It is composed of the three environment ministers from the three countries and meets at a minimum of once yearly. The council is responsible for overseeing all the activities of the secretariat, including its budget and annual program. The "overarching responsibility of the Council is to promote and facilitate cooperation between the parties through strategic selection of the Secretariat's workplan, strengthening cooperation on the development and continuing improvement of environmental laws and regulations, and expanding public access to information concerning the environment."[101]

The secretariat is located in Montreal and handles the day-to-day operations of the CEC. It is headed by an executive director who is chosen by the council for a three-year term, which may be renewed once. The secretariat's primary functions are the preparation of an annual report of the CEC, preparation of reports on other matters, and handling submissions on enforcement matters. It has an annual budget of over U.S.$10 million with equal contributions from the three members.

The JPAC is a fifteen-member multistakeholder advisory board responsible for advising the council on any matter within the scope of NAAEC. The JPAC meets once a year in public session at the same time as the regular session of the council. There are additionally national advisory committees (NACs) and governmental advisory committees (GACs) responsible for providing advice on CEC matters.

The CEC has an annual program with a number of projects in such areas as environmental conservation, the protection of human health and environment, enforcement cooperation and law, and information and public outreach. Some argue that the work of these projects has already begun to contribute to enhancement of the quality of the North American environment.[102] Some of the more notable achievements have been the development of a regional action plan aimed at reducing and eliminating the use of pesticides (chlordane and DDT) and the toxic industrial chemicals (PCB), improved environmental enforcement efforts in the tracking of illegal transborder movements of hazardous substances and wastes, the establishment of a North American Pollutants Release Inventory, and the development of the first set of North American eco-maps illustrating the baseline biodiversity of eco-regions. In 1995, the CEC established a North American Fund for Environmental Cooperation (NAFEC) in order to fund community-based projects throughout North America by engaging the "energy and imagination of the people of North America in achieving the goals and the objectives of the NAAEC." The total allocation of the NAFEC in 1996 was $1.6 million. It seeks to fund projects with concrete results at the local level and possibly larger-scale impacts. To date, thirty-five projects have been funded from NAFEC.

Enforcement and Investigation of Environmental Issues

The area of the NAAEC with the highest expectations for results are the provisions that allow it to investigate matters of environmental significance throughout North America. Article 13 of the NAAEC, which allows the secretariat to cast a "roving spotlight" on environmental issues, has been used to complete three reports. The first report concerned the high number of bird deaths at the Silva Reservoir in Mexico but concluded that the Mexican government was not wholly responsible for the problem. A scientific panel was established that resulted in the CEC issuing detailed recommendations of how to deal with the problem, namely, recommendations concerning sewage treatment and industrial waste. Some commentators felt that the final recommendations of council fell short, as they recommended only that the Mexican government conduct a comprehensive evaluation of the problem and propose recommended solutions. Thus, the potential for real improvement was limited by the council because, as the experts' work moved up the institutional hierarchy of the NAAEC, it resulted in only further study and "best efforts."[103] Others have argued that the report had significant political impact in Mexico.[104]

The second report investigated the long-range transport of air pollutants throughout North America. In contrast to the Silva Reservoir report, this report was proactive in nature and helped "establish the technical basis for developing coordinated policy work on air pollution in North America."[105] The third report examined migratory bird resting stops in southern Arizona. Here the CEC acted both reactively and proactively as it began with a specific submission on the part of citizens' groups that eventually formed the basis of a broader study.

Article 14 of the NAAEC permits individuals or ENGOs to submit to the CEC an allegation that a party to NAFTA is failing to effectively enforce its environmental law. The secretariat then decides whether the submission meets the requisite criteria and thus merits a response from the concerned country. The council may order that a factual record be developed. In extreme cases of persistent nonenforcement, the parties may become involved and trade sanctions and monetary penalties may be imposed.

With twenty-three submissions through 2000, this has been the most widely used provision of the NAAEC (see table 6.1). The first submission was filed in 1995 by the Biodiversity Legal Foundation. It alleged that fiscal restraining legislation passed in the United States resulted in an effective failure to adequately enforce the U.S. Endangered Species Act. The CEC did not pursue the complaint, finding that "Articles 14 and 15 of the Agreement were intended to address failures by enforcement agencies or departments, and not inaction mandated by law" and that "the enactment of legislation which specifically alters the operation of pre-

Table 6.1   Registry of Submissions on Article 14/15 Enforcement Matters

Submitters	Date Submission Filed
Biodiversity Legal Foundation et al.	June 30, 1995
Sierra Club et al.	August 30, 1995
Comité para la Protección de los Recursos Naturales, A.C. et al.	January 18, 1996
Aage Tottrup, P. Eng	March 20, 1996
The Friends of the Oldman River	September 9, 1996
The Southwest Center for Biological Diversity et al.	November 14, 1996
Comité por Limpieza del Río Magdalena	March 15, 1997
B.C. Aboriginal Fisheries Commission et al.	April 2, 1997
Centre québécois du droit de l'environnement (CQDE)	April 9, 1997
Canadian Environmental Defence Fund	May 26, 1997
Animal Alliance of Canada et al.	July 21, 1997
The Friends of the Oldman River	October 4, 1997
Instituto de Derecho Ambiental	October 10, 1997
Hector Gregorio Ortiz Martínez	October 14, 1997
Instituto de Derecho Ambiental	January 9, 1998
Department of the Planet Earth et al.	May 27, 1998
Sierra Club of British Columbia et al.	June 29, 1998
Academia Sonorense de Derechos Humanos	July 23, 1998
Grupo Ecológico Manglar, A.C.	October 20, 1998
Environmental Health Coalition et al	October 23, 1998
Methanex Corporation	October 18, 1999
Alliance for the Wild Rockies et al.	November 19, 1999
Rosa María Escalante de Fernández	January 27, 2000

Source: North American Commission for Environmental Cooperation, <www.cec.org> (February 2000).

existing environmental law in essence becomes a part of the greater body of environmental laws and statutes on the books."[106] Thus, in this instance, the obligation to enforce environmental law was limited as it was found that "such an obligation does not extend to a requirement that nonenvironmental legislation not frustrate such enforcement."[107]

In contrast, one of the more publicized cases concerned the failure of the government of Mexico to conduct an adequate environmental review of a project involving the construction of a cruise ship pier in Cozumel, Mexico, that endangered fragile coral reefs in the area. In this case, the council ordered that a factual record be established. It was subsequently released to the public, stalling the building of the pier.

While none of these cases has resulted in formal actions against NAFTA parties (leading to criticisms that the CEC has failed in its role as an environmental enforcer), Kirton and Audley argue that to label the process as a failure would be misleading. They find an overall positive contribution, as the CEC is an "institution dedicated to enhancing regulatory compliance and enforcement of environmental laws through cooperative means, rather than sanctioning mechanisms."[108] In addition, the enforcement processes have heightened public awareness on critical environmental issues and thus served as a deterrent to potential violators.

Yet since its inception, the CEC has been criticized as being a toothless ineffectual organization with little potential to create any positive environmental impacts.[109] Some groups argue that the CEC has done little to counteract worsening environmental conditions during the five years of NAFTA's existence.[110] Such criticism fails to take account of the significance of the fact that citizens are able to challenge environmental enforcement activities within North America, a power that has never before been available. However, given the mandate of the CEC, which is focused more on regime building than actual microenvironmental change, its work has arguably been a success over its first five years. It has been crucial in developing a political and institutional landscape where concrete, albeit incremental, environmental change can take place. Most important, however, and probably the point most neglected because of political sensitivities, is that through cooperation and shared technical expertise, the operation of the CEC and the implicit threat of the application of the NAAEC rules have helped significantly in bringing Mexican environmental protection up to a level more comparable to Canada and the United States.

Thus, while the actual harmonizing effect has been minimal in terms of substantive environmental law, the application of the NAAEC enforcement rules has likely had a political and institutional impact. While it seems that there is further scope for enhanced social welfare through more meaningful environmental enhancing policy action, the NAAEC has been useful at building "understanding between domestic regulators and a transnational network of NGOs regulators [which] has been enabled through these institutions, which may eventually lead to the knowledge and trust required for more concrete steps toward more ambitious regulatory co-operation."[111]

NAFTA-INSPIRED BILATERAL INSTITUTIONS:
THE BECC AND THE NADBANK

Two related institutions were created at the same time as NAFTA but established through separate agreements to deal with critical and highly politically charged environmental issues on the U.S.-Mexico border. Here the harmonization of institutional structures and policies was arguably needed to deal with spillover environmental problems and externalities. Rules adopted by one jurisdiction can result in costs imposed on other jurisdictions. In the border area, the domestic activity on each side of the border has imposed costs on each respective transborder neighbor. Thus, the lack of an effective coordinated regulatory and policy regime to address such problems has resulted in serious environmental degradation. The institutions created to address border environmental issues were born primarily of the concern that increased trade resulting from liberalization would place even more environmental stress on the region. In this instance, harmonization of policy goals and institutions should have proven to be very effective in attacking very serious environmental issues.

The U.S.-Mexico border area is particularly vulnerable to transborder spillovers, as cities on both side use common basins and aquifers, air sheds, and ecosystems, leading one report to conclude that "events on one side of the border affect the other side almost equally."[112] Given this ecological interdependence, the report noted the following:[113]

- More than 32 million tons of toxic waste are produced annually by 150 industrial facilities in the border region.
- There are 460 endangered species in the border region.
- The New River, which flows across the border near Calexico, California, has been labeled the most polluted river in the United States, carrying more than 280 million gallons a day of industrial waste and sewage. The New River is a major contributor to poor regional health: Fifteen viruses, including hepatitis, polio, cholera, and typhoid, have been identified in its waters.
- Air quality in many border communities often falls far below U.S. federal standards. Many border area residents are exposed to health-threatening levels of air pollutants, including ozone, particulate matter, carbon monoxide, and sulfur dioxide.

The Border Environment Cooperation Commission (BECC), located in Ciudad Juarez, Mexico, is charged with facilitating the development of environmental projects within 100 kilometers of the U.S.-Mexican border. It is a joint U.S.-Mexican organization that attempts to help states, localities, and the private sector develop and find financing for environmental infrastructure projects, primarily water and solid waste initiatives. "The primary roles of the BECC are to provide technical assistance to border communities and to certify environmental infrastructure projects in the border region for financing consideration by the NADBank and other sources."[114]

The BECC's sister institution, the North American Development Bank (NAD-Bank), is located in San Antonio, Texas, and is responsible for assistance in the financing of BECC approved projects. The NADBank also provides financial and managerial advice to applicants. Authorized capital for the NADBank is U.S.$3 billion, and 90 percent of the NADBank funds are designated for U.S.-Mexico border infrastructure projects. The remainder is allocated to finance community adjustment and investment projects.

Through 2000, BECC has certified and assisted in the implementation of twenty-seven border infrastructure projects, with a combined estimated cost of almost $625.6 million, to the benefit of almost seven million border residents.[115] Fifteen of these projects are located in the United States and twelve in Mexico. The BECC-NADBank projects have included the construction of a $24.8 million water treatment facility in Brawley, California; a $4.1 million project to improve the wastewater system in Mercedes, Texas; a $830,000 water supply and wastewater treatment facility in Naco, Sonora; and a number of municipal solid waste treatment facilities in Sonora.[116] The NADBank has approved $108.9 million in loans, guaranties, and/ or grant resources to over fourteen infrastructure projects as of March 1999, representing a total investment of $408.5 million.[117]

One criticism leveled at the BECC is that its process is not transparent and that there has been a lack public outreach. Despite the fact that "public comments have been routinely solicited and the BECC has established a level of openness to public comment and participation in certification decisions that is unusual among public entities . . . activists have charged that community participation has been hampered by failure to provide documents to the public sufficiently in advance of meetings."[118] This has led to the observation that "non-governmental organizations still need to be convinced that the BECC will in fact fully consider public views."[119] In some respects the larger problem stems from the fact that the BECC operates within parameters and an environment that create an inherent conflict between moving promptly to certify worthy projects and avoiding situations where speedy consideration deprives the public of a meaningful opportunity to participate in the process.[120] For such a harmonization of institutional processes to be successful, public participation is crucial. Public institutions, such as the BECC, must be responsive to the constituencies, communities, interests, and concerns that it was created to protect. The BECC has responded to this concern, and there have been initiatives outside the BECC institutional framework itself that have allowed for greater public participation. And the BECC has been open to these new ideas and modes of communication.[121] However, this must be balanced against the possibility that the BECC become overly sensitive to *every* interest group.

Others are critical of the BECC because of its limited mandate, which restricts it to projects that clean up waterways, sewage, and solid waste within 100 kilometers on both sides of the border.[122] Critics go as far as saying that the BECC and the

NADBank are a drop in the bucket. They are not going to solve all the border pollution problems—maybe one-half of 1 percent, such air pollution that is caused by the "swelling numbers of cars, tractor trailers waiting in incredibly long lines . . . [and] a host of threats to area species and their habitats."[123] It is true that the emphasis on waterways, sewage, and solid waste do not address all the border pollution problems. However, the BECC is not the only institution capable of addressing the environmental related border problems. For critics to hold the BECC responsible for dealing with all issues of border pollution is unrealistic. Furthermore, the BECC coexists and complements other institutions and mechanisms where these specific concerns can be addressed. For example, the Border XXI Program is a comprehensive plan of action agreed to by the United States and Mexico to address a multitude of border issues relating to the environment.

There have been a number of criticisms of the NADBank in operation. First, it has been slow to release funds and certify projects. Second, the rates on NADBank loans are above market, and cheaper funds can often be found elsewhere. Third, the NADBank has a cumbersome application process, "especially for many small towns unaccustomed to planning large-scale infrastructure projects."[124] Fourth, projects are limited by the requirement that they "generate sufficient revenues, by user fees otherwise, to be self-sustaining, or that funds will be available from other sources to meet debt servicing obligations."[125] While the NADBank has responded to many of these concerns and has introduced a number of initiatives to deal with these shortcomings,[126] the NADBank had approved only $108.9 million in loans by 2000, despite $3 billion in authorized capital.

The BECC and the NADBank harmonized institutional processes to deal with issues of environmental concern. They are not environmentally related trade instruments but rather are better characterized as bilateral environmental agreements adopted as a result of general concerns about the impact of liberalized trade. The public perception that these institutions have failed to meet their mandates is unwarranted. Although there is room for improvement, the creation and operation of the BECC and NADBank have resulted in fundamental and positive transformations in how environmental issues are handled in the border region.[127] The nascent years of the BECC and NADBank have been focused on capacity building: the incorporation of sustainable development principles into environmental infrastructure development, increased public participation, and the democratization of decision making. There are continual challenges facing the organizations, such as limited private-sector participation and limited community resources and overall capabilities. With that foundation in place, the BECC and the NADBank are thus expected to deliver more concrete results.

CONCLUSION

This chapter has found that NAFTA has incorporated elements of both national treatment and harmonization as a means to handle the trade and environment interface. In general, NAFTA uses national treatment as a primary response and harmonization as a secondary response to trade and environment issues. There may be room for additional welfare gains from trade to be made from further harmonization. While an attractive proposition, this is probably unlikely, as the parties to NAFTA did not seek to achieve the "deep level of economic integration envisioned by the EC."[128] Moreover, deeper or more substantive harmonization with Mexico may resurface fears that U.S. and Canadian environmental protection would be compromised.[129]

This chapter found that while substantial autonomy remains with each national government to regulate the environment, there are many areas in which NAFTA has advanced a harmonization agenda. Rule harmonization, the substantive harmonization of specific environmental rules (as per Leebron's first category), is generally of a voluntary and cooperative nature only within NAFTA. Here harmonization has been effected through NAFTA's committees, subcommittees, and working groups. These NAFTA institutions are working on an issue-by-issue basis through the types of standards and regulations that inhibit trade. Harmonization from these groups has been generally welfare enhancing. The work of the Working Group on Pesticides provides an apt example. It has increased global and domestic welfare in two ways. First, it has made considerable progress in managing and working through trade irritants, thereby allowing trade in agricultural products to expand within North America. Second, it has worked to bring Mexican pesticide regulation and capacity to manage such regulation up to the levels of Canada and the United States. It is important for regulators to be mindful of the fact that, in the case of the harmonization of environmental regulation and standards, the burden often falls most heavily on Mexico. It is also important to remain cognizant of the trade-offs involved when making the decision to harmonize, as there certainly will be instances where less extreme tools than harmonization may be appropriate.

NAFTA has facilitated extensive institutional harmonization (Leebron's fourth category). There has been a strong harmonization of the institutional structure of regional environmental management, as evidenced through the NAAEC, the CEC, the BECC, and the NADBank. While real, concrete environmental achievements may be less impressive than was originally hoped by the groups who most heavily lobbied for those institutions, there has been substantial harmonization in an upward direction of various management and cooperation processes that have laid important groundwork for further achievements.

Less successful has been the use of the national treatment model in Chapters 7 and 9 of NAFTA, intended to discipline trade-restricting environmental regulation. Here there has been a mixture of national treatment and process harmonization. Although the Chapter 20 process was amended to be sensitive to environmental concerns, access to the use of such mechanisms is restricted to national governments that have not used them since the inception of NAFTA, despite the often severe welfare losses that stem from the many trade-restricting environmental regulations that currently exist, with little or no social welfare justifications. This is not a fault of the national treatment model itself but rather that of the process, as the nongovernment actors who are affected most by the trade-restricting regulation are not free to directly initiate litigation. Where parties are able to directly initiate litigation, as in Chapter 11, environmental regulations that have affected foreign investment have been increasingly challenged. While few Chapter 11 cases have yet completed the dispute settlement process, the nontransparent nature of the process is problematic and could potentially result in a chilling effect on environmental regulation and thus a decrease in social welfare.

NOTES

The author gratefully acknowledges the financial support of the SSHRC Strategic Themes Research Grant on Globalization and Social Cohesion and the Olin Fellowship in Law and Economics. I am grateful for the guidance of Michael Trebilcock and John Kirton of the University of Toronto and Robert Howse of the University of Michigan. Excellent research assistance was provided by Peter Vinh Nguyen.

1. Alan M. Rugman and Julie A. Soloway, "An Environmental Agenda for APEC: Lessons from NAFTA," *The International Executive,* 39, no. 6 (1997): 735–44. See also Alan M. Rugman, John Kirton, and Julie A. Soloway, *Environmental Regulation and Corporate Strategy: A NAFTA Perspective* (Oxford: Oxford University Press, 1999), and J. O. Saunders, "NAFTA and the North American Agreement on Environmental Cooperation: A New Model for International Collaboration on Trade and the Environment," *Colorado Journal of International Environmental Law and Policy* 5, no. 2 (1994): 273–304, also in Alan M. Rugman and John Kirton, eds., with Julie A. Soloway, *Trade and the Environment: Economic, Legal and Policy Perspectives* (Cheltenham: Edward Elgar, 1998).

2. John Kirton, "NAFTA's Trade-Environment Institutions: Regional Impact, Hemispheric Potential" (paper presented at the Conference of International Studies Association and the Mexican Association of International Studies, Manzanillo, Mexico, December 11–13, 1997).

3. Robert Howse and Michael Trebilcock, "The Myth of NAFTA's Regulatory Power: Rethinking Regionalism as a Vehicle for Deep Economic Integration," in G. B. Doern et al., eds., *Changing the Rules: Canadian Regulatory Regimes and Institutions* (Toronto: University of Toronto Press, 1999), 336–60.

4. For example, suppose that country A is a large producer of lawn mowers and would like to protect its market from cheaper, foreign-made imports. Standards relating to the lawn mower's maximum allowable noise level in decibels differ from standards that mandate exact technological specifications of how that lawn mower must achieve the reduced noise level. And suppose that country A drafted such regulations that applied equally to both foreign and domestic producers. One could imagine a situation where those regulations would, in fact, favor a specific domestically patented technology in noise reduction, thereby favoring its own producers.

5. David Leebron, "Lying Down with Procrustes: An Analysis of Harmonization Claims," in Jagdish Bhagwati and Robert Hudec, eds., *Fair Trade and Harmonization: Prerequisites for Free Trade?* vol. 1 (41–118) (Cambridge: MIT Press, 1996). Far more complex classifications of harmonization can be devised; see Daniel C. Esty and Damien Gerardin,

"Market Access, Competitiveness and Harmonization: Environmental Protection in Regional Trade Agreements," *Harvard Environmental Law Review* 21, no. 2 (1997): 265.

6. Ibid., 44.

7. Ibid., 45.

8. Ibid., 46.

9. For a full discussion on this point, see ibid.

10. Howse and Trebilcock, "The Myth of NAFTA's Regulatory Power," 38.

11. Leebron, "Lying Down with Procrustes."

12. Michael J. Trebilcock and Robert Howse, "Trade Liberalization and Regulatory Diversity: Reconciling Competitive Markets with Competitive Politics," *European Journal of Law and Economics* 6 (1998): 5.

13. Ibid.

14. Michael J. Trebilcock and Robert Howse, *The Regulation of International Trade*, 2nd ed. (London: Routledge, 1999).

15. Richard Steinberg, "Trade-Environment Negotiations in the EU, NAFTA and WTO: Regional Trajectories of Rule Development," *American Journal of International Law* 9, no. 2 (1997): 231.

16. Raymond B. Ludwiszewski and Peter E. Seley, "Reconciling Free Trade and Environmental Protection," in Seymour J. Rubin and Dean C. Alexander, eds., *NAFTA and the Environment* (1–24) (The Hague: Kluwer Law International, 1996).

17. John J. Audley, *Green Politics and Global Trade: NAFTA and the Future of Environmental Politics* (Washington, D.C.: Georgetown University Press, 1997), 115.

18. See "United States—Import Prohibition of Certain Shrimp and Shrimp Products" (Report of the WTO Appellate Body, AB-1998–4, 1998).

19. Convention on International Trade in Endangered Species of Wild Fauna and Flora, March 3, 1973, 993 U.N.T.S. 243.

20. Montreal Protocol on Substances That Deplete the Ozone Layer, September 16, 1987, 28 I.L.M. 657 (amended June 29, 1990).

21. Basel Convention on Transboundary Movements of Hazardous Waste and Their Disposal, March 20–22, 1989, 28 I.L.M. 657. The United States has not ratified this agreement, although both Canada and Mexico have ratified it.

22. The Agreement between the United States of America and the United Mexican States on Cooperation for the Protection and Improvement in the Border Area, La Paz, Baja California Sur, August 14, 1983.

23. Howse and Trebilcock, "The Myth of NAFTA's Regulatory Power," 341.

24. Robert Howse and Michael J. Trebilcock, "The Fair Trade–Free Trade Debate: Trade, Labour and the Environment," *International Review of Law and Economics* 16 (1996): 61–79.

25. Convention on Biological Diversity, June 5, 1992, Can. T.S. 1993 No. 24.

26. United Nations Framework Convention on Climate Change, May 9, 1992, U.N.T.S. 1771/107, Can. T.S. 1994 No. 7 (entered into force in Canada, May 21, 1994).

27. Audley, *Green Politics and Global Trade,* 116.

28. Ibid.

29. Howse and Trebilcock, "The Myth of NAFTA's Regulatory Power," 342.

30. See NAFTA Article 724 for a full definition.

31. For detailed case studies of SPS trade irritants, see Alan M. Rugman et al., "An Environmental Agenda for APEC."

32. Jon R. Johnson, *The North American Free Trade Agreement: A Comprehensive Guide* (Aurora, Ont.: Canada Law Book, 1994), 238.

33. "EC Measures concerning Meat and Meat Products (Hormones)" (Report of the Appellate Body, AB-1997–4, 1998).

34. Michael I. Jeffrey, "The Legal Framework for Environmental Regulation," in Seymour J. Rubin and Dean C. Alexander, eds., *NAFTA and the Environment* (The Hague: Kluwer Law International, 1996), 214.

35. Commission for Environmental Cooperation, *NAFTA's Institutions: The Environmental Potential and Performance of the NAFTA Free Trade Commission and Related Bodies,* Environment and Trade series 5 (Montreal: Commission for Environmental Cooperation, 1997), 37.

36. <http://www.epa.gov/oppfead1/international/naftatwg/>.

37. Ibid.

38. Ibid.

39. Commission for Environmental Cooperation, *NAFTA's Institutions.*

40. Ludwiszewski and Seley, "Reconciling Free Trade and Environmental Protection," 7. See also Rugman et al., "An Environmental Agenda for APEC."

41. In the Matter of: Puerto Rico Regulations on the Import, Distribution and Sale of U.H.T. Milk from Quebec, USA-93-1807-01, June 3, 1993. Ultra-high-temperature (UHT) milk is produced by heating milk to 138 degrees Celsius for a minimum of two seconds. The milk is then cooled and packaged in hermetically sealed boxes. UHT milk has a shelf life of between six and twelve months at room temperature.

42. D. Orden and E. Romano, "The Avocado Dispute and Other Technical Barriers to Agricultural Trade under NAFTA" (paper presented at the conference "NAFTA and Agriculture: Is the Experiment Working?" San Antonio, Texas, November 1996).

43. Ibid., 34.

44. Ibid.

45. Commission for Environmental Cooperation, *NAFTA's Institutions.*

46. Julie A. Soloway, "Institutional Capacity to Constrain Suboptimal Welfare Outcomes from Trade-Restricting Environmental, Health and Safety Regulation under NAFTA" (S.J.D. thesis, University of Toronto, 2000).

47. Alan M. Rugman and Julie A. Soloway, "Corporate Strategy and NAFTA When Environmental Regulations Are Barriers to Trade," *Journal of Transnational Management Development,* 3 (1997): 231.

48. For an elaboration of those institutional developments in the context of NAFTA, see Soloway, "Institutional Capacity to Constrain Suboptimal Welfare Outcomes from Trade-Restricting Environmental, Health and Safety Regulation under NAFTA."

49. This was due to the fact that the agreements were negotiated virtually at the same time with many less powerful nations in the case of NAFTA and perhaps by the same individuals. For example, the same Canadian government negotiators responsible for the SPS Agreement under the WTO were at the table for NAFTA's SPS provisions. See John Kirton and Julie A. Soloway, "Assessing NAFTA's Environmental Effects: Dimensions of a Framework and the NAFTA Regime," Trade and Environment Working Paper Series No. 1 (Montreal: North American Commission for Environmental Cooperation, 1996).

50. Johnson, *The North American Free Trade Agreement,* 245.

51. TBT Agreement, Article 2.5. See also Johnson, *The North American Free Trade Agreement,* 246.

52. "United States—Restrictions on Imports of Tuna" (complaint by Mexico) 39th Suppl. (1991–1992) BISD 155 (1991).

53. Commission for Environmental Cooperation, *NAFTA's Institutions.*

54. Ibid.

55. Howse and Trebilcock, "The Myth of NAFTA's Regulatory Power," 342.

56. Ibid.

57. Ibid.

58. Ibid.

59. "United States—Restrictions on Imports of Tuna."

60. Ludwiszewski and Seley,"Reconciling Free Trade and Environmental Protection," 8.

61. NAFTA Article 2006(1) and ibid.

62. NAFTA Article 2007(4) and Ludwiszewski and Seley, "Reconciling Free Trade and Environmental Protection," 8.

63. NAFTA Article 2008(1).

64. As discussed in Ludwiszewski and Seley, "Reconciling Free Trade and Environmental Protection," 9–10.

65. Commission for Environmental Cooperation, *Dispute Avoidance: Weighing the Values of Trade and the Environment under the NAFTA and the NAAEC.* Environment and Trade series 3 (Montreal: Commission for Environmental Cooperation, 1996).

66. Ibid., 12.

67. See Soloway, "Institutional Capacity to Constrain Suboptimal Welfare Outcomes from Trade-Restricting Environmental, Health and Safety Regulation under NAFTA."

68. Esty and Gerardin, "Market Access, Competitiveness and Harmonization," 280.

69. Ibid.

70. Ibid.

71. For details of these cases, see Julie A. Soloway, "Environmental Regulation as Expropriation: The Case of NAFTA's Chapter 11," *Canadian Business Law Journal* 33 (February 2000): 92, and "NAFTA's Chapter 11: The Challenge of Private Party Participation," *Journal of International Arbitration* 16, no. 2 (1999): 1.

72. For a populist overview of the NGO point of view, see Tony Clarke and Maude Barlow, *MAI: The Multilateral Agreement on Investment and the Threat to Canadian Sovereignty* (Toronto: Stoddart Publishing, 1997), and *MAI Round 2: New Global and Internal Threats to Canadian Sovereignty* (Toronto: Stoddart Publishing, 1998); see also Stephen Kobrin, "The MAI and the Clash of Globalizations," *Foreign Policy* 112 (fall 1998): 97–109, and Michelle Sforza, Scott Nova, and Mark Weisbrot, "Writing the Constitution of a Single Global Economy: A Concise Guide to the Multilateral Agreement on Investment: Supporters' and Opponents' Views" (available at <http://www.preamble.org/MAI/maioverv.html>, 1999).

73. There is no one complete public data set on NAFTA Chapter 11 dispute settlement. Neither the filed briefs nor the tribunal decisions are required to be made public. More recently, in an effort to increase transparency of the Chapter 11 process, the government of Canada has been more forthcoming and has made a number of briefs filed against it available to the public. In this way statements regarding the totality of claims can be viewed as qualified. See generally Rugman et al., "An Environmental Agenda for APEC."

74. See Dani Rodrik, *Has Globalization Gone Too Far?* (Washington, D.C.: Institute for International Economics, 1997). For an insightful perspective on globalization and risk regu-

lation, see Robert Howse, "Democracy, Science and Free Trade: Risk Regulation on Trial at the World Trade Organization" (presented at Harvard Law School, spring 1999). For a critique of the NGO attack on the Multilateral Agreement on Investment, see Alan M. Rugman, "Negotiating Multilateral Rules to Promote Investment," in Michael R. Hodges, John J. Kirton, and Joseph P. Daniels, eds., *The G8's Role in the New Millennium* (143–57) (Aldershot: Ashgate, 1999).

75. Stephen J. Kobrin, "The MAI and the Clash of Globalizations," *Foreign Policy* 112 (fall 1998): 97–109.

76. See the entire issue titled "It's the Global Economy, Stupid: The Corporatization of the World," *The Nation*, July 15, 1996, and the Inside Globalization section of *Monetary Reform* (fall/winter 1998–99).

77. Forty-two percent of Canada's GDP is derived from exports. See John Kirton, "NAFTA Foreign Direct Investment and Economic Integration: A Canadian Approach," in Organization for Economic Cooperation and Development, *Migration, Free Trade and Regional Integration in North America*, OECD Proceedings (181–94) (Paris: OECD).

78. "NAFTA—The Sting in Trade's Tail," *The Economist*, April 18, 1998, 70.

79. Ibid.

80. Kobrin, "The MAI and the Clash of Globalizations."

81. NAFTA Article 1131.

82. David Vogel and Alan M. Rugman, "Environmentally Related Trade Disputes between the United States and Canada," *American Review of Canadian Studies* 27, no. 2 (1997): 271–92.

83. See Johnson, *The North American Free Trade Agreement*.

84. See ibid. and Edward M. Graham, "Regulatory Takings, Supernational Treatment and the Multilateral Agreement on Investment: Issues Raised by Nongovernmental Organizations," *Cornell International Law Journal* 31 (1998): 3, and David Schneiderman, "NAFTA's Takings Rules: American Constitutionalism Comes to Canada," *University of Toronto Law Journal*, 46 (1996): 499, at note 11.

85. Evan Atwood and Michael J. Trebilcock, "Public Accountability in an Age of Contracting Out," *Canadian Business Law Journal* 27, no. 1 (1996): 45.

86. Robert Howse and Jonathan Feldman, "A Brief Analysis of the MAI," *Canada Watch* 6, no. 2 (March 1998). See also Graham, "Regulatory Takings, Supernational Treatment and the Multilateral Agreement on Investment."

87. See Richard Epstein, *Takings: Private Property and the Power of Eminent Domain* (Chicago: University of Chicago Press, 1985). See also Graham, "Regulatory Takings, Supernational Treatment and the Multilateral Agreement on Investment."

88. See Johnson, *The North American Free Trade Agreement*.

89. See Nihal Sherif, "Canada Seeks to Limit Investor-State Provisions in NAFTA Review," *Inside U.S. Trade* 16, no. 50 (December 18, 1998): 1–3; "Canadian, Mexican Ministers Differ on Investor-State Clause," *Americas Trade* 6, no. 4 (February 25, 1999): 3; and "Administration Split on Changes to NAFTA Investor-State Provisions," *Inside U.S. Trade* 17, no. 2 (January 15, 1999) 1–2.

90. See Clarke and Barlow, *MAI* and *MAI Round 2*.

91. Ibid.

92. John Kirton, "The Commission for Environmental Cooperation and Canada-U.S. Environmental Governance in the NAFTA Era," *American Review of Canadian Studies* 27(3) (autumn 1997): 459–86, 461.

93. Ibid.

94. Ibid.

95. Kirton and Soloway, "Assessing NAFTA's Environmental Effects."

96. Steinberg, "Trade-Environment Negotiations in the EU, NAFTA and WTO."

97. John J. Kirton and John J. Audley, "NAFTA's Commission for Environmental Co-operation: North American Performance, Hemispheric Promise" (paper prepared for a publication of the National Wildlife Federation, Washington, D.C., 1997), 1.

98. The NAAEC Objectives are to (1) foster the protection and improvement of the environment in the territories of the parties for the well-being of present and future generations; (2) promote sustainable development based on cooperation and mutually supportive environmental and economic policies; (3) increase cooperation between the parties to better conserve, protect, and enhance the environment, including wild flora and fauna; (4) support the environmental goals and objectives of the NAFTA; (5) avoid creating trade distortions or new trade barriers; (6) strengthen cooperation on the development and improvement of environmental laws, regulations, procedures, policies, and practices; (7) enhance compliance with, and enforcement of, environmental laws and regulations; (8) promote transparency and public participation in the development of environmental laws, regulations, and policies; (9) promote economically efficient and effective environmental measures; and (10) promote pollution prevention policies and practices.

99. Saunders, "NAFTA and the North American Agreement on Environmental Cooperation."

100. Ibid., 289.

101. Kirton and Audley, "NAFTA's Commission for Environmental Cooperation."

102. Ibid.

103. See "Four Year Review of the North American Agreement on Environmental Cooperation" (Report of the Independent Review Committee, June 1998).

104. Ibid.

105. Ibid., sec. 3.3.2.

106. Secretariat's Determination under Article 14(2) (September 21, 1995).

107. Howse and Trebilcock, "The Myth of NAFTA's Regulatory Power."

108. Kirton and Audley, "NAFTA's Commission for Environmental Cooperation," 2.

109. Public Citizen. *NAFTA's Broken Promises* (Washington, D.C.: Public Citizen, 1995).

110. Economic Policy Institute. *The Failed Experiment: NAFTA at Three Years* (Washington, D.C.: Economic Policy Institute, 1997) (available at <http://www.epn.org/epi>).

111. Howse, "Democracy, Science and Free Trade," 345.

112. U.S.-Mexico Chamber of Commerce, "Border Issues: Some Basic Facts" (available at <http://www.usmcoc.org/border1.html>).

113. Ibid.

114. BECC and NADBank, "Joint Status Report" (1999), 3.

115. Ibid.

116. The White House, *Study on the Operation and Effect of the North American Free Trade Agreement* (report submitted to Congress by President William J. Clinton, July 1997).

117. BECC and NADBank, "Joint Status Report."

118. D. Gantz, "The North American Development Bank and the Border Environment Cooperation Commission: A New Approach to Pollution Abatement along the United States–Mexican Border," *Law & Policy in International Business* 27 (1996): 1027, 1047.

119. Ibid., 1051.

120. Ibid., 1052.

121. See the discussion of the BECCnet in S. E. Gaines, "Bridges to a Better Environment: Building Cross-Border Institutions from Environmental Improvement in the U.S.-Mexico Border Area," *Arizona Journal of International and Comparative Law* 12 (1995): 429, 460–61; Gantz, "The North American Development Bank and the Border Environment Cooperation Commission," 1045–46; and N. Mikulas, "An Innovative Twist on Free Trade and International Environmental Treaty Enforcements: Checking in on NAFTA's Seven-Year Supervision of the U.S.-Mexico Border Pollution Problems," *Tulane Environmental Law Journal* 12 (1999): 497, 510–11.

122. D. S. Perwin, "Maquila Problems and Governmental Solutions BECC and NAD-Bank: Can They Stop the Destruction?" (1997) 23 *Thurgood Marshall Law Review* 23 (1997): 195 225, citing A. Wheat, "Troubled NAFTA Waters," *Multinational Monitor* 17, no. 4 (April 1, 1996) (available in WL 13094200).

123. Ibid., 225–26.

124. Jacqueline McFadden, "NAFTA Supplemental Agreements: Four Year Review," Institute for International Economics Working Paper Series No. 98–4, 10.

125. The NADBank Chapter, Chapter II: North American Development Bank, Article 3, Section 6:2(2).

126. McFadden, "NAFTA Supplemental Agreements."

127. Mark Spalding and John Audley, "Promising Potential for the US-Mexico Border and for the Future: An Assessment of the BECC/NADBank Institutions" (report issued as a result of meetings between the authors and those involved in the BECC and NADBank activities, 1997) (available at <mspalding@ucsd.edu>, 3).

128. Esty and Gerardin, "Market Access, Competitiveness and Harmonization," 319.

129. Ibid.

7

The Free Trade Area of the Americas: Lessons from North America

Sanford E. Gaines

In 1994, a decade of vigorous bipartisan U.S. policy to liberalize trade swelled in a crescendo of activity. On January 1, the North American Free Trade Agreement[1] (NAFTA) came into effect, liberalizing trade with two of the United States' largest trading partners. In April, the U.S. trade representative and the vice president traveled to Marrakesh to sign the multilateral trade-liberalizing agreements of the Uruguay Round.[2] In November, the United States persuaded the heads of state of the Asia Pacific Economic Cooperation (APEC) group to commit to a schedule for negotiating freer trade arrangements in Asia and the Pacific.[3] In early December, the Clinton administration secured congressional approval of the Uruguay Round agreements;[4] the new, more powerful World Trade Organization (WTO) was set to come into being on January 1, 1995. Riding this wave of market-opening initiatives, the Clinton administration also orchestrated the Summit of the Americas, held in Miami in December 1994, the centerpiece of which was a hemispheric commitment to "begin immediately to construct a Free Trade Area of the Americas."[5]

Although there was little official consideration of trade and environment at Miami, U.S. trade policy during this active period had already incorporated attention to the environmental implications of international trade rules. NAFTA set important precedents by including some novel environmental clauses and two side agreements on environmental issues addressing broader concerns.[6] In other forums, the United States touted NAFTA as a model for addressing environmental considerations in future trade agreements. Multilaterally, the United States secured some late

189

environmental provisions similar to NAFTA's in the Uruguay Round agreements,[7] and it worked actively in the Organization for Economic Cooperation and Development (OECD) on a trade-environment policy declaration that affirmed the value of policy integration.[8] With respect to the Free Trade Area of the Americas (FTAA), it was expected in 1994 that the first step would be Chile's accession to NAFTA itself, including the environmental side agreements, and Chile had already begun to consult with NAFTA governments about its environmental programs in anticipation of the negotiations.[9] The Clinton administration also included authority to negotiate on environmental issues in its 1994 draft of legislation for renewed authority from Congress to negotiate trade liberalization under "fast-track" approval procedures.[10]

In the seven years since Miami, the Western Hemisphere nations have pursued their resolution to "construct" an FTAA. They have held periodic meetings of trade ministers and have worked diligently through various committees to lay the technical foundations for FTAA negotiations.[11] At the Santiago summit in April 1998, the hemisphere's heads of state agreed to open formal talks in September 1998, pledged "concrete progress" toward an FTAA by end of 2000, and reaffirmed the Miami target date of 2005 for a final agreement.[12] A November 1999 meeting of trade ministers in Toronto agreed to come up with a draft treaty by the spring of 2001, with negotiations to "take into account" the need to "better protect the environment."[13] In January 2001, a heavily bracketed FTAA negotiating text was completed in advance of trade ministerial and summit meetings in March and April 2001. The hemispheric leaders agreed in Quebec to make this bracketed text publicly available, which they did on July 3, 2001.[14] The FTAA remains a core element of U.S. foreign policy toward Latin America.[15]

It has not been consistently obvious that the countries of the hemisphere would sustain the initiative for the FTAA.[16] A key missing ingredient has been clear authority for the U.S. administration to negotiate significant trade agreements.[17] What in 1994 seemed would be a brief hiatus in the president's congressionally delegated authority to negotiate trade-liberalizing agreements dragged on into an extended altercation within the political parties and between the president and the Congress over the fundamental objectives of U.S. trade policy.[18] A focal point of the domestic debate has been the question of what connection, if any, to make between the core trade-liberalizing elements of a free trade agreement and policies directed to the protection of the environment.[19] President George W. Bush has pledged to conclude the FTAA and has asked Congress for "trade promotion" authority, but it remains unclear in mid-2001 how the administration itself, much less a fractured Congress, will address the trade-environment linkage.

The kaleidoscope of political relationships that allowed specific trade-environment links to be forged in NAFTA began to shift even before the Miami summit. In the fall of 1994, President Clinton dropped his request for new negotiating authority to avoid a fight over the trade-environment issue during the approval of the Uruguay Round.[20] The trade politics that emerged since then portend a different but as yet undefined trade-environment linkage for the FTAA. On one side, most

U.S. environmentalists seem to have concluded that the environmental provisions in the NAFTA itself are inconsequential and that the environmental side agreements have been inadequate to fill the gaps.[21] After a post-NAFTA period of dormancy, the environmental nongovernmental organizations (ENGOs) reappeared in 1997 as pivotal players in U.S. domestic trade politics. Their insistence on a strong linkage between commercial trade objectives and environmental protection measures was a significant factor in forcing President Clinton to withdraw his fast-track bill from Congress in November 1997.[22] On the other side of the debate, the American business community, which accepted the modest environmental clauses and agreements in NAFTA, reverted quickly to a more traditional opposition to environmental provisions in trade agreements.[23] The fundamental split between U.S. business and environmental groups is not changed by the election of George W. Bush, who has been opposed to a trade-environment linkage. The United States lacks, for the time being, the necessary consensus at home to lead the hemisphere in defining what trade-environment linkage, if any, should be part of the FTAA.[24]

Without a trade-environment linkage, loud street protests against free trade and globalization erupted in Seattle in 1999 at the WTO ministerial meeting and recurred at the 2001 Summit of the Americas in Quebec. In the face of such protests, an unfettered free trade policy cannot be easily sustained. Hence, the political leaders of the Americas will need to address the trade-environment linkage eventually,[25] and the November 1999 declaration of the hemisphere's trade ministers acknowledging the issue[26] suggests that the linkage may be established in the FTAA negotiations. The ENGOs in Latin America are using the opportunities of more pluralistic democracy to gain a measure of political clout.[27] Chile agreed to the NAFTA environmental provisions and most of the environmental side agreement in its free trade agreement with Canada in 1996[28] and in late 2000 opened negotiations on a bilateral trade agreement with the United States that U.S. officials say will include integrated trade provisions on observance of national environmental standards. Though few governments have enthusiasm for the trade-environment linkage, political imperatives in the United States as well as changes in their own constituencies will put pressure on the hemisphere's leaders to make more vigorous official commitments to environmental protection as part of any broad free trade arrangements for the Americas.[29]

This chapter will assess the prospects for incorporating environmental protection measures in the hemispheric movement toward free trade. A trade-environment link in the context of an FTAA could take a number of forms, from common market structures that go beyond NAFTA to fully integrate environmental and economic issues throughout the hemisphere at one end of the spectrum to a pattern of discrete national environmental initiatives concurrent with market-access agreements through bilateral or regional arrangements at the other end.[30] The form that will emerge will be shaped by the negotiating leverage that can be exercised by each of the parties to the negotiations, which in turn will depend on the domestic political dynamics constraining the negotiating space for key nations. On the domestic side,[31] each country will first need to shape its own preferences for the linkage.[32] The United States, having had major public debates on the issue in 1993, 1997, and 1999 in advance of the Seattle WTO ministerial and most recently in the 2000 presidential election, provides the richest context for understanding the contending political forces. Internationally, the negotiating nations will then meld and compromise their respective national policies to forge a specific agreement. Here, strategic foreign policy considerations become an important overlay on domestic economic and environmental preferences and may influence countries either to accept stronger trade-environment linkages than they would prefer, as Canada and Mexico did in NAFTA, or to settle for less than they wanted, as the United States did in the Uruguay Round.

The negotiation of environmental undertakings in connection with NAFTA and their implementation during the first six years provide important lessons for evaluating both the policy merits and the political prospects of the various trade-environment linkages in an FTAA.[33] This chapter will draw out those lessons with reference to both the domestic and the international aspects of the political economy in the Americas. The first section of this chapter will provide a framework for the analysis by briefly setting forth the principal arguments for and against integrating trade and environmental policies. The second section will show how the negotiation of the environmental agreements associated with NAFTA derived from just two of the arguments for linkage and expresses skepticism that those arguments have legitimate application in the hemispheric context. The third section proposes exploiting the third argument in favor of linkage—advancing sustainable development—in the FTAA context and assesses the early work of the North American Commission for Environmental Cooperation (CEC) as an example of the benefits of pursuing a sustainable development agenda. In the conclusion, I argue that although the CEC is not itself a suitable institution for the whole hemisphere, it offers a model for managing the hemispheric trade-environment linkage that is normatively satisfactory and may be achievable in the current political context.

WHY LINK TRADE AND THE ENVIRONMENT?

Policy Rationales for and against Linkage

A number of analytical frameworks have been developed for thinking about the relationship between trade flows and trade policies on the one hand and environmental effects and environmental protection policies on the other.[34] In a political context such as that surrounding the FTAA, these analytical frameworks can be reduced to three leading justifications for addressing environmental issues when negotiating agreements for freer trade and two arguments against such linkage.[35]

Noting that trade liberalization agreements are intended to bolster economic productivity and facilitate the international flow of goods and services, the first argument for linkage holds that there should be corresponding commitments to address the environmental effects of the hoped-for changes in production and transport among the trading partners.[36] While increased shipments of goods under free trade regimes can cause direct environmental effects in terms of transportation infrastructure and fuel consumption, the larger issue is the environmental consequences of the expanded and redistributed production taking advantage of the new terms of trade.[37] The challenge here is that the new economic activities and their environmental consequences take place largely through a multitude of discrete, incremental business decisions not amenable to precise prediction or site-specific ex ante control by governments.[38]

A second justification for linking trade and environment is to avoid possible competitive imbalances from differences in environmental standards between trading partners. Environmentalists, labor leaders, and businesspeople alike subscribe to the notion that producers in countries with "low" environmental standards will enjoy a competitive advantage against U.S. producers because of lower environmental compliance costs. Mixing concern about polluted conditions in other countries with traditional fears about losing market share or jobs to "cheap" imports creates a potent political brew that favors protectionism over trade liberalization. Although numerous economic analyses show that the presumed competitiveness effect scarcely appears in the real world,[39] the argument has an intuitive logic that is hard to resist.[40] Politically, therefore, environmentalists seem to think that their strongest argument for attaching environmental conditions to trade agreements is to "level the playing field" by setting some basic standards for environmental performance by trading partners.[41] In the United States, this goal is usually expressed in terms of pressuring other countries to raise their environmental standards toward the "high" level of standards that we apply domestically, counteracting the specter of a competition-driven downward spiral of environmental standards in a "race to the bottom."[42]

Pursuit of the all-encompassing goal of sustainable development, a concept embraced at least rhetorically by political leaders around the world,[43] provides a third argument for linking trade and environmental protection. As articulated in a general way at the Rio Earth Summit[44] and more specifically in such pronouncements as the preamble to the Agreement Establishing the World Trade Organization[45] and the 1995 declaration of the OECD on the relationship between trade and the environment,[46] sustainable development requires that agreements to liberalize international trade incorporate consideration of the environmental consequences of the changes in national and international economic activity that they will promote.[47] The sustainable development justification for linking trade and environment overlaps the first justification—dealing with the direct environmental consequences of production changes induced by trade liberalization—but goes beyond that to take in a full integration of economic and environmental planning and analysis in national and international policy. Sustainable development also provides a foundation in international law and diplomatic rhetoric for the linkage, making it more attractive, or at least more palatable, to political leaders and foreign policy bureaucrats. Substantively, sustainable development counsels that freer trade without accompanying provision for environmental cooperation threatens to create unsustainable systems that would eventually undermine the very economic development it intends to promote.

Opponents of building legal and institutional links between trade and environment voice two main arguments in response to the three justifications for linkage just presented. One counterargument holds that environmental protection is primarily a matter of national policy, to be determined by each government separately rather than through international coercion. The argument gains substantial credibility from the many economists and other policy analysts who view the variation in environmental conditions and environmental preferences between countries as legitimate bases for differences in national standards.[48] Looking at the competitiveness argument from the other side, developing countries in particular want to maintain their freedom to gain some competitive advantage (however illusory) for their exporting producers from lower environmental standards. The undertone of defense of national prerogatives against neoimperialist imposition of U.S. environmental values gives this argument added political appeal.

The second argument against linkage portrays it as a threat to the core legal elements of the liberalized trade regime of the General Agreement on Tariffs and Trade (GATT), on which NAFTA and other trade regimes are also based. With many tariffs reduced to modest levels, current trade policy, even for free trade areas, emphasizes removing or limiting the effects of various nontariff barriers to trade. A strong apprehension exists, especially among economic policy experts, that environmental conditions, once introduced into the trade context, will erode the basic disciplines against nontariff barriers through which the economic benefits of trade liberalization are secured. Constraints on market access in the name of environmental protection, they fear, will open the door to whole new worlds of nontariff barriers to protect commercial rather than bona fide environmental interests, becoming, in essence, "green protectionism."

The antitrade rhetoric of U.S. environmentalists stresses the alleged competitiveness effect of low environmental standards and seeks to bar entry into the United States for goods produced in countries with less exacting environmental regimes. The ENGOs have formed a close alliance with organized labor, which also favors using trade leverage to influence national worker rights and workplace standards policies in other countries. The conjunction of environmental protection goals with the long-standing protectionist tendencies of organized labor deepens the conviction of free trade advocates that environmental conditionality of trade would be used by governments to legitimize breaches of free trade disciplines for economic protectionist purposes at the behest of domestic producers and their workers. President Clinton's public endorsement of the trade-labor agenda during the WTO ministerial in Seattle in 1999 contributed to the breakdown of the fragile global support for broadened trade liberalization initiatives.

International Relationships Influencing the Trade-Environment Linkage

The preceding arguments for and against linkage of trade and environmental policy are applied by governments to shape their policy goals. The expression of those goals and the opportunity to achieve them in international negotiations will also be influenced by the relationships among the participating countries—ecological, economic, and political—and how a new trade agreement would alter them.[49]

The ecological relationships among countries in the Americas include the nature of the distinct, often unique ecosystems within countries or regions as well as how those ecosystems connect and interact in larger continental and hemispheric patterns. Any environmental conditions in trade agreements or parallel agreements should correspond to the ecological resources and regions of interest to the parties. Renewed commitment to and improvement of national regimes to protect the environment of each nation may be one focus of interest, especially in connection with a trade agreement. Such a focus would comport with both the competitiveness and the sustainable development justifications. Transboundary[50] environmental effects are the other possible target for an international agreement, consistent with the justification of dealing with direct environmental effects of trade, as well as sustainable development and general principles of international law.

In the case of the Western Hemisphere as a whole, strong ecological connections exist at the regional or even continental scales,[51] but ecological ties between the land masses on either side of the Panamanian isthmus are attenuated.[52] Competitiveness effects aside, therefore, it is not apparent what specific environmental protection objectives of hemispheric scope should be pursued through a hemisphere-wide linkage of trade and environment beyond galvanizing the collective response of the Americas to shared or global problems, such as deforestation and climate change. The weak connection between ecological and trade issues at the hemispheric scale becomes even more attenuated when we take into account the imperfect application of trade rules and national environmental policies to the resource-extractive exports that are an important part of international trade to many Latin American countries.[53]

By definition, the economic relationship within the hemisphere is also central to the FTAA. The paramount economic factor in the Americas is the overwhelming market power of the NAFTA combination as an economic unit and of the United States as a single national market.[54] The motivation for the FTAA for most countries is to gain tariff-free access to the enormous U.S. market, to control U.S. protectionist behavior (such as antidumping duties and agricultural quotas), and to seek disciplines and dispute settlement mechanisms to control the massive U.S. exports of goods, services, and investments.[55] But the United States is not the only market of interest. Existing regional economic arrangements in the Americas, especially NAFTA and MERCOSUR, and the negotiation of free trade agreements between some Latin American countries and the European Union create a complex layering of economic incentives and disincentives for a hemispheric free trade area for members of those regional groups or countries aspiring to associate with them.[56] Thus, for example, in negotiating an FTAA, Mexico will be calculating the costs of heightened competition with products of Argentina or Brazil in the U.S. market, where it now enjoys special preferences, against the benefits of greater access for Mexican products in the markets of Argentina and Brazil.[57]

A third important aspect of the relationships among the countries is politics. Outside the already established free trade areas of North America and the Southern Cone, trade flows within the hemisphere are relatively modest, so the commitment to negotiate the FTAA is as much a political act as it is an expression of economic policy. The political overlay on the complex economic web in the hemisphere has important ramifications for the relations between and among different nations, exemplified by the decision of Chile to associate itself with its neighbors in MERCO-SUR after the prospects for its early accession to NAFTA faded and Brazil's preference for strengthening MERCOSUR (in which it is the dominant player) rather than encouraging the FTAA.[58] Consequently, no one country, not even the United States, appears to hold enough political power to control the FTAA agenda. Such political polycentricity diminishes the likelihood that the FTAA will strongly link environmental issues with the trade agreement.[59] With global flows of capital and information, it is also clear that the lines between foreign policy and domestic politics have blurred as national political actors become open to external influences such as foreign investors or the expanding networks among ENGOs.[60]

In addition to these three fundamental relationships, the influence of personalities and historical accidents adds a fourth dimension that should not be overlooked. The strengths, weaknesses, and personal preferences of key individuals can occasionally make a significant difference in defining the possibilities for agreement or the success of policy implementation. For example, Chile's position as the prime candidate for association with NAFTA derives not from its size or even its natural endowments but primarily from a stable, open economy that resulted from policy choices made by the Pinochet regime and sustained through the transition to elected governments.[61]

In sum, the form of the trade-environment linkage that evolves in the context of hemispheric trade liberalization will depend on a combination of the policy objectives that the participating players (businesses and NGOs as well as governments) bring to the table and the opportunities to induce or impose agreement that emerge from the relationships among those participants.

NAFTA'S TRADE-ENVIRONMENT LINKAGES: LESSONS FOR THE FTAA

The negotiation of NAFTA from 1991 to 1993 catalyzed many reactions to the already deepening integration of peoples and economies within North America. One of the more politically salient was the insistence of environmental advocates that the expansion of economic activity promised by free trade should be conditioned on explicit commitments to protect the environment at the same time.[62] Two of the justifications for linkage discussed previously—addressing the environmental consequences of trade and warding off competitiveness effects—emerged as the fundamental and politically salient concerns. Do these same concerns apply in the case of the FTAA?

Direct Environmental Consequences

The concern of U.S. environmental organizations with the direct environmental consequences of NAFTA arose from Mexico's experiences during the 1970s and 1980s with proliferating environmental problems. These were especially noticeable in the U.S.-Mexico border area, where the rapid influx into northern Mexico of export-oriented manufacturing operations under Mexico's *maquiladora* program caused serious problems of air and water pollution and waste disposal, some of which spilled over into U.S. communities like El Paso and San Diego.[63] National environmental leaders foresaw adverse consequences of NAFTA-led growth for Mexico, where industrial development was outstripping the capacity of the government to promulgate or enforce environmental controls.[64] They also feared that NAFTA would exacerbate the industrialization of the ecologically fragile border area, creating additional environmental problems in the United States as well as for Mexico. Border area environmental leaders also saw the national focus on NAFTA as a way to draw media and political attention to issues that had been long neglected by capital-centered national governments.

This constellation of interests compelled national attention to the border environment. The George H. W. Bush administration in the United States and the Salinas administration in Mexico each made some gestures to address these direct consequences of economic activity. The Clinton administration came up with a more substantial response that gained significant support for the NAFTA from border community leaders: a bilateral NAFTA side agreement with Mexico establishing a Border Environment Cooperation Commission and a North American Development Bank to oversee and fund environmental infrastructure projects in the border area.[65]

As already noted, the ecological relationship between North America and the rest of the hemisphere is much weaker than the obvious pollutant flows and migratory pathways that link Mexico, the United States, and Canada. Apart from some migratory birds and fish that travel between North and South America, our common hemispheric interests are limited largely to generic or global environmental questions, such as biodiversity and habitat conservation,[66] tropical deforestation, deterioration of coral reefs, and widespread extinction of species. The interest of the United States in these matters is not nearly so vivid as our interest in water pollution or improper waste disposal in Mexico that occurs within sight of the United States and has immediate environmental effects on the U.S. side of the border. Likewise, Brazilians or Peruvians are scarcely affected by how North Americans manage the Great Lakes or the salmon fisheries of the Pacific Northwest. The weak ecological relations, in turn, mean that there is little political constituency in any country for a hemispheric mechanism for addressing the direct environmental consequences of the FTAA. Rather, those consequences are likely to be left for each nation to address on its own, as is true for all regional free trade arrangements except NAFTA and the European Economic Community.[67]

Preventing Competitive Imbalances

The concern with competitiveness effects of lower environmental standards emerged slowly in the NAFTA debate but became, at the end, the critical trade-environment issue. Ross Perot, who coined the phrase "giant sucking sound" as an image for his claim that substantial U.S. production would move to Mexico under NAFTA, debated the competitiveness effect with Vice President Al Gore on national television weeks before the NAFTA vote. The product standards provisions of NAFTA address a small part of the competitiveness argument by ensuring the right of an importing country to reject goods that do not conform to regulatory standards.[68] So does the environmental provision in the investment chapter, in which the countries agree not to become "pollution havens," that is, not to lower their environmental standards to attract or keep foreign investment.[69] The larger part of the competitiveness concern, however, has to do with lax environmental controls at manufacturing facilities located in a foreign jurisdiction. In trade jargon, this is the issue of processes and production methods (PPMs), and most PPMs still lie beyond the reach of trade controls on the resulting goods.[70]

During the NAFTA negotiations, U.S. environmental groups proposed an ingenious device to deal, at least partially and indirectly, with the competitiveness issue: a trinational commission with enforcement powers that would ensure that the separate national environmental laws of the three countries would be enforced with uniform rigor. Although the CEC that resulted from the ensuing year of negotiations lacks the supranational enforcement authority originally proposed,[71] the competitiveness issue provided strong impetus to the creation of the CEC and underlies the most often cited provision of the agreement.[72] Separate from the establishment of the CEC, the agreement provides a government-to-government dispute resolution mechanism, including trade sanctions, if one government believes that another government has exhibited a "persistent pattern" of failure to enforce its environmental laws that is having effects on the terms of competition between the two countries.[73] The United States insisted on these provisions in the agreement against resistance from Canada and Mexico in order to have a strong counter to the competitiveness argument in the then-looming congressional debate on NAFTA approval.

Several factors unique to the circumstances of the NAFTA enabled the United States to get Canada and Mexico to agree to the withdrawal-of-NAFTA-benefit sanction. To begin with, the ambivalence of the American public toward a free trade agreement with Mexico made the influence of organized U.S. ENGOs with certain members of Congress a potentially decisive factor.[74] Since the final trade agreement would need congressional approval, it became important for the administration to secure the endorsement of NAFTA by enough ENGOs to neutralize the environmental issues as a reason (or excuse) for members of Congress to vote against NAFTA.[75] President Clinton raised the political stakes further during his 1992 campaign by conditioning his support for NAFTA on separate agreements on environment, labor, and import surges.[76] The domestic politics of NAFTA in the United States made it imperative for the Mexicans and Canadians to accept most of the U.S. terms on environmental provisions and agreements in order to get reasonable assurance that the NAFTA would come into effect.[77] The economic and political relationships among the NAFTA parties, however, allowed little room for maneuver on the environmental agenda within the trade agreement itself. Although NAFTA went beyond the original "parallel track" concept to include a few provisions specifically addressing environmental concerns, all the governments concurred in dealing with more substantial environmental issues through ancillary programs and agreements.

The specific proposal to address a broad range of environmental issues through a trinational commission afforded an opportunity to link the environment with trade through agreements that impinged only remotely on their fundamental trade goals. Part of its attractiveness was that it made ecological sense. There are significant movements and interactions of air, water, oceans, and wildlife that connect the three countries of North America.[78] Binding binational agreements on transboundary environmental problems have long been a prominent element of U.S. relations with both Canada and Mexico, so it required only a small shift in policy for all three governments to move from the bilateral context to a trinational agreement, even though a continent-wide environmental institution with broad powers breaks significant new ground in international environmental law. To deal with the politics of the competitiveness issue, however, the environmental agreement had to have some "teeth" against lax enforcement.

Recent history and individual personalities contributed to the willingness of the NAFTA partners to be politically venturesome on environmental matters. President Salinas made repeated earnest claims of the Mexican government's (and his own personal) commitment to protect the environment and took symbolic actions to demonstrate that commitment. His posture made Mexico surprisingly supple in responding to multiple U.S. demands for unilateral actions and binding commitments on environmental protection and made it awkward for Mexico to reject a commitment to enforcement of its own laws. In the United States, William Reilly, a strong administrator of the Environmental Protection Agency with a deep interest in international affairs and a good personal relationship with President George H. W. Bush, supported the initial proposal for the commission. The inauguration of the Clinton administration in 1993 brought President Clinton, who had made strong campaign appeals to environmentalists; Vice President Gore, who had just published a book urging greater consideration to environmental issues in economic policy;[79] and U.S. Trade Representative Mickey Kantor, a lawyer with roots in public interest law and a personal confidant of the president.

All these factors converged to induce the negotiators to satisfy the major demands of the environmentalists on the competitiveness issue while carefully shielding the essential economic bargain of the trade agreement itself. Although the political alignment at the time of NAFTA will never recur, similarly strong environmental conditions could be included in agreements on the FTAA if U.S. domestic politics demand it and other key countries see enough economic advantage in improved access to the U.S. market to accept unwanted side conditions. Those are big "ifs," however. The economic stakes for individual countries are not as high in the FTAA as they were in NAFTA. The trade flows between the NAFTA "bloc" and the rest of the hemisphere are significant enough but very modest in comparison to the massive flows of trade among the three NAFTA partners. In proportional terms as well, no country in Latin America begins to rank with Mexico and Canada, the first- and second-largest trading partners for the United States.[80] By the same token, Latin and Caribbean countries depend less heavily than Mexico or Canada on trade with the United States for their own success. These economic realities make it unlikely that FTAA negotiators will be prepared to make major concessions to the United States on environmental issues in order to secure a free trade agreement.[81]

Neither do the complex political relationships within Latin America and between Latin countries and the United States offer any prospect for real traction on the trade-environment linkage. The MERCOSUR countries seem reasonably satisfied with their regional trade arrangement and show little eagerness to embrace the much different trade liberalization approach of NAFTA. Quite the contrary, they show signs of trying to strengthen and expand the MERCOSUR to create a substantial southern alternative to NAFTA.[82] If that strategy succeeds, free trade in the Americas may ultimately take the form of a trade agreement between distinctly different northern and southern regional markets. Such a scenario appears unlikely to lead to much environmentally favorable linkage between trade and the environment beyond routine trade agreement language allowing certain carefully controlled trade restrictions for the protection of human, animal, or plant life, health, or safety.

THE CEC AS AN EXAMPLE OF THE SUSTAINABLE DEVELOPMENT APPROACH

To recapitulate, the competitiveness argument for environmental protection provisions in the FTAA raises contentious issues and seems politically implausible under current circumstances. The argument that the trade agreement or a parallel agreement should address the environmental consequences of the new terms of competition within the trade area is much less politically sensitive but seems to have little objective merit in the FTAA, which would bring together widely dispersed countries with relatively small trade flows among them. But the third argument for linking trade and environment policy—the strengthening imperative to promote sustainable development—has relevance for all countries and perhaps a special resonance in Latin America, host to the 1992 Earth Summit in Rio, which enshrined the concept, and the 1996 Summit of the Americas on Sustainable Development in Bolivia. Moreover, the concept has been embraced by Brazil, Paraguay, and Uruguay, as evidenced by their support for the hortatory MERCOSUR draft environmental protocol. Sustainable development may offer an affirmative and progressive basis for trade-environment integration that avoids pitting environmental protection against trade growth and economic development.

The unheralded cooperative work of the NAFTA-linked CEC during its first six years provides us with some empirical evidence for assessing the value of building robust international institutions dedicated to sustainable development within or linked to new or expanded regional trade frameworks. The CEC experience particularly merits consideration because of its close linkage with the terms and institutions of NAFTA itself and the still-flickering anticipation that it will be expanded to include Latin American adherents to NAFTA.

The very structure of the CEC as an institution advances sustainable development by penetrating some of the barriers between governments and citizens, enhancing opportunities for individual citizens and NGOs to shape the continental environmental agenda. The Commission comprises three elements: a Council, a Secretariat, and a Joint Public Advisory Committee (JPAC). Only the Council, which is composed of the environmental ministers of the three countries, represents government authority. The Secretariat and the JPAC, both independent of direct government control, have played the more active roles.

The Secretariat is a professional staff of civil servants under the management of an executive director. It has autonomous authority to receive and make initial determinations on citizen petitions to the CEC for investigation into alleged national failures to enforce environmental laws.[83] Moreover, it has discretion under Article 13 of the Agreement to investigate and develop recommendations on matters brought to its attention by citizens in cases that raise issues within the scope of the annual work program.[84] Private citizens or NGOs thus have the power to "force" the governments to give greater attention to certain issues than they might have without the pressure of a secretariat inquiry. The Secretariat also consults independently with experts and organizations in civil society in determining its work program and carrying it out.

The third constitutional component of the CEC is the JPAC. This unique body of fifteen private citizens (five from each country, appointed by their respective national presidents) has a mandated role in the administration of the CEC. It was created deliberately to ensure responsiveness of the CEC to the wider interests of citizens throughout the continent. Since more participatory decision making is a fundamental element of the sustainable development concept, the JPAC contributes directly to the sustainable development mission of the CEC.[85] The JPAC helps link individual citizens and officials making decisions at international levels through public hearings and other channels of communication.[86] Such direct links between citizens and international decision makers are increasingly important; the credibility and legitimacy of international trade policies and international environmental protection efforts depend on nurturing public support and creating opportunities for direct public input into decisions that will affect their lives.[87] At the same time, such channels for citizen input challenge traditional patterns of nonparticipatory decision making that still prevail, especially with respect to trade policy. The JPAC also helps to hold the CEC secretariat and the ministers themselves accountable to the broader public through their official role as advisers to the CEC and reviewers of CEC activities.[88]

In its first six years, the CEC has launched a wide range of cooperative activities on major aspects of a sustainable development agenda for North America. It has collected and disseminated data on environmental conditions throughout North America; established a basic library of environmental laws in the three countries; instigated standardization of air quality monitoring to assure continent-wide comparability of data as a prelude to cooperative air quality management; published ecosystem maps; convened federal, state, and local officials to develop plans for ecosystem-based management of surface and groundwater in a transboundary watershed; and disbursed funds to grassroots organizations and nonprofit groups undertaking local and regional collaborative projects aimed toward sustainable development.[89] Even in its disposition of matters first brought to its attention through claims of nonenforcement of environmental laws, the CEC has given more prominence to affirmative recommendations for solutions to complex problems and much less attention to the task of retrospective assessment of enforcement practices.

Many advocates of a strong link between trade and the environment fault the CEC for not giving priority to its mission to assess the environmental effects of NAFTA.[90] To begin with, it should be noted that the CEC has not neglected that part of its mandate altogether. In 1998, it released for public consideration a methodological framework for doing such analyses and three sectoral studies that piloted the methodology.[91] A final methodology, established in 1999, led to a series of independent studies discussed at an October 2000 CEC workshop on NAFTA's environmental effects. More important, the relative lack of success in the study of NAFTA's environmental effects and the greater success of the CEC's cooperative activities confirm the value of conceiving the collective environmental agenda for trading partners in terms that attend to, but do not overemphasize, the role of trade rules and institutions in contributing to their common environmental problems. Without neglecting its mandate to study NAFTA's effects on the environment, the CEC has devoted more of its resources to matters such as global warming, persistent organic pollutants, and patterns of urban air quality degradation that are determined largely by domestic economic activities without special regard to patterns of trade. In my judgment, the CEC, understood as both the three environmental ministers acting in concert and as the permanent secretariat staff, has properly set its priorities by the environmental significance of issues and the particular contributions that the three nations can make through concerted action rather than allowing itself to be driven by the NAFTA effects agenda. Its current emphasis on ecology and conservation— critical but often neglected environmental issues for all three countries—exemplifies this approach.

Though eminently justifiable as a cooperative enterprise to promote sustainable development on a continental scale, the CEC would not have come into being except for the political pressure to address environmental concerns on the occasion of significantly deepening and broadening the economic exchange relationship of the NAFTA partners. Despite its roots in concerns about direct effects and competitiveness, however, the effectiveness of the CEC on issues not directly NAFTA related argues for the advantages of multinational environmental mechanisms that are parallel to rather than embedded within or tightly integrated with trading institutions. This view is in keeping with the judgment of most trade experts as well as environmentalists that it would not be appropriate to give the WTO environmental responsibilities.[92] Even if parallel rather than fully integrated systems for trade and environment policy are preferred, the question remains what links to forge between the two policy spheres. Although the CEC is tightly bound to NAFTA in terms of politics and perception, the legal and institutional linkages between the CEC and the NAFTA trade mechanisms are in fact very weak. As of this writing, the NAFTA governments have yet to convene a joint meeting of the trade and environment ministers. The CEC's staff and consultants rarely have contact with trade officials, and a CEC report indicates that most NAFTA-established intergovernmental committees on trade issues rarely consider the environmental implications of their work.[93] Given the rather scant attention to specific environmental issues in NAFTA itself and the limited resources of the CEC, the weak linkage is arguably suitable to the circumstances.

CONCLUSION: HOW TO LINK TRADE AND ENVIRONMENT IN THE AMERICAS

Former Quebec Premier Pierre Marc Johnson, writing about trade and environment at the world level, suggests that, "ultimately, the success or failure of the WTO will depend on . . . reconciliation of trade, environment, and development agendas under a broadened system of global governance."[94] The same observation applies to the Western Hemisphere and the success (or failure) of the FTAA.

The CEC is a first step toward trade, environment, and development reconciliation and international governance. It has been moderately successful as a new institution tackling environmental problems on a continental scale among three neighboring countries that share many ecosystems, have deeply interwoven economies (even before NAFTA), and are bound to each other by geography and history in close, if sometimes contentious, political relations. Can the CEC be adapted to link with the FTAA, which will bring together more than thirty hemispheric cohabitants with diverse and often tenuous ecological, economic, and political connections? This chapter has developed an argument in favor of the CEC as an environmental protection institution parallel to NAFTA that emphasizes sustainable development policies for North America. Canada and Mexico, having paid a political price to expend resources and yield certain powers to a trinational environmental authority that neither would have agreed to except for the politics of gaining NAFTA approval in the United States, understandably insist (at least officially) that the CEC should be expanded to include any other country, like Chile, that wishes to accede to NAFTA.[95] Expanding the existing North American CEC is not the right approach, however, to building an environmental institution for the hemisphere linked to an FTAA. Rather, the CEC should be maintained, indeed strengthened, as a North American enterprise while serving as a model for structuring a similar but distinct institution to promote sustainable development throughout the Americas.

The existing CEC could, perhaps, be institutionally adapted to a larger membership and geographic scope, but to restructure it in this way would put this important new North American environmental institution at risk. Consider the implications of adding just one country, Chile. Compelling Chile to accede would necessarily divert some of the CEC's attention from matters of specific concern to North America in favor of issues in which Chile has some stake or role to play. The Secretariat and the JPAC would need to be expanded, at considerable expense associated with getting the secretariat staff and the JPAC to Chile from time to time. Expanding the CEC would also allow Chile to have a voice in deciding on environmental policies affecting primarily North America, creating the potential for diplomatic game playing or logrolling, with unpredictable results.[96] Finally, taken to the FTAA level, Chile's accession would establish the precedent that any other new NAFTA or FTAA party must join the CEC, creating substantial uncertainty about future changes to the CEC's structure and agenda if the FTAA becomes the vehicle for more extensive free trade.

Even if the CEC were easily expanded through a single action related to the establishment of the FTAA or by creating a second sphere of operations for Latin American "associate" members,[97] North America would lose in that process an institution with a specific continental purpose that has fostered greater awareness of the need for, and capacity to provide, international cooperation to address environmental issues previously seen only in domestic or bilateral terms. The CEC's achievements in its first six years of operation have established momentum and institutional credibility, but support for the CEC remains fragile and needs to be carefully nurtured. The CEC must still be considered an experiment in international environmental management on a continental scale. Failure to build steadily and without serious interruption on the CEC's record to date could diminish its stature and effectiveness, if not cause it to atrophy altogether. Bringing new members or associate members into the CEC in the near future risks structural instability and a loss of focus.

On balance, the political and institutional risks inherent in expansion of the CEC outweigh the benefits of enlarging its scope and modestly supplementing its resources.[98]

Though expansion of the CEC through NAFTA accession seems a poor strategy for both North America and Latin America, the hemispheric scope of the proposed FTAA opens completely new vistas for parallel hemispheric environmental cooperation that should be pursued vigorously and linked to the FTAA, just as the CEC was politically linked to NAFTA. Linkage is possible, despite ecological, economic, and political connections weaker than in the NAFTA context. The hemispheric commitment to construct the FTAA and the substantial preparatory work the countries have invested in the project reflect shifting economic realities and give the FTAA political momentum and symbolic importance as well. The United States is motivated in part by the increasing importance of the Americas in its trading relationships. The hemisphere is the destination for 20 percent of U.S. exports, Brazil outranks China as a U.S. trading partner, and Chile and Argentina outrank Russia and India. In a world in which economic politics is gaining in importance compared to traditional geopolitical considerations, these economic realities imply the increasing strategic political importance of the Americas in U.S. foreign policy as well. By the same token, most countries in the Americas would like to cement closer political relations with the United States as well as gain preferential access to the U.S. market.

Throughout the Americas, environmental issues are gaining political attention on the national and international levels.[99] Chile has substantially strengthened its national environmental program, Ecuador is reasserting control over the environmental effects of petroleum production in its Lacondan region, Brazil has recently enacted new legislation to curb deforestation of the Amazon, and Costa Rica has enjoyed substantial economic benefits from eco-tourism to its forest reserves. In short, the governments see the political imperative to show progress on environmental issues. The Summit of the Americas on Sustainable Development in Bolivia at the end of 1996 showed a special willingness to address environmental issues in a sustainable development framework, which would presumably include technology transfer and other benefits or concessions by the developed countries to the developing countries to help them overcome structural obstacles to development that also have adverse environmental consequences.

Sustainable development recognizes the links between trade, economic development, and environmental protection and the need to integrate economic and environmental policies. The negotiation of the FTAA is thus a particularly appropriate context for the hemispheric partners to construct a Commission for Sustainable Development in the Americas. The agenda for such a commission should include the leading environmental challenges for the hemisphere, many of which have at least an indirect connection to traded goods and services. Forests, both tropical and temperate, are one of the hemisphere's great natural resources. A hemispheric approach to sustainable forest management might facilitate the compromises necessary for new policy initiatives, compromises that have proved impossible to negotiate at the world level. Management of coffee plantations for the protection of migratory songbirds is one issue of forestry and agricultural policy where there are strong ecological and economic connections between North America and the rest of the hemisphere that could provide a firm basis for hemispheric programs and management practices. Other matters that could benefit from cooperation throughout the Americas range from specific problems, such as the environmental impacts of mining activities, to more subtle but widespread problems, such as the decline of coral reefs. At its most ambitious, a hemispheric commission could address such complex sustainable development issues as habitat and cultural protection and pollution prevention in areas inhabited by indigenous peoples.

Regional approaches to such matters have proved successful in the past, often serving as mechanisms for implementation of general international aspirations or as constructive steps toward more broadly multilateral agreements. The cooperation of many countries on issues affecting the Caribbean Sea under the auspices of the UN Regional Seas Program is one example in the hemisphere.[100] A Commission on Sustainable Development for the Americas could also be an effective forum for addressing shared problems of urban pollution in such cities as São Paulo and Mexico City, shared problems of the environmental effects of oil production, energy supply and distribution, and environmentally sound management of river basins and other water resources. These are mighty challenges that are being addressed to some extent by national governments and multilateral programs but perhaps could be addressed more effectively if the nations of the hemisphere view themselves, in terminology that is now passé, as "good neighbors" who have a common interest in helping each other address the sustainability of their neighborhood in return for the economic advantages of working together to develop it. In that sense, perhaps, the promises of the Rio Declaration can be realized, with poetic as well as environmental justice, in the greater vicinity of Rio.

A single Commission for Sustainable Development in the Americas is one plausible institutional structure for marshaling resources and focusing attention on hemisphere-wide and shared environmental challenges. Other structures can also be imagined, such as four or five regional councils (including the North American CEC) under the umbrella of a hemispheric coordinating body or a sustainable development program operated through the Organization of American States (OAS). Whatever the structure, it should incorporate the best elements of the CEC model. These include an independent, professional staff; defined mechanisms for private individuals or organizations to submit issues needing attention (and decision-making criteria for evaluating such submissions); and a citizen's advisory committee with specific powers and responsibilities and defined opportunities to shape the agenda of the organization. Sustainable development itself demands such specific opportunities for the public to participate in determining the agenda and influencing the decisions of the international organization. The political liberalization that is already under way throughout the hemisphere and the demonstrable environmental improvements associated with that liberalization should be a motivation to all governments to move in this direction.[101]

Finally, if the parallel commission model that I propose is to win sufficient political support to get established, the question of how to ensure cooperation of governments with the environmental agenda must be addressed. Full compliance by all governments with an international agreement on sustainable development would be an impossible goal; even national legal systems cannot promise perfect enforcement. Plausible and effective incentives and sanctions can be devised through multilateral decision-making and dispute resolution structures, backed up by the endless variety of other pressures and inducements that governments can apply to each other in their international relations. International environmental agreements such as the Montreal Protocol and the Convention on International Trade in Endangered Species of Fauna and Flora have developed effective systems of reporting, monitoring, and international review of compliance. The only trade pressure applied under these agreements is the multilaterally agreed bar to trade in the regulated products by participating nations with nations that are not complying with the international system.

Most environmental organizations in the United States, who are the chief *demandeurs* for trade-environment linkage, continue to advocate a broad right of unilateral market access restrictions or other trade sanctions for environmental derelictions of our trading partners. Recent experience shows that this insistence on self-judged and self-implemented trade leverage to coerce compliance jeopardizes the substantial environmental benefits that will flow from economic development and exchange. Conditionality of trade is perilous in a realm such as environmental policy where multiple scientific, social, and political factors determine each country's or region's choice of environmental standards. In any case, the fear of international economic competition based on the presumed production cost advantage of "lower" environmental standards finds no support in the record of the past twenty-five years of expanding international trade and more stringent but differentiated environmental control strategies at the national level.[102] Stringent environmental conditionality would effectively preclude the United States from ongoing international negotiations, including the all-important multilateral negotiations on agricultural trade. This would be unfortunate for our efforts to improve environmental performance in agriculture and other sectors, at home as well as abroad. A more politically pragmatic and culturally deferential strategy is called for if we are to move toward true integration of environmental protection and conservation into economic policymaking at the international level.

NOTES

1. North American Free Trade Agreement, December 17, 1992, Canada-Mexico-United States, 32 I.L.M. 289 (1993).

2. General Agreement on Tariffs and Trade, Final Act Embodying the Results of the

Uruguay Round of Multilateral Trade Negotiations, done at Marrakesh, April 15, 1994, 33 I.L.M. 1125 (1994).

3. With strong urging by the United States, the APEC leaders at their 1994 meeting agreed to work toward "free and open trade and investment" by 2010 for the developed members and by 2020 for the developing members. Lyuba Zarsky and Jason Hunter, "Environmental Cooperation at APEC: The First Five Years," *Journal of Environment and Development* 6 (1997): 222, 231.

4. Uruguay Round Agreements Act, Public Law 103-465, 108 Stat. 4809 (1994).

5. Summit of the Americas: Declaration of Principles and Plan of Action, 34 I.L.M. 808, 811 (1995). See generally Frank J. Garcia, " 'Americas Agreements'—An Interim Stage in Building the Free Trade Area of the Americas," *Columbia Journal of Transnational Law* 35 (1997): 63, 82–86.

6. See Pierre Marc Johnson and André Beaulieu, *The Environment and NAFTA: Understanding and Implementing the New Continental Law* (Washington, D.C.: Island Press, 1996) (describing the NAFTA environmental provisions and the North American Agreement for Environmental Cooperation); Sanford E. Gaines, "Bridges to a Better Environment: Building Cross-Border Institutions for Environmental Improvement in the U.S.-Mexico Border Area," *Arizona Journal of International & Comparative Law* 12 (1995): 429 (describing the U.S.-Mexico agreement establishing the Border Environment Cooperation Commission and the North American Development Bank).

7. The preamble to the Agreement Establishing the World Trade Organization includes recognition by the WTO members that trade and economic relations should "[allow] the optimal use of the world's resources in accordance with the objective of sustainable development, seeking both to protect and preserve the environment and to enhance the means for doing so." Some late modifications to the Agreement on the Application of Sanitary and Phytosanitary Measures brought the multilateral text closer to the comparable provisions of the NAFTA.

8. "Procedural Guidelines on Integrating Trade and Environmental Policies," Report of the Joint Sessions of Trade and Environment Experts to the Council at Ministerial Level, June 1993, OCDE/GD(93)99. The policy work at the OECD has continued since then, most notably in "Guiding the Transition to Sustainable Development: A Critical Role for the OECD," Report of the High Level Advisory Group on the Environment to the Secretary General of the OECD, November 25, 1997, which includes a section on "Ensuring Policy Integration."

9. Informal and preliminary consultations with Chile were held at the Office of the U.S. Trade Representative in the first half of 1994. What motivated Chile's environmental law reforms is more difficult to assess. Rafael X. Zahralddin-Aravena, "Chilean Accession to NAFTA: U.S. Failure and Chilean Success," *North Carolina Journal of International Law & Commercial Regulation* 23 (1997): 53, 54, suggests that anticipation of free trade talks was one of the stimuli. Heraldo Muñoz, "Free Trade and Environmental Policies: Chile, Mexico, and Venezuela," in Gordon J. MacDonald, Daniel L. Nielson, and Marc A. Stern, eds., *Latin American Environmental Policy in International Perspective* (Boulder, Colo.: Westview Press, 1997), 113, 116–17, connects the environmental reform more with the democratization of Chile during the late 1980s and early 1990s.

10. "Administration Seeks Extension of Fast Track for Seven Years," *International Trade Reporter* 11 (June 22, 1994): 978.

11. See Sherry M. Stephenson, "Standards, the Environment, and Trade Facilitation in the Western Hemisphere: Negotiating in the FTAA," *Journal of World Trade* 31, no. 6 (December 1997): 137 (discussion of preparatory work on the FTAA, especially standards issues, by an attorney with the Organization of American States); Jeanette M. E. Tramhel, "Free Trade in the Americas: A Perspective from the Organization of American States," *Houston Journal of International Law* 19 (1997): 595 (same).

12. Calvin Sims, "Free-Trade Zone of the Americas Given a Go-Ahead," *New York Times,* April 20, 1998, 1. The Santiago Declaration, done at Santiago, Chile, April 19, 1998, is available at <http://www.ftaa.alca.org/ministerials/chile_e.asp>. The Quebec Summit of the Americas in April 2001 reaffirmed the 2005 target date for final agreement and set a schedule for sectoral negotiations beginning in the spring of 2002. See USTR Fact Sheet, April 7, 2001 (available at <http://www.ustr.gov/regions/whemisphere/ftaafactsheet.pdf>).

13. The reference to environmental protection occurs in the context of a "reiteration" that the trade negotiations shall "take into account the broad social and economic agenda contained in the Santiago and Miami Declarations of Principles and Plans of Action." Free Trade Area of the Americas, Declaration of Ministers, Fifth Trade Ministerial Meeting, Toronto, November 4, 1999, para. 5 (available at <http://www:ftaa-alca.org/ministerials/minis_e.asp>).

14. U.S. Office of the Trade Representative, Press Release, Publication of Draft FTAA, July 3, 2001 (available at <http://www.ustr.gov/release/2001/G7/01.51.pdf>). The bracketed text is now available at <http://www.ftaa-alca.org/FTAADraft/Eng/draft_e.doc>.

15. Promoting it was a central mission of President Clinton's state visits in the region in the fall of 1997. See, for example, Howard La Franchi, "Clinton Plays Catch Up in South America," *Christian Science Monitor,* October 14, 1997, 1; Paul Blustein, "Making a Case for South America: White House Prepares Arguments on Trade in Advance of Clinton," *Washington Post,* October 12, 1997, A32.

16. For example, Jane Bussey, "Americas Trade Conference Hits Early Bumps," *Miami Herald,* September 30, 1998, reported on a lack of funding that was making it "difficult for organizers to set up the secretariat to run the trade talks" and that Jamaican ambassador Richard Bernal said that "very little substance had been discussed so far. . . . 'We are still setting the parameters within which we negotiate.'" Jane Bussey, "Negotiators Plan to Show Progress in Americas Free Trade Area," *Miami Herald,* December 10, 1998, reported "a sense that the momentum for the [FTAA] undertaking was being lost because of the slow pace of procedures and governments' inability to convey the importance of trade agreements to the public." FTAA negotiators were still focusing on small-bore issues like customs clearance procedures and that such work was "far from the lofty goals" of the 1994 Summit of the Americas. Statement of William T. Pryce, Council of the Americas, before the House Committee on Ways and Means, Subcommittee on Trade, March 4, 1999 (Federal News Service, available on Lexis), observed that "the goal of reaching interim agreements by 2000 in order to achieve the 'concrete progress' referred to in the Miami Summit declaration appears increasingly difficult to achieve."

17. Sims, "Free-Trade Zone of the Americas Given a Go-Ahead," A10 (national ed.), reported that trade experts at the Santiago summit acknowledged that the lack of fast-track authority for President Clinton had "hurt the United States' credibility on free trade." Richard Feinberg observed that the absence of fast-track authority is slowing the FTAA; "the energy and enthusiasm with which it is being pursued is certainly being diluted by congressional

hostility." Jim Christie, "Trade Expert Feinberg on EU/Latin America Trade Talks," *Investor's Business Daily,* July 6, 1999, A4. More recently, a senior Costa Rican trade official was quoted as saying, "The FTAA has lacked political support because of U.S. and Brazil. . . . The rest of the countries are strongly in favor." Edward Alden et al., "U.S. Push for Free Trade Deal Faces Hurdles," *Financial Times* (London), February 11, 2001, 9 (in LEXIS/NEXIS CUR-NWS Library).

18. Congress defeated a Republican-sponsored fast-track bill, H.R. 2621, on September 25, 1998. Rossella Brevetti and Cheryl Bohlen, "House Defeats Fast-Track Bill by 180–243 in Debate Marked by Strong Partisanship," *International Trade Reporter* 15 (September 30, 1998): 1623. In neither 1999 nor 2000 did the administration and Congress agree to move forward on fast-track legislation.

19. In 1999, the administration proposed a compromise position that would not directly link environmental protection efforts by other countries to the conclusion of trade agreements but would ensure that the president "have full authority to negotiate agreements [that are] in the best interests of the United States," including environmental agreements. Gary G. Yerkey, "USTR Seeks to Distance Fast Track from Progress on Labor, Environment," *International Trade Reporter* 16 (June 30, 1999): 1080, reporting on testimony of Ambassador Charlene Barshefsky before the Senate Agriculture Committee.

20. "Administration Withdraws Proposal to Include 'Fast Track' in GATT Bill," *International Trade Reporter* 11 (September 14, 1994): 1388.

21. The new assertiveness of the environmentalists appeared early in 1994 when they criticized the Clinton administration proposal on fast track for its lack of specific objectives on trade-environment issues. "Environmental Groups Oppose Administration's Fast Track Plan," *International Trade Reporter* 11 (July 20, 1994): 1138. The groups opposing the administration included groups that had supported NAFTA. See also Joseph F. DiMento and Pamela M. Doughman, "Soft Teeth in the Back of the Mouth: The NAFTA Environmental Side Agreement Implemented," *Georgetown International Environmental Law Review* 10 (1998): 651.

22. Thomas Edsall and John Yang, "Clinton Loss Illuminates Struggle within Party," *Washington Post,* November 11, 1997, A1; Brennan Van Dyke, "Clinton Reaps What He Sowed: Nothing," *Los Angeles Times,* November 17, 1997, B5 (op-ed).

23. "U.S. Chamber Opposes House Accord Linking Trade to Labor, Environment," *International Trade Reporter* 11 (August 24, 1994): 1293.

24. Indeed, as Jeffrey Dunoff suggested and the 1997 fast-track debate indicated, the very notion of a linking trade and environment may lie at the root of the political deadlock over American trade policy. Jeffrey L. Dunoff, " 'Trade and': Recent Developments in Trade Policy and Scholarship—and Their Surprising Implications," *Northwestern Journal of International Law & Business* 17 (1996–97): 759, 764–68.

25. This proposition is also supported by Stephenson, "Standards, the Environment, and Trade Facilitation in the Western Hemisphere," 168–69; Pierre Marc Johnson, "Beyond Trade: The Case for a Broadened International Governance Agenda," *Policy Matters* 1, no. 3 (June 2000).

26. See note 13.

27. The situation in Chile, for example, is nicely summarized in Scott C. Lacunza, "From Dictatorship to Democracy: Environmental Reform in Chile," *Hastings International & Comparative Law Review* 19 (1996): 539, and in Zahralddin-Aravena, "Chilean Ac-

cession to NAFTA," 76–78. More generally, see Stephen P. Mumme and Edward Korzetz, "Democratization, Politics, and Environmental Reform in Latin America," in MacDonald et al., eds., *Latin American Environmental Policy in International Perspective,* 40; Blanca Torres, "Transnational Environmental NGOs: Linkages and Impact on Policy, in MacDonald et al., eds., *Latin American Environmental Policy in International Perspective,* 156. In July 1997, Mexico's Partito Verde (Green Party) made strong showings in Mexico City and many other parts of the country. Howard LaFranchi, "Sprouting of Young Party May Yield Earth-Friendlier Mexico," *Christian Science Monitor,* July 11, 1997, 1.

28. Canada-Chile Free Trade Agreement, December 5, 1996, 36 I.L.M. 1693 (1997); "U.S., Chile Trade Talks to Encompass Labor, Environment," *National Journal's Congress Daily,* December 5, 2000.

29. Alden, "U.S. Push for Free Trade Deal Faces Hurdles," noting that many Democrats in the U.S. Congress demand FTAA provisions to protect the environment, "a view that has little support in Latin America." Canada, too, currently opposes addressing environmental issues in the FTAA. Ian Jack, "Don't Link Free Trade to Other Issues, Say Minister," *National Post,* June 15, 2000, C12, quoting International Trade Minister Pierre Pettigrew. See also Stephenson, "Standards, the Environment, and Trade Facilitation in the Western Hemisphere," 168: "For the FTAA to be a complete and forward-looking agreement in the area of standards, it will have to deal with standards-related environmental measures. In this regard it will, of necessity, have to go beyond existing WTO provisions."

30. Basically, there are six models for trade-environment linkages. There are three basic choices about the degree of linkage: (1) full integration of trade and environment policy in a single agreement; (2) partial integration, such as in the NAFTA side agreements; and (3) complete separation. The three choices can be applied to either of two basic models of trade liberalization: (1) full economic integration through a customs union or (2) free trade agreements that facilitate flows of goods and services but stop well short of economic integration.

31. The policy debate over the proper relationship between trade and environment also continues in several multilateral contexts, notably the WTO Committee on Trade and Environment and the OECD. The positions of the various countries in those multilateral discussions, however, simply reflect the combination of domestically determined policy preferences and foreign policy considerations. The multilateral discussions may refine or inform national policies, but they have so far had little independent effect on how countries approach these issues. Whether the chorus of calls by the United States and Europe for the WTO to develop some substantive policy reforms on trade and environment issues alters this situation remains to be seen. Frances Williams and Guy de Jonquières, "Brittan Welcomes Clinton Trade Talks Call," *Financial Times,* May 20, 1998, 8, reported support by Prime Minister Tony Blair and President Nelson Mandela for President Clinton's appeal to the WTO to be more open to environmental views but skeptical reactions from Australia and India, among others.

32. In fact, many linkages exist between national law and international trade agreements, and national policies thus shape preferences for particular patterns of international trade and the international rules that govern them. As one writer has observed, "Should a FTAA be established, it will have repercussions beyond the sphere of imports and exports. In the late twentieth century, the term 'trade law' is another name for general rulemaking. As more and more subjects are brought into the sphere of international trade negotiation, the adoption of rules that affect trade in goods and services influences our societies on multiple levels: public and private, national and international, centralized and local." Stephen Zamora, "Allocating

Legislative Competence in the Americas: The Early Experience under the NAFTA and the Challenge of Hemispheric Integration," *Houston Journal of International Law* 19 (1997): 615, 618. For consideration of the broad patterns of interaction between domestic policies and international trade policies in the Americas, see Rodrigo Fuentes, "La Política Comercial Chilena y el Futuro del Libre Comercio en el Continente Americano," in Sergio López Ayllón, ed., *El Futuro del Libre Comercio en el Continente Americano* (Mexico, D.F.: Universidad Nacional Autónoma de Mexico, 1997), 149; Bernardo Sepúlveda Amor, "International Law and National Sovereignty: The NAFTA and the Claims of Mexican Jurisdiction," *Houston Journal of International Law* 19 (1997): 565.

33. NAFTA is naturally looked on not only as a model relevant to the Americas but also as offering guidance for trade-environment linkages worldwide. See, for example, Mark J. Spalding, "Lessons of NAFTA for APEC," *Journal of Environment & Development* 6 (1997): 252.

34. For example, John H. Jackson, "World Trade Rules and Environmental Policies: Congruence or Conflict?," *Washington & Lee Law Review* 49 (1992): 1227; Peter L. Lallas, NAFTA and Evolving Approaches to Identify and Address "Indirect" Environmental Impacts of International Trade, *Georgetown International Environmental Law Review* 5 (1993): 519, 523–38; Geza Feketekuty, "The Link between Trade and Environmental Policy," *Minnesota Journal of Global Trade* 2 (1993): 171, 186–96; and Richard H. Steinberg, "Trade-Environment Negotiations in the EU, NAFTA, and WTO: Regional Trajectories of Rule Development," *American Journal of International Law* 91 (1997): 231, 234–35. The analytical approach of the governments reflects some of the specific controversies that have arisen at the interface of trade and environment. OECD Secretariat, "Report on Trade and Environment to the OECD Council at Ministerial Level," OECD Document OCDE/GD(95)63 (1995); WTO, "Report (1996) of the Committee on Trade and Environment" (available in WTO/Press/TE 014, November 18, 1996).

35. I make no claim to originality here. Daniel C. Esty, *Greening the GATT: Trade, Environment, and the Future* (Washington, D.C.: Institute for International Economics, 1994), 42, identifies four environmental critiques of international trade rules, responses to which become the justification for the trade-environment linkage. Thomas Schoenbaum, "International Trade and Protection of the Environment: The Continuing Search for Reconciliation," *American Journal of International Law* 91 (1997): 268, 280, adopts Esty's four issues. Although I phrase the issues differently, my list of three is similar to Esty's four. I choose to omit from my list the issue of assuring that imported goods meet high national environmental standards because that is already substantially addressed by well-accepted trade rules in the WTO Agreements and in the NAFTA governing product standards. See, for example, Steinberg, "Trade-Environment Negotiations in the EU, NAFTA, and WTO," 237–38, 245–46, and Sanford E. Gaines, "Environmental Laws and Regulations after NAFTA," *U.S.-Mexico Law Journal* 1 (1993): 199. As noted by Stephenson, "Standards, the Environment, and Trade Facilitation in the Western Hemisphere," however, acceptance of the basic disciplines on products still leaves significant work to do in national legislation, in mutual recognition and conformity assessment across countries, and in areas such as eco-labeling, all of which reinforce national product standards (ibid., 155–57).

36. The preambles to the NAFTA and the WTO Agreements both make rhetorical nods in this direction. The NAFTA parties, for example, resolve to "undertake each of the preceding [economic policies] in a manner consistent with environmental protection and conservation."

37. These are sometimes referred to generically as questions of "the projected impacts of the trade policies and agreements on the scale and structure of economic activity and . . . their resulting potential environmental effects." Organization for Economic Cooperation and Development, Trade and Environment, June 1993, OECD Document OCDE/GD(93)99, Annex 1, item II.2. Muñoz, "Free Trade and Environmental Policies," discusses both the positive and the negative environmental effects of changes in scale and structure of trade in the Latin American context.

38. Consequently, the pre-NAFTA evaluation of the environmental effects of the NAFTA offered only very general conclusions about most effects. Executive Office of the President, "The NAFTA: Report on Environmental Issues (1993)," reprinted in North American Free Trade Agreement, Supplemental Agreements and Additional Documents, House Document 103–160, 103rd Cong., 1st sess. (1993), 143. Post-NAFTA assessments have been more intensive and methodologically rigorous but still must grapple with multiple complexities. The Final Analytical Framework (Draft) for Assessing Environmental Effects of the North American Free Trade Agreement (NAFTA), published in June 1999 by the Commission for Environmental Cooperation, identifies four "critical linkages" that will mediate the effect of NAFTA on the environment: production, management, and technology; physical infrastructure; social organization; and government policy (available at <http://www/cec/org/english/profile/coop/frame.cfm?format = 1>). The potentially large magnitude but diffuse nature of trade-induced environmental effects encourages many environmentalists to oppose trade liberalization altogether. The *maquiladora* plants developed both before and after NAFTA along Mexico's border with the United States to take advantage of special tariff concessions, which have attracted lots of regulatory attention in both Mexico and the United States, are an exceptional case. Even for *maquiladoras,* however, the post-NAFTA experience is vastly different from the pre-NAFTA predictions because of the exogenous and largely unforeseen variable of the 1994–95 devaluation of the Mexican peso.

39. I have examined these issues closely in Sanford E. Gaines, "Rethinking Environmental Protection, Competitiveness, and International Trade," *University of Chicago Legal Forum* (1997): 231. Although numerous factors may account for the absence of real-world competitiveness effects, the principal explanation is that environmental compliance is a negligible cost factor for most firms (ibid., 259–60).

40. As one commentator has noted, "This received economic wisdom [finding little competitiveness effect] does not, however, comport with political reality, where competitiveness concerns arising from environmental standards are a major issue." Esty, *Greening the GATT,* 21–22.

41. A variant on this theme, a concern about diverting investment flows through waiver of environmental standards, led to a special clause against such "pollution havens" in the NAFTA; NAFTA Article 1114.2. Broader concerns about inhibitions on local control over the environmental effects of foreign direct investment led to the shelving of a proposed "Multilateral Agreement on Investment" being negotiated under the auspices of the Organization for Economic Cooperation and Development.

42. This justification naturally generates an equal and opposite argument from developing countries against a trade-environment link, as described in this chapter in the text following note 48.

43. Bolivia, which has a national ministry of Sustainable Development and Environment, hosted a Summit of the Americas on Sustainable Development in December 1996 pursuant to the Plan of Action from the Miami summit.

44. The Rio Declaration and Agenda 21 refer repeatedly to "sustainable development" but never define it. The common reference point is the work of the World Commission on Environment and Development that laid much of the intellectual foundation for the UN Conference on Environment and Development in Rio: "Sustainable development is development that meets the needs of the present without compromising the ability of future generations to meet their own needs." World Commission on Environment and Development, *Our Common Future* (Oxford: Oxford University Press, 1987), 43.

45. The WTO parties recognize that their economic objectives should also allow "for the optimal use of the world's resources in accordance with the objective of sustainable development." Agreement Establishing the World Trade Organization, Preamble.

46. Organization for Economic Cooperation and Development, "Report on Trade and Environment to the OECD Council at Ministerial Level," Document OCDE/GD(95)63 (1995).

47. At a high level of generality, the nations of the Americas already endorse such policy interface. The Summit of the Americas on Sustainable Development, for example, included in its Plan of Action the following commitment: "Promote coordination and complementarity between the processes for follow-up and implementation of the Plan of Action of the Summit of the Americas and the Plan of Action on Sustainable Development. To achieve this objective the Inter-American Committee on Sustainable Development (CIDS) and the Summit Implementation Review Group (SIRG) should exchange the relevant information." Permanent Council of the Organization of American States, Draft Plan of Action for the Sustainable Development of the Americas, OEA/Ser.G, GT/CCDS-52/96 rev. 1, November 29, 1996.

48. For an authoritative exposition of this argument, see Jagdish Bhagwati and T. N. Srinivasan, "Trade and the Environment: Does Environmental Diversity Detract from the Case for Free Trade?" in Jagdish N. Bhagwati and Robert E. Hudec, eds., *Fair Trade and Harmonization: Prerequisites for Free Trade?* (Cambridge, Mass.: MIT Press, 1996), 159.

49. Ambassador Richard Fisher, deputy U.S. trade representative, made just this point in speaking to environmental issues in NAFTA and in the FTAA, noting that "each negotiation is different" and that "we need to think about environmental issues in terms of the specific context of each negotiations." "NAFTA's Integration of Trade and Environment: A U.S. Perspective on the Relevance to the FTAA" (remarks at the Conference on the Environment in the FTAA Process, April 26, 2000 (available at <http://www.ustr.gov/speech-test/fisher/fisher_26.html>).

50. I use this general term to embrace both local cross-border effects such as pollution flows and larger regional or global effects arising from multiple sources and having widespread consequences.

51. For example, in North America there are many transboundary ecological regions, and the whole continent is linked by airflows and by migratory patterns of fish and birds. The Commission for Environmental Cooperation has generated maps of the nine border-spanning ecological regions of the continent. See <http://www.cec.org/english/resources/ecoregion> for text of the CEC publication "Eco Region"; the maps are mentioned in *Eco Region* 1, no. 2 (fall 1995). The CEC has also documented specific connections; see Commission for Environmental Cooperation, *Continental Pollutant Pathways* (Montreal: Commission for Environmental Cooperation, 1997), which traces and analyzes air pollution flows among the three countries. In South America, the Andes form one obvious multinational ecological nexus and the Amazon River another.

52. Indeed, proposals over the years to complete the Pan American highway by building an overland route through the impenetrable jungles and swamps of the Darien Gap in eastern Panama and northwestern Colombia have met with strong environmental opposition precisely because the highway would breach what has so far been an almost impervious ecological barrier between the northern and southern halves of the hemisphere. See *Sierra Club v. Coleman*, 405 F.Supp. 53 (D.D.C. 1975), *rev'd sub nom. Sierra Club v. Adams*, 578 F.2d 389 (D.C. Cir. 1978) (case on adequacy of environmental impact statement on highway project in Colombia and Panama, reviewing the environmental concerns). A number of migratory birds and fish travel between North or Central America and South America. Other ecological links are sporadic.

53. Gordon J. MacDonald and Marc A. Stern, "Environmental Politics and Policies in Latin America," in MacDonald et al., eds., *Latin American Environmental Policy in International Perspective*, 1, 2–3, suggest greater environmental policy reform in Latin America on urban and pollution issues as compared to natural resource issues. Muñoz, "Free Trade and Environmental Policies," 116–19, notes positive environmental effects from trade liberalization in Chile in some industrial sectors but continued dependence on exports of resources and consequent overexploitation.

54. The United States accounts for 85 percent of the economy of the entire hemisphere. Sims, "Free-Trade Zone of the Americas Given a Go-Ahead," A10.

55. Several countries or trade blocs in Latin America have negotiated or are negotiating trade deals with the European Union, in part to use the European Union as a political counterweight to the United States. Larry Rohter, "Latin America and Europe to Talk Trade," *New York Times*, June 26, 1999, C2; BBC Summary of World Broadcasts, November 18, 2000, giving text from the Brazilian newspaper *Gazete Mercantil*, November 8, 2000, "MERCOSUR, EU Begin to Negotiate Free Trade Agreement" (from LEXIS/NEXIS CURNWS Library).

56. Maurice Wolf, "Americas Choice: The Slow Path to Global Trade Cooperation," in López Ayllón, ed., *El Futuro del Libre Comercio en el Continente Americano*, 75, provides an overview of the interlocking trade relations and incentives for or against trade liberalization. David Lopez, "Dispute Resolution under MERCOSUR from 1991 to 1996: Implications for the Formation of a Free Trade Area of the Americas," *NAFTA: Law & Business Review of the Americas* 3 (1997): 3, focuses on the important effect of the deepening and expanding Southern Cone trade arrangement.

57. As one illustration of these complex connections, Samsung, the Korean maker of televisions, computers, and other electronics, established a major facility in Tijuana, Mexico, from which it can export freely to the United States and Canada and on favorable terms to Chile and other Latin American destinations as well, thanks to Mexico's growing network of bilateral and regional trade agreements. For a concise, elegant study of the trade effects of regional trade agreements that reports on empirical work indicating that the MERCOSUR countries have sharply increased the proportion of their trade within MERCOSUR, see Jaime Serra et al., *Reflections on Regionalism: Report of the Study Group on International Trade* (Washington, D.C.: Carnegie Endowment for International Peace, 1997).

58. The latest flurry of jockeying for position and recalibration of interests was prompted by Chile's agreement to negotiate bilaterally with the United States. Brazil and Argentina downplayed the significance of this shift. "Splits regarding Chile-USA Free Trade Talks, FTAA Put into Perspective," BBC Summary of World Broadcasts, December 16, 2000 (sum-

marizing a December 14, 2000, article in Le Nación, Buenos Aires) (from LEXIS/NEXIS CURNWS Library).

59. Steinberg, "Trade-Environment Negotiations in the EU, NAFTA, and WTO," 266, underscores the importance of political power of environmentally motivated countries in making the trade-environment connection and expresses skepticism that the United States can muster the requisite political power on the FTAA.

60. See Peter J. Spiro, "New Global Potentates: Nongovernmental Organizations and the 'Unregulated' Marketplace," *Cardozo Law Review* 18 (1996): 957. Former Mexican President Miguel de la Madrid Hurtado briefly makes similar observations about the globalization of politics and society as well as the economy in "Foreword: National Sovereignty and Globalization," *Houston Journal of International Law* 19 (1997): 553.

61. Lacunza, "From Dictatorship to Democracy"; Zahralddin-Aravena, "Chilean Accession to NAFTA," 56–61.

62. Johnson and Beaulieu, *The Environment and NAFTA,* gives an excellent capsule history.

63. There are many sources describing these circumstances. I review the leading environmental problems of the border area in Gaines, "Bridges to a Better Environment," 435–43.

64. Although the earlier U.S.-Canada Free Trade Agreement stimulated new trade and new economic activity in both countries, environmentalists showed little concern for direct environmental consequences from that trade, presumably because they had substantial confidence in the willingness and ability of governments in Canada to protect the environment.

65. Agreement between the Government of the United States of America and the Government of the United Mexican States concerning the Establishment of a Border Environment Cooperation Commission and a North American Development Bank, signed at Washington, D.C., November 16, 1993, and at Mexico, D.F., November 18, 1993, 32 I.L.M. 1545 (1993). This bilateral agreement was made an integral part of the NAFTA "package" submitted to Congress for approval in November 1993. For a description of its provisions, see Gaines, "Bridges to a Better Environment," 448–59.

66. This topic is addressed to some extent in the Convention on Nature Protection and Wildlife Preservation in the Western Hemisphere, concluded at Washington, D.C., October 12, 1940, 161 U.N.T.S. 193, T.S. 981.

67. Steinberg, "Trade-Environment Negotiations in the EU, NAFTA, and WTO," provides cogent explanations for the trade-environment linkages in Europe and North America and the absence of such linkages elsewhere. He notes in both instances the overwhelming economic and political force of environmental leader nations and the sensitivity of those nations to the trade-environment link when economic relations are integrated tightly.

68. See NAFTA Chapters 7B and 9.

69. See NAFTA Article 1114. This provision stops short of creating a binding obligation, however, leading to calls for reinforcement of the commitment through a side agreement.

70. Schoenbaum, "International Trade and Protection of the Environment," 288–301, gives a thorough analysis of the PPMs issue. Arguably, the general exceptions of GATT Article XX would allow national control over PPMs, but to date there is still not a single instance in which the GATT or the WTO has approved such national measures under Article XX.

71. See, for example, John Audley, "Why Environmentalists Are Angry about the North American Free Trade Agreement," in Durwood Zaelke, Paul Orbuch, and Robert F. Housman, eds., *Trade and the Environment: Law, Economics, and Policy* (Washington, D.C.: Island Press, 1993), 191, 194–96.

72. The trinational agreement creating the Commission for Environmental Cooperation (CEC), also known as the environmental "side agreement," is the North American Agreement on Environmental Cooperation between the Government of the United States of America, the Government of Canada, and the Government of the United Mexican States, signed at Washington, D.C., September 9 and 14; at Ottawa, September 12 and 14; and at Mexico, D.F., September 8 and 14, 1993, 32 I.L.M. 1480 (1993). The most widely available version of the text is a "final draft" dated September 13, 1993. For an excellent description and analysis, see Johnson and Beaulieu, *The Environment and NAFTA*. The CEC is not an enforcement agency, however. As its name indicates, the emphasis is on cooperation. The CEC's mandate covers a broad sweep of environmental issues of continental dimension or common interest to the three countries. Article 10.2 of the North American Agreement on Environmental Cooperation lists topics from "(a) comparability of techniques and methodologies for data gathering and analysis, data management, and electronic data communications on matter covered by this Agreement" to "(r) eco-labeling," not to mention the catchall "(s) other matters as it [the council of ministers] may decide." For Mexico in particular, commitment to cooperation on continental environmental matters nicely counterbalanced the investigative- and compliance-oriented provisions, making the agreement as a whole politically palatable. It allows Mexico to play a constructive environmental role, and it creates substantial opportunity for Mexico to obtain expert advice and assistance in defining and resolving some of its serious environmental problems. The third section of this chapter comments on the operation of these cooperation provision in the first six years.

73. See, generally, Johnson and Beaulieu, *The Environment and NAFTA,* for a detailed exposition of the agreement's provisions.

74. The influence of the environmentalists had made itself felt at the outset of the negotiations, when their congressional allies compelled President Bush to commit to consideration of environmental issues on a "parallel track." President George Bush, "Response of the Administration to Issues Raised in Connection with the Negotiation of a North American Free Trade Agreement," transmitted to Congress May 1, 1991.

75. This political imperative was identical for both the Bush and the Clinton administrations, though their responses to that imperative differed somewhat.

76. Remarks by Governor Bill Clinton at the Student Center at North Carolina State University, Raleigh, Federal News Service, October 4, 1992 (available in LEXIS, Nexis Library, Executive File).

77. For an insightful discussion, see Torres, "Transnational Environmental NGOs," 169–77.

78. The Commission for Environmental Cooperation has documented one example, the flow of air pollution across North America's borders, in its report "Continental Pollutant Pathways," 1997.

79. Albert Gore Jr., *Earth in the Balance* (Boston, Mass.: Houghton Mifflin, 1993).

80. In 1999, the U.S. two-way trade with Canada was $365 billion and with Mexico $197 billion. The largest trading partner elsewhere in the Americas, Brazil, had just $25 billion of trade with the United States. Data from the Department of Commerce (available at <http://www.ita.doc.gov/TSFrameset.html>).

81. One sign of reluctance to engage the trade-environment linkage has come, ironically and ominously, from Mexico. According to one report, "As talks continue to create a Free Trade Area of the Americas by 2005, negotiators are complaining, privately, about Mexico's

fierce objections to linking trade and the environment. Mexico objects to any process that might be created under the FTAA to bring international pressure on a nation for its environmental policies. . . . In interviews, a top Mexican trade negotiator and high-level environmental policy-maker argues that dialogue with environmental and other groups is best done on a domestic level and has no place in international trade accords." Kevin G. Hall, "Mexico Adamant about Keeping Environment out of Trade Talks," *Journal of Commerce,* January 11, 1999, 1A.

82. The summit between the European Union and Latin America in Rio in June 1999 was one manifestation of this political approach.

83. North American Agreement on Environmental Cooperation, Article 14. Through the end of 1998, the CEC had received twenty submissions from citizens. In two cases, one involving Mexico and the other Canada, the secretariat's independent inquiry led it to recommend to the Council the development of a more thorough investigation, known as a "factual record," under Article 15 of the Agreement. The Council approved both requests. The factual record on the *Cozumel Pier* case was completed in 1997 and seemed to influence the Mexican government's decision to suspend completion of the project. The factual record in the *British Columbia Hydro* case was completed in 2000.

84. The secretariat has used this authority twice, once to investigate the cause of a bird kill on the Silva Reservoir in Mexico and once to examine water resources management in the San Pedro River Basin, which spans the border of Sonora, Mexico, and Arizona. The final report on the Silva Reservoir, Commission for Environmental Cooperation, "Secretariat Report on the Death of Migrating Birds at the Silva Reservoir" (1995), has resulted in corrective actions described in a follow-up report, "Silva Reservoir: An Example of Regional Environmental Cooperation in North America" (available at <http://www.cec.org/english/resources/publications/silva-e.cfm?format = 1>). The San Pedro study resulted in a final report, Commission for Environmental Cooperation, "Ribbon of Life: An Agenda for Preserving Transboundary Migratory Bird Habitat on the Upper San Pedro River," June 1999. The CEC study has also catalyzed cooperative transboundary work on San Pedro issues at both the local and the federal levels.

85. Despite its unique composition and role, the JPAC has received little attention from legal commentators. For example, an otherwise useful discussion of the CEC by Alicia Samios, "NAFTA's Supplemental Agreement: In Need of Reform," *New York International Law Review* 9, no. 2 (1996): 49, completely misses the novel and vital role of the JPAC. Political scientists seem more attuned to its significance. See Stephen P. Mumme and Pamela Duncan, "The Commission for Environmental Cooperation and Environmental Management in the Americas," *Journal of Interamerican Studies & World Affairs* 39, no. 1 (winter 1997–98): 41.

86. One vivid example of the JPAC's role and influence relates to the procedural guidelines for the citizen submission process under Articles 14 and 15, described previously. In June 1998, the Council of Ministers put forward a government-negotiated draft of changes to the guidelines that would have made submissions more difficult and limited the secretariat's discretion. Under pressure, the Council agreed to have the JPAC manage a public notice and comment process on the proposed changes. As a result of that process, the JPAC reported back a recommendation that the guidelines not be modified. Consequently, at its 1999 meeting, the Council finally adopted a much reduced and largely benign set of amendments to the guidelines. Much of this story can be found in CEC and JPAC press releases and reports available on the CEC's Web site at <http://www.cec.org>.

87. Mumme and Duncan, "The Commission for Environmental Cooperation and Environmental Management in the Americas," 48–55. Lacking authority to press a substantive trade agenda, the Clinton administration began emphasizing increased public participation and transparency in trade forums. That was President Clinton's main message at the fiftieth anniversary celebrations at the WTO in Geneva in May 1998. U.S. Trade Representative Charlene Barshefsky was quoted as saying, "We want to discuss how best to ensure the institution does not remain mysterious. Secrecy in institutions does nothing but breed suspicions." Guy de Jonquières and Frances Williams, "World Trade Party-Goers Look for the Next Big Leap Forward," *Financial Times,* May 18, 1998, 7. "Other governments are starting to recognise that unless the WTO does more to spread the word about the benefits of free trade, it risks losing the public relations battle to increasingly vocal opponents of liberalisation and globalisation" (ibid.).

88. Supplementing the JPAC are the National Advisory Committees and Governmental Advisory Committees authorized by the agreement. All three countries have constituted National Advisory Committees and convene them regularly. Only the United States has a Governmental Advisory Committee of state, local, and tribal officials.

89. Details on these and other activities can be found in the annual reports of the CEC and in other documents available on the CEC's Web site at <http://www.cec.org>.

90. Those advocates note negatively the political maneuvering within and between governments on the NAFTA effects work. These difficulties point up the political sensitivity of efforts to integrate trade and environment policy. Significant methodological problems in isolating the economic effects of NAFTA from other economic factors and in identifying specific environmental effects have also contributed to the slow pace and thus far preliminary nature of the work.

91. The methodological framework is in note 38. The CEC held a symposium in 2000 to review the methodology. The three sector studies, released in 1999, study electricity, feedlot production of cattle in the United States and Canada, and maize production in Mexico. All these documents are available through the CEC's Web site at <http://www.cec.org>.

92. See Dunoff, " 'Trade and,' " 763–64. Some environmentalists argue that a strong multinational environmental organization would have value as a counterweight to the WTO in multilateral policymaking on trade and environment. Esty, *Greening the GATT.*

93. Commission for Environmental Cooperation, *NAFTA's Institutions: The Environmental Potential and Performance of the NAFTA Free Trade Commission and Related Bodies* (Montreal: The Commission for Environmental Cooperation 1997).

94. Johnson, "Beyond Trade."

95. In pursuit of that policy, Canada replicated most of the CEC system in its bilateral free trade agreement with Chile.

96. For example, on the subject of the CEC secretariat's development of a factual record on compliance with Mexican law in the granting of permits for the construction of a cruise ship pier and associated onshore facilities on the island of Cozumel, Mexico's environmental minister, Julia Carabias Lillo, was quoted in the Mexican press objecting to the interference of the CEC in Mexico's domestic environmental policies. If Chile were a CEC member, it might have seconded those concerns and offered Mexico political support to block the CEC inquiry.

97. Mexican lawyer Alberto Székely, who has served on an independent review committee for the CEC, made the suggestion for an associate membership category in a personal conversation with the author, October 1997.

98. This proposition is also supported by Mumme and Duncan, "The Commission for Environmental Cooperation and Environmental Management in the Americas," 55–58, offering additional analytical support for this view from the literature of political science study of international institutions.

99. See, generally, the chapters by various authors in MacDonald et al., eds., *Latin American Environmental Policy in International Perspective.*

100. Convention for the Protection and Development of the Marine Environment of the Wider Caribbean Region, done at Cartagena, March 24, 1983. See UN Environment Program, "The Current Situation of International Environmental Law in Latin America and the Caribbean" (report by Alberto Székely for the Meeting of Legal Experts, Mexico City, February 1993), 36–37. Ambassador Székely views the Caribbean convention and a similar one for the Southeast Pacific as the most effective regional environmental programs in the hemisphere (ibid., 46).

101. On the process of political liberalization in the hemisphere and its relation to environmental policy, see the contributions by Mumme and Korzetz, "Democratization, Politics, and Environmental Reform in Latin America"; Muñoz, "Free Trade and Environmental Policies"; and Torres, "Transnational Environmental NGOs," all in MacDonald et al., eds., *Latin American Environmental Policy in International Perspective.*

102. By the same token, however, trade officials, especially trade officials from developing or newly industrializing economies, must overcome their equally misguided fear that the incorporation of reasonable environmental factors into the disciplines of international trade will impair the competitiveness of local producers and impede their nations' economic development.

8

APEC: The "Sustainable Development" Agenda

Lyuba Zarsky

In the early 1990s, popular concern about mounting ecological degradation swept the world. The historical moment was crystallized in the 1992 UN World Conference on Environment and Development, known popularly as the Rio Summit. Attended by over 100 heads of state, the Summit coalesced around the concept of "sustainable development," the idea that environmental protection could and should be built into the design of economic development plans and policies rather than addressed as an aftermath of economic growth. The Summit produced a sweeping plan of action called "Agenda 21" and called for both states and international organizations to implement it.

From another direction as well, environmental issues began to trickle into—and bump up against—global consciousness and institutions, especially the General Agreement on Tariffs and Trade (GATT; later the World Trade Organization [WTO]). At the GATT/WTO, however, the framework for grappling with new environmental concerns was based on a "trade and environment" formulation that stressed the primacy of maintaining neoliberal trade rules and ensuring that national environmental regulation not be a mask for trade protectionism. First convened in 1995, the WTO Committee on Trade and Environment has focused discussion primarily on confining the environmental parameters for trade sanctions and trade restrictions.[1] During the 1990s, when national level efforts to protect global resources—such as sea turtles and dolphins—were challenged, the WTO ruled every time that trade trumps environment. In the early 1990s, environmental issues gained rapid momentum in the Asia Pacific Economic Cooperation forum (APEC), whose approach to the environment was an anomaly. While the organization is focused mainly on trade liberalization, APEC's attempts to grapple with environmental issues flowed in the "sustainable development" current. APEC focused not on resolving conflicts between trade and environmental policies but on developing practical, voluntary initiatives and broad principles of environment-economy integration in the context of trade liberalization. Like its trade diplomacy, APEC's actions on environmental policy grew out of a consensus-building, nonbinding, "soft law" approach to international cooperation. In style and substance, it was more akin to a UN than a WTO model of international collective action.

Given the narrowness, contentiousness, and gridlock of environmental diplomacy at the WTO, APEC's broad scope and "nuts and bolts" approach seemed promising. Moreover, global environmental and trade negotiations typically are conducted in separate institutions. Discussing them under one APEC roof suggested seeds of possibility for the integration of environmental and economic objectives in a regional trade regime.

Between 1994 and 1997, a series of high-profile meetings of APEC environment ministers initially yielded an innovative set of "sustainable development" principles and triggered a plethora of "capacity-building" seminars and workshops. Despite early hopes, however, the substantive results were meager. No collective policy initiatives were charted or debated, let alone embraced; environmentally sensitive sectors, including forests and agriculture, were treated like any other commodity by overeager trade diplomats; and no effective institutional mechanisms emerged either to coordinate APEC's environment work at the governmental level or to provide an interface with scientists, nongovernmental organizations (NGOs), and other "civil society" groups.

Moreover, despite APEC's stated commitment to "economy-environment integration," environmental and trade diplomacy were tightly kept on separate and parallel tracks, both within individual APEC economies and in APEC as an institution. The possibility of scrutinizing APEC's trade initiatives on environmental grounds was thus strictly off the agenda. Divorced from both popular domestic political forces and from APEC's high-powered trade and investment track, environmental cooperation remained mired in the lackluster province of bureaucrats and technocrats. Well before the Asian financial crisis took the wind out of APEC's economic sails, the environmental track had gotten stuck in the doldrums.

This chapter describes and assesses APEC's "sustainable development" diplomacy in the 1990s. The first part outlines the analytical and political contours of environmental regionalism in Asia-Pacific. After surveying some of the region's most pressing environmental problems, the chapter develops a theoretical framework to show why economic interdependence requires nations to coordinate both trade-impacting environmental policies and environment-impacting trade policies. The second part examines the politics of environmental diplomacy at APEC and analyzes the "value-added" domain of environmental cooperation. The third part describes APEC's environmental initiatives between 1993, when environmental issues moved into the mainstream, and June 1997, when APEC's third—and last—environment ministerial was held. It also describes the emergence of NGO activism on APEC. The fourth part evaluates APEC's foray into sustainable development and argues that the reasons for its lackluster performance include poor leadership and the lack of a coordinating institutional structure, popular opposition in Asia to APEC's "free trade" agenda, and, most fundamentally, the lack of political will within APEC countries to integrate trade and environment issues. The fifth part concludes that APEC made a high-profile but ultimately false start in the 1990s toward a regional approach to trade, environment, and sustainable development. Like other large-scale international efforts—perhaps Agenda 21 itself—APEC's environmental initiatives were dissipated by the disconnect between "top-down" pressures and "bottom-up" demands.

The fundamental issues that APEC tried to wrestle with, however, have not been resolved. The high level of ecological degradation and the burgeoning role of civil society throughout Asia ensure that social and environmental issues will be deeply embedded in future debates about development. Given that East Asian countries will continue to be highly integrated in the regional and global economy, these debates will spill over into regional trade and investment diplomacy.

While the future of APEC itself is uncertain, trade-linked environmental issues will be on the agenda at the WTO, in bilateral trade agreements, or in some new regional trade grouping. An increasingly strong popular voice in Asia is demanding that environmental protection must be one of the pillars of global economic governance—not in a framework that blindly asserts the primacy of trade but in a new approach based on the coequal status of economic development, environmental protection, and social justice.

ASIA-PACIFIC REGIONALISM
AND THE ENVIRONMENT

For much of the past fifty years, trans-Pacific politics were delineated by the Cold War. With the end of the Cold War in 1991, new imperatives to cooperate in building regional institutions were unleashed, not the least of which is the need to manage the changing regional power balance between China, Japan, and the United States.[2] For the United States, APEC offered a vehicle for political engagement on a regional basis.

The primary driving force behind the founding and evolution of APEC, however, was economic, namely, the increasing market-driven integration of APEC economies in the 1980s and 1990s. Nearly 70 percent of total APEC trade was intraregional in 1994.[3] Capital flows also became highly concentrated in APEC. About 65 percent of Japan's foreign direct investment outflows, for example, went to APEC countries in 1990, some 46 percent to the United States alone.[4] Within APEC, North America and East Asia form two highly integrated economic subregions. In 1990, about 40 percent of total East Asian trade was to other East Asian countries; for North America, the figure was roughly 37 percent.[5]

Most East Asian nations have pursued development strategies that have two overarching features. First, they are based on "linkage-led" growth, that is, on promoting trade and investment with developed countries, especially Japan and the United States. Second, they are based on an economic paradigm that excludes environmental "externalities" and social concerns, including human rights.

Linkage-led growth made East Asia the world's economic dynamo during the 1980s and much of the 1990s. In most Southeast Asian nations, gross national product (GNP) grew more than 5 percent per year throughout the 1980s and early 1990s. In China, GNP has been growing at an annual rate of about 10 percent or more for nearly two decades.[6]

The good news is that rapid growth raised the standard of living for millions of people.[7] The bad news is that rapid, socially and environmentally blind growth has exacerbated poverty in the countryside and created severe problems of ecological degradation.[8] In its first comprehensive report on the state of Asia's environment, the Asian Development Bank concluded in 2001 that environmental pollution and resource degradation are so "pervasive, accelerating and unabated" that they risk human health and livelihood.[9]

Regional Environmental Problems

While environmental woes are many, three are especially salient to international politics in the region: (1) air, atmospheric, and water pollution, especially those related to energy production and use; (2) resource depletion and degradation; and (3) demographic shifts, including rural out-migration, food security, and urbanization.

Among the most pressing problems for both the developed and the developing countries of APEC is the cluster of issues related to energy production and use, including air and atmospheric pollution.[10] In East Asia, commercial energy demand has been projected to nearly double between 2000 and 2010, propelled by high rates of economic growth. In China alone, electricity-generating capacity has been expected to nearly quadruple in the same period.[11] Projected growth in generation and transmission in Northeast Asia has been projected to require an investment of $72 billion per year for the fifteen years after 1997.[12] If future investment decisions resemble those of the past, power sector development will be based heavily on fossil fuels, including "dirty" high-sulfur- and/or carbon-emitting coal.

Energy-related air pollution, especially "acid rain" induced by sulfur emissions from power plants in northern China, is among the most severe regional environmental problems in Northeast Asia.[13] According to the World Bank/ADB RAINS-Asia model, sulfur dioxide emissions in Northeast Asia totaled 14.7 million tons in 1990. Under a "business-as-usual" scenario, sulfur dioxide emissions will more than double that figure by 2010 and nearly triple by 2020; emissions of nitrogen oxide (NO_X) will more than triple between 1990 and 2020. Even under a "higher-efficiency forecast" scenario, in which governments make targeted efforts to increase energy efficiency and institute reasonable fuel substitution measures, sulfur dioxide emissions would double in those thirty years.[14] The lion's share of the emissions will emanate from China and could double the levels of acid rain in neighboring countries, including Japan and the two Koreas.

Rapid growth in coal-based energy, as well as motorized urban transport, is also responsible for projected large increases in greenhouse gas emissions in Asia, especially carbon dioxide. Between 1990 and 2000, the growth of carbon dioxide emissions in Asia was calculated to more than triple that of the rest of the world.[15] As a whole, Asia accounted for about 20 percent of worldwide greenhouse gas emissions in 1985; by 2000, its share was 30 percent. By the year 2025, China is projected to be the world's largest annual emitter of greenhouse gases.[16]

Problems of energy demand and use are not restricted to the East Asian members of APEC. The United States, Canada, and Australia are among the world's four highest per capita carbon emitters.[17] In the United States, energy use is encouraged by financial and environmental resource subsidies. Besides helping to make Americans energy guzzlers,[18] the subsidies distort global energy prices.

Rapid industrial development is also an important source of both air and water pollution. The pollution intensity of industry is increasing in all the rapidly industrializing countries of East Asia.[19] Water pollution, especially generated by high organic pollution loads, is a serious problem throughout the region.[20] The increase in pollution intensity is a result of both an overall increase in manufacturing and the sectoral growth of pollution-intensive industries within manufacturing. In Thailand, for example, hazardous waste–generating industries accounted for 58 percent of industrial gross domestic product (GDP) in 1989, up from only 29 percent in 1979.[21] In Indonesia, manufacturing output doubled in volume every six to seven years during the 1970s and 1980s and was projected by the World Bank to expand another thirteen-fold between 1990 and 2020.[22]

Besides air and atmospheric pollution, APEC economies suffer high rates of resource depletion and degradation. East Asia has the world's highest rate of deforestation and loss of original habitat. According to the Asian Development Bank, Asia has lost half its forest cover, and the region's remaining timber reserves will be depleted by the year 2034.[23] The marine environment and fisheries, both coastal and offshore, are also under severe stress in many APEC countries. In Canada, policy neglect precipitated a collapse of northeastern fisheries. In Northeast Asia, the Sea of Japan suffers a high level of marine pollution stemming from oil exploration and transport, radioactive waste disposal, and shipping and industrial waste dumping.[24] Throughout East Asia, coastal zones are threatened by flows of urban, industrial, port and riverine wastes. Intensive shrimp aquaculture ponds, mostly for export, have damaged significant areas of coastal mangrove forests throughout China and Southeast Asia. A marked increase in fishing effort has resulted in the overexploitation of several important species in Southeast Asian seas, one of the world's most productive fisheries.[25]

Interwoven into the human-nature interface in Asia are demographic factors, including population growth, rural-urban migration, and urbanization. The population of Asia was about 3.4 billion in 1995 and is projected to rise to 4.9 billion in 2025. As of 1994, about 34 percent of all people in Asia lived in cities, up from only 22 percent in 1965.[26] In APEC as a whole, 44.5 percent of the population lived in urban areas in 1995; by 2015, over 64 percent will be urban dwellers.[27]

While the urbanized population is rising rapidly, environmental infrastructure, such as clean water, sewerage systems, and public transport, is not keeping pace. Problems of air pollution in many East Asian cities are severe, generated by high levels of particulates, lead from leaded gasoline, and emissions from households, vehicles, and small industry. In the Western countries of APEC, widely dispersed cities, coupled with lack of public transport, make automobile dependence high, with associated problems of local and atmospheric pollution.[28]

Interrelationships between natural resource degradation and demographic change are not well charted.[29] While simplistic formulations should be eschewed, there is ample evidence that unplanned and large jumps in the number of people living in a given area can increase ecological degradation.[30] Throughout Asia, high levels of rural-urban migration are driven by the prospect of employment and higher incomes on the one hand and the demise of traditional sources of livelihood in rural areas due to marketization and resource depletion on the other.[31]

The shift from agricultural production and rural living to industrial work and urban habitation has been a feature of all countries in the process of industrialization. In Asia, however, the shift is occurring on an unprecedented scale—and at great speed, stimulated by "structural adjustment" economic policies.[32] A rapid, broad, and deep liberalization of agricultural trade—as presaged by APEC—would likely speed the rural-urban migration process further, leaving potentially millions of poor displaced peasants without secure sources of food.

Besides its human and ecological impacts, it is likely that environment-blind development is more costly in financial and economic terms than environmentally sensitive development. According to the World Bank, by the late 1990s the annual health costs from air pollution in Bangkok, Jakarta, and Kuala Lumpur totaled about $5 billion—about 10 percent of city income. In Jakarta, unsafe drinking water was generating health costs of $300 million per year. A study in Vancouver found that traffic congestion in the late 1990s cost the city $200 million per year.[33] Given the region's projected large increases in energy and industrial growth, one of the central environmental management issues for the next twenty years will be the creation of incentives for the "greening" of investment and "innovative financing" for the provision of public goods.[34]

The Domain of Regional Environmental Cooperation

Environmental and resource management are largely the unilateral preserve of nation-states. There are three cases, however, when cooperation between two or more nations is needed to govern ecosystems and resources: first, when ecosystems or natural resources straddle national borders (transboundary); second, when a resource is wholly or partially outside the jurisdiction of any state (commons); and third, when two or more nations are highly integrated economically (globalization).

It is commonly understood that the management of transboundary and common resources require international collective action. APEC could conceivably serve this function by acting as an umbrella under which Asia-Pacific nations develop regimes to manage common resources, especially the western Pacific Ocean and fisheries. However, APEC is highly dispersed geographically. With land masses spread on four continents, few resources are truly regional. On the other hand, APEC could help catalyze or support cooperation on subregional transboundary issues, such as acid rain in Northeast Asia or fisheries in Southeast Asia. It could help build consensus around Asia's role in managing global commons, such as the oceans or the atmosphere.

Given its character as an economic organization, APEC's primary "value added" is more likely to lie in promoting better governance of the environment-economy interface in the context of globalization. In this vein, there are four key tasks: (1) vision—developing a common paradigm and norms of ecologically sensitive development at a national level and a long-term sense of direction at the regional level; (2) capacity building—developing capacities for environmental and resource management by closing national gaps between richer and poorer countries and by creating new, regional capacities to monitor and raise environmental performance; (3) policy coordination—undertaking common policies aimed at creating market incentives to improve environmental performance; and (4) institutional strengthening—developing regional institutional mechanisms to coordinate, evaluate, and stimulate environmental initiatives and to provide avenues for public information and input.

In the 1990s, APEC focused on building norms and capacities. While it did not generate a compelling overarching vision, progress was made toward articulating common principles (see the following discussion). On the capacity-building side, the primary emphasis was on building capacities to build capacities, that is, on analyzing problems and exchanging information. The need to develop institutional mechanisms, at least for better coordination, was discussed, debated—and rejected. The highly controversial realm of coordinated policy initiatives, however, was largely uncharted.

The rationale for focusing on regional economy-environment cooperation, especially policy coordination, stems from the high level of Asia-Pacific economic integration in the regional and global economy. Under conditions of globalization, the environmental policies and commitments of nations are highly conditioned by those of major trade and investment partners and competitors. Environmental degradation—and good environmental management—imposes costs. Unless specific measures are taken, these costs are not reflected in market prices but are borne socially, today or in the future.[35] Many environmentalists and commentators have suggested that an individual country (or business) that takes significant measures to internalize its own local or global environmental costs could be priced out of export markets or lose attractiveness as a production site for domestic or foreign investors. Even if the actual change in relative costs is negligible, the fear of such an effect might act to politically paralyze policymakers, especially if there were implications for job loss and campaign contributions.[36]

This logic suggests that there are strong market-driven incentives for domestic environmental management standards, especially for production and harvesting processes, to converge toward and remain close to those of primary competitors.[37] Product standards, on the other hand, tend to be drawn toward large-market countries, such as the United States and Japan.[38] Moreover, standards within particular industries are likely to converge toward those of market leaders.

Beyond market forces, policymakers have an incentive to harmonize environmental policy in order to facilitate trade and investment by reducing transactions costs, that is, the costs to business of getting information about and meeting different environmental requirements. Transnational firms as well can reduce learning and management costs by adopting global rather than country-specific standards.

What do market-driven convergence pressures mean for environmental performance?[39] On the one hand, product standards of the worst performers are likely to be drawn up toward an Organization for Economic Cooperation and Development (OECD) average. On the other hand, production and process standards may be drawn up or down, depending on the structure of global competition in the particular sector or industry. Over time, the long-term trend might even be positive, that is, toward better environmental performance because of market-driven processes of technological and managerial innovation and better allocation of resources.

The problem is that, with each nation (or firm) reluctant to take bold unilateral measures that could impose costs on domestic producers, the *average level* of environmental performance in particular sectors, industries, and nations is likely to be too low to be ecologically sustainable, and, most important, the *rate of innovation* in improving environmental performance will be slow.[40] Given projected rapid growth in the Asia-Pacific region, with associated high levels of ecological degradation, the rate of improvement is a crucial variable. Besides generating a level of performance that is too low and a process of change that is too slow, a purely market-driven process of convergence is bound to be too blunt. Good ecosystem and resource management requires sensitivity to local ecological and social conditions. Diversity of goals and approaches both across and within nations will yield a better environmental outcome than uniformity. Without policy coordination, markets are likely to promote harmonization without fully incorporating specific environmental objectives.

Market competition among open economies, in short, creates a drag on bold, unilateral policy initiatives.[41] In some cases, globalization might indeed press standards down in a "race to the bottom," at least in the short term, while in other cases it might push standards up. Overall, however, it is likely that standards are "stuck in the mud," that is, that the rate of improvement is slow because policymakers are looking over their shoulders at their competitors and engage in intense "local competition" for investment.[42] For international market forces to promote *sustainable* development, governments must set common policy frameworks that expressly create incentives for better environmental performance, especially for sectors exposed to the global economy.

Coordinated action would change the terms of the "level playing field" in which all firms compete. An example would be a common commitment to reduce or eliminate environmentally damaging financial subsidies, including for energy use and the commercial use of resources.[43] While countries could reduce subsidies unilaterally, the sectoral impacts on competitiveness create powerful domestic oppositional lobbies. As a 1996 OECD workshop concluded, "Overcoming opposition to subsidy reform will be substantially easier if countries can be convinced to react *together*, rather than *separately*, in reducing subsidies/tax concessions to particular industries or sectors."[44]

APEC AND THE POLITICS OF
ENVIRONMENTAL DIPLOMACY

APEC's ability to effectively undertake the tasks of regional environmental governance depends ultimately on politics and leadership. During the 1990s, environmental politics at APEC were intimately bound up with the regional politics of trade diplomacy and the global politics of environmental diplomacy.

During the 1990s, APEC could have been described as a "club of winners," at least until the financial crisis of 1997. And within three years after the crisis, most APEC countries resumed rapid growth. APEC embraces two of the world's three largest industrial economies, Japan and the United States; two of the world's most populous and rapidly developing nations, China and Indonesia; and a clutch of the most successful newly industrialized economies, including South Korea, Singapore, Taiwan, Chile, Thailand, Malaysia, and Indonesia.

Little wonder that the membership of APEC grew rapidly—from twelve in 1989 to twenty in 1998.[45] The membership issue—whom to let in and when—is a recurrent and contentious theme. Should APEC continue to expand to include big, powerful developing countries like India, its modus operandi and even raison d'être could change substantially.

Besides economic interdependence, APEC is characterized politically by discrepancies in economic size and thus political power. In 1999, the United States and Japan together accounted for about 80 percent of the total GDP of APEC countries.[46] The United States alone accounted for nearly 50 percent.[47] In nearly all Asian APEC countries, however, exports comprised a growing share of GDP during the 1980s and 1990s.[48]

Market-driven economic integration and the gaps in national economic capacities have shaped the "two legs" of APEC diplomacy: (1) trade and investment liberalization and facilitation, primarily the lowering of tariff and nontariff trade barriers in East Asia, the creation of a nondiscriminatory investment regime, and measures to reduce regulatory and procedural barriers to trade, and (2) economic and technical cooperation, dubbed "Eco-Tech," promoting economic and human resource development primarily in APEC's poorer economies. Slotted into the second leg, environmental cooperation has been premised largely on the notion that the poorer countries have the problems while the richer countries have the solutions rather than a need to tackle problems common to all.

APEC diplomacy, on both trade and environment tracks, has been characterized by differences in the priority different members accord to the two legs. APEC's original focus was on economic cooperation, including trade facilitation. In 1993, however, the Western countries, led by the United States, began to press hard for liberalization.[49] In 1994, APEC leaders meeting in Bogor, Indonesia, accepted a broad vision of "free and open trade and investment" by 2020 for the developing and 2010 for the developed countries. In November 1995, an Action Agenda was accepted in Osaka, and in November 1996, "Individual Action Plans" for liberalization were presented to APEC ministerial meetings in Manila.[50] Since the financial crisis of 1997, however, key parts of that agenda have stalled.

On the surface, APEC member economies have developed a broad consensus on the desirability of free trade and investment. Below the surface, however, are deep tensions between Western and Asian elites over the scope and pace of liberalization. In Asian countries hit hard by the financial crisis in late 1997 to early 1998, these tensions were exacerbated by the structural adjustment policies imposed by the International Monetary Fund (IMF) as a condition of bailout. The refusal of the United States to entertain Japan's proposal for a regional solution to the crisis in the shape of an Asian Monetary Fund further inflamed anti-Americanism.

There is also contention about APEC's role in global trade diplomacy. It is unclear whether APEC could and will act primarily to implement commitments made under the GATT/WTO or will go beyond them. In other words, will APEC be a leader or a follower in the push toward global free trade? On the one hand, APEC's broad vision of "free trade by 2020" is much more sweeping than any free trade goals yet embraced by the WTO. On the other hand, the Individual Action Plans put forward by APEC countries in 1996 pointed in the direction of a follower: Few new "GATT-Plus" commitments were offered by any country.[51] Changing tack, APEC trade ministers in 1997 designated fifteen broad sectors as targets for "Early Voluntary Sector Liberalization" (EVSL). While progress toward trade liberalization was made in some sectors, the EVSL strategy has not yielded brilliant success. Indeed, one of the sectors, forest and wood products, was stalemated at APEC by Japan and nudged into the WTO arena.

On the environment side, APEC diplomacy has yielded outcomes almost exactly inverse to the trade track. On the one hand is a plethora of activity: By the late 1990s, over forty environmentally oriented projects had been launched. On the other hand, no broad vision of "sustainable development by 2020" emerged to integrate the myriad projects either with each other or with APEC's trade and economic diplomacy.

An egregious example of this failure at integrating trade and environment tracks at APEC was the designation of two resource-intensive sectors—forest and wood products and fisheries—as targets for EVSL with virtually no consideration of their environmental impacts. Environmental groups protested loudly that there was no environmental impact assessment, including an evaluation of whether existing policies—such as financial and environmental subsidies—and management capacities would be adequate or appropriate under a changed trade regime.[52]

Three characteristics of APEC inhibit more substantive environmental cooperation: (1) cultural and economic differences among members, which have fueled trade conflicts and Asian nationalism; (2) the complex and confused politics of leadership, especially the preponderant but nonhegemonic power of the United States; and (3) APEC's particular "consensus-building" style and flaccid institutional structure.

Cultural Diversity and Trade Conflict

Within APEC is found a high degree of cultural diversity and economic disparity. Income per capita, for example, is about thirty times greater in Japan, APEC's richest country, than in the Philippines, one of its poorest.[53] Northeast Asia is predominantly Confucian, while Southeast Asia is a mixture of Buddhist, Muslim, Christian, and other religions. Western countries have strong legal, juridical traditions, while East Asian and Latin APEC countries generally do not. Western countries also have strong democratic traditions, with noisy civil society groups who press their governments to act on social and environmental issues. In much of East Asia, strong civil society organizations are young or nascent.

One political dividing line in APEC could be drawn as "North-South," that is, between developed and developing/newly industrialized countries; another between East and West; and a third between the Association of Southeast Asian Nations (ASEAN) and the rest. One of the primary fault lines stems from different models of development. Over the past twenty years, rapid growth and industrialization in several East Asian countries, including South Korea, have come as a result of strong "developmental" state policies, including import protection and export promotion.[54] The large growth in production and export capacities, however, has generated large and persistent trade deficits with the United States.[55] Threats by the United States and, occasionally, actions to restrict domestic market access unless Asian markets are opened to American goods, services, and investment have shaped bilateral and regional relations with East Asia since the early 1980s.

Broad East-West differences in development strategies and political-economic cultures, as well as a newfound sense of power and identity, have fueled an East Asian nationalism within APEC, centered especially in ASEAN.[56] Jealous to guard its own status as a regional organization, ASEAN initially blocked the formation of

APEC in the 1980s. In the 1990s, Prime Minister Mahathir of Malaysia called for the creation of an "East Asian Economic Organization" as an alternative to APEC that would exclude Western nations. The proposal failed, primarily because of the overriding economic interests of ASEAN in Western capital and export markets as well as security concerns about Japan and China. Nonetheless, an APEC East Asian Caucus was established at APEC, and in November 2000, China proposed a free trade area within ASEAN.[57]

Differences in levels of economic development, as well as political culture, have created gaps among APEC nations in capacities for environmental and resource management. For APEC's Western nations and Japan, environmental regulation and legislation began in earnest in the late 1960s or early 1970s. For most of East Asia, environmental awareness and regulation was sparked only in the early 1990s. While there is some potential for fast-growing Asian economies to "leapfrog" Western technology and avoid the West's ecological sins, environmental managers in both the public and the private sectors are often playing "catch-up" with the West. Economic managers, in turn, resist the rapid imposition of environmental requirements that could impose costs and slow growth.

As in other international environmental fora, gaps in management capacities and development priorities have generated tension in APEC over the weight given to a "development" versus an "environment" agenda. While the tension has not dead-locked progress toward environmental cooperation, it has slowed the pace and com-plicated the articulation of a common vision. To date, discussion of political differ-ences about environmental postures and development priorities has been muted, with general consensus on the need to establish common principles and focus on noncontroversial aspects of capacity building.

The Politics of Leadership

The second feature of internal politics at APEC is the preponderant power—and the unilateralist leadership style—of the United States. With the largest economic and military capability, the United States has been called the "800-pound gorilla" of APEC.[58] East Asia, however, is highly dynamic. For example, between 1980 and 1995, Japan's share of APEC's GDP increased from about 22 percent to about 33 percent;[59] since 1995, however, its share started to decline slightly. If China contin-ues its current growth rates of 7 to 10 percent per year, it will emerge as an even more significant economic player over the next fifteen years. Until the financial cri-sis, ASEAN as well was emerging as an increasingly important political player in Asia.

The United States, often with its Western allies, tends to take leadership in APEC on all-important issues, including the environment. The success of unilateral U.S. initiatives, however, is not ensured, especially in the gap between acquiescence and implementation. To be truly successful, initiatives require skillful leadership to de-fine a sense of common self-interest and to build supporting coalitions. The support of ASEAN is especially important. Trained during a period of U.S. hegemony, many U.S. diplomats do not operate effectively as coalition builders.

Environmental cooperation at APEC has been promoted primarily by the United States and by Canada, which promised in 1993 to "green APEC."[60] The North American push has been driven primarily by the need to maintain domestic support for free trade ever since the bruising domestic battles over NAFTA and creation of the WTO and the hope that the "environment track" can reinforce the goals of trade liberalization. In addition, there is an increasing recognition of the intrinsic importance of good environmental management, stemming both from changes in norms and from rising costs of environmental degradation. Finally, American and Canadian, as well as Japanese and Australian, governments and businesses see commercial opportunity in the export of environment management products and services as well as in cleaner, leading-edge technologies generally.

There are also security incentives for regional environmental cooperation. Japan, for example, has taken leadership on energy issues, largely out of concern for security of energy supplies, as well as export opportunities. Diplomats in the U.S. State Department have increasingly come to view environmental cooperation as a "second crop" of seedlings to nurture not only economic but broader U.S. security interests in Pacific regionalism.[61] When the Labor party was in government, Australia promoted the notion that environmental cooperation enhanced Australia's trade interests and vice versa.[62]

The leadership of the United States and Canada has been short of brilliant. For the United States, the pursuit of narrow, sectoral trade interests has often trumped efforts to articulate and implement an overarching strategic vision of long-term U.S. economic, environmental, and security interests in Asia-Pacific. While there is a general consensus in Washington about the importance of trade liberalization and of Asia—there is confusion over U.S. commercial versus strategic priorities in APEC and little articulation of how environmental objectives fit in with or are important to U.S. interests in their own right. Moreover, there has been some tug-of-war between the State Department and the Office of the U.S. Trade Representative.

This confusion plays itself out in the different signals the United States gives APEC. On the one hand, the United States has taken the lead to promote specific environmental initiatives—including clean technology and marine conservation. On the other hand, the United States has promoted rapid liberalization without regard to environmental impacts or management capacities. Moreover, environmental issues tend to get sidelined within the Office of the U.S. Ambassador on APEC, who adopted a wary posture toward a broad, sustainable development agenda for fear that environmental concerns could slow progress toward free trade or raise demands for increased development aid.[63] When Asian governments press for "development cooperation," U.S. diplomats recite the mantra that technology transfer will be on a commercial basis only.

Eschewing the old model of development aid, the United States has pressed for "public-private partnerships" that increase the role of markets in virtually every

APEC initiative, including the environment. The United States has also tried—unsuccessfully—to nudge the environmental agenda toward policy discussion within its favored initiatives. The reluctance to offer aid or concessional financing to help build environmental management capacities suggests that the United States seeks environmental leadership "on the cheap."

In 1994, Canada catalyzed environmental cooperation at APEC when it organized and hosted APEC's first meeting of environment ministers (see the third part of this chapter). In 1997, shortly after taking the helm as APEC chair, the Canadian government announced that it would make environment the "key theme" for the year's activity. As the months unfolded, however, Canada produced no bold initiatives and diluted the focus on environment by adding other, vote-attracting themes, such as women and youth.

Like the United States, Canada is highly trade dependent—exports comprised almost 40 percent of its GDP in 1995—and faces a persistent trade deficit with East Asia.[64] Moreover, although its diplomats often display a high level of diplomatic skill, Canada has found it difficult to articulate specific environmental initiatives and has been unable to design an institutional process to pursue its priority issue: sustainable cities. Besides running into conflicts with its own trade bureaucracy, Canada's environmental push was hampered by a domestic fiscal crisis in the late 1990s that undercut financial support for APEC-oriented bureaucrats, even as Canada pursued a plethora of initiatives. Faced with proliferating demands—Canada hosted six ministerials in total—Canada's APEC-oriented foot soldiers were too constrained and overextended to effectively generate and guide an environmental agenda.

Japan also attempted to guide an environmental agenda at APEC in the 1990s. While Canada waved the banner of integration of environment and economy, Japan steered toward development goals, especially energy. In 1995, its proposal for a program on the "3Es"—environment, economy, and energy—was taken up and elaborated by APEC leaders, who called for a scoping of issues related to the interrelationship of food, energy, environment, economy, and population issues (see the following discussion). Japan also established and funded a central fund for APEC projects and was instrumental in establishing the APEC Energy Resource Center (APERC), based in Tokyo.

Japan's focus on development was welcomed by many Asian governments. However, Japan's strong self-interest in ensuring security of energy supply and promoting its energy technologies make other APEC economies, both Western and Asian, wary. Japan's proposals for developing-developed country partnerships often include a "tied aid" component that Western countries consider contrary to the push for trade liberalization and that Asian countries consider a violation of sovereignty.

Other Asian voices on environmental issues include the Philippines, which, as the 1996 chair of APEC, strongly promoted a new focus on "sustainable development," and Taiwan, which collaborated with the United States in designing APEC's Clean Technology initiative. For East Asian newly industrialized countries (NICs) and developing countries, incentives for regional environmental cooperation stem from the desire to enhance domestic management capacities, both technological and managerial; maintain market access in developed country markets; and encourage "green" foreign investment. Taiwan, for example, faces enormous problems of water and soil pollution and is eager to embrace market-oriented approaches to cleanup, such as ISO 14,000.

Like the trade side, the "action" of APEC environmental diplomacy often rests in domestic political economy. In the Philippines, presidential promises to turn APEC's course toward sustainable development and transform the Philippines into a "green tiger" aimed, in part, to assuage domestic criticism of a push toward liberalization. The other target of Filipino diplomacy was to pull the United States and its Western allies toward a greater focus on development issues generally, an effort that ultimately did not succeed.

Weak Institutions and "Soft Law": Governance without Government?

The third defining feature of APEC politics is a consensus-building, nonbureaucratic institutional style that has been dubbed the "APEC way."[65] By design, APEC is not a forum in which binding regional agreements are negotiated—on trade, environment, or any other issue.[66] Moreover, APEC members are generally keen to limit bureaucracy and constrain formal institutional development. Instead, APEC aims to be primarily task oriented and to promote private-sector initiatives. The chair of APEC rotates every year, the secretariat is purposefully kept very small, the ten working groups and three committees do most of the work, and coordinating mechanisms, if they exist, are built into existing committees. Moreover, initiatives can easily be undertaken to fill issue vacuums. Indeed, APEC may be the quintessential model of a nonbinding "soft law" approach to regulation in a global economy. Lacking sanctions, the "soft law" approach relies for enforcement on self-interest, common norms, and citizen watchdogging in the design and implementation of international agreements and initiatives.[67]

The consensus-building approach was important in gaining East Asian participation in APEC as a whole and the environmental agenda in particular. It has helped head off actual or perceived attempts by Western countries to define environmental issues primarily in terms of their links to market access. However, the requirement to move ahead only in ways and on issues in which there is unanimity—or at least, in which there is no strong objection—derails the discussion of controversial issues and makes progress painfully slow. Moreover, a resistance to formalizing institutional development creates an organizational flaccidity that mitigates against effective coordination of APEC's various initiatives, clouds the transparency of APEC processes, and inhibits public input.

One characteristic of this approach is that it provides substantial leeway to APEC's annual chair to raise the profile of specific areas of interest. In 1996, the Philippines championed a "sustainable development" paradigm of economic growth. In broad terms, the paradigm stresses the integration of environmental and social objectives into the design of trade and investment regimes, both nationally and regionally.[68]

One of the key political issues in moving toward a new, sustainable development paradigm is the role of civil society. Throughout Asia, civil society groups are blossoming and seeking to engage governments as both critics and partners. Within APEC, however, the principle of stakeholder participation, including environmental and other NGOs, has not yet been embraced either within member economies or in APEC as an organization. Indeed, unlike the United Nations, there are no policies or procedures for NGOs to interface with APEC. Only a few APEC members, including Canada, the United States, the Philippines, and Indonesia, have included NGOs in official delegations to environmental or other ministerials.[69] Even this meager attempt at transparency and inclusion has drawn criticism from other APEC members.

Without institutional mechanisms for stakeholder participation in the creation of common norms and in pressing governments to be accountable to them, the effectiveness of the "soft law" approach in actually changing behavior is limited. The push by the Philippines, for example, ignited little popular passion or discussion outside Manila. The adoption by APEC leaders of sustainable development language in their 1996 statement reflected more a rhetorical than a political process or commitment.

ENVIRONMENTAL COOPERATION: THE 1990s

Environmental issues have been on APEC's agenda virtually since its inception. At the founding conference in 1989, ministers agreed to examine national issues related to energy, fisheries, and marine pollution. In 1991, the Seoul Declaration defined equity and sustainable growth to be within the scope of APEC. But it was in 1993, with the launching of the "Sustainable Development Dialogue" by APEC heads of state, that environmental issues moved unmistakably onto APEC's radar screen.

Environmental Initiatives "at the Top"

The milestones of environmental cooperation at APEC have been propelled primarily "at the top" by initiatives taken by leaders and environment ministers. In 1993, Canadian Prime Minister Chretien promised to "green" APEC and offered to host APEC's first environment ministerial. Held the following March in Vancouver, the ministerial produced an environmental vision statement and a framework of principles for integrating economy and environment.[70]

Following the spirit of the Rio Declaration, the environmental vision statement established APEC's goal to be the pursuit of sustainable development. "We are committed to develop policies that are sound economically and environmentally," the statement proclaims. It calls on senior officials to "develop a strategic approach, based on sustainable development principles, for environment considerations to be fully integrated into the program of each APEC working group and policy committee."[71] To help implement the vision statement, the ministers generated a framework of nine principles, including the precautionary principle and the principle of making trade and environment policies mutually supportive. After approval by APEC ministers and leaders, the vision statement and framework were sent to senior officials. In a crucial initiative, the senior officials in 1995 directed all of APEC's ten working groups and three committees to include environmental issues in their annual reporting process.

When the sectorally structured working groups began to grapple with implementation of the directive, it became clear that crucial issues of sustainable resource and environmental management cut across sectors. At the 1995 Osaka meeting, leaders directed the Economic Committee to consider crosscutting issues in an initiative called "FEEEP": Food, Energy, Environment, Economic Growth, and Population. A FEEEP Symposium held in September broke new ground in including both governmental and nongovernmental participants. However, it generated no substantive initiatives.

Environmental cooperation also evolved toward defining *regional* priorities and developing a regional work program. In July 1996, the Philippines hosted a second ministerial meeting on sustainable development issues that produced consensus on developing an "Action Programme" in three priority areas: (1) Sustainable Cities, put forward and supported especially by Canada, Japan, and the Philippines; (2) Clean Production/Clean Technology, put forward by the United States and Chinese Taipei; and (3) Sustainability of the Marine Environment, put forward by the United States.[72]

Over the following year, "Action Strategies" were developed for the Clean Technology and the Marine Environment priority areas, largely at the initiative of the United States.[73] Shepherded by the Industrial Science and Technology Working Group, the Clean Production strategy is focused on building capacities for better environmental management at two levels: industry sectors, through the adoption of cleaner technologies, policies, and practices, including ISO 14,000 and environmental performance indicators, and (2) crosscutting, through institutional, professional, and private-sector partnerships, including the facilitation of demonstration projects and mechanisms to diffuse best practices.

The Strategy for the Sustainability of the Marine Environment, developed and shepherded by the Marine Resource Conservation Working Group, established that APEC cooperation would focus on integrated approaches to coastal management, the reduction of marine pollution, and sustainable management of marine resources. The primary "tools" are the familiar APEC litany: information and technology exchange, training and education, and public-private sector participation and partnership.

The three action strategies were adopted by APEC's third meeting of environment ministers, held in Toronto in June 1997. With Canada as APEC chair in 1997, environmentalists had hoped that the ministerial would propel a "great leap forward." In the event, it took a few small steps. The Clean Technology strategy *could* offer a way out of the North-South conundrum over technology transfer. The Sustainable Cities program *could* point APEC toward an integrative, crosscutting approach to sustainable development. The Marine strategy *could* point toward a Pacific-wide regime of sustainable coastal and ocean management.

The fulfillment of this potential, however, has not been realized. "Many people have real doubts about whether APEC can evolve into a credible force for environmental protection," Eileen Claussen, the head of the U.S. delegation, told the ministers. "It is true that we certainly have not become one yet."[74]

In 1998, Malaysia assumed the chairmanship of APEC. Fatigued with the activity of 1997 and caught up in financial crisis, Malaysia announced it would focus only on trade and finance. The environmental push "at the top" to link environmental and economic policy issues went flat. In 1999, New Zealand chaired APEC and could have revived high-level interest in the environment, but it did not. In short, environment programs in APEC have not regained the momentum that seemed to be building prior to the 1997 financial crisis.

"Nuts and Bolts": Working Groups

While the leaders and ministers have been the architects of the environmental agenda, the working groups and three committees have been the engineers. The most active has been the working group on Regional Energy Cooperation, which defines it objective as maximizing "the energy sector's contribution to the region's economic and social well being," including, through regional discussion, how to respond to "energy related issues such as the greenhouse effect."[75]

Since 1996, the Regional Energy Cooperation working group has focused primarily on developing an information base and stimulating regional discussion. It has begun to move, however, into policy-related areas with the proposed "Joint Regional Action on Appliance Efficiency Improvement and Harmonization of Standards." This is a "nuts and bolts" initiative in the management of policy convergence and, if undertaken, should have a demonstrable positive effect on regional environmental performance by pulling regional appliance standards up. The working group is also expanding into regional capacity-building efforts with the newly established Asia Pacific Energy Research Centre in Tokyo.

Another working group achievement is the creation of an "APEC Sustainable Development Information and Training Network." Launched in October 1996, the network was the brainchild of the Economic Development Department of the State of Oregon. Seeking to promote local environmental management industries in Asia-Pacific, the department stumbled on APEC and creatively developed a "win-win" proposal to enhance basic capacities of middle-level governmental environment managers.[76] The network will be under the purview of the Human Resources Development Working Group.

Other working groups with environment-related outputs include Tourism, which is developing regional "Sustainable Tourism" guidelines; Human Resources Development, which is promoting environmental training; Marine Resources Conservation, which is spearheading the Regional Action Programme component on Sustainability of the Marine Environment; and Industrial Science and Technology, which is spearheading the Clean Technology component of the Regional Action Programme.

While the quantity of output is impressive, the working groups suffer from lack of technical expertise and resistance to the discussion of policy issues. Moreover, initiatives related to "environment" are only part of what working groups do. In their other work, the working groups are pursuing agendas that may have far greater and potentially negative impacts on the environment, such as liberalization of resource-intensive trade and harmonization of vehicle emissions standards.

Finally, the overall orientation and technical capacities of working groups reflect their original raison d'être, namely, to promote trade and investment liberalization and facilitation on a sectoral basis. The Fisheries Working Group, for example, undertook a four-year study aimed primarily at examining trade barriers, including, in the fourth year, the issues of subsidies. Whether they will focus on environmental impacts of subsidies and propose ways to integrate trade and environmental objectives will depend more on external advocacy than bureaucratic directive.

"Track Two" Diplomacy

As long as APEC remained primarily a forum for broad regional economic consultation, it captured little public imagination or concern. With APEC's turn toward trade activism in 1993, nongovernmental and private sector groups throughout the region began to consider how to engage APEC on both trade and environmental issues. The business-oriented Pacific Basin Economic Council, for example, organized a Task Force on the Environment in May 1996.

In the 1990s, environmental advocacy was strongest among nongovernmental and quasi-governmental think tanks. Between 1994 and 1996, a series of NGO workshops and seminars aimed to scope out the parameters and articulate an agenda for regional trade-environmental cooperation.[77] In addition, activist NGOs targeted specific initiatives and working groups. In Australia, for example, a coalition of environment and development groups challenged a meeting of APEC energy ministers in July 1996 to focus on social and environmental rather than purely commercial aspects of energy development.[78]

Efforts to engage APEC on environmental issues have been somewhat successful in countries that have established institutional mechanisms for the regular interface of NGOs with government, like the Philippines Council for Sustainable Development. Such mechanisms, however, are few and far between. Even in the United

States, there is no regular avenue for environmental groups to consult with policy-makers on issues related to U.S. policy on APEC.[79]

Among Asia-Pacific-based activist and community groups, APEC's "free trade" push in the early 1990s generated a storm of controversy and opposition, including on environmental grounds. In 1995, NGOs held a "parallel conference" to the official APEC November ministerial.[80] In 1996, five separate NGO conferences were held, including the Manila People's Forum, which drew over 500 people from a wide range of groups working on human rights, environment, women's empowerment, and economic development.

United in their rejection of socially and environmentally blind "free trade," APEC-based NGOs were less sure about their posture toward APEC itself. A debate over whether to "engage or oppose" APEC emerged in Kyoto in 1995, raged in Manila in 1996, and was politely pushed under the table in Vancouver in 1997. The central argument of the oppositionists was that there is "no *there* there," namely, that APEC is mostly a figment of instrumental American imagination. Attempts to engage it on any issue, including environment, would simply lend legitimacy to the U.S.-imposed free trade thrust. Those seeking to engage APEC argued that NGOs should be not only oppositional but also propositional. APEC provides a vehicle, they suggested, by which they can not only challenge but also generate alternatives to the "free trade" orthodoxy.

The emergence of "track two" diplomacy is a two-edged sword for many APEC governments. On the one hand, NGOs and other groups can proffer creative and constructive proposals, and their increased activism deepens APEC's region-building process. On the other hand, NGOs can and often do clash with and retard governmental objectives, especially the push toward free trade, as well as force issues into the political spotlight that governments would rather keep obscure.

CONCLUSION: WHITHER SUSTAINABLE DEVELOPMENT?

APEC made a high-profile—but ultimately false—start in the 1990s toward regional cooperation for sustainable development. It accepted the principle that environmental issues are a legitimate part of APEC, defined a framework and developed a capacity-building approach that spawned a host of initiatives and avoided political stalemate, and, by embracing a "sustainable development" framework, steered away from the contentious and largely barren paradigm of trade versus the environment.

Given the political, economic, and ecological diversity of its members, the achievement of regional consensus on any program for environmental cooperation was no small feat. Moreover, lodging environmental concerns within an organization concerned preeminently with trade and investment holds promise for environmental governance of the global economy.

The actual programmatic initiatives were meager, however, and there emerged little sign of coherent leadership or enduring political will to grapple with deeper, thorny issues of environment and development in the design of a regional trade regime. Moreover, the popular passions that APEC did ignite tended to undermine rather than promote APEC's prospects as a catalyst for sustainable development. Indeed, the future of APEC itself is in question, as East Asian nations increasingly turn toward bilateral and subregional arrangements.

Hence, early in the first decade of the twenty-first century, despite its promise and early momentum, cooperation for sustainable development at APEC seems to be the doldrums. The fundamental problem was and continues to be the lack of political demand at home—in virtually all APEC countries—for APEC to grapple seriously with creating a framework for sustainable trade and investment in the region. Without domestic demand and the political will it generates, APEC's initiatives will tend to be narrow and shallow and follow the strategic and commercial interests of its strongest members.

Political demand, in turn, is constrained by the lack of institutional openings at APEC and within APEC countries for the participation by NGOs and other civil society groups. Without organic connection to social groups, international efforts at environmental governance will remain trapped in rhetoric. APEC is not the only international organization to find environmental initiatives dissipated by the disconnect between "top-down" bureaucratic initiatives and "bottom-up" popular concerns.

Moreover, APEC's sustainable development thrust lost steam because environmental and trade diplomacy was not integrated. Some of the major issues of sustainable development—massive private investment in clean energy and industrial technologies, the reduction of subsidies for the commercial exploitation of natural resources, common standards to improve environmental performance, and the protection of the rights of marginal groups to environmental amenities and resources—are deeply integrated with trade and investment rules and norms. Shunting environmental cooperation into calm waters safely away from trade negotiations might avoid debilitating controversy, but it also dampens motivation.

Whether at APEC, an East Asia Free Trade Area, the WTO, or other fora, popular and commercial pressures suggest that environmental issues will be linked to economic governance over the next decade. The governance imperatives generated by economic integration, namely, a convergence toward common environmental standards, remain extant. Most important, civil society organizations are increasingly pressing for new approaches to economic development that explicitly target environmental and social objectives. The ability of ENGOs, on both sides of the Pacific, to coalesce into a significant regional political voice is likely to be the single most important determinant of the scope and direction of environmental governance, whether at the regional or the global level. To truly promote sustainable development, environmental goals must be linked to and integrated with trade and investment rules and norms—neither in a neoliberal "trade-environment" framework that blindly asserts the primacy of trade nor in a bland "sustainable development" approach that eschews new trade rules and economic policies. What is needed—and what popular forces in Asia are increasingly demanding—is a new "values-based" approach to the governance of trade and investment based on coequal status of economic development, environmental protection, and social justice. It is a tall order. But it is one worth fighting for.

NOTES

Earlier versions of this chapter appeared in *Asian Perspectives,* University of Oregon in Portland, fall 1998, and in the *Journal of Environment and Development* of the University of California at San Diego.

1. Environmental issues at the World Trade Organization are primarily the purview of the Committee on Trade and Environment (CTE). For an ongoing report on the Committee's activities, see World Trade Organization, *Trade and the Environment,* CTE newsletter, December 1996.

2. Jenelle Bonnor, "APEC's Contribution to Regional Security," in Hadi Soesastro and Anthony Bergin, eds., *The Role of Security and Economic Cooperation Structures in the Asia Pacific Region, Indonesian and Australian Views* (45–56) (Jakarta: Centre for Strategic and International Studies in cooperation with the Australian Defence Studies Centre, 1996).

3. International Monetary Fund, *Direction of Trade Statistics* (Washington, D.C.: International Monetary Fund, 1995).

4. United Nations, *World Investment Directory, Volume III: Developed Countries* (New York: United Nations, 1993).

5. Ippei Yamazawa, "On Pacific Integration," in R. Garnaut and P. Drysdale, eds., *Asia Pacific Regionalism: Readings in International Economic Relations* (Pymble, New South Wales: Harper Educational Publishers, 1994), table 16.4.

6. World Resources Institute, *World Resources 1994–1995* (New York: Oxford University Press, 1994), table 15.1.

7. United Nations Development Program, *Human Development Report* (New York: United Nations, 1998), table 1.

8. Vinod Anuja, Benu Bidan, Francisco Ferreira, and Michael Walton, *Everyone's Miracle? Revisiting Poverty and Inequality in East Asia* (Washington, D.C.: World Bank, 1997); Asian Development Bank, *Emerging Asia: Changes and Challenges* (Manila: Asian Development Bank, 1997).

9. Asian Development Bank, *Asian Environmental Outlook 2001* (Manila: Asian Development Bank, 2001), 2.

10. In addition to environmental impacts, there are security implications to energy development choices in Northeast Asia, including potential conflicts erupting over insecurity of supply and the potential for nuclear weapons proliferation arising from the widespread development of nuclear power. See Kent E. Calder, *Pacific Defense, Arms, Energy, and America's Future in Asia* (New York: William Morrow, 1996), and the Energy, Security and Environment in Northeast Asia Project of the Nautilus Institute (available at <http://www.nautilus.org.esena>).

11. Fesharaki Fereidun, Sara Banaszak, and Wu Kang, "Energy Supply and Demand in Northeast Asia" (paper presented at the Seventh Meeting of the Northeast Asia Economic

Forum, Ulan Bataar, Mongolia, August 17–21,1997); International Energy Agency, *World Energy Outlook* (Paris: OECD, 1996).

12. H. Razawi, "The Impact of Financing on Sustainability of Energy Development in North East Asia," in *Energy, Security and Environment in Northeast Asia Project* (Berkeley, Calif.: Nautilus Institute for Security and Sustainable Development, March 1997), table 1.

13. Lyuba Zarsky, "Energy and the Environment in Asia-Pacific: Regional Cooperation and Market Governance," in Pamela Chasek, ed., *Global Environments in the 21st Century* (Tokyo: United Nations University Press, 1999).

14. David G. Streets, "Energy and Acid Rain Projections for Northeast Asia," in *Energy, Security and Environment Project.*

15. C. Brandon and R. Ramankuty, R. (1993). *Toward an Environment Strategy for Asia,* World Bank Discussion Paper No. 224 (Washington, D.C.: World Bank, 1993), figure 2.

16. China is also the world's most populous country. Historically, it has been the rich, relatively unpopulated countries that have been the primary emitters. For a discussion of the ethical and historical dimensions of allocating responsibility for greenhouse gas emissions, see P. Hayes and K. Smith, eds., *The Global Greenhouse Regime: Who Pays?* (1997).

17. The fourth is Saudi Arabia. Jeffrey S. Hammer and Sudhir Shetty, *East Asia's Environment, Principles and Priorities for Action,* World Bank Discussion Paper No. 287 (Washington, D.C.: World Bank, 1995), 4.

18. High energy use in the United States and Canada also stems from urban design patterns: Widely dispersed cities with few public transport services encourage a high level of dependence on cars. See J. Kenworthy and F. Laube, "Indicators of Transportation Efficiency in Global Cities and Their Implications for Urban Sustainability" (paper presented to the Workshop on Toward Sustainable Cities in APEC, National Roundtable on the Environment and Economy, Vancouver, British Columbia, May 5–6, 1997).

19. V. Wangwacharakul, "Trade, Investment and Sustained Development" (paper presented to the ESCAP/ADB Expert Meeting on Trade, Economic and Environmental Sustainability, October 23–27, 1989).

20. M. T. Rock, "Industry and the Environment in Ten Asian Countries: Synthesis Report of US-AEP Country Assessment" (Washington, D.C.: U.S-Asia Environmental Partnership, USAID, October 9, 1996).

21. D. Reed, *Structural Adjustment and the Environment* (Boulder, Colo.: Westview Press, 1992), 113.

22. World Bank, *Indonesia Environment and Development* (Washington, D.C.: World Bank, 1994), 74.

23. Asian Development Bank, *Emerging Asia* (Manila: Asian Development Bank,1997), 199; Asian Development Bank, *The Environment Program of the Asian Development Bank, Past, Present, and Future* (Manila: Asian Development Bank, 1994), 4.

24. Energy, Security and Environment in Northeast Asia Project, *Energy, Environment and Security in Northeast Asia* (Berkeley, Calif.: Nautilus Institute and the Center for Global Communications, March 2000).

25. A. Soegiarto, "Sustainable Fisheries, Environment and the Prospects of Regional Cooperation in Southeast Asia" (paper presented to the Workshop on Trade and Environment in Asia Pacific: Prospects for Regional Cooperation, Nautilus Institute, East-West Center, Honolulu, September 22–24, 1994).

26. World Resources Institute, *World Resources 1994–1995,* table 17.1.

27. R. Gilbert, "Reducing Urban Air Pollution in APEC Economies" (paper presented to the Workshop on Toward Sustainable Cities in APEC, National Roundtable on the Environment and the Economy, Vancouver, British Columbia, May 5–6, 1997, table 2). The definition of "urban" and "rural" differs among nations, making cross-national comparisons problematic. This estimate is based on UN data, which simply sums figures submitted by governments.

28. Kenworthy and Laube, "Indicators of Transportation Efficiency in Global Cities and Their Implications for Urban Sustainability."

29. One detailed study concluded, "Population density and natural resource degradation cannot be correlated in any fixed way since factors such as poverty and land-tenure policies mediate what happens to the resource base." Comparing Costa Rica and the Philippines, the study showed inter alia that, despite much lower population density, Costa Rican soils were relatively more damaged because of large-scale conversion of forest to cattle pasture. See M. C. Cruz, C. A. Meyer, R. Repatto, and R. Woodward, *Population Growth, Poverty, and Environmental Stress: Frontier Migration in the Philippines and Costa Rica* (Washington, D.C.: World Resources Institute, 1992), p. vii and passim.

30. See papers of the Project on Environment, Population and Security, a collaboration of the Peace and Conflict Studies Program, University of Toronto, and the Population and Sustainable Project of the American Association for the Advancement of Science, Washington, D.C. Papers are available from the AAAS, 1200 New York Ave. N.W., Washington, D.C. 20005.

31. World Resources Institute, *World Resources 1996–97: The Urban Environment* (New York: Oxford University Press, 1996), 11.

32. W. Cruz and R. Repetto, *The Environmental Effects of Stabilization and Structural Adjustment Programs: The Philippines Case* (Washington, D.C.: World Resources Institute, 1992); Lyuba Zarsky, "Lessons of Liberalization in Asia: From Structural Adjustment to Sustainable Development," in *Financing Environmentally Sound Development* (Manila: Asian Development Bank, 1994); D. Reed, *Structural Adjustment, the Environment and Sustainable Development* (London: Earthscan, 1996).

33. Michael Harcourt (paper presented at the Sustainable Cities Workshop, National Roundtable on the Environment and the Economy, Vancouver, British Columbia, March 4–6, 1997).

34. David P. Angel and Michael T. Rock, eds., *Asia's Clean Revolution: Industry, Growth and the Environment* (Sheffield: Green Leaf Publishing, 2000).

35. While gains in eco-efficiency can offer "win-win" solutions on the micro-level, deeper problems stemming from too large a total ecological load and poor land use planning require more costly, macro-measures.

36. J. A. Hoerner and F. Muller, "Carbon Taxes for Climate Protection in a Competitive World," Environmental Tax Program, Center for Global Change, University of Maryland at College Park, June 12, 1996.

37. More subtly, there is a tendency for the total costs to business of meeting environmental management requirements to converge. Total costs include compliance costs as well as information, regulatory, and other transactions costs. More efficient regulatory regimes may generate a higher level of environmental performance for the same cost. See C. L. Anderson and R. A. Kagan, "Adversarial Legalism, Transaction Costs, and the Industrial Flight Hypothesis," draft paper, Carleton University, Ottawa, October 1996, 17.

38. D. Vogel, *Trading Up: Consumer and Environmental Regulation in a Global Economy* (Cambridge, Mass.: Harvard University Press, 1995). For the rich countries of the OECD, primary competitors and export markets are typically other OECD countries. The newly industrializing countries (NICs) typically compete with other NICs for foreign investment and export opportunities while at the same time being drawn toward the product standards of the large-market countries. There is thus likely to be more than one "equilibrium" convergence point at a global level at any given time.

39. Some analysts have argued that the process of policy convergence will be a "race to the bottom" in terms of environmental performance standards. For an exposition and critique, see Richard L. Revesz, "Rehabilitating Inter-State Competition: Rethinking the 'Race to the Bottom' Rationale for Federal Environmental Regulation," *New York University Law Review* 67 (1992): 1210.

40. Lyuba Zarsky, "The Asia-Pacific Economic Cooperation Forum and the Environment: Regional Governance in the Age of Economic Globalization," *Colorado Journal for International Environmental Law and Policy* 8 (summer 1997): 323. An example is the inability of the European Union, the United States, and Australia to enact even a very small carbon tax. In the United States, the proposal was defeated by a strong business lobby, including aluminum producers. In Australia, an aluminum industry–dominated business lobby argued successfully that, even though the actual cost of the proposed tax to producers was negligible, a perception of added cost and of rising environmental commitment would dampen foreign investment. See Hoerner and Muller, "Carbon Taxes for Climate Protection in a Competitive World."

41. A similar argument is made by Daniel C. Esty in "Environmental Regulation and Competitiveness: Theory and Practice," in Simon S. C. Tay and Daniel C. Esty, eds., *Asian Dragons and Green Trade* (33–48) (Singapore: Times Academic Press, 1996).

42. Lyuba Zarsky, "Havens, Halos, and Spaghetti: Untangling the Relationship between FDI and Environment," in *Foreign Direct Investment and the Environment* (Paris: OECD, 1999).

43. Gareth Porter, "Natural Resource Subsidies and International Policy: A Role for APEC," *Journal of Environment and Development* 6, no. 3 (September 1997): 276–91.

44. C. Ford Runge and T. Jones, "Subsidies, Tax Disincentives and the Environment: An Overview and Synthesis," in Organization for Economic Cooperation and Development, *Subsidies and Environment: Exploring the Linkages* (Paris: OECD, 1996), 12.

45. Russia and Peru joined in December 1997. Hong Kong will retain its separate membership in APEC, as in all international fora, for fifty years after reunification with China in July 1997.

46. World Bank, *World Development Indicators* (Washington, D.C.: World Bank, 2000), table 4.2.

47. Ibid.

48. Ibid., table 4.21.

49. The "broad vision" was developed by an Eminent Persons Group chaired by Fred Bergsten of the United States. APEC, *A Vision for APEC: Towards an Asia Pacific Economic Community* (Singapore: APEL Secretariat, October 1993).

50. Asia Pacific Economic Cooperation Forum, *Selected APEC Documents, 1995* (Singapore: APEC Secretariat, 1995).

51. APEC's utility as a leader in the global push toward free trade is constrained by the

differences in diplomatic styles between the and APEC. In the WTO, tariff reductions and other market access offers are made on a "tit-for-tat" reciprocal basis. APEC, by contrast, is not a negotiating forum. Trade liberalization is presumed to be in the self-interest of all members, and any actions to increase market access are offered unilaterally. WTO negotiators are reluctant, therefore, to give up bargaining chips at APEC that they could use in Geneva.

52. The campaign to raise environmental concerns about liberalization was led by the Pacific Environment Resource Center in Sausalito, California (perc@pop.igc.org).

53. World Resources Institute, *World Resources 1996–97,* table 7.1.

54. Peter Evans, *Embedded Autonomy: States and Industrial Transformation* (Princeton, N.J.: Princeton University Press, 1995).

55. U.S. Department of Commerce, "Goods and Services Deficit Increases in 2000," Bureau of Economic Analysis, February 21, 2001 (available at <http://www.census.gov/indicator/www/ustrade.html>). In 1996, East Asia accounted for nearly 50 percent of the total U.S. trade deficit.

56. Some Southeast Asian analysts argue that it is important for industrializing countries in Asia to retain flexibility in trade policy, that is, to retain the option to undertake import protection/export promotion strategies in particular sectors. See Walden Bello, *Presentation to Forum on APEC and Its Implications for Asia and the Pacific* (Washington, D.C.: School of Advanced International Studies, The Johns Hopkins University, October 1996). However, reliance on external market access limits the political viability of developmental state policies: U.S. threats to limit market access carry political weight.

57. Fred Bergsten, "Brunei: A Turning Point for APEC?" Institute for International Economics, Washington, D.C., February 2001.

58. Bello, *Presentation to Forum on APEC and Its Implications for Asia and the Pacific.*

59. World Bank, *World Development Indicators* (Washington, D.C.: World Bank, 1997), 174–76, table 4.2.

60. The analysis in this section is based largely on interviews with a variety of government officials in the United States and Canada.

61. Joseph Hayes, interview with the author, Office of Economic Policy, U.S. State Department, June 1996. In April 1996, U.S. Secretary of State Warren Christopher made a widely publicized speech about integrating environmental issues into U.S. foreign policy. See U.S. Secretary of State, "Integrating Environment Issues into the Department's Core Foreign Policy Goals," memorandum, February 14, 1996. Since then, the State Department has announced the creation of six regional "environmental hubs," including in Bangkok for Southeast Asia. See U.S. Department of State, *Environmental Diplomacy* (available at <http://www.state.gov/www/global/oes/earth.htm/>).

62. P. Keating, prime minister of Australia, foreign policy speech, Singapore National University, February 1996.

63. Lyuba Zarsky, Report from Sustainable Development Ministerial, Manila, Nautilus Institute (available at <http://www.nautilus.org.aprenet>, July 1996).

64. World Bank, *World Development Indicators* (2000), table 4.21.

65. Yoichi Funabashi, *Asia Pacific Fusion: Japan's Role in APEC* (Washington, D.C.: Institute for International Economics, October 1995) 142–44.

66. "The value of APEC is not that we are going to do trade agreements in APEC," claimed a U.S. trade official in 1995. "I mean, if that's all APEC were, we could do it in Geneva. We don't need it. The value of APEC is that it will help create the conditions for commercial and economic integration." Quoted in Funabashi, *Asia Pacific Fusion,* 146.

67. Edith Brown Weiss, ed., *International Compliance with Nonbinding Accords* (Washington, D.C.: American Society of International Law, 1997).

68. For a sampling, see Center for Alternative Development Initiatives, *What Is Sustainable Development: Asia-Pacific Initiative?* (Quezon City: Center for Alternative Development Studies, October 1996); National Round Table for the Environment and Economy, *The Environment and Economy in APEC: Realizing Convergence,* March 1996; and Lyuba Zarsky, "The Asia Pacific Economic Cooperation Forum and the Environment: Regional Environmental Governance in An Age of Globalization," *Colorado Journal of Environmental Law and Policy* (Sept. 1997): 323–58.

69. The organizations that participated in the 1996 Ministerial on Sustainable Development in Manila were the Philippine Commission on Sustainable Development, the National Round Table on the Environment and Economy (Canada), and the Nautilus Institute for Security and Sustainable Development (United States). These three organizations also participated in the 1997 Environment Ministerial in Toronto. In addition, a representative from a women's organization in Indonesia participated.

70. APEC Environmental Vision Statement, APEC Secretariat, Vancouver, British Columbia (available at <http://www.apecsec.org.sg>, March 1994; also available from the Nautilus Institute at <http://www.nautilus.org>).

71. APEC Environmental Vision Statement, March 1994.

72. APEC Declaration, APEC Ministerial Meeting on Sustainable Development, Manila, July 1996 (available from the Nautilus Institute at <http://www.nautilus.org>).

73. For the full text of both strategies, see <http://www.nautilus.org/aprenet/library>.

74. Eileen Claussen, U.S. assistant secretary of state for oceans and international environmental and scientific affairs, Opening Statement, Environment Ministerial Meeting on Sustainable Development, APEC, June 9, 1997 (available at <http://www.nautilus.org/aprenet/library>).

75. The Regional Energy Cooperation Working Group has expert groups focused on five key themes: (1) energy supply and demand; (2) energy and the environment, which aims to promote clean coal technologies; (3) energy efficiency and conservation; (4) energy research and development and technology transfer, with a priority on new and renewable energy technologies; and (5) minerals and energy exploration and development. See the Regional Energy Cooperation Working Group's home page at <http://www.dpie.gov.au/resources.energy/energy/apec/APEC_Energy.html>.

76. APEC, Organizing Conference, Sustainable Development Training and Information Network, *Initial Conference Report,* October 1996.

77. These include workshops organized by the Canadian National Round Table on the Environment and Economy in March 1996 and by the Nautilus Institute for Security and Sustainable Development, held at the East-West Center in Honolulu in September 1994. ASEAN also held a series of conferences during 1995.

78. Even more specifically, an NGO has formed to target the minerals-oriented work of the Regional Energy Committee. See D. Kennedy, "Project Underground," International Rivers Network, Berkeley, California, 1997 (dannyk@moles.org).

79. The Office of the U.S. Trade Representative established a Trade and Environment Policy Advisory Committee in 1994. However, the agenda has been tightly focused on narrow issues relating to trade-environment conflicts at the WTO.

80. The first NGO parallel conference was slated for Indonesia in 1994. However, Indonesia refused to grant permission or visas for the gathering, and it was hastily relocated to Bangkok. In 1995, an NGO conference held in Kyoto drew over 150 participants from throughout the region to discuss the environmental and social costs of "free trade."

III

A BUSINESS-LED
ORGANIZATION

9

The International Organization for Standardization: Drafting of the ISO 14000 Series

Naomi Roht-Arriaza

The International Organization for Standardization (ISO) is a trade organization unlike any other. It can only be called a trade organization at all because its stated purpose is to facilitate international trade through the creation and harmonization of technical standards. As long as the ISO's work involved nothing more than creating uniform rules for screw widths, lightbulb sizes, and the like, its work was barely noticed and rarely controversial. However, as the organization has moved into the more wide-ranging areas of quality control and especially environmental management standards, its decision-making processes have increasingly come under scrutiny.

This chapter examines the genesis of the ISO's environmental management series of standards. These standards are designed for voluntary application by industry and do not require state implementation or enforcement. I focus on the process of their elaboration and accompanying debates, which took place in a context of a formally open negotiating process dominated in fact by developed country corporate interests. These players had both a domestic agenda—stimulating regulatory rollback—and an international one—preempting substantive international environmental action that might impede trade. An understanding of these crosscutting domestic and international agendas, and of their intersection with North-South debates over trade liberalization, is needed to better understand the outcomes of the negotiations over ISO 14000.

The first part of this chapter describes the ISO and summarizes the content of the ISO 14000 series standards. The second part looks at the drafters of the standards, and the third part recounts some illustrative debates during the drafting process. The fourth part considers the politics of the negotiations and speculates on why the actors took certain positions. The fifth part looks at how the standards will be used. The sixth part concludes.

WHAT ARE THE ISO 14000 STANDARDS?

The ISO and the Genesis of the ISO 14000 Series

The ISO was founded in 1946 to promote international standards that would facilitate global trade. It is a federation of over 100 national standards bodies, each of which is that body "most representative of standardization in its country."[1] Each national standards body determines its own composition; while some are almost entirely composed of private interests, others have substantial government representation. The organization's complex structure is based on technical committees (TCs), which may, as needed, establish their subcommittees (SCs) and working groups (WGs). The member organizations provide most of the financing, staffing, and administrative and technical services for the committees. Each national group delegates its own members and decides the positions they will take in the ISO TCs and SCs. This may be done through the formation of technical advisory groups (TAGs) to develop a unified national position on a proposed standard; these may, in turn, subdivide into sub-TAGs. By the beginning of 1994, there were 187 TCs, 552 SCs, 2,100 WGs, and 19 ad hoc study groups. Each TC or SC has a secretariat, while the less formal WGs have conveners.[2] The ISO's headquarters in Geneva has a central secretariat that handles voting procedures, a general assembly, a governing council, and a technical board.

The ISO's work products are known as International Standards. To date, there are 13,025 standards, mostly in the fields of mechanical engineering, basic chemicals, nonmetallic materials, information processing, graphics, and photography.[3] The process of creating a standard starts with the formation of a TC by the ISO Council. The members of the TC organize the work into its component parts, assigning tasks to SCs and WGs. Participants negotiate and discuss the drafts in the various SCs and WGs as well as in the national TAGs. The various SC and WG drafts are eventually integrated into a Committee Draft (CD), which must be approved by consensus. After the TC approves the draft, it becomes a "draft international standard" and is circulated to the entire ISO membership for a vote. A substantial majority must approve the standard for it to be published as an international standard.[4]

Documents approved by the ISO may be either specification standards, which frame the standards' requirements and form the basis for third-party certification or verification, or guidance documents that set out suggested methods and approaches for achieving the standard but do not themselves serve as the basis for certification. A given area may include a specification standard and a number of related guidance documents and aids to implementation.

Until the late 1980s, the ISO's work focused on harmonizing existing national technical specifications. Then ISO pioneered a global standard for quality control management, the ISO 9000 standard series.[5] ISO 9000 was the first ISO standard developed more or less from scratch and also the first to apply across a broad range of industries and processes. ISO 9000 set out procedures and systems to ensure adequate feedback and control systems for quality management, subject to periodic auditing as well as regular verification by a private outside entity who certifies that the organization conforms to the standard.[6] ISO 9000 quickly became a de facto requirement for doing business in Europe and with large customers elsewhere.[7] From the beginning, some industries voiced concerns that certification requirements were simply disguised trade barriers.[8]

The success of ISO 9000 and of an international management systems approach led to discussions about applying such an approach in the environmental arena. The 1992 UN Conference on Environment and Development and the subsequent adoption of an action program that envisioned a new role for industry and industry standards in sustainable development also played a role.[9] In addition, global businesses were concerned about the proliferation of eco-labeling programs in different countries as well as of private corporate codes of conduct.[10] These approaches aimed at using consumer pressure to spur environmental improvements, but they involved inconsistent methodologies and multiple reporting requirements that threatened over time to become a significant burden to business.

Most important, the European Community adopted a regulation setting up an Eco-Management and Auditing Scheme[11] (EMAS). Under EMAS, industrial sites voluntarily establish systems to analyze and improve the effects of their activities on the environment; they can then register these sites through national registration bodies.[12] Companies based outside Europe began worrying that such a scheme might provide an unfair advantage to European producers in European markets and so pushed for a global standard on environmental management and auditing.[13]

A technical committee, TC 207, was officially launched in October 1992. The result is the ISO 14000 series. The series includes standards in the areas of environmental management systems, environmental auditing, environmental performance evaluation (indicators of environmental performance), environmental labeling programs, life-cycle analysis, and environmental aspects of product standards. Almost from the start, the environmental management systems standard (EMS) has been the focus of much of the attention. In part this is because the EMS will be the certification standard, while those in other areas will be merely guidance documents amplifying or supporting the EMS standard,[14] and in part because the EMS standards were placed on a "fast track" since a global standard needed to be ready quickly to fit into the EMAS timetable. From 1992 through mid-1995, a number of large meetings (in Canada, France, Australia, and Norway) and many more small ones took place to hash out the content of an EMS standard. By mid-1996, the final EMS standards were in place, along with several auditing guidances.

The Content of the ISO 14001 Environmental Management System Standard

The EMS standard, in essence, sets out procedures that an organization's management can implement to ensure that environmental issues are properly dealt with at all levels of the organization. The EMS shall consist of a stated environmental policy defined by top management, which must include a commitment to continual improvement, to compliance with relevant law and other requirements, and to prevention of pollution. It must have a documented framework for setting and reviewing environmental objectives and targets. It shall include a "procedure to identify the environmental aspects of its activities, products, and services that it can control and over which it can be expected to have an influence in order to determine those which have or can have significant impacts . . . and to ensure that the aspects related to these significant impacts are considered in setting its environmental objectives."[15] The organization must then define environmental objectives, specific targets, and a management program. The management shall designate responsibility for achieving targets and determine the means and time frames for both new and existing activities.[16] Management is to provide human and financial resources essential to implementation, appropriate training, periodic monitoring, and corrective or preventive action in cases of nonconformance.[17] The organization must also periodically audit its EMS performance, and top management must review the system's suitability and effectiveness.[18] Each of these steps is specified and elaborated on in the specification document and, in greater detail, in the guidance document.

WHO WERE THE DRAFTERS?

The ISO attempts to create legitimacy through formal requirements for broad-based participation. The ISO's constituent national groups are to bring together the interests of producers, users (including consumers), governments, and the scientific community.[19] A balance of interests among producers, users, and others within the ISO is presumably ensured because each national standards organization is required by its own rules to seek such balance.[20] Other internal rules attempt to ensure procedural fairness: Comments must be addressed, all negative votes must be considered[21] during vote casting, and a supervisory body must ensure that proper procedures have been followed.[22]

However, in practice full representation of major stakeholders has been missing, especially at the early stages, where the basic "architecture" of the standards was put in place. Despite the stated goal of balance, the membership of TC 207 is heavily concentrated in large global industry, industry trade associations and consultants, and industry-related government standard-setting bodies. The chairpersons of the TC subcommittees included representatives of the Merck and Bayer pharmaceutical giants, chemical and electronics companies, consulting firms, and national standard-setting institutes.[23] At the work group level, where most of the drafting work is done, ten of the sixteen conveners came from large corporations or industry federations.[24] As late as the May 1994 plenary meeting of the TC, only one consumer organization attended, as an "external liaison" rather than a participant.[25]

In practice, those who consistently attend meetings and participate in the actual drafting work decide the content of the ISO standards. The drafting committees are considerably less representative than the formal TC membership and have been dominated, especially in the United States, by large corporate interests. Small businesses and consumer and environmental groups have been underrepresented.[26] This is so in part because the costs of participation add up: Recent international meetings were held in Australia, France, Korea, Norway, Brazil, and South Africa. While the intent is to distribute evenly the costs of travel, the result is that only those who can afford to pay thousands of dollars in travel costs may consistently attend meetings.[27] Those tend to be representatives of the global corporations who have the most to lose or gain by how a standard is drafted. The dominance of transnational corporations is magnified by the existence of corporate subsidiaries in a number of participating countries. Thus, the same corporate or industry interests have multiple entry points into the drafting and decision-making process.[28]

The presence of government, small business, and nongovernmental organization (NGO) interests on TC 207 did improve over time as word of the possible implications of the ISO's work began to spread. The Netherlands provided a one-time, two-year grant to pay travel costs of underrepresented interests and countries,[29] although for the long term the travel issue remains unresolved. Government agencies like the U.S. Environmental Protection Agency (EPA), which had preferred until 1994 to watch the process from afar, began taking a more active role. Large, relatively well funded NGOs like the Environmental Defense Fund and the Worldwide Fund for Nature also began regularly attending meetings. Nonetheless, NGO input has been largely in the form of damage control rather than being able to shape the form and content of the standards.[30] By the time these new actors became engaged in the process, most of the basic decisions (at least on the ISO 14001 and other EMS documents) had already been made.

Although it may have happened too late, the private process, once composed almost exclusively of those with a pecuniary stake in the outcome of the exercise (either as regulated entities or as certifiers/practitioners/consultants), over time began to look more like the public one, with its messy, time-consuming, but ultimately legitimacy-enhancing proliferation of interest groups. In addition, over time the proportion of professional lawyers and public standard setters compared to technical and engineering personnel also increased. These actors were not simply lobbyists but actually sat at the table. In many ways this could be seen as an improvement over the public process, where NGOs may find themselves pacing the halls or relegated to meeting sites far from the centers of decision.[31] Moreover, standards are more likely to be actually implemented when the "real parties in interest," those industries expected to use them, are at the drafting table and can take the product back and "sell" it to their respective organizations.

In addition to the predominance of transnational corporate interests (and lack of small business, consumer, and environmental interests), another potential problem is the predominance of delegations from large industrial countries. Just as in public international negotiations, formal equality of national delegations masks functional inequality. The lack of timely developing country input poses the danger that the standards, even if implemented, may be ineffective in the conditions of many developing countries.

In theory, a wide range of countries participated in crafting the standards: Forty-nine participating country and seventeen observing country delegations had expressed interest in the work of the TC as of 1996.[32] However, in practice far fewer countries have attended, and fewer still participated actively in the drafting and debate process. For example, at a May 1994 plenary session held in Australia (to facilitate the attendance of industrializing Asian countries), only five of twenty-six delegations (Brazil, Malaysia, China, Korea, and Thailand) came from non-OECD (Organization for Economic Cooperation and Development) states.[33] In contrast, fourteen European states attended.[34] Attendance by less developed country (LDC) delegations at meetings held in the United States and Europe was even more sparse, although by July 1995, as the importance of the standard became more obvious, a sizable number of developing country delegations were able to attend the plenary.[35] The most substantive disputes in the TC have involved the United States, Europe, and, to a lesser degree, Japan, Australia, Canada, New Zealand, Korea, and South Africa.[36] Moreover, while most developed countries can send only one or two delegates, about seventy people formed part of the U.S. delegation to the July 1995 plenary session.[37]

Obstacles to LDC participation may include the cost of attending meetings as well as difficulties in obtaining critical documents in a timely manner.[38] There may also have been a sense among some participants that the developing countries entered the process so late that they would have no choice but to fall in line with whatever standard is finally approved. This perception may in part be due to experience with ISO 9000, which became a de facto requirement for developing countries wishing to compete in European markets. Nonetheless, as word of the potential implications of the ISO standards has spread, more and more LDCs have expressed interest. While participants in the ISO process seem aware of the dangers posed by a lack of developing country participation, concern only belatedly translated into some action, with developed countries granting limited and temporary travel funds for LDC delegates to attend plenary sessions.[39]

The process limitations of the current ISO effort shade over into substantive shortcomings. Perhaps the greatest concerns revolve around the watering down of the standards to a lowest common denominator. The lowest common denominator problem results from the consensus nature of the process and the need for widespread conformity with the final product if the standards are to be voluntarily implemented.[40] Although the ISO rules do not require absolute consensus, and indeed drafts have been advanced to draft international standard (DIS) status over the objections of some participants,[41] an effort is made to accommodate the views of at least the major players. The danger is that disputed points will be omitted or papered over, leaving a standard with few specifics and fewer teeth. To the extent the standards replace or complement other forms of regulation, their relative lack of stringency implicates public policy concerns; it is especially worrisome if the standards are being set by those who have the greatest financial stake in their leniency.

DEBATES OVER THE CONTENT OF THE STANDARD

Debates over the content of the EMS standard can be considered along five interrelated dimensions.

Substance versus Procedure

From the start, the debates over drafting the standard revolved around the extent to which it would contain substantive, performance-based obligations or would be only a set of prescribed procedures and management techniques. A purely procedural approach allows maximum flexibility for management but does not necessarily, as the standard itself recognizes, guarantee optimal environmental outcomes.[42] It has the advantage of forcing internal discussion prior to establishing goals and priorities, making it perhaps more likely that organizations will take the resulting plans seriously rather than seeking minimal or halfhearted compliance with externally imposed rules. However, the danger is that because the goals and priorities are entirely self-chosen, they will be implemented only up to the point where changes no longer result in cost avoidance or cost savings within the short term; investments that require a longer investment horizon or that will in fact impose some costs will be avoided. Indeed, because there is no prescribed floor or minimum standard beyond compliance with local law, companies that set and meet extremely lenient goals will conform to the standard to the same or greater extent than those companies that set themselves more ambitious and harder-to-realize objectives.

The EMS standard makes clear that it "does not establish absolute requirements for environmental performance beyond commitment, in the policy, to compliance with applicable legislation and regulation and to continual improvement."[43] An annex elaborates: "The rate and extent of [continual improvement] will be determined by the organization in the light of economic and other circumstances. . . .

The establishment and operation of an EMS will not, in itself, necessarily result in an immediate reduction of adverse environmental impact."[44]

Disputes over procedure versus substance cropped up in several places. One of the most contentious involved the definition of "continual improvement" and whether evaluation of the EMS would involve evaluation only of improvements in the system itself or also in its actual results. The European EMAS requires evaluation of a specified group of parameters, including resource use, waste avoidance, and the like; it then requires continual improvement of a participating site's actual performance in these areas. The United States and some other participants pushed for a definition of "continual improvement" that did not impose minimum rates of emissions or toxics reduction. European delegates, led by Denmark, Austria, the United Kingdom, and Germany, wanted language directly linking continual improvement with improvement in *performance,* not just of the system's operation.

After considerable debate, the final standard specifies that the term merely means "the process for enhancing the EMS to achieve improvements in overall environmental performance, in line with the organization's environmental policy. Note: The process need not take place in all areas simultaneously."[45] The tie-in between continual improvement and the organization's "policy" was enough to obtain the agreement of the European delegates. However, the definition of "environmental performance" refers only to the "measureable results of the EMS relating to an organization's control of the environmental *aspects* of its activities" (emphasis added). An earlier draft made the difference clear: It defined performance as the "measureable outputs of the EMS, relating to an organization's control of the *impacts* of its activities . . . on the environment" (emphasis added).[46]

Along similar lines, the United States and some other non-European delegations wished to limit evaluation of performance to conformance of the management system itself—whether it operated as intended, whether feedback loops were operational, and the like—rather than of actual environmental performance. They argued that an international standard should not be driven by European Union requirements. Thus, it should focus on management systems, leaving performance to other regulatory tools and other parts of the standard-setting process. At the July 1995 meeting, compromise language was worked out that, according to at least some participants, clarifies that the EMS covers objectives and targets and that continual improvement refers not only to refinements in the system itself but also to improvement of objectives and targets.[47] While an improvement from an environmental standpoint over prior drafts, the standard still leaves no way to judge whether the improvements are sufficient, and it permits a company starting from a very low baseline to "improve" without ever meeting any international benchmark for adequate performance beyond compliance with local law.

Substantive Differences

Another aspect of this debate concerned the extent to which the standard would require a specific level of pollution control technology. At one point some European representatives pressed for a standard of "viable and achievable best available technology."[48] While such a standard might have little practical effect in much of Europe, where it would add little to existing laws,[49] the U.S. participants worried that in the United States it would change substantive legal requirements and could result in enormous civil and/or criminal liability. As a result, the standard's introduction merely provides that "the EMS should encourage organizations to consider implementation of best available technology where appropriate and where economically viable. In addition, the cost effectiveness of such technology should be fully taken into account."[50] It also specifies, in a late addition, that the standards "are not intended to be used to . . . increase or change an organization's legal obligations."[51]

The definition of environmental policy in the standard does have some more substantive components, but even these are limited. One requirement is "a commitment to comply with relevant environmental legislation and regulations, and with other requirements to which the organization subscribes."[52] However, organizations seeking certification presumably are already under a legal obligation to comply with local law; there is no additional requirement that, for example, an organization with operations in several countries apply the same rules or the most stringent rules to all its operations worldwide.[53] The ISO definition of "organization" allows each operating unit of a corporation to be considered a separate organization. This may be useful in ensuring that each operating unit must independently qualify for certification, but it also means there is no way to hold transnational firms operating in several countries to a higher standard than local law allows in each one. It is also far from clear that a "commitment to comply" is the same as actual compliance, at least from an auditing perspective.

The other substantive requirement worth noting is that the policy include efforts at "pollution prevention." This language, inserted by the U.S. delegation, is positive in that it goes beyond compliance with existing laws and is in line with the thrust of much current thinking on environmental protection. However, objections from the United States and some Asian countries watered down the definition perhaps beyond the point of usefulness. At the July 1995 Oslo meeting, the definition was changed to include processes to *control* pollution, which may include recycling, *treatment,* and others.[54] According to the EPA and many other experts,[55] neither simple pollution control nor after-the-fact treatment or off-site recycling is really *prevention,* which focuses on changes in process, practices, and materials to avoid introducing pollutants into the environment at all.

Specificity and Public Nature of Evaluation

A third area of debate concerned the specificity and public nature of requirements for evaluation of environmental impacts. The original British standard that served as a model for the ISO draft contained a requirement for an "environmental effects register." Under that standard, organizations must establish and maintain a register of significant direct and indirect environmental effects of activities, products, and services.[56] While the purpose of an environmental effects register is to identify areas for improvement, U.S. participants worried that, in the U.S. legal and regulatory climate, a document listing detrimental environmental impacts of corporate activity could be requisitioned by regulators or discovered in litigation, with disastrous consequences.[57] The draft ISO standard thus contains no mention of an environmental register, only references to a "procedure to identify the environmental aspects of its activities, products and services that it can control and over which it can be expected to have an influence, in order to determine those which have or can have significant impacts on the environment."[58] The organization need only "consider" the aspects related to these significant impacts in setting objectives and targets. An annex specifies air emissions, releases to water, waste management, and the like as possible environmental parameters but contains nothing mandatory, leaving it up to each organization to consider such parameters "where appropriate."[59]

Furthermore, the procedure and its results need not be made public. The U.S. delegation argued that requiring environmental policies and objectives to be publicly available would discourage companies from setting ambitious, meaningful objectives rather than listing vague platitudes.[60] European representatives, on the other hand, argued that credibility depended on making at least basic information publicly available. In addition, EMAS requires public disclosure, and the external pressure presumably generated by such pressure is central to its effectiveness.[61] The draft standard requires the organization's environmental policies to be publicly available, but on the more important issue of publication of its environmental impacts, it requires only that "the organization shall consider processes for external communication on significant environmental aspects of its activities and record its decision."[62]

Application along the Supply Chain

The reach of the ISO standards is more limited than that of EMAS, which requires firms to "ensure that suppliers and those acting on the organization's behalf comply with the company's environmental policy as it relates to them."[63] The draft ISO 14000 standard is more vague as to the registered companies obligations, requiring only "communication of relevant procedures and requirements to suppliers and contractors."[64] The idea that ISO-certified companies might require outside parties to meet any similar requirements was specifically rejected.[65]

Verification and Audits

A final area of controversy concerned the relationship between the EMS and environmental audits.[66] The EMAS requires a public statement, contains (in Annex 2) detailed requirements for audits, and requires the use of an external "verifier."[67] The audit required under EMAS covers not only the management system but also the factual data on environmental performance. Here again, European participants urged a system of audits that included independent audit verification and publication of at least a summary of audit results as necessary for both credibility and real pressure for improvement. Other delegations, led by the United States, found the costs of third-party verification excessive and often unnecessary,[68] especially after the U.S. experience with quality control, where verifiers had to be hired from Europe.[69] In the end, the U.S. position prevailed. The standard requires only an internal audit of the management system itself—to determine whether it conforms to the standard and has been properly implemented and maintained.[70] It also requires a management review to ensure the "continuing suitability, adequacy and effectiveness [of the EMS]."[71] The audit is designed to serve a strictly internal function; the organization may decide whether the audit is to be internal or external. There is no obligation to make the audit results public.

In all these instances, the main lines of debate pitted European participants against a "rest-of-the-world" camp led by the United States. The U.S. position was generally to seek less substantive, more procedural and flexible positions that preserved management prerogatives and corporate secrecy.[72] European representatives, in contrast, wished to ensure that compliance with the ISO standard would also constitute compliance with the EMAS regulation,[73] and EMAS, as well as existing national European standards, imposed several more substantive obligations. Countries that worried about the possible trade-restrictive or competitiveness effects of substantive standards tended to support the U.S. delegation; this included many developing country delegations. For the most part, the U.S. positions prevailed, as reflected in the draft standard.

Viewed objectively, it would have seemed to be in the best interests of the United States to push for a strong, substantively "green" standard. After all, existing domestic legal obligations in the United States already required a good deal in the way of installation of best available technology, disclosure of information, and the like. A predictable position on the part of the United States would have been to push to "level the playing field" by drafting a standard that would make other countries' industry have to meet some of the same requirements that the United States was already subject to. But this was not the position assumed by the corporate-heavy U.S. delegation. Rather, the United States used the rhetoric of the developing countries—fear of disguised trade barriers and the need for flexibility—to champion a watered-down version of standards. A perspective that focused only on the U.S. "national interest" would therefore not predict the actual positions taken.

Two sets of concerns might begin to explain this outcome: trade-related concerns and the interplay with domestic agendas. First, the use of voluntary, management-based standards responded to prevailing concerns around the expansion of global trade and increasing demands for environmental considerations to be built into the global trading order. Environmental management standards allow for procedural harmonization without substantive harmonization, so that countries need not change their domestic rules to come up to an international minimum (or to conform to an international ceiling). They impinge far less on national sovereignty than substantive standards while providing at least an environmental patina that may be used to defer or deflect other efforts at creating industry- or sector-specific rules. Moreover, ISO standards are considered "international standards" and thus given a presumption of legality under current trade law. More stringent or demanding standards then face a heavy burden of justification.[74] The U.S. delegation may have seen the opportunity to use this trade-related aspect of ISO standards to preempt more substantive international efforts.

At the same time, developing countries worried that even voluntary standards can become de facto mandatory and could have a detrimental effect on their exports to "big market" countries. These countries forecast that any substantive requirements in such voluntary standards would be more difficult for them to meet, both because of the need to import pollution control machinery and technical expertise and because the lack of a developed regulatory structure has allowed them to operate in the past with far less in the way of environmental controls or reporting requirements than their developed country competitors. The U.S. delegation could use these concerns to argue for a watered-down standard.

Second, U.S. companies may have wanted to ensure consistency between their efforts at ISO and their domestic deregulatory agenda. This agenda takes the form of pushing for self-regulation, for self-set goals, and for a limit on prescriptive government standards. Many companies in the United States have been in the forefront of recent efforts to shield the results of voluntary environmental audits from public and regulatory scrutiny and were not about to let international standards undermine their domestic positions.[75] Thus, by looking at the internal imperatives of the predominant forces in the U.S. delegation, the U.S. positions become easier to explain.

On the European side as well, a focus on internal factors explains the positions taken at the ISO. In addition to the European imperative to make the standard acceptable to the European Commission for EMAS purposes, many of the differences originated in divergent legal cultures and norms between Europe and the United States. In Europe, discovery rules are more protective,[76] and the threat of large-scale liability or criminal prosecutions is more remote.[77] There is no European-wide enforcement agency equivalent to the EPA, and national enforcement of environmental law varies greatly among European states.[78] Regulatory compliance and liability concerns drive the move toward environmental management and auditing standards in the United States, while proving that a company is "green" is a more salient motivator in Europe.[79]

HOW WILL THE STANDARDS BE USED?

The ISO 14001 EMS standard is designed to be voluntarily adopted by organizations. Companies may choose to implement an EMS for a number of reasons, both internally and externally imposed. Those companies that adopt the standard for internally generated reasons are most likely to take it seriously and to stress performance, while those "conscripts" who feel pressured or forced into too-quick adoption may see it more as yet another paper-shuffling enterprise.

Internal Reasons

A first group of reasons for implementation concerns the companies' own needs. Implementation of an EMS may allow firms to improve their compliance with existing national laws, reducing exposure to enforcement actions, lawsuits, or community distrust. Backers of systems approaches point to the savings and increased efficiency that can be generated through waste minimization or input substitutions identified through the EMS process.[80] Moreover, an EMS may allow companies in highly sensitive or consumer-focused industries to cultivate a "green" image, increasing their market share or distracting attention from past failures. In all these concerns, it is the implementation of the EMS itself, not necessarily its certification, that is paramount.

Implementation through Regulation

In some places industry self-regulation may be touted as an alternative to "command-and-control," and users may hope for decreased regulatory scrutiny if they show compliance with an EMS.[81] This decreased scrutiny may take many forms: fewer inspections, quicker permitting, or waiver of certain requirements. Creation of an EMS may also be imposed after a violation has taken place, as part of remediation for environmental violations, or as part of a cleanup plan.[82]

To date, no regulatory agency has relaxed its scrutiny simply on the basis of compliance with ISO 14000. Indeed, some industry and government officials have said that ISO 14001 should be kept separate from regulatory uses. Nonetheless, several APEC economies have incorporated use of an EMS into voluntary programs that trade increased documented and supervised self-regulation for relaxed permitting and monitoring requirements. For example, Victoria, Australia, allows use of an EMS as one element of an integrated license.[83] South Korea's Ministry of Environment is implementing a program for Environmentally Friendly Companies that requires an environmental management system, an environmental assessment and improvement plan, and a demonstration of actual improvement; the ministry inspects prior to designating the site as "friendly" and exempting it from surprise compliance inspections.[84] A number of U.S. states and the EPA are considering its use as one element in a "superior performance" track that also includes disclosure and community involvement components. A multistate working group of environmental officials and others is monitoring over 100 pilot projects to test the relationship between EMS implementation and improved performance.[85] Further regulatory strategies await the results.

Implementation through the Market: The Use of Supply Chains

A final impetus for adoption of an EMS is market pressure on the supply chain. As large global businesses begin preferring certified entities or requiring proof of certification to ISO 14001 or another EMS standard of their suppliers, demand for certification will grow. Especially as global business structures increasingly resemble dense networks of large and small suppliers and contractors, the leverage exercised by large transnational businesses over other firms in their supply chain is potentially quite powerful.[86]

Similarly, although it has not happened to date, government procurement practices could begin to incorporate certification preferences or requirements. If they do, companies seeking contracts will be likely to seek out certification. This was indeed the result after the introduction of the ISO 9000 quality control standard,[87] and a similar snowballing effect may occur here. The result, at least in theory, will be pressure emanating down the supply chain to encompass a wide range and size of producers. On the other hand, because ISO 9000 is concerned with product quality, it has much stronger requirements for suppliers than does ISO 14001, which makes compliance optional; this may dampen any supply chain effect. In some markets, pressure from banks and insurance companies anxious to minimize their own potential environmental liabilities or from investors looking for a quick investment "green screen" or to comply with regulatory disclosure rules may also create pressure for certification.[88]

It is as yet unclear whether and under what circumstances large global industries will see a business advantage either in complying with ISO 14001 themselves or in encouraging such compliance in their suppliers. Unlike ISO 9000, no immediate impact on product quality or usability is associated with better environmental management. Certification requirements may be limited to high-profile companies or sectors, where a major accident or discharge would reflect badly on the entire sector. On the other hand, fear of legal liability in more litigious cultures or of public opprobrium and damage to reputation being passed up the supply chain may extend a desire for added assurance to suppliers even those in places where liability is of far less concern. If suppliers are less likely to be subject to government shutdowns or fines, the indirect benefits in timeliness and reliability of output may help convince other large purchasers to require EMSs. Large developed country–based global enterprises, driven by their own liability or reputational concerns, may thus serve as transmission belts not only for the existence of a certified EMS but also for real performance improvement among their suppliers. If so, such enterprises may also be instrumental in providing the training and capacity building to enable suppliers to meet their requirements. Early research in this area seems to show that while large businesses do impose some environmental qualifications on their suppliers, they are generally not tied to ISO 14001 certification.[89] As of 1999, ISO 14001 had over 10,000 certifications in over fifty-five countries. Japan had the most certifications, followed by western Europe. Interest in North America had lagged until recently, with many companies declaring that they would implement their own EMS but not necessarily one that conformed to the ISO 14001 specifications. Nonetheless, major U.S. manufacturers, including IBM, Ford, and Xerox, have implemented the standard.[90]

Work has begun on the five-year revision of the ISO 14001. In preparation for that revision, a group led by U.S. state and federal officials and NGOs has been pushing for changes in the standard to strengthen its disclosure and performance requirements. However, at the latest plenary meeting of TC 207, delegates decided to move forward very slowly if at all, agreeing only to keep the question of whether revisions were needed "under review." With the possible exception of making the ISO quality control and environmental management standards more compatible, it seems that a majority of ISO TC 207 delegates do not want to risk widespread acceptance of the standard by making it more difficult to implement.

On the procedural front as well, change is slow. After NGOs publicly expressed their displeasure with access and openness in ISO, a negotiating group was formed. As of 1999, however, the negotiations had resulted only in agreement for preparation of a white paper for future presentation to all delegates expressing NGOs concerns about standard-creating procedures.[91] Similarly, while concerns continue to be raised about the lack of developing country input into standards development, the program that had previously brought developing country participants to plenary meetings had no funds left to sponsor participants to the 1999 plenary.[92]

CONCLUSION

As a general matter, it was perhaps predictable that the United States would favor weaker, less stringent measures in the area of environment-related standards; that Europeans would want "greener" rules; and that developing countries would worry primarily about trade effects. The ISO is surely not the only recent international forum where the U.S. delegation has played a conservative role. What makes the ISO example interesting is both the multiactor nature of the forum, where government officials have no primacy of place vis-à-vis corporate interests, and the further insights to be gained by applying a liberal lens that allows a look into the domestic agendas helping to shape national positions on the international front. By doing so, the positions of the U.S. delegation, which at first blush might seem contrary to the "national interest," become more comprehensible.

NOTES

This chapter contains material published in a number of earlier versions, including Naomi Roht-Arriaza, "Environmental Management Systems and Environmental Protection: Can

ISO 14001 Be Useful within the Context of APEC?" *Journal of Environment and Development* 6 (1997): 292; "Developing Countries, Regional Organizations, and the ISO 14001 Environmental Management Standard," *Georgetown International Environmental Law Review* 9 (1997): 583; "Private Voluntary Standard-Setting, the International Organization for Standardization and International Environmental Lawmaking," *Yearbook of International Environmental Law* 6 (1995): 107; and "Shifting the Point of Regulation: The International Organization for Standardization and Global Lawmaking on Trade and the Environment," *Ecology Law Quarterly* 22 (1995): 479.

1. International Organization for Standardization, Memento 3 (1995). While all developed countries have full ISO membership, only about half the developing countries participate. United Nations Council on Trade and Development, *ISO 14001: Five Key Questions for Developing Country Officials* (draft) (Geneva: UNCTAD, 1996), 9.

2. While conveners oversee the actual draft standard writing at the WG level (see Office of Pollution Prevention and Toxics, U.S. EPA, ISO 14000: International Environmental Management Standards 1 [1995]), the committees and subcommittees, headed by secretariats, are the bodies that promulgate the draft international standards that members vote on. ISO in Figures, Jan. 2001, at <http://www.iso.ch/iso/en/aboutiso/ISOinfigures.Jan.2001.pdf>.

3. Ibid.

4. No more than 25 percent of the national bodies may vote against the draft standard, and two-thirds must affirmatively vote in favor of it (ISO Memento). In general, "ISO work is based on the principle of reaching consensus as far as possible." Dick Hortensius and Mark Barthel, "Beyond 14001: An Introduction to the ISO 14000 Series," in Christopher Sheldon, ed., *ISO 14000 and Beyond* (London: Greenleaf Publishing, 1997), 42.

5. See, generally, Perry L. Johnson, *ISO 9000: Meeting the New International Standards* (New York, N.Y.: McGraw-Hill, 1993).

6. For a fuller description, see, for example, ibid.

7. See Charles W. Thurston, *Quality Is a Global Affair: Worldwide Adoption of International Organization for Standardization Program, Quality '94,* 246 Chemical Marketing Reporter SR-10 (1994).

8. This suspicion was fueled by the preponderance of European firms among accredited certifiers and by the insistence of the European Community that only European-accredited certifiers were acceptable.

9. See, for example, Agenda 21, which recommends that industry "establish environment management systems, including environmental auditing of production or distribution sites" (20.13[i]) and "share their environmental management experiences with the local authorities, national Governments, and international organizations (30.22). Nonetheless, in the standard itself, all references to sustainable development have disappeared. See UNCTAD, *ISO 14001,* 43.

10. In 1991, the Business Council for Sustainable Development (BCSD) began creating international standards that would allow businesses in various sectors to measure their environmental impacts according to comparable criteria. See Stephan Schmidheiny, *Business Council for Sustainable Development, Changing Course: A Global Business Perspective on Development and the Environment* (Cambridge, Mass.: MIT Press, 1992), 30. The BCSD's initiative dovetailed with that of a coalition of socially responsible investors in the United States, who in 1989 published the Valdez Principles, a set of voluntary commitments intended to be used by investors to favor environmentally responsible corporations. The Valdez Principles

have now become the CERES Principles. Coalition for Environmentally Responsible Economies, "1990 CERES Guide to the Valdez Principles," reprinted in John R. Salter, *Corporate Environmental Responsibility: Law and Practice* (London: Butterworths, 1992), 257, appendix. Corporations that signed on to the principles were supposed to minimize pollutants, resource and energy use, and waste generation; inform consumers of the environmental impacts of their products and services; complete and make public an annual self-audit of environmental progress and work toward creation of independent environmental audit procedures to be made available to the public; and establish management and Board structures to oversee environmental performance. Other similar initiatives include the Business Charter for Sustainable Development and the Global Environmental Management Initiative (GEMI). To join, companies simply sign up; public pressure is the only means of monitoring compliance with the commitment. Sectoral codes of conduct, such as the Chemical Manufacturers Association's "Responsible Care" program, also appeared.

11. Council regulation 1836/93. The regulation became effective as of April 1995, and a revised version, expanding the scope of the regulation, entered into force in April 2001. Council Reg. 761/2001, March 19, 2001.

12. Ibid.

13. See Stanley A. Marash, "The Future of ISO 9000," The Corporate Board, May 1994, available in Lexis, News Library, MAGS File, 20. This worry was based in part on experience with ISO 9000. A 1994 study noted that of the more than 50,000 ISO 9000 certificates issued worldwide, only some 4,000 were issued to companies in the United States. "SusService Announces Registration to ISO 9001 Standard," Business Wire, April 24, 1995, available in Lexis, Nexis Library, BWIRE File.

14. The EMS draft standard states, "There is an important distinction between this specification which describes the requirements for certification/registration and/or self-declaration of an organization's environmental management system and a non-certifiable guideline intended to provide generic assistance to an organization for implementing or improving an environmental management system." ISO/TC 207/DIS 14001, Introduction (July 1995).

15. Ibid., 4.2.1.

16. Ibid., 4.2.3, 4.2.4.

17. Ibid., 4.3, 4.4.

18. Ibid., 4.4.4, 4.5.

19. International Organization for Standardization, "Information about ISO," Geneva, January 1993 (on file with author).

20. Ibid.

21. Negative votes may, however, be rejected as "not related" or "not persuasive." See Robert W. Hamilton, "The Role of Nongovernmental Standards in the Development of Mandatory Federal Standards Affecting Safety or Health," *Texas Law Review* 56 (1978): 1329, 1357–58 (describing process of ASTM, a constituent member of ANSI responsible for most U.S. standard setting). According to Hamilton, some consumer representatives felt their objections were often rejected on these grounds (ibid.).

22. American National Standards Institute, *ANSI Procedures for the Development and Coordination of American National Standards* (Washington, D.C.: ANSI, 1995), 3.3.

23. Global Environmental Management Initiative, "Organizational Structure of ISO/ TC207: Environmental Management and U.S. Participation" (chart), February 1994. In drawing conclusions from this list, one must keep in mind that although participants were delegated

from their corporation to participate in the process, they often come from the corporation's environmental compliance shop rather than top management, and it is unclear to what extent they represent the views, and commitment, of the corporation's leadership.

24. Ibid.

25. At some point in the process, nonparticipation by NGOs may be the result of an assessment that the standards will have little substantive impact and so are not worth spending scarce resources to influence. But that result in turn may reflect an earlier lack of NGO input into the decisions on the procedural or substantive content of the standards.

26. These problems seem endemic to voluntary consensus standard setting. In a 1978 article on elaboration of U.S. safety or health standards, Professor Robert Hamilton found that the U.S. standard-setting committees suffered from a lack of qualified representatives for some important interests, uneven attendance, and a lack of balance on important working groups (Hamilton, 1355). Hamilton expressed concern that standards may have been developed with insufficient participation by consumers, workers, and small business and that certain noneconomic interests may have been given inadequate consideration in developing a consensus when most of the participants were representatives of economic interests (ibid., 1386). Similar concerns apply in an international context.

27. Formal requirements for participation in national groups seem minimal. In the United States, for example, members of the TAG are largely self-selected: on payment of $250, anyone can request membership; fact sheet from ASTM, U.S. Administrator of the TAG (on file with author). Prospective members' names are periodically distributed to existing members of the TAG. Existing members must specifically vote to exclude applicants, and this rarely happens. Correspondence from ASTM; interview with Gordon Bellen, U.S. TAG member.

28. The TC leadership is aware of the lack of balance and the price paid in lessened credibility of the final standards, although they see the proindustry slant of some delegations internationally as balanced by the government- or consultant-heavy bias of others. Joe Cascio (program director for environment, health and safety standardization of IBM and head of the U.S. TAG), "International Environmental Management Standards," *ASTM Standardization News,* April 1994, 48. In addition, any tendencies of corporate-dominated drafting groups toward lax standards is to some degree mitigated by the professional norms of the environment, health, and safety specialists like Cascio who often represent the corporation. As another example, Joel Charm, head of one of the working groups, is the director of occupational health in the corporate health, safety, and environmental sciences office of Allied Signal.

29. Mary McKiel, U.S. EPA, "Report on Annual Meeting of the ISO Technical Committee for Environmental Management" (1995), 2–3 (on file with author).

30. For example, NGO representatives reintroduced the idea of the environmental objective of labeling programs, which the United States had earlier managed to delete from the eco-labeling draft. Meeting minutes, November 30, 1995. NGOs were also extremely active in the fight to scuttle a Canadian/Australian initiative to create specific management standards on forestry.

31. For example, both the NGO forum for the 1992 Rio Conference on Environment and Development and the NGO forum for the 1995 Beijing 4th World Conference on Women were located far from the site of government deliberations, and many NGOs had problems obtaining access. See "Chinese Government Angers Delegates as Women's Forum Opens," *Deutsch Presse-Agentur,* August 30, 1995.

32. ISO Secretariat, "The ISO 14000 Environment," March 1996, 2.

33. Minutes of Australia meeting, May 1994 (on file with author).

34. Ibid.

35. An unofficial listing of TC 207 members present includes Colombia, India, Chile, Malaysia, South Africa, China, Korea, Mexico, Thailand, Brazil, Indonesia, Mauritius, Vietnam, Jamaica, Trinidad-Tobago, and Zimbabwe. Thirteen European states, the United States, Australia, New Zealand, Canada, Israel, Russia, Japan, and Turkey also fielded delegations. McKiel, "Report on Annual Meeting of the ISO Technical Committee for Environmental Management," 7.

36. For example, a consensus draft on Type I eco-labeling schemes was hammered out in May 1994 by delegations from France, the United States, the United Kingdom, Germany, Japan, Korea, Canada, and Australia. June 10, 1994, correspondence re SC3/WG1 (on file with author); the initial draft of an annex to the EMS standard, intended to overcome U.S.-European differences, was drafted by a small group consisting of Austria, Canada, Japan, Germany, the United Kingdom, New Zealand, the United States, and the International Chamber of Commerce. July 20, 1994, correspondence (on file with author).

37. Of course, in public environmental treaty negotiations, many of the same problems and discrepancies arise, but over time, mechanisms, including travel subsidies and the use of NGO advisers for small states, have arisen to ameliorate the problems. To date those mechanisms are absent in the ISO context.

38. A number of delegates from developing countries claimed that they did not receive critical documents from the TC secretariat before the July 1995 plenary meetings. "Small and Medium-Size Businesses, along with Developing Nations, Face Challenges," *Quality Systems Update*, July 1995, SR-10.

39. Support for an ISO mandate to provide travel funds for underrepresented states might come from the GATT's Agreement on Technical Barriers to Trade, which provides that "Members shall take such reasonable measures as may be available to them to ensure that international standardizing bodies and international systems for conformity assessment are organized and operated in a way which facilitates active and representative participation of relevant bodies in all Members, taking into account the special problems of developing country Members." TBT Agreement, 12.5.

40. See Peter Sand, *Lessons in Global Environmental Governance* (Washington, D.C.: World Resources Institute, 1990).

41. For example, the EMS Specification standard was approved by a vote of 28–2, the guidance standard by a vote of 26–3. Minutes, July 1995 meeting, TC 207, SC 1 (on file with author).

42. ISO 14001, Introduction.

43. Ibid.

44. Ibid., Annex A (Informative), A.4.0.

45. ISO 14001, 3.1.

46. Benchmark Environmental Consulting/EEB, "ISI 14001: An Uncommon Perspective: Five Public Policy Questions for Proponents of the ISO 14000 Series," November 1995, 15.

47. Interview with Dick Hortensius, chief negotiator of the Dutch delegation, and Jose Cascio, head of the U.S. delegation to TC 207, 18 *International Environment Reporter (BNA)* 18 (July 12, 1995): 555, 556. The changed wording comes in the definition section of the specification standard. The previous definition of "environmental management system" was

"the organizational structure, responsibilities, practices, procedures, processes and resources for implementing and maintaining environmental management." ISO/TC207/SC1/N 47, 3.6. In the July 1995 draft, the new definition reads "that part of the overall management system which includes organization, structural changing activities, responsibilities, practices, procedure, process and services for developing, implementing, achieving, reviewing and monitoring the environmental policy." The key change is the reference to policy at the end: The environmental policy section includes commitments to compliance, continual improvement, and pollution prevention and to setting and reviewing environmental objectives and targets. Thus, at least according to some delegates, the policy becomes an auditable part of the EMS. "International Environmental Systems Update," July 1995, SB-27. However, this may be minimally useful, as attempts to extend audit requirements to objectives and targets failed. Ibid., SB-33.

48. Interview with Christopher Bell, Sidley & Austin, member of the TC, April 7, 1994. EMAS requires participating companies to aim at reducing environmental impacts to levels not exceeding those corresponding to economically viable application of best available technology. Council Reg. 1836/93, *Supra* note 11.

49. For example, German law has far-reaching emissions control duties requiring the imposition of best available technology, for example, in Section 5[1], no. 2, of the Federal Emission Control Act and Section 7a of the Water Management Act. See generally H. Hohmann, *Precautionary Legal Duties and Principles of Modern International Environmental Law* (London: Graham & Trotman, 1994), 11. In the United States, in contrast, most existing sources have to comply with less stringent technological requirements, at least for nontoxic pollutants. W. Rodgers, *Environmental Law,* 2d ed. (St. Paul, Minn.: West Publishing Co., 1994), 54–55; 228–29.

50. ISO 14001, Introduction. Note that the Introduction is not part of the specification part of the standard but merely provides guidance.

51. Draft, 1. This language is missing from the May 1994 draft.

52. The guidance annex specifies that "other requirements" may include industry codes of practice, agreements with public authorities, or nonregulatory guidelines. Annex, A4.2.2.

53. See, for example, Alan Neff, "Not in Their Backyards, Either: A Proposal for a Foreign Environmental Practices Act," *Ecology Law Quarterly* 17 (1990): 477; see also Benchmark Environmental Consulting/EEB, "ISI 14001," 23–24.

54. It now reads, *"Prevention of Pollution*: Use of processes, practices, materials, or products that avoid, reduce or control pollution which may include recycling, treatment, process changes, control mechanisms, efficient use of resources, and materials substitutions." DIS, Section 3.14.

55. See U.S. EPA, *Policies for Pollution Prevention* (Washington, D.C.: U.S. Government Documents. 1991); Kenneth Geiser, "The Unfinished Business of Pollution Prevention," *Georgia Law Review* 29 (1995): 473.

56. The register was to include, as appropriate, air and water emissions; wastes; land contamination; use of land, water, fuels, and energy and other natural resources; noise; visual impact; and effects on specific ecosystems arising from both normal operations and accidents and such information regarding future planned activities. BSI BS 7750, 4.4.3, and Annex A.4. As noted, EMAS requires similarly detailed evaluations.

57. Interview with Bell. Similar concerns were raised about requiring an audit verifying compliance with local laws. "Committee Draft on Management Standards Includes Two New

U.S.-Backed Requirements, *BNA InternationalEnvironment Daily,* February 28, 1995 (Joe Cascio, head of the U.S. TC, says that some U.S. industry representatives were concerned that compliance audits might become public and be used for enforcement purposes).

58. Draft, 4.2.1.

59. Annex, A4.2.1.2. Those parameters are to be systematized and harmonized through the work of the Environmental Performance Evaluation (EPE) subcommittee of TC 207, expected to be ready by 1998. The EPE is a "process to measure, analyze, assess, and describe an organization's environmental performance against agreed criteria for appropriate management purposes." It defines a system for measurement and reporting of performance improvements, such as units of measurement and base time periods. Originally, the subcommittee divided into working groups on generic and sector-specific EPE. The Europeans, especially the Norwegians, pushed for a standard that would specify, for some five to ten priority industry sectors, maximum allowable emissions of key pollutants. Christopher Bell and James Connaughton, "New Global Standards May Guide Industry on Environmental Issues," *National Law Journal,* September 6, 1993, S4. Others, including the United States, considered the effort as too ambitious and too fraught with difficulties stemming from regional and local variation. They wanted more general criteria, to be used primarily as internal evaluation tools. The U.S. position prevailed: As of April 1994, development of industrial sector indicators was abandoned, and the EPE group reconfigured into working groups on management system EPE and operational system EPE. The operational system EPE is to develop a series of diagnostic tools for measuring environmental performance. These will include such measures as quantity per unit of production of effluents, emissions and wastes, changes in output over time, and compliance record. Companies will be free to pick and choose among the indicators; however, none will be required.

60. Ibid.

61. Caroline London and Brizay London, "Disclosure Obligations and Due Diligence Practices in Europe," C764 ALI-ABA, September 24, 1992, 667, 670–71 (discussing EC Directive of June 7, 1990, requiring freedom of access to information on the environment); "European Community: Business Warned of More Disclosure, Environmental Audits in Europe," *BNA Environmental Reports,* April 22, 1992. Also, Article 5 of EMAS requires a published environmental statement, including a summary of data on emissions, wastes, consumption of raw materials and energy, and other factors. EMAS, Council Reg. 1836/93, *supra* note 11.

62. DIS, ISO 14001, 4.3.3. Communication with stakeholders is also limited: When establishing its objectives, an organization is to consider the views of interested parties, but it is unclear on the basis of what information such parties are to form their views or to what extent companies must act on the views expressed. DIS 4.2.3.

63. EMAS, Council Reg. 1836/93, *supra* note 11.

64. ISO 14001 4.3.6.(c) is entitled "control procedures for routine operations." It requires the organization to "establish and maintain procedures related to the significant environmental aspects of goods and services used by the organization and communication of relevant procedures and requirements to suppliers and contractors." Elsewhere, the Annex warns that "the control and influence over the environmental aspects of products vary significantly, depending on the market situation of the organization." Annex A4.2.1.

65. *International Environmental Systems Update* (July 1995): SB-32.

66. A separate subcommittee within TC 207 is developing specific auditing standards.

Detailed procedural requirements for audits are laid out in separate draft standards dealing with general audit principles (ISO 14010), auditing of environmental management systems (ISO 14011/1), and qualification criteria for environmental auditors (ISO 14012), all of which were approved as DISs in July 1995. They deal with such issues as periodicity of audits, confidentiality of audit results, appropriate training for auditors, and the like. Other auditing standards on compliance/performance audits and auditing of environmental status were deleted, while a new proposal for environmental site assessments is to be decided on next year. ISO 14000 Series Standards—Document Status, *Quality Systems Update,* Special Report, July 1995, R-4.

67. EMAS, Article 4.3.

68. By one estimate, third-party certification had added 20 percent to the cost of registration with the ISO 9000 standard. J. Cascio, "International Environmental Management Standards," 45.

69. See discussion in notes 7 and 8 (ISO 9000).

70. DIS at 4.4.4.

71. Ibid., 4.5.

72. Some of these debates are described here. On the other hand, the U.S. delegation was responsible for inserting language requiring efforts at "pollution prevention" of all organizations seeking certification. While this could be seen as a positive step in that it goes beyond compliance with existing laws, there are no guidelines to date for what will be considered pollution prevention activity for purposes of the standard. See *BNA International Environment Daily,* March 1995.

73. International Environmental Management Standards, ISO/TC 207, Update, May 1994 (on file with author). See discussion.

74. The Agreement on Technical Barriers to Trade (TBT), which is part of the GATT '94, covers government regulations on products, like those relating to size, quality, or emissions levels. It states, "Where technical regulations are required and relevant international standards exist or their completion is imminent, Members shall use them, or the relevant parts of them, as a basis for their technical regulations." Final Act Embodying the Results of the Uruguay Round of Multilateral Trade Negotiations, Agreement on Technical Barriers to Trade, April 15, 1994, reprinted in H.R. Document 316, 103rd Cong., 2d sess. (1994), Art. 2.2, 1428. The text continues, ". . . except when such international standards or relevant parts would be an ineffective or inappropriate means for the fulfillment of the legitimate objectives pursued, for instance because of fundamental climatic or geographical factors or fundamental technological problems." Ibid., Art. 2.4. Although this qualifier allows states to impose their own standards, it puts the burden on them to justify such departures.

75. Industry representatives are now attempting to have information generated in the process of conducting an "environmental audit," very broadly defined, declared confidential. Under heavy corporate pressure, seven states have enacted legislation creating a broad "self-evaluative" privilege for anything termed an audit report, while twenty-one others have legislation pending. "More States Adopt Audit Privilege Laws; EPA Calls Federal Legislation Ill-Advised," *Environment Report* 25, no. 44 (March 10, 1995): 2186. A proposed federal "Environmental Audit Protection Act" would allow any document labeled an "environmental audit report" or its supporting documentation to be kept confidential. The theory is that if regulators or the public could obtain information contained in an audit that was not required under the law, the thoroughness of the audit would suffer. Opponents respond that unscrupulous

corporations will be able to cover almost anything, including evidence of legal violations, under the rubric of an "environmental audit report" and will use the audit process strategically to disclose some violations but not others. Under EPA's current audit policy, EPA will not routinely request access to a firm's audits in the course of enforcement activities but reserves the right to demand access to audits on a case-by-case basis. U.S. EPA, "Restatement of Policies Related to Environmental Auditing," *Federal Register* 59, no. 38455 (July 28, 1994): 4. The current ISO draft environmental audit standards neither require nor forbid publication of audit results by the client, although they do require the auditee's permission where the client and auditee are different. Draft guidelines for environmental auditing, auditing of environmental management systems, ISO/TC207/SC2/N64, February 1, 1995, 5.4.3. For a fuller discussion, see Sanford Lewis, "Corporate Environmental Audits and the Public's Right to Know," February 1, 1995 (unpublished report on file with author), and David Ronald, "The Case against an Environmental Audit Privilege," *Chemical Waste Litigation Reporter* 29 (1995): 167, 168–69, and "No Audit Privilege in Interim EPA Policy; Lack of Prosecution, Punitive Fines Possible," *Environment Report* 25, no. 48 (April 7, 1995): 2411.

76. See, for example, Elli Louka, "Bringing Polluters before Transnational Courts: Why Industry Should Demand Strict and Unlimited Liability for the Transnational Movements of Hazardous and Radioactive Wastes," *Denver Journal of International Law & Policy* 22 (1993): 63; see also Peter Roorda, "The Internationalization of the Practice of Law," *Wake Forest Law Review* 28 (1993): 141.

77. See, for example, Barbara A. Boczar, "Toward a Viable Environmental Regulatory Framework: From Corporate Environmental Management to Regulatory Consensus," *DePaul Business Law Journal* 6 (1994): 291, and Gert Bruggermeir, "Enterprise Liability for 'Environmental Damage' in German Law and EC Law," *New European Law Review* 2 (1994): 17.

78. See Deborah A. Nelson, "European Environmental Agency," *Colorado Journal of Environmental Law and Policy* 10 (1999): 153, and Mark E. Allen, "Slowing Europe's Hazardous Waste Trade: Implementing the Basel Convention into European Union Law," *Colorado Journal of Environmental Law and Policy* 6 (1995): 163.

79. See Linda Spedding, "Environmental Auditing and International Standards," *Review of European Community and International Environmental Law* 3 (1994): 14, 15.

80. See, for example, Office of Technology Assessment, U.S. Congress, "Serious Reduction of Hazardous Waste: For Pollution Prevention and Industrial Efficiency," OTA-ITE-317 (1986).

81. See, for example, "External Concerns Drive EMS Implementation and Certification," Business and the Environment's ISO 14000 Update, December 1996, 1; "Are Voluntary Incentives Offering the Right Incentives?," *Business & the Environment* 7, no. 11 (1996): 2. For a summary of U.S. state government interest in using EMSs as alternatives or supplements to regulation, see "Interest High in States but Keyed to Compliance," *International Environmental Systems Update,* March 1996, 9.

82. In Canada, for instance, an Alberta court imposed an obligation on Prospec Chemicals, Inc., to obtain ISO 14001 certification by June 1998 and to deposit a bond to guarantee its compliance as part of a sentence for exceeding allowable sulfur emissions. *Business & the Environment* 7, no. 3 (March 1996): 2.

83. The Victoria accredited license scheme involves, in addition to an EMS, a good track record of performance, an environmental improvement plan, an environmental audit system

that at some point involves a government auditor, and industry-community liaison groups. Industries receive in exchange the ability to operate within broad environmental parameters, with lessened permit, reporting, and inspection requirements. Dr. Brian Robinson, "ISO 14000: Eagle or Albatross" (paper presented on July 2, 1996, in Canberra at the Australian Centre for Environmental Law). In California, a proposed "Consolidated Permit Zone Pilot Project" would allow ISO 14001 to be used as part of a Facility Compliance Plan, which must be approved by state authorities as part of a larger process. Draft Regulations Pursuant to SB 1299, Title 27 Environmental Protection (1996).

84. UNCTAD, *ISO 14001*, 72–73.

85. Erik J. Meyers, "Leading to Greener Pastures," *The Environmental Forum* 16 (March/April 1999): 28.

86. For a discussion of the far-ranging implications of large-to-small producer links involving product stewardship, audit, and training requirements, see Neil Gunningham, "Environment, Self-Regulation, and the Chemical Industry: Assessing Responsible Care," *Law & Policy* 17 (1995): 57, 84.

87. ISO certification was required for certain "regulated products" covered by EC directives as well as for some government contracts. Johnson, *ISO 9000*, 9.

88. In the case of banks and insurers, their leverage depends highly on market conditions. For example, in a market with too many banks and too few borrowers, conditions like ISO 14001 certification are unlikely. On the other hand, Malaysia and Japan, among others, are considering the imposition of rules regarding disclosure of potential environmental liabilities like those now required by the U.S. Securities and Exchange Commission. Interview with David Nelson, September 30, 1996.

89. U.S.-Asia Environmental Partnership, "Global Environmental Management: Candid Views of Fortune 500 Companies," (Washington, D.C.: U.S.-AEP, October 1997).

90. See *Business & the Environment*'s ISO 14000 Update for status reports on companies adhering to the standard.

91. *Business & the Environment*'s (5, no. 7 [July 1999]) ISO 14000 Update, "White Paper to Address NGO Concerns about ISO 14000 Drafting Process."

92. Ibid., "Task Force Reports on ISO 14000 Standards' Potential as Trade Barrier," September 1998.

IV

CONCLUSION

10

Explaining Similarities and Differences across International Trade Organizations

Richard H. Steinberg

This volume has examined how trade-environment issues have been addressed in many of the world's most prominent international trade organizations. Three political-economic theories (classified in chapter 1 as "realist," "institutionalist," and "liberal") have been used to understand how trade-environment rules are developing in trade organizations. Each of these approaches has helped highlight different trade-environment problems and solutions. Moreover, analysis through these alternative lenses has helped show why interlocutors on the topic—environmentalists, trade experts, economists, sociologists, political scientists, and lawyers, from developed and developing countries—often seem to be talking past one another; they are often using different vocabularies and analytic tools and focusing on different aspects of a problem. But at least one set of questions seems to be of interest to everyone concerned with trade-environment issues: To what extent are trade rules developing in an environment-friendly way, and why? Which international trade organizations are the most environment-friendly? Which are the least environment-friendly? What accounts for that variance?

Environmentalists want to understand the extent to which various international organizations are developing rules in an environment-friendly way, and why, because that understanding may provide insight into which policy strategies are likely to be most effective in securing greener international trade law. Those who want to limit the inclusion of environmental issues in the trade agenda of particular international organizations want answers for their own purposes. And scholars examining trade-environment issues need to understand how and why these rules are developing across trade organizations so that they can better evaluate trade rules, their effectiveness and efficiency, the underlying politics and sociology of international trade organizations, and for a host of other reasons particular to various inquiries.

This chapter evaluates the extent to which the international trade organizations examined in this volume are developing environment-friendly rules, offers a power- and interest-based explanation for variance in that development across international trade organizations, considers some of the limits of that explanation, and suggests some of the policy implications of the analysis.

VARIANCE IN THE EXTENT OF ENVIRONMENT-FRIENDLY RULE DEVELOPMENT IN INTERNATIONAL TRADE ORGANIZATIONS

International trade rules may develop in a manner that is environment-friendly or in a manner that is not environment-friendly. On each of the four dimensions of trade-environment policy issues identified in chapter 1, a balance may be struck that is more or less environment-friendly. Thus, the extent of environment-friendliness may be measured with respect to each of those four categories: the extent to which national trade measures may be used by a state to protect domestic health, safety, and environment; the extent to which trade measures may be used by a state to influence extrajurisdictional activity, such as foreign activity that generates pollution; the extent to which trade organizations have become involved in remediating polluted transboundary territory; and the extent to which institutional rules (e.g., rules regarding legal competence of the institution to consider or act on environmental concerns and rules regarding who may participate in providing information, framing issues, offering policy arguments, and offering legal arguments before judicial panels regarding the environment) permit and favor consideration of and action on environmental concerns. In assessing the environment-friendliness of rules, those that constitute binding obligations on states (i.e., "hard law") are considered more environment-friendly than rules that are merely hortatory (i.e., "soft law").[1]

Using these four categories, most of the organizations examined in this volume may be compared with each other fruitfully in terms of the development of environment-friendly rules and institutions. The GATT/WTO, EU, NAFTA, FTAA, and APEC—and some other trade organizations not studied in this volume, such as the Southern Cone Common Market in Latin America (MERCOSUR)[2] and the ASEAN[3] Free Trade Area (AFTA)—are each "state-centric" international organizations in that only the governments of states (i.e., neither natural persons, nongovernmental organizations, nor business organizations) have formal legal standing to participate directly in the negotiation and establishment of each of these four categories of trade-environment rules. The most environment-friendly of these international trade organizations have adopted measures, administered policies, and developed institutions that further environmental goals in all four categories of trade-environment issues. The least environment-friendly of these organizations have done little or nothing to further environmental goals in any of the four categories.

The ISO cannot be compared fruitfully to these other international organizations along the four dimensions. As seen in chapter 9, the private sector—not the government of a state—formally drives ISO negotiations and rule making. The ISO has no legal authority to negotiate or establish trade-environment rules that restrict states from imposing trade measures for domestic or extrajurisdictional environmental purposes. In other words, the ISO lacks the legal competence to adopt the first two dimensions of trade-environment policy considered in state-centric international organizations. Therefore, including the ISO in a comparison and analysis of the development of trade-environment rules along with the other international organizations examined here would be systematically biased. Indeed, a general consideration of the ISO in this volume was warranted in part because its contrast to the other organizations has highlighted their state-centric similarity.

State-centric international trade organizations may be classified into four categories: those with no environment-friendly hard law (APEC, MERCOSUR, and AFTA), those with little environment-friendly rule development (WTO), those with moderately environment-friendly rule development (NAFTA and perhaps the FTAA), and those with the most environment-friendly rule development (EU).

International Trade Organizations with No Environment-Friendly Hard Law: AFTA, APEC, and MERCOSUR

As seen in chapter 8, APEC has not developed any environment-friendly rules. Despite efforts by NGOs and the U.S. government to establish such rules in APEC—despite high-profile meetings of APEC environment ministers, agreement on a set of "sustainable development" principles, and several "capacity-building" seminars and workshops—no trade-environment rules have been adopted, no collective trade-environment policies debated, and no effective trade-environment institutions developed. Nothing of substance has emerged.

APEC is not the only trade organization that has not developed environment-friendly hard law or institutions. For example, neither AFTA nor MERCOSUR has developed any environment-friendly hard law. Nongovernmental organizations in South America and Southeast Asia have lobbied to put environmental issues on the MERCOSUR and ASEAN trade agendas, respectively. In ASEAN, these efforts have been unsuccessful. MERCOSUR member states have considered a draft protocol on environmental matters[4] that has been championed by Brazil (the country with the region's most advanced and effective environmental management system), but the protocol's terms are entirely hortatory, and Argentina has blocked its adoption.[5]

International Trade Organizations with Little Environment-Friendly Rule Development: GATT/WTO

Trade-environment issues have been a topic of hot debate in the GATT/WTO system, but trade-environment rules are less well developed and less environment friendly in the GATT/WTO than in various other trade organizations, such as the NAFTA and the EU.

Three sets of GATT/WTO rules are most relevant to defining the conditions under which a green country can ban imports that threaten the maintenance of its chosen levels of domestic health, safety, and environmental protection. First, Article XX—the GATT's "general exceptions"—allows import bans, discrimination against imports, and other deviations from the GATT's rules in specified circumstances, including some relating to the conservation of exhaustible natural resources and some relating to human, animal, or plant life, health, or safety. Second, the Uruguay Round Agreement on the Application of Sanitary and Phytosanitary Measures (SPS)[6] covers measures relating to human, animal, and plant health and safety in agriculture, including, inter alia, pesticide and fungicide tolerances and inspection rules for meat. Third, the Agreement on Technical Barriers to Trade (TBT)[7] was designed mainly to ensure that technical standards and regulations not addressed by the SPS Agreement are not used for protectionist purposes. The general rule under the GATT, the SPS Agreement, and the TBT Agreement is that each country may maintain regulations necessary to protect domestic life and health and conserve exhaustible natural resources and may determine for itself the level of risk it deems appropriate to embody in its product standards.[8] In general, the importation of products not meeting those standards may be prohibited. Each country may provisionally prohibit imports of goods while national control, inspection, and approval procedures (e.g., FDA approval) are under way.[9] These environment-friendly rules are qualified to ensure that they are not used as disguised means of protectionism. Hence, product standards that limit imports must be applied on a most-favored-nation (MFN) basis,[10] must be subject to national treatment disciplines,[11] must not "arbitrarily or unjustifiably discriminate" against imports,[12] and must not be "more trade restrictive than necessary"[13] to achieve the chosen level of environmental protection.[14] The SPS measures either must conform with international standards, guidelines, or recommendations—in which case they are deemed GATT consistent—or must not be maintained "without sufficient scientific evidence" of a relationship to the harm to be avoided.[15] This balance may be considered friendly to the environment within the jurisdiction of a WTO member with relatively stringent environmental standards, inasmuch as members can generally ban imports that would undermine their domestic environmental protection. However, qualifications of that right may be used to attack the WTO legality of national environmental laws, as the decision in the WTO Beef Hormones case[16] has shown. Moreover, the GATT/WTO approach will not likely increase environmental protection in countries with relatively weak standards to the same extent that harmonization at a high level of protection would.[17] The net result of these GATT/WTO rules will be maintenance of, but little improvement in, the level of global environmental protection.

The GATT/WTO dispute settlement system has only once condoned a challenged trade restriction aimed at extrajurisdictional environmental activity—and in that case it did so only provisionally and only after guidelines implementing the restriction were substantially amended to comply with a previous WTO Appellate Body decision ruling the restriction WTO illegal. Developing countries have consistently opposed a right of importing countries under the GATT to impose any trade restriction or duty surcharge on goods produced in countries with less stringent processes and production methods (PPMs).[18] In addition, there has been no agreement to harmonize PPMs at a high level of environmental protection. GATT Article XX provides exceptions to the GATT's liberal trade rules, including actions necessary for the protection of human, animal, or plant life or health[19] or the conservation of exhaustible natural resources.[20] Those provisions were interpreted, in the *Tuna II* decision,[21] to permit import restrictions for the protection of health or exhaustible natural resources only within the national jurisdiction of the importing party.[22] The subsequent and more authoritative 1998 *Shrimp-Turtle* Appellate Body Report[23] effectively overrules the *Tuna II* decision on the jurisdictional limitation of the relevant Article XX exception, suggesting that the exhaustible natural resources in question need not be located within the jurisdiction of the country imposing import restrictions. As argued in chapters 2 and 3, this represents a potentially major environment-friendly shift in GATT/WTO jurisprudence. However, that Appellate Body Report expressly avoided a decision on the jurisdictional scope of Article XX(g), analyzed several factors that must be considered in determining whether such import measures might be deemed WTO illegal on grounds that they were "arbitrary" or unjustifiably "discriminatory," and ruled that the U.S. shrimp-turtle law then in effect was WTO inconsistent. After substantial changes in the guidelines implementing the U.S. shrimp-turtle law and serious ongoing U.S. efforts to negotiate a multilateral agreement on sea turtle conservation, both of which were catalyzed by the 1998 *Shrimp-Turtle* Appellate Body Report, a WTO Panel held in June 2001 that the U.S. shrimp-turtle law was being applied in a WTO-consistent manner. Nonetheless, that Panel suggested that the U.S. law could be considered WTO consistent only provisionally, as long as there were serious ongoing efforts to negotiate a multilateral agreement. Moreover, as suggested in chapter 3, the factors considered by the *Shrimp-Turtle* Appellate Body limit the circumstances under which unilateral import measures aimed at extrajurisdictional activity would be found WTO legal. And the GATT and WTO dispute settlement systems still have never upheld a challenged import restriction that the importing country tried to justify solely on grounds that it considered the way those goods were produced or obtained environmentally unsound. Developing countries have cheered the stringency of this doctrine and the associated legal outcomes, fearing "eco-imperialism" by the United States and other relatively green countries.

Transboundary remediation efforts have never been negotiated under GATT auspices or in the shadow of GATT negotiations. In 1994, in meetings associated with establishing a work program for the WTO's Committee on Trade and Environment (CTE), the possibility of addressing transboundary remediation was met with assertions that such work would extend beyond the GATT's legal competence.[24]

Finally, the GATT/WTO institutions for addressing trade and environment issues have very limited mandates, offering limited avenues for the development of trade-environment rules and participation by environmental NGOs. Trade-environment issues are discussed primarily in three fora: the Committee on Sanitary and Phytosanitary Measures, which administers the SPS Agreement; the Committee on Technical Barriers to Trade, which administers the TBT Agreement; and the CTE. The CTE was effectively created in a 1994 ministerial decision[25] at the signing of the Uruguay Round Final Act and was charged with reporting to the WTO's trade ministers on several trade-environment topics, such as "the relationship between environmental policies relevant to trade and environmental measures with significant trade effects and the provisions of the multilateral trading system" (i.e., the domestic health, safety, and environmental protection issues) and "the relationship between the provisions of the multilateral trading system and trade measures for environmental purposes, including those pursuant to multilateral environmental agreements" (i.e., one dimension of the extrajurisdictional activity issue).[26] As described in chapter 2, the CTE process has deadlocked along North-South lines in its efforts to reach agreement on new trade-environment rules.

The WTO dispute settlement process adjudicates trade-environment disputes, but resolution of these disputes entails scrutinizing the trade friendliness of environmental laws—not whether a WTO member's actions or laws are appropriately green.[27] The 1998 *Shrimp-Turtle* Appellate Body Report makes clear that WTO dispute settlement panels may accept amicus curiae briefs from NGOs or others, but the panels are not obligated to do so, and many developed countries have warned against panels doing so. Moreover, only the governments of WTO members have standing to request dispute settlement and participate directly in the adjudicative process, and only officials of WTO member governments and members of the WTO secretariat may attend oral argument and receive most official WTO documents relating to the dispute, whose distribution to persons outside government is prohibited—-despite U.S. government demands, described in chapter 2, for broader participation and greater transparency in WTO dispute settlement.

International Trade Organizations with Moderately Environment-Friendly Rule Development: NAFTA and Perhaps the FTAA

The system of trade-environment rules and institutions established by the NAFTA and the North American Agreement on Environmental Cooperation (NAAEC)[28] (hereafter the "NAFTA/NAAEC system") are far more developed and environment-friendly than in the GATT/WTO. And, as suggested in chapter 7, while trade-environment rules in an FTAA are unlikely to be as developed and environment-friendly as those in NAFTA, there is good reason to believe that they might be more developed and environment-friendly than those in the GATT/WTO. An evaluation of the NAFTA/NAAEC system is followed by speculation on the environment-friendliness of the FTAA rules currently being negotiated.

The NAFTA rules on the use of trade measures to protect domestic human, animal, plant, and environmental health and safety are similar to those in the GATT/WTO. The NAFTA provisions on sanitary and phytosanitary measures were adapted from nearly final versions of the Uruguay Round SPS Agreement, described previously.[29] On technical barriers to trade, the parties to the NAFTA expressly agreed to adhere to the GATT/WTO TBT Agreement[30]—again adopting the GATT/WTO approach.[31] Both the NAFTA and the GATT/WTO rules establish the right of a party to ban imports that in its view do not meet the appropriate level of domestic health, safety, and environmental protection, subject to some general tests intended to ensure that the restrictions are not a disguised means of trade protectionism.

Problems raised by extrajurisdictional activity are addressed more fully and in a more environment-friendly way in the NAFTA/NAAEC system than in the GATT/WTO. The NAFTA/NAAEC system expressly permits a party, in specified circumstances, to impose an import ban as legitimate retaliation for environmental activities that would otherwise be considered beyond its jurisdiction.[32] The NAFTA prohibits most import restrictions unless they are used to protect health or to conserve exhaustible natural resources within the jurisdiction of the importing country. However, unlike the GATT/WTO, the NAFTA expressly provides that import restrictions may be applied to enforce specified multilateral environmental agreements (MEAs), such as the Convention on International Trade of Endangered Species of Wild Fauna and Flora (CITES),[33] the Montreal Protocol on Substances That Deplete the Ozone Layer,[34] and the Basel Convention on the Control of Transboundary Movements of Hazardous Wastes and Their Disposal.[35]

More significant, the NAFTA/NAAEC system effectively increased the stringency of *applied* PPMs in Mexico. At the time the NAFTA was negotiated, reviews of Mexican PPMs suggested that, on the books, they were generally equivalent to those in the United States; the bigger problem was that Mexican PPMs were not enforced.[36] As explained in chapter 6, the NAAEC resolves the problem by providing that a party government may have recourse to dispute settlement to challenge another party's "persistent pattern of failure to enforce" domestic environmental measures; demonstration of such a pattern and the failure to cure it gives rise to a monetary fine against the nonenforcing party and, eventually, a right to trade retaliation if the pattern of failure to enforce is not cured.[37] The NAFTA also permits environmental NGOs to submit a formal report "that a Party is failing to effectively enforce" to specified trinational authorities, which may then prepare a factual record on the issue; that record may serve as a basis for further action by the parties on enforcement matters.[38] This set of solutions to problems associated with Mexican environmental law enforcement appears to have been enormously successful.[39]

In the shadow of the NAFTA negotiations, motivated by the same political forces that demanded a solution to other trade-environment issues, and building on foundations established in the 1983 La Paz Agreement on transboundary pollution,[40] Mexico and the United States agreed to a multi-billion-dollar cleanup and environmental infrastructure development project that concentrates on a 100-kilometer area on either side of the border.[41] These activities are financed partly by the North American Development Bank (NADBank), which is jointly managed and operated by Mexico and the United States and coordinated in part by a Mexico-U.S. Border Environment Cooperation Commission (BECC), created, inter alia, to certify border cleanup and environmental infrastructure projects that are eligible for NADBank financing. The United States and Mexico each pledged to contribute half the NADBank's $450 million of paid-in capital and half the $2.55 billion in callable capital.[42] While it was estimated that this $3 billion capitalization might be leveraged to support up to $9 billion in border cleanup projects,[43] to date the NADBank has not been used to finance as many projects as originally projected.[44]

Finally, NAFTA/NAAEC trade-environment institutions are substantially more well-developed and environment-friendly than those in the WTO. Legislative and administrative issues concerning trade and environment matters are entertained in multiple fora that are analogous to their GATT/WTO counterparts.[45] But unlike the GATT/WTO, which has only the CTE to focus exclusively on trade-environment issues, the NAAEC created a broad set of institutions charged with that exclusive focus and with ensuring adherence to specified standards of environmental protection. These institutions perform legislative, judicial, and administrative functions. The Commission for Environmental Cooperation (CEC) is run by the Council, which is composed of cabinet-level representatives from each of the three member states and is empowered, inter alia, to oversee implementation of the NAAEC and assess the environmental impact of proposed projects likely to cause significant transboundary environmental effects. The CEC Council is serviced by a secretariat, which provides technical and administrative support, prepares factual reports on matters subject to the Agreement on Environmental Cooperation, and considers submissions from NGOs regarding a party's failure to enforce its environmental measures. The Joint Public Advisory Committee, composed of five members of the public from each party, advises the Council and provides information to the secretariat. Like the GATT/WTO, the NAFTA/NAAEC system has a dispute settlement process that grants standing only to party governments. But unlike the GATT/WTO, the NAAEC allows environmental NGOs to take formal action that may indirectly initiate a dispute.[46] Moreover, given the political sensitivity of trade-environment issues to both the United States and Mexico, especially in the light of the substantive legal standards (e.g., "persistent failure to enforce"), an extraordinary dispute settlement procedure was established whereby persistent nonenforcement may lead to trade sanctions.[47] In addition, under the NAFTA/NAAEC system, several entities monitor not only the trade-friendliness of national environmental measures (as in the GATT/WTO) but also the environment-friendliness of national measures. Monitoring is conducted not only by complainant party governments (as in the GATT/WTO) but also by the CEC Secretariat, the CEC Council, the Joint Public Advisory Committee, and NGOs, which may submit data, reports, or complaints to the CEC Council or Secretariat. In contrast to the GATT/WTO institutions, this is a complex web of institutions focusing exclusively on trade-environment issues, performing many more environment-friendly functions and comprising several distinct function-specific units, each with a clearly defined trade-environment mandate and multiple sources of input from governments, NGOs, and scientific and technical experts.

Any analysis of trade-environment rules to be developed in an FTAA would be speculative, of course, since those rules are the subject of ongoing negotiation. But there is reason to believe that the FTAA may embody somewhat environment-friendly rules and institutions. In 1998, the U.S. government—representing the most powerful single country participating in the FTAA negotiations—"insisted on" and won establishment of an FTAA committee to hear views from environmentalists, which the U.S. Trade Representative said would ensure that environmental measures are considered in the FTAA.[48] And in 1999, the developing countries agreed to the inclusion of environmental issues and standards in the negotiations.[49] Moreover, four of the countries participating in the negotiations—Canada, Chile, Mexico, and the United States—are already parties to trade agreements that embody significant trade-environment undertakings.[50] Hence, there is a sense among negotiators that the final product may contain trade-environment provisions that are more environment-friendly than those in the WTO agreements.

Nonetheless, it is unlikely that trade-environment undertakings in the FTAA will be as well developed or as environment-friendly as those in the NAFTA/NAAEC system. As argued in chapter 7, hemispheric concerns about environmental issues are more diffuse than those in the U.S.-Mexico border region. Moreover, U.S. power to dictate outcomes is less concentrated in the hemispheric context than in North America. Hence, trade-environment rules in the FTAA will likely fall somewhere between the GATT/WTO and the NAFTA/NAAEC system on the environment-friendly rule development continuum.

The International Trade Organization with the Most Environment-Friendly Rule Development: The European Union

The analysis in chapter 5 suggests that Europe has developed quite environment-friendly rules and institutions. Indeed, of the organizations examined in this volume, the European Union maintains the most well-developed and environment-friendly trade-environment rules and institutions.

The European Union permits member states to prohibit the import of goods insofar as "necessary" to meet the importing country's chosen level of environmental or health risk.[51] This right is circumscribed by a set of tests that do not consider environmental concerns alone but the principle of free trade as well: The import restriction must be maintained in a manner that provides for national treatment and MFN treatment, and evidence that harm would result from nonapplication of the measure must be based on sound science.[52] But the European Union also provides for "harmonization" of member states' environmental, health and safety standards.[53] As EU environmental measures[54] must be based on "a high level of protection,"[55] the EU harmonization process may be described as "upward harmonization" (i.e., harmonization of standards at a high level of environmental, health, and safety protection). Taken together, these approaches have led to more extensive cross-national environment-friendly convergence on the domestic environmental protection issue than in any other international organization.

The European Union goes further than any other international trade organization in addressing extrajurisdictional activities of concern to the greener members. Its rules specifically permit some import bans directed at poor environmental protection that is taking place outside a member state's jurisdiction. For example, EU member states are required to ban imports from other member states and from outside the Community of goods embodying animal parts covered by CITES (plus all species of dolphin and cetacean products), the EC fur seal ban (1983), and the EC whale ban (1981). In addition, under some directives the member states are required to ban imports of goods from outside the Community not produced in accordance with specified EU PPMs.[56] And at least one European Court of Justice (ECJ) decision suggests that a member state may maintain a national environmental rule that is more stringent than EU or international standards and that bans the importation of goods from other member states, with the intention of protecting animal life outside its border.[57] Perhaps more significant, the European Union has engaged in an upward harmonization or approximation exercise of dozens of PPM standards and has adopted over 200 directives dealing with air, water, waste, and chemicals.[58] Those exercises have been subject to the requirements that the directives use a "high level of protection," and member states are generally allowed to maintain more stringent standards.[59]

Transboundary remediation also takes place under EU auspices and action, pursuant to Title XIX of the European Community (EC) Treaty or in the shadow of Community activity. For example, the 1979 Directive on Conservation of Wild Birds requires some member states to restore wild birds' habitat. Directives contemplated under Article 174 of the EC Treaty would require polluters throughout the Community to remediate specific sites where toxic wastes have contaminated soil.[60] And the Convention on the Protection of the Rhine against Chemical Pollution, which was negotiated in the shadow of Community environmental cooperation, accepted by the European Union, and made to conform with EU directives on discharging certain dangerous substances into the aquatic environment, provides for remediation of the Rhine River.[61] National cost sharing or EU support for remediation is either provided for expressly in legal instruments prescribing the remediation, as in the case of the Rhine River,[62] or effected by means of payments from the Cohesion Fund [63] or other funds.[64]

Finally, EU trade-environment institutions are highly developed, perform many functions, and provide many avenues for participation by NGOs. The absence of a unanimity requirement makes environmental and standards harmonization in the European Union easier to undertake than in any other organization examined in this volume, and safeguards ensure that national environmental measures will not be replaced by less stringent EU standards.[65] Issues concerning legislation and administration of trade-environment matters may be raised by member states in the Council; private individuals, NGOs, or corporate lobbyists before the Commission; scientific and technical advisers before standards-setting bodies organized by the Commission; and political parties in the European Parliament.[66] The ECJ adjudicates trade-environment disputes and offers standing to member states, private individuals, business organizations, and the Commission.[67] Moreover, in contrast to the domestic status of law promulgated by the other trade organizations examined in this volume, EU law enjoys unqualified supremacy in all member states.[68] And some EU laws have direct effect in all member states.[69] Therefore, the status of EU law in the member states creates the possibility of legislating environmental regulations or creating other environmental rules in Brussels that must be enforced by the national courts of all member states despite inaction by a national legislature or the existence of prior inconsistent national law; this possibility does not exist in any other international trade organization. Compliance with all major aspects of EU trade-environment measures is monitored, including the trade-friendliness of national environmental measures, the environment-friendliness of national measures, national implementation of Community standards, and national implementation of remediation requirements.[70] Finally, a member state's infringement of an environmental directive (which generally does not have direct effect in member states) is subject to several legal procedures intended to establish compliance.[71]

The Environment-Friendliness Rule Development Continuum

Figure 10.1 depicts a continuum illustrating the extent to which different international trade organizations are developing environment-friendly rules and institutions. Based on the foregoing analysis, trade organizations are ranked in terms of the extent to which their rules and institutions are environment-friendly. The most complex, well-developed, and environment-friendly rules are those of the European Union. At the other extreme, environment-friendly hard law has not yet developed in AFTA, APEC, or MERCOSUR. The other trade organizations rest in between and may be ranked in ascending order of environment-friendliness: the WTO, FTAA (probably), and the NAFTA/NAAEC system.

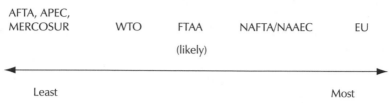

Figure 10.1   Trade-Environment Rule Development in International Trade Organizations

EXPLAINING THE EXTENT OF ENVIRONMENT-FRIENDLY RULE DEVELOPMENT IN INTERNATIONAL TRADE ORGANIZATIONS: STATE POWER AND INTERESTS

What explains the extent of environment-friendly rule development in the international trade organizations considered here? The case studies in this volume have shown that trade-environment rule development in international trade organizations is mostly a result of bargaining among the organization's members. In some organizations, like the EU and the GATT/WTO, judicial action may have marginally advanced the development of environment-friendly rules, but almost always within the bounds of substantive rules consented to by the members.

Institutionalist analyses suggest functional reasons for cooperation on trade-environment issues, and they may theorize about why international organizations vary in the extent of rule development,[72] but they cannot explain variance among the organizations in the environment-friendliness of their rules. Rationalist-institutionalist accounts are good at explaining the demand for international organizations: International organizations help solve cooperation problems and other market failures, facilitating Pareto-improving outcomes among constituent member states.[73] This implies that highly developed international organizations, such as the European Union, will solve many market failures, presumably including those relating to the environment (e.g., reducing transactions costs among members,[74] offering monitoring that solves prisoners' dilemmas by enhancing assurance and verification,[75] reducing the risk of a "race toward the bottom,"[76] internalizing environmental externalities, and so on) and will have broad and deep rules. But such analyses offer little basis for explaining or predicting the extent to which a particular international organization's rules will be environment-friendly largely because specification of the environmental interests of particular nations are exogenous to the models.

Moreover, even if an institutionalist model could specify the environmental interests of particular nations, the basis of a complete explanation for reconciling competing state interests is exogenous to institutionalist models. Faced with competing state interests, institutionalists often turn to decision-making rules for an explanation, but those rule are only part of the story. Decision-making rules on trade-environment issues themselves change, as seen in the case of the European Union. And in some organizations, such as the WTO, a consensus decision-making rule prevails, a rule that offers no obvious explanation as to how competing state interests are reconciled. Hence, if different nations have different interests (e.g., some are greener than others), whose interests will prevail? Will a regulatory floor that prevents a "race toward the bottom" be high or low? To what extent will the organization facilitate a solution to environmental externalities? Will internalization costs be borne by the polluter (i.e., "polluter pays") or by those who would otherwise bear the cost of the externality in a Coasian bargain? Rationalist-institutionalist accounts cannot fully explain variance in the environment-friendliness of trade organization rule development.

Liberal accounts may be better at explaining the sources and range of trade-environment interests represented by national governments in international organizations, but these analyses also provide incomplete explanations of variance across organizations in the extent of environment-friendliness. For example, liberal neofunctionalists[77] might argue that environmental issues are a "spillover" that comes onto the trade agenda as integration deepens. And what some have called a "structural liberal" account[78] might suggest that environmental NGOs champion environmental protection in international trade organizations, that business interests are less keen on environment-friendly rule development, and that developed countries (in which environmental NGOs are often powerful domestically) are more likely than developing countries to champion environment-friendly rule development. But what is the outcome of the resulting confrontation on trade-environment issues between developed and developing countries in a particular international organization? Why? What are the processes by which the confrontation resolves? How is the confrontation likely to evolve? Liberal answers to those questions are bound to be incomplete since liberalism offers no account of relative state power (in terms of national capacity to affect outcomes)—no account as to which states prevail among those championing and those opposing environment-friendly rule development in an organization, the contexts in and processes by which power is exercised to resolve the confrontation, and (more dynamically) the frequency with which those contexts and processes emerge. Therefore, liberalism cannot fully explain variance in the environment-friendliness of rule development across international trade organizations.

Ultimately, any complete explanation of the extent of environment-friendly rule development in an international organization must account for state power. As explained in chapter 1, for realists, powerful states set the rules of international organizations, and those rules advance the interests of powerful states.[79] Yet, as also suggested in chapter 1, realism offers a very limited account of state interests: Interests must usually be assumed or derived from a model (often a liberal model of preference formation)[80] that supplements realism.

An explanation of variance in environment-friendly rule development across international trade organizations requires understanding the structure of state power and interests in each organization. The extent of environment-friendly rule development in an international organizations depends on the extent of northern state power in the organization, the extent of economic integration in the organization (since the salience of trade-environment issues in northern countries is directly related to the extent of integration), and the geographic scope of the organization (since the salience of environmental externalities and other environmental concerns dissipates as geographic scope increases). Elaboration of these findings is served by considering the structure of trade-environment interests and power in international trade organizations.

The Structure of State Interests on Trade-Environment Issues

The structure of state interests on trade-environment issues is defined by three relationships. First, in the trade-environment context, richer is greener. Richer countries tend to adopt more stringent environmental standards and regulations than poorer countries,[81] which suggests that richer countries are more likely than poorer countries to be concerned about international environmental externalities and a possible "race toward the bottom." For reasons beyond the scope of this volume, Japan is the only major trading power that provides an exception to the rule.[82] But in accordance with the "richer is greener" expectation, only highly developed countries (e.g., the United States and Germany) have been the *demandeurs* of substantially more environment-friendly hard law in international trade organizations. And in trade organizations where there are no highly developed countries, either trade-environment issues have not been raised (e.g., as in AFTA) or trade-environment principles have been raised by a *relatively* affluent member of the organization but its proposal has been merely hortatory (e.g., the draft protocol championed by Brazil in MERCOSUR). The trade-environment agenda is driven by relatively wealthy states with relatively stringent environmental regulations.[83]

Second, deeper integration is greener. As integration deepens through liberalization among members of a trade organization, the richer, greener countries' interest in the development of environment-friendly rules also increases. This increased interest may be considered a "spillover" from initial, previous, or ongoing efforts at integration.[84] As integration deepens among members of a trade organization, previously "domestic" regulations (such as environmental rules, product standards, intellectual property rules, and competition policy) find their way onto the integration agenda:[85] Once overt border protection (such as tariffs and quotas) is withdrawn, leveling the playing field may require, inter alia, harmonizing or approximating technical and product standards and PPMs. Domestic interest groups in richer countries with relatively well developed and stringent regulatory regimes find many regulatory issues increasingly salient as integration deepens. This perception applies, in particular, to environmental NGOs, consumer groups, and labor unions in these countries, which lobby their governments to address those issues in an environment-friendly way.[86]

The logic of this relationship between deeper integration and the interest of richer, greener countries in the development of environment-friendly rules becomes clearer by considering each of the four sets of trade-environment issues that have received the most attention in the last decade. Environmentalists, consumer advocates, and labor unions often argue that liberalization increases the threat posed by imports to domestic health and safety standards, as imports with unsafe or dirty characteristics will face fewer trade barriers. From the perspective of those who want states to be able to maintain trade measures aimed at extrajurisdictional activity because they are worried about a "race toward the bottom," liberalization increases the probability that production will be located in poorer countries with less stringent environmental standards since liberalization means that goods produced there will face lowered barriers to their export into wealthier, greener countries. Liberalization increases concerns about border-area environmental degradation, as more people and goods travel through the border region and as trade creation combines with consideration of transportation costs to yield the establishment of more industries in border regions, thereby raising interest in transboundary remediation. And as liberalization increases the salience of the foregoing trade-environment concerns, it also raises the question whether institutions are constituted to perform appropriate functions. Thus, ceteris paribus, in trade organizations with one or more highly developed countries, deeper integration is greener.

A comparison of the results of the NAFTA and WTO Uruguay Round trade-environment negotiations helps illustrate the "deeper integration is greener" relationship. These negotiations were concluded within a year of each other, by the same U.S. administration. The NAFTA established deeper integration, of course, than the Uruguay Round. American demands in the NAFTA negotiations—and the results—were more environment-friendly than those in the Uruguay Round. Similarly, the European experience is consistent with the "deeper integration is greener" relationship: As suggested in chapter 5, as integration has deepened in Europe, greener countries like Germany and Denmark have demanded—and obtained—increasingly environment-friendly rules in the treaties that have governed the EC.[87]

Third, trade organizations with at least one highly developed country and member states in close proximity to each other are greener. Richer, greener countries have more reason to be concerned about trade-environment problems with countries in close proximity than with countries located far away. Countries in close proximity to each other may share common watersheds, air basins, and other tightly connected ecosystems. Environmental externalities from neighboring country sources are likely to impose greater costs than externalities from sources in countries located far away. The threat of a "race toward the bottom" is more serious in situations when investment and production can move just across the border than when it would have to relocate much farther away. Hence, countries in close proximity have a greater interest in joint environmental management than countries located far away from each other. Thus, for example, chapter 7 shows that for these reasons, U.S. interest in highly developed, environment-friendly rules and institutions in the NAFTA context has been more pronounced than its interest in highly developed environment-friendly rules in a hemispheric FTAA.

The Structure of State Power on Trade-Environment Issues

Richer countries not only are the *demandeurs* in trade-environment negotiations but also tend to be more powerful in trade negotiations than poorer countries. In the international trade context, "power" may be seen as a function of relative market size.[88] In all the trade organizations that have developed trade-environment rules, the richer, greener states have used their power to exert environment-friendly pressure on international trade-environment rules, coercing poorer countries into accepting greener rules (usually by threatening to close their markets to goods from those countries),[89] compensating them for doing so (usually by promising to keep open or further open their markets to those countries),[90] or signaling likely coercion or compensation.[91] For example, the United States effectively forced a resistant Mexico into signing the North American Agreement on Environmental Cooperation by refusing to conclude the NAFTA (with its attendant market opening commitments) until Mexico signed. Germany (as well as Denmark) insisted that the EC exercise in approximating environmental, health, and safety standards could move forward only if the Treaty of Rome were amended to provide that environmental directives must be based on "a high level of protection."[92] Similarly, Germany insisted that the EC's PPMs approximation exercise could take place only if the EC Treaty were amended to require that the associated directives use a "high level of protection" and if member states were generally allowed to maintain more stringent standards.[93]

Similarly, power has been the means by which the richer, greener countries have gotten the poorer, dirtier countries to accept the GATT/WTO trade-environment provisions. Most developing countries acceded to the GATT in the 1960s, and, in obtaining the guarantee of access to developed country markets implicit in accession, they had to accept the environmental exceptions of Article XX. At the conclusion of the Uruguay Round, in effect through compensation and coercion, the developing countries were induced to accept all the WTO's multilateral agreements. The European Union and the United States achieved this result by means of a legal-political maneuver that simultaneously threatened to withdraw most-favored-nation (MFN) treatment of developing country goods if those countries refused to sign the Uruguay Round's "single undertaking" (which included the SPS and TBT agreements and the Decision on Trade and the Environment) and offered them new MFN treatment with lower tariff levels if they did sign. Failure by developing countries to sign the Uruguay Round's single undertaking would have jeopardized MFN treatment of their goods because the United States and the European Union were withdrawing from GATT 1947 and joining GATT 1994, the latter of which constitutes an integral part of the single undertaking. And signing the single undertaking gave developing countries increased access to the U.S. and EU markets on an MFN basis by virtue of the decrease in tariff barriers embodied in the WTO Agreements.[94]

The relative power of richer, greener states varies across trade organizations. The more poor nations in a trade organization and the more impoverished they are, the less power richer, greener countries have to solve trade-environment problems, ceteris paribus. This is because the currency of rich-country power in trade negotiations—access to rich-country markets—has to be spread more thinly across more poor countries.

This point may be illustrated by considering the environment-friendliness of rules in regional trade organizations with different distributions of power. The NAFTA, FTAA, and APEC are regional trade organizations that have either established a free trade area or are in the process of negotiating one. As argued in chapter 7, U.S. power to solve trade-environment problems in the NAFTA/NAAEC system (where the U.S. market is a source of great power over Mexico) is greater than its power to solve trade-environment problems in the hemispheric FTAA context, which helps explain why it appears that the FTAA's rules will be less environment-friendly than those in the NAFTA/NAAEC system. By the same reasoning, of all the regional trade organizations in which the United States is a member, U.S. power to influence trade-environment outcomes is probably weakest in APEC, where other great trading nations (like China and Japan) exert considerable influence; hence, despite U.S. demands in APEC, no environment-friendly rules have been adopted there.

By similar reasoning, while U.S. power to solve trade-environment problems through the NAFTA/NAAEC system (where the U.S. market is a source of great power over Mexico) may be roughly equivalent to the power of various northern European countries (such as Germany, Denmark, the Netherlands, Sweden, and Finland) to solve trade-environment problems through the European Union (where those northern European markets are a source of great power over Greece, Portugal, Spain, and Italy), combined U.S. and northern European power is less effective in the WTO because that market power must be used to solve trade-environment problems with scores of developing countries. This helps explain why the WTO is less environment-friendly than the EU and the NAFTA/NAAEC system.

Thus, power and interests explain why environment-friendly rules are most well developed in the European Union (the organization in which integration is deepest and the market power of northern European countries suffices to bring about such rules), why they are moderately well developed in the NAFTA/NAAEC system (and perhaps will be in the FTAA), why they are poorly developed in the WTO (an organization in which, by comparison to the foregoing, integration is shallow and the power of richer, greener countries' markets to bring about trade-environment solutions is not high), and why there is environment-friendly hard law in neither APEC (an organization with little integration and where U.S. power is very limited) nor AFTA or MERCOSUR (where there are no rich, green *demandeur* countries).

CONCLUSION: REGIONAL TRAJECTORIES, QUALIFICATIONS TO THE APPROACH, AND IMPLICATIONS FOR POLICY

The Dynamics of Regime Building and the Regionalization of Trade-Environment Rule Development

This model also helps explain and predict how trade-environment rules are likely to develop over time. In accordance with the expectation and observation that environment-friendly solutions to trade-environment issues assume more importance for richer, powerful countries as trade barriers fall, the cases examined in this volume show that when powerful countries engage in an integration-deepening exercise, they require enhanced trade-environment solutions as part of the package they bring home for domestic ratification.[95] Hence the related argument, consistent with earlier studies by this author[96] and others such as David Vogel:[97] As liberalization becomes more extensive among members of a trade organization, powerful green states both demand an increasingly environment-friendly web of trade-environment rules and institutions in the organization and use their power to get it.

Thus, for example, in the GATT/WTO system, it is only since 1990 that economic integration seems to have reached a threshold at which trade-environment issues have become highly salient. The only trade-environment issues raised by GATT/WTO negotiators in the first forty years of the GATT's existence related to the right of a country to restrict imports for purposes of domestic environmental protection, health, or safety. The other trade-environment issues emerged only in 1990—seemingly from out of nowhere—after decades of trade-deepening and in the final phase of the Uruguay Round, which was the GATT system's deepest integration exercise. Within only a few years, trade-environment issues had become among the most high-profile topics being considered in the WTO. In 1999, when WTO ministers met in Seattle to try to launch another round of trade-deepening negotiations, the trade-environment debate heated up into a clear North-South confrontation, while environmentalists protested (and some rioted) in the streets.

The history of the EU provides a more complete illustration of the dynamic relationship between series of deepening integration and environment-friendly rule development. The will of Germany and other green EU member states to use their power on trade-environment issues has increased as European integration has deepened:[98] With each exercise in deepening, these countries have insisted on and obtained more environment-friendly convergence. Accordingly, environmental policy in Europe's poorer countries has proliferated in large part because of European integration.[99] Specifically, with each step of deepening, the European Union has adopted legislative rules that make it easier to achieve environment-friendly convergence. The Treaty of Rome nowhere mentions the environment; until 1987, harmonization of standards had to be undertaken pursuant to what was Article 100 of the treaty,[100] by unanimous vote, under the theory that harmonization was necessary to stop distortion of competition.[101] As deeper integration was pursued under the Single European Act (SEA), legislative processes for harmonization (or approximation) and environmental decisions were made more environment-friendly. Harmonization decisions under what was Article 100A of the EC Treaty, as amended by the SEA[102]—relating to completion of the single market—could be taken by qualified majority voting (QMV), subject to codecision, provided that standards were based on a "high level of protection" and member states could maintain more stringent standards. In addition, Articles 130r to 130t[103] were added, permitting the adoption of environmental measures unrelated to completion of the single market by a unanimous vote of the Council, with a right of member states to adopt more stringent measures.[104] With a step toward still deeper integration via the Maastricht Treaty, what was Article 100 was left largely untouched, while what were Articles 130r to 130t were made even more environment-friendly. At Germany's insistence,[105] most decisions taken on the environment under those articles have since been taken by QMV, subject to coparticipation, provided that they "shall aim at a high level of protection." The right of member states to adopt more stringent measures has remained intact.[106] And with the most recent, relatively small step toward deeper integration, via the Treaty of Amsterdam, the former Article 100A was amended to expressly permit any member state, subject to a review procedure, to introduce new national law based on new scientific evidence relating to protection of the environment on grounds that a problem specific to that member state has emerged subsequent to adoption of a harmonizing measure.[107]

This relationship between deepening integration and the greening of trade law, combined with a pattern of economic integration that has taken a decidedly regional turn in the last twenty years,[108] explains why trade-environment rules are developing increasingly along regional trajectories and less along a multilateral path. In the past two decades, trade liberalization has taken place more rapidly and deeply in regional organizations than in the GATT/WTO multilateral system. Since 1979, the GATT/WTO system has launched and concluded only one trade round. In the same period, the NAFTA, AFTA, APEC, and MERCOSUR were created, FTAA negotiations were launched, and the EC has deepened considerably through the Single European Act, Maastricht, and Amsterdam. As economic integration has deepened more rapidly on a regional than multilateral basis, so has the development of environment-friendly rules. Moving forward, realist theory[109] and recent developments[110] provide reason to expect that the GATT/WTO system will continue to face big obstacles to rapid liberalization and to trade-environment rule development and that regional economic integration and regional environment-friendly rule development will continue to develop more rapidly. Indeed, limited northern power to advance the trade-environment agenda is becoming one of the obstacles to further multilateral trade liberalization. Together these relationships explain the enhancement of Western environmental protection as it relates to trade but suggest that further development of trade-environment rules will take place along regional paths, particularly in Europe and the Americas.

Some Qualifications to the Analysis

This account of trade-environment rule development has some significant limits and qualifications.[111] For example, in explaining state interests, it simplifies the domestic politics of developed states. Indeed, at its most structural realist, parsimonious extreme, the model presented here deduces state interests in trade-environment rules from level of development, extent of integration among member states, and geographic scope of the organization,[112] ignoring details on the operation of domestic politics. In so doing, the approach risks losing precision in its evaluation of state interests. For example, this model implies that trade-environment issues are on the international policy agenda to stay since economic integration has reached a threshold depth in several international organizations with highly developed countries. Consistent with that expectation, for example, it seems highly unlikely that vocal support and demonstrations for trade-environment rule development will wither away in the United States. Nonetheless, some U.S. trade policy analysts have suggested the possibility that business interests opposed to developing trade-environment rules might begin consistently trumping the power of environmental NGOs in U.S. trade politics, yielding a U.S. government position that does not champion environment-friendly rule development. To the extent that the model used here delves into reductionist domestic politics, it loses some of its realist character and parsimony and becomes an increasingly liberal story.[113]

In addition, the approach used here (realism supplemented by a structural liberal theory of preference formation) does not intrinsically admit or explain the possible impact of institutional procedural rules feeding back onto underlying state interests.[114] Some contributors to this volume have suggested that trade-environment rule development may depend on the extent to which institutional rules and procedures offer avenues for participation to environmental NGOs. In chapters 2 and 8, these institutionalists show that in places like the WTO and APEC, where NGOs are not given a chance to participate directly in the international organization processes, trade-environment rules are not developing. A modified structural realist[115] or transnational liberal might admit the possibility that procedures offering direct civil society participation could accelerate the development of environment-friendly trade rules: As richer, greener countries facilitate the development of such procedures, along with environment-friendly rules, direct environmental NGO participation could accelerate the development of even more environment-friendly rules. A structural realist or structural liberal argument, "unadulterated" by such a fundamentally institutionalist argument, cannot admit this possible dynamic.

Some Implications for Policy

Despite its limitations and through consciousness of them, the analysis here has demonstrated a powerful capacity at post hoc explanation of trade-environment rule development. The resulting model also has important prescriptive implications, emphasizing the importance and nature of international, top-down pressure for increased environmental protection in international trade organizations. It suggests at least three sets of policy considerations that can help facilitate the development of environment-friendly rules in trade organizations.

First, while some have suggested that trade liberalization is bad for the environment,[116] the analysis here shows that as integration deepens through liberalization in a trade organization, richer, greener countries become more interested in environment-friendly solutions to trade-environment problems and use their market power in trade negotiations to yield those solutions.[117] Therefore, this argument suggests, the development of environment-friendly rules can be facilitated by pursuing more extensive trade liberalization.

Second, the development of environment-friendly rules in trade organizations will be facilitated by actions that enhance the will and capacity of richer, greener countries to compensate poorer, dirtier countries or coerce them into action. The capacity of richer, greener countries could be enhanced in the WTO and APEC through adoption of a common position by richer, greener countries that could be presented to the developing country members. Adoption of a common position by the most powerful countries would effectively concentrate their market power in favor of a single environment-friendly proposal, helping overcome one of the primary obstacles to reaching a solution in each of those organizations: the existence of a relatively dispersed power structure. In addition, environmental NGO activity in richer, greener countries can increase the will of those countries' governments to use their power in support of environment-friendly rule development in international trade organizations.

Finally, the extent to which environment-friendly rules develop will depend in large part on which international organization is chosen as the forum for action. U.S. policymakers are currently addressing trade-environment issues in at least four alternative fora: APEC, FTAA, the NAFTA/NAAEC system, and the WTO. Some prominent commentators[118] have recommended the creation of still other international fora for resolving trade-environment issues, fora that would be multilateral and could address environmental issues more broadly defined than the trade-related issues. And some commentators and environmentalists have suggested moving multilateral trade-environment negotiations out of the WTO.[119] This study suggests that those who want trade-environment rules to develop in an environment-friendly manner may be ill-advised to move these issues into nontrade fora: It is precisely by linking trade and environment that the developed countries have gained the leverage necessary to yield environment-friendly developments. The analysis also suggests that the United States will be most successful at pursuing the development of environment-friendly trade rules through the NAFTA/NAAEC system and the FTAA: The market power of the United States in those fora is relatively favorable for advancing U.S. trade-environment preferences and will facilitate deeper integration through those organizations, which together will help spread environment-friendly rules throughout the Americas. In contrast, progress is likely to be slow in the GATT/WTO and APEC: The prospects for deeper integration in these organizations (and associated agreement on trade-environment rules) are limited by more diffuse power structures. This problem will worsen in the WTO as China, a powerful country opposed to environment-friendly rules in the WTO, accedes to membership.

NOTES

Some parts of this chapter were published previously in *The American Journal of International Law,* © The American Society of International Law. They are reproduced here with permission.

1. Law is conventionally classified as "hard" or "soft" according to whether it imposes binding obligations. While some have recently argued that soft law may be effective under particular circumstances, it is difficult to argue that soft law is more likely than hard law to result in the behavior suggested by the rule. H. L. A. Hart, *The Concept of Law* (Oxford: Clarendon Press, 1961), 77–96. For arguments suggesting the effectiveness of soft law, see, for example, Kal Raustiala and David G. Viktor, "Conclusions," in David G. Viktor, Kal Raustiala, and Eugene B. Skolinkoff, eds., *The Implementation and Effectiveness of Environmental Commitments: Theory and Practice* (Cambridge: MIT Press, 1998), 685. There have been recent efforts to redefine whether law is "hard" or "soft" along additional dimensions. See, for example, Kenneth W. Abbott and Duncan Snidal, "Hard Law and Soft Law in International Governance," *International Organization* 54, no. 3 (summer 2000): 421–56.

2. Comprising Argentina, Paraguay, Uruguay, and Brazil, the Southern Cone Common Market (MERCOSUR) represents a total population of 190 million individuals, living in an area larger than the total surface of the European continent, covering more than 12 million square kilometers. In 1993, the combined gross domestic product of these four nations was approximately U.S.\$715 billion. See <http://www.americasnet.com/mauritz/mercosur/english/page01.html>, visited January 20, 2000.

3. The Association of Southeast Asian Nations was established by the Bangkok Declaration in 1967. The original nations were Indonesia, Malaysia, Singapore, the Philippines, and Thailand. By 2000, membership had expanded to also include Brunei, Laos, Myanmar, and Vietnam.

4. Protocolo Adicional al Tratado de Asunción Sobre Medio Ambiente (on file with author).

5. On the absence of progress in MERCOSUR generally, see Diana Tussie and Patricia Vasquez, "Regional Integration and Building Blocks," in Diana Tussie, ed., *The Environment and International Trade Negotiations: Developing Country Stakes* (London: Macmillan, 2000).

6. The SPS Agreement was concluded as part of the Uruguay Round agricultural negotiations and catalyzed primarily by EU-U.S. rows over health and safety measures relating to beef, wine, and other agricultural products. Agreement on the Application of Sanitary and Phytosanitary Measures, April 15, 1994.

7. The TBT Agreement is applied multilaterally through the Uruguay Round Final Act. Agreement on Technical Barriers to Trade, April 15, 1994.

8. Agreement on the Application of Sanitary and Phytosanitary Measures, April 15,

1994, Articles 2 and 5, Agreement Establishing the World Trade Organization, Annex 1A, in Final Act Embodying the Results of the Uruguay Round of Multilateral Trade Negotiations, Marrakesh, April 15, 1994, p. 69 (hereinafter Final Act); Agreement on Technical Barriers to Trade, April 15, 1994, preamble, ibid., 17; GATT. See also GATT Dispute Panel, Thailand-Restrictions on Importation and Internal Taxes on Cigarettes (hereinafter *Thailand Cigarettes*), November 7, 1990, GATT, B.I.S.D. (37th Supp.) (1990), 200.

9. SPS Agreement, Article 5.7 and Annex C; TBT Agreement, Articles 2–4.

10. SPS Agreement, Article 2.3; TBT Agreement, Article 2.1.

11. SPS Agreement, Article 2.3; TBT Agreement, Article 2.1.

12. SPS Agreement, Article 2.3; TBT Agreement, preamble.

13. SPS Agreement, Article 2.2; TBT Agreement, Article 2.2. The SPS Agreement uses the word "necessary," while the TBT Agreement uses the word "required." See also GATT, Article XX; *Thailand Cigarettes.*

14. A footnote in the SPS Agreement clarifies the meaning of this language: To challenge an import restriction successfully under this language, the challenging party must show that another measure that would achieve the same level of protection is "reasonably available" and would be "significantly less restrictive to trade." SPS Agreement, note 3.

15. SPS Agreement, Article 2.2.

16. "European Communities—Measures concerning Meat and Meat Products (hereinafter *Beef Hormones*), Report of the Appellate Body," adopted on February 13, 1998, WTO Document WT/DS26/AB/R, WT/DS48/AB/R.

17. The GATT/WTO approach may nonetheless result in some upward harmonization via two means. First, the SPS Agreement regards conformity to international standards as GATT consistent, creating an incentive for poor countries that cannot afford testing simply to default and choose the international standard, which is generally more stringent than current developing country standards. Second, the right of wealthy green countries to ban imports that do not conform to their relatively stringent standards is likely to create market pressures on developing countries to produce products for export that meet those higher standards. On this latter point, see David Vogel, *Trading Up: Consumer and Environmental Regulation in a Global Economy* (Cambridge, Mass.: Harvard University Press, 1995).

18. WTO member governments have stated that they are committed "not to introduce WTO-inconsistent or protectionist trade restrictions or countervailing measures in an attempt to offset any real or perceived adverse domestic economic or competitiveness effects of applying environmental policies." WTO Committee on Trade and Environment Report, WTO Document PRESS/TE 014, para. 7 (November 14, 1996) (hereinafter WTO CTE Report), para. 169. The OECD secretariat defines PPM standards as standards that "specify criteria for how a product is manufactured, harvested, or taken. They encompass emission and effluent standards, certain performance or operations standards, and practices prescribed for natural resource sectors. Terms such as 'made with,' 'produced by' and 'harvested by' signify a PPM standard. . . . All PPM standards apply to the production stage, i.e., before a product is placed on the market for sale. These standards specify criteria for how a product is produced or processed. However, the PPM standard may address the environmental effects of a product all during its life-cycle, i.e., effects which may emerge when the product is produced, transported, consumed or used, and disposed of." *Typology of Trade Measures Based on Environmental Product Standards and PPM Standards: Note by the Secretariat,* Joint Session of Trade and Environment Experts, OECD Environment Directorate and Trade Directorate, COM/ENV/TD(93)89 (September 28–30, 1993).

19. GATT, Article XX(b).

20. Ibid., Article XX(g).

21. GATT Dispute Panel Report, "United States—Restrictions on Imports of Tuna," 33 I.L.M. 839 (1994) (hereinafter *Tuna II*); see also WTO CTE Report.

22. See Thomas J. Schoenbaum, "International Trade and Protection of the Environment: The Continuing Search for Reconciliation," *American Journal of International Law* l 91, no. 2: 279–78. See also WTO CTE Report (esp. para. 7).

23. "United States—Import Prohibition of Certain Shrimp and Shrimp Products, Report of the Appellate Body," WTO Document WT/DS58/AB/R, October 12, 1998 (hereinafter *Shrimp-Turtle Appellate Body Report*).

24. Confidential interview with a member of the WTO secretariat, Washington, D.C. (February 1995). This also seems to be the current view of the WTO Committee on Trade and Environment. See WTO CTE Report, para. 8. A discussion of the GATT/WTO's legal competence is beyond the scope of this chapter, but it is likely that an argument could be made that such negotiations and activities would be within the GATT's legal competence pursuant to Article XXV of the General Agreement and within the WTO's legal competence pursuant to Article III of (and the first paragraph of the preamble to) the Agreement Establishing the World Trade Organization. See Agreement Establishing the World Trade Organization, in Final Act. On the scope of GATT legal competence generally, see Frieder Roessler, "The Competence of GATT," *Journal of World Trade Law* 21 (1987): 73.

25. WTO Trade and Environment Ministerial Decision, adopted April 14, 1994, GATT Document MTN.TNC/MIN(94)/1/Rev.1 (April 11, 1994), 33 I.L.M. 1267 (1994).

26. At the insistence of many developing countries, the CTE was also charged with considering, inter alia, the "environmental benefits of removing trade restrictions and distortions" and "the need for rules . . . for the promotion of sustainable development."

27. This follows from the WTO's substantive provisions, which constrain environmental laws to the extent they are inappropriately trade restrictive (as defined in WTO rules) but do not affirmatively require any level of environmental protection.

28. North American Agreement on Environmental Cooperation, December 17, 1993, U.S.-Can.-Mex., pt. V, 32 I.L.M. 1480 (1993) (hereinafter NAAEC).

29. In December 1991, a Uruguay Round draft SPS agreement was circulated by GATT Director-General Arthur Dunkel. Draft Final Act Embodying the Results of the Uruguay Round of Multilateral Trade Negotiations, GATT Document MTN.TNC/W/FA (December 20, 1991) (hereinafter Dunkel text). That draft, known as the "Dunkel text," became the basis of the final Uruguay Round text: No significant changes were made to the trade-environment provisions of the Dunkel text, and essentially the same text is included in the Final Act. Compare Dunkel text with Final Act. The approach in the Dunkel text was incorporated into the draft NAFTA in 1992. See "Chapter Seven: Agriculture and Sanitary and Phytosanitary Measures, Section B—Sanitary and Phytosanitary Measures," Summary of NAFTA Provisions, Background, in *Message from the President of the United States Transmitting the North American Free Trade Agreement*, H.R. Document 103–159, vol. 1 (1993) (hereinafter *Presidential Message*), 89. Canadian, Mexican, and U.S. negotiators reasoned that since many countries had already agreed to those provisions in the Uruguay Round negotiations, they could also agree to them as the NAFTA's solution. And if the Uruguay Round were not successfully concluded, which was a real possibility in 1992, the NAFTA would establish an acceptable set of rules on the subject. Hence, the NAFTA negotiators adopted the Uruguay

Round rules and principles, with some minor differences that some commentators see as environment-friendly. See, for example, Jennifer Schultz, "The GATT/WTO Committee on Trade and the Environment—Toward Environmental Reform," *American Journal of International Law* 89 (1995): 427–30.

30. North American Free Trade Agreement, December 8, 11, 14, 17, 1992, Article 712.1, U.S.-Can.-Mex., 32 I.L.M. 289 (1993) (hereinafter NAFTA), Article 903.

31. "Chapter Nine: Standards-Related Measures," Summary of NAFTA Provisions, Background, in *Presidential Message,* 120–21. At the request of U.S. negotiators, the other parties agreed to make more explicit an underlying principle in the WTO TBT Agreement: The NAFTA states expressly that each party may "establish the level of protection it considers appropriate." NAFTA, Article 904(2). The only significant difference from the corresponding GATT/WTO rules is that a technical standard that has been adopted by an international standards-setting body is accepted as in compliance with the NAFTA. Since the standards adopted by international standards-setting bodies are usually more stringent than those established in poor countries, this NAFTA rule was intended by U.S. negotiators to put upward pressure on some of Mexico's technical standards; it also relieved the Mexican government's concerns that the United States might otherwise attack other Mexican standards as illegal technical barriers to trade under the NAFTA, despite their compliance with internationally agreed levels of protection.

32. For example, limited retaliation is permitted if a member state is found to have engaged in a "persistent pattern of failure to enforce" its environmental measures and does not pay NAAEC-imposed fines for that failure. NAAEC, Articles 14 and 15.

33. Convention on International Trade in Endangered Species of Wild Flora and Fauna, March 3, 1973, 27 U.S.T. 1087, 993 U.N.T.S. 243 (hereinafter CITES).

34. Montreal Protocol on Substances That Deplete the Ozone Layer, September 16, 1987, Senate Treaty Document 10, 100th Cong., 1st sess., 26 I.L.M. 1541 (1987) (hereinafter Montreal Protocol).

35. Basel Convention on the Control of Transboundary Movements of Hazardous Wastes and Their Disposal, March 22, 1989, Senate Treaty Document 5, 102nd Cong., 1st sess. (1991), 28 I.L.M. 649 (1989) (hereinafter Basel Convention).

36. See Jack I. Garvey, "Trade Law and Quality of Life-Dispute Resolution under the NAFTA Side Accords on Labor and the Environment," *American Journal of International Law* 89 (1995): 442; Kevin W. Patton, "Dispute Resolution under the North American Commission on Environmental Cooperation," *Duke Journal of Comparative and International Law* 87 (1994): 90; confidential interviews with U.S. government officials (from the Office of the U.S. Trade Representative and the Environmental Protection Agency) who negotiated NAFTA trade-environment issues, Washington, D.C. (September 1994).

37. NAAEC, Articles 14 and 15.

38. Ibid.

39. Richard H. Steinberg, "Trade-Environment Negotiations in the EU, NAFTA, and WTO: Regional Trajectories of Rule Development," *American Journal of International Law* 91, no. 2 (April 1997): esp. 249–53.

40. Agreement on Cooperation for Protection and Improvement of the Environment in the Border, August 14, 1983, U.S.-Mex., TIAS No. 10,827.

41. Agreement concerning the Establishment of a Border Environment Cooperation Commission and a North American Development Bank, November 16, 18, 1993, U.S.-Mex., 32 I.L.M. 1545 (1993).

42. Ibid., chap. II, Article II, sec. 1(b).

43. "Use of NADBank's Capital," in NADBank, NADBank's Operations and Benefits (1996) (available at <http://www.quicklink.-com/mexico/NADBank/ning1.htm>). But see Raul Hinojosa-Ojeda, "The North American Development Bank: Forging New Directions in Regional Integration Policy," *Journal of the American Planners' Association* 60 (1994): 301 (suggesting that it could be leveraged to support up to $20 billion in cleanup projects).

44. Steinberg, "Trade-Environment Negotiations in the EU, NAFTA, and WTO," 251–53.

45. The NAFTA's Committee on Sanitary and Phytosanitary Measures, Committee on Standards-Related Measures, and the North American Council are analogous to the WTO's SPS and TBT Committees and the WTO General Council, respectively.

46. An NGO may petition the CEC under NAAEC Article 13, requesting that the CEC secretariat prepare a factual record on an environmental matter for consideration by the CEC Council. Alternatively, an NGO may choose a more confrontational path, petitioning the CEC under NAAEC Article 14, alleging a party's failure to enforce its environmental law and requesting that the CEC secretariat prepare a factual record on the matter for consideration by the CEC Council. Publication of a factual record may draw enough political attention to a matter for it to be resolved; it could also lead to the establishment of a dispute settlement panel.

47. Two of the three NAFTA members must agree to send a trade-environment dispute to dispute settlement; the penalty for "persistent failure to enforce" is a fine against the losing government, not to exceed a specified amount (set initially at $20 million); nonpayment of the fine can lead to trade sanctions.

48. "Barshefsky Says Early FTAA Results Must Not Hurt Final Agreement," *Inside U.S. Trade* 16, no. 12 (March 27, 1998); "Crane Subcommittee Blasts Fisher on Fast Track, FTAA Progress," *Inside U.S. Trade* 16, no. 13 (April 3, 1998).

49. Steven Pearlstein, "Progress Made toward Western Hemisphere Free Trade Zone," *International Herald Tribune,* November 6, 1999, 8.

50. The three North American countries are, of course, parties to the NAFTA, and Chile has concluded a free trade agreement with Canada that contains some environmental obligations.

51. Consolidated Version of the Treaty Establishing the European Community, as amended by the Treaty of Amsterdam, done at Maastricht, Rome, and Amsterdam, February 7, 1992, March 25, 1957, and October 2, 1997, 37 I.L.M. 56 (1998) (hereinafter TEEC), Article 30. See also case 302/86, *Commission v. Denmark,* 1988 E.C.R. 4607, 1 C.M.L.R. 619 (1989) (Danish rules that certain beverages be sold only in recyclable bottles not inconsistent with Treaty of Rome, despite effects on intra-Community trade) (hereinafter *Danish Bottles* case). An EU member state may also impose an import ban provisionally where it has not yet established the level of risk it is willing to accept for a particular additive or emission. Case 53/80, *Officier van Justitie v. Koninklijke Kaasfabriek Eyssen BV,* 1981 E.C.R. 409, 2 C.M.L.R. 20 (1982) (European Court of Justice [ECJ] upheld Dutch ban on the use of nisin in processed cheese until clear health risks were established for maximum permissible intake) (hereinafter *Dutch Nisin* case).

52. The European Union also has a rule suggesting that the import restriction must be the least trade restrictive means necessary to effectuate the measure's legitimate purpose. See case 120/78, *Rewe-Zentral AG v. Bundesmonopolverwaltung für Branntwein,* 1979 E.C.R. 649

(German ban on French Cassis, on theory that French Cassis was low in alcoholic content and so could confuse German consumers into consuming too much alcohol, held inconsistent with Treaty of Rome) (hereinafter *Cassis de Dijon* case), and case 130/80, *Criminal Proceedings against Fabriek voor Hoogwaardige Voedingsprodukten Kelderman BV,* 1981 E.C.R. 527 (Dutch ban on French brioches held inconsistent with common market principles in the Treaty of Rome). And the European Court of Justice has interpreted the rule as requiring "proportionality"—a balancing test between the trade restrictiveness of the measure and the purpose of the measure. *Cassis de Dijon* case; case 178/84, *Commission v. Germany,* 1987 E.C.R. 1227, 1 C.M.L.R. 780 (1988) (German beer purity law, Reinheitsgebot, held to interfere impermissibly with intra-Community trade) (hereinafter *German Beer* case). It may be argued that this invites a determination by the ECJ as to the importance of the measure's purpose, effectively substituting the Court's judgment about risk aversion for that of national authorities. However, the ECJ has been careful about intruding on national judgments in adjudicating disputes over import restrictions adopted for the purposes of domestic health or environmental protection. For example, in some well-known cases, the Court has upheld national laws apparently intended for these purposes. *Danish Bottles* case; *Dutch Nisin* case. But it has struck down other national laws that do not appear to have been legitimately so intended. *German Beer* case; *Cassis de Dijon* case.

53. The European Union has engaged in a massive exercise in harmonization of product additive and emission standards. These efforts began in the late 1960s but were not successful on a large scale until the exercise culminating in the Single European Act (1987–92). By the end of 1992, the European Community had harmonized or approximated seventy-five SPS measures (including directives that established maximum allowable pesticide residues in cereals, fruits, and vegetables; a directive on the use of hormones for growing cattle; a directive on appropriate slaughterhouse veterinary and cleanliness standards; and a directive prohibiting the sale in the Community of foodstuffs that have come into contact with any type of plastic not on a positive list) and eighteen other food law measures (including directives on milk and eggs and a directive requiring member states to permit the use of 412 food additives approved by the EC Scientific Office—although each member state could still decide how much of each additive could be used and in which foods). Baker and McKenzie, *Single European Market Reporter* 29, nos. 1–4 (1994). In addition, the Community had established harmonization of EC-wide automobile emissions standards. See William F. Dietrich, "Harmonization of Automobile Emission Standards under International Trade Agreements: Lessons from the European Union Applied to the WTO and the NAFTA," *William and Mary Environmental Law and Policy Review* 20 (1996): 199.

54. That is, action taken under the TEEC, Title XIX.

55. At Germany's insistence, the Single European Act, the Maastricht Treaty, and the Treaty of Amsterdam provide that harmonized or approximated standards (i.e., action taken under the TEEC, Article 95) and EU environmental measures (i.e., action taken under the TEEC, Article 175) are to be based on "a high level of protection." TEEC Articles 95(3) and 147(2). Moreover, at Germany's and Denmark's insistence, where Community standards for purposes of completing the internal market are adopted only by "qualified majority voting" (i.e., where legislation is adopted by population-weighted voting by member states in the Council, so that the legislation may become EU law despite the objection of any particular member state), member states may maintain their own more stringent standards. Ludwig Kramer, "The Single European Act and Environment Protection: Reflections on Several New

Provisions in Community Law," *Common Market Law Review* 24 (1987): 680. See also Dirk Vandermeersch, "The Single European Act and the Environmental Policy of the European Economic Community," *Common Market Law Review* 12 (1987): 417–19. TEEC, Article 95. See also *Danish Bottles* case. And for all other Community environmental measures, member states may maintain or adopt their own more stringent standards. TEEC, Article 176. Each member state must permit imports of products from other member states that comply with unanimously established Community standards. While harmonization or approximation measures are sometimes phased in or provide for derogations by the poorest member states, most harmonization and approximation directives have required that the member states eventually meet standards that are as high as those then in place in Germany. Hence, the EU exercise in upward harmonization or approximation of standards has generally maintained domestic health and environmental protection within the greenest northern European importing countries and simultaneously increased the stringency of pesticide, fungicide, product additive, and emissions standards in the dirtier European countries.

56. For example, the EU directive on animal testing of cosmetics requires each member state to ban the importation of all cosmetics produced by companies that unnecessarily use animals to test the safety and health effects of these products. Directive 86/609/EEC, OJ L 358 (Dec. 18, 1986) and Directive 76/768/EEC, Sixth Amendment, 93/35/EC, OJ L 151 (June 23, 1993).

57. Dicta in *Dutch Red Grouse* case, described in Environment Directorate and Trade Directorate, Typology of Trade Measures Based on Environmental Product Standards and PPM Standards, OECD Document COM/ENV/TD(93)89 (September 28–30, 1993). For the *Dutch Red Grouse* case, see case 169/89, *Commission v. Netherlands,* 1990 E.C.R. 2143.

58. European Commissioner Ritt Bjerregaard, *EUROPE*, April 1996, 27.

59. For example, each member state must now limit emissions of nitrogen oxides and sulfur dioxide in accordance with the large-scale combustion directive; reduce lead content in gasoline and offer unleaded gasoline in accordance with the EC emissions directives; reduce water pollution in accordance with the water effluent directive; control or restrict the use of chemical substances in accordance with EC chemicals directives; and recycle a specified proportion of solid wastes in accordance with the solid wastes directive.

60. Remedying Damage to the Environment: Green Paper from the European Commission, COM(93)47 final.

61. Convention on the Protection of the Rhine against Chemical Pollution, December 3, 1976, reprinted in 16 I.L.M. 242 (1977). See Alexandre Kiss and Dinah Shelton, *Manual of European Environmental Law* (Cambridge: Cambridge University Press, 1993); Thomas Bernauer, "International Financing of Environmental Protection" (paper presented at the annual meeting of the American Political Science Association, New York, September 1–5, 1994) (on file with author).

62. Ibid.

63. The scope of environmental side payments made through the Cohesion Fund is set forth in Article 161 of the TEEC and the Protocol on Economic and Social Cohesion attached to the TEEC. David Wilkinson, "Maastricht and the Environment: The Implications for the EC's Environment Policy of the Treaty on European Union," *Journal of Environmental Law* 4 (1992): 225–32.

64. Kramer, "The Single European Act and Environment Protection," 673.

65. See discussion on pp. 285–86.

66. NGOs, business interests, and even political parties may participate in the several institutions that help develop Community environmental standards, which may be embodied in products or PPMs. The member states participate in standards setting through the Council and its committees, such as the Standing Committee on Foodstuffs, which was established in 1969. Scientific and technical advisers participate via committees organized by the Commission, such as the experts from the member states that constitute the Scientific Committee on Food, which was established in 1974, and the Consultative Committee on Food, which was established in 1976. Business organizations and NGOs, like the Consumers in the European Community Group, lobby the Commission on standards issues. And political parties, such as the Green Party, participate in environmental standards setting in the European Parliament.

67. And the Court may consider input from scientific and technical advisers in rendering a decision. Kramer, "The Single European Act and Environment Protection," 673; Rolf Wagenbaur, "The European Community's Policy on Implementation of Environmental Directives," *Fordham International Law Journal* 14 (1991): 470–71.

68. Case 106/77, *Amministrazione delle Finanze dello Stato v. Simmenthal S.p.A.*, 1978 E.C.R. 629.

69. Case 26/62, *Van Gend & Loos v. Nederlandse Administratie der Belastingen*, 1963 E.C.R. 1, 2 C.M.L.R. 105 (1963).

70. Monitoring is conducted by officials in former DG XI and the European Environment Agency and by means of complaints by competing member state or business organizations or NGOs. Moreover, member states are required to notify the Commission as to the status and content of national implementing legislation.

71. Under the Article 226 procedure, a letter of formal notice is sent from the Commission to a suspected infringer; that letter may be followed by a "reasoned opinion" from the Commission setting forth the factual and legal basis for concluding that a directive has been infringed; and if the situation is not remedied within two months of receiving the reasoned opinion, the Commission may take the member state before the ECJ for a declaration of infringement and an order to comply. For a more complete analysis of the Article 226 procedure, formerly known as the Article 169 procedure, see Wagenbaur, "The European Community's Policy on Implementation of Environmental Directives," 462–63, and Alan Dashwood and Robin White, "Enforcement Actions under Articles 169 and 170 EEC," *European Law Review* 14 (1989): 388. Continued noncompliance may be subject to a lump sum "penalty payment" and, ultimately, to the freezing of sizable payments from the EC Structural Funds. TEEC, Article 228. At least one commentator thinks that this latter penalty will be used only rarely. See Heinrich Kirschner, "The Framework of the European Union under the Treaty of Maastricht," *Journal of Law and Commerce* 13 (1994): 233. Wilkinson, "Maastricht and the Environment," 233. Compliance is also encouraged less directly by ECJ cases holding that a member state may be held liable for damages to an individual for failure to implement a directive, the so-called Francovich liability (cases C-6/90 and C-8/90, *Francovich v. Italian Republic*, 1991 E.C.R. I-5357). See also James E. Hanft, "Francovich and Bonifaci v. Italy: EEC Member State Liability for Failure to Implement Community Directives," *Fordham International Law Journal* 15 (1991/92): 1237, and Melanie L. Ogren, "Francovich v. Italian Republic: Should Member-States Be Directly Liable for Nonimplementation of European Union Directives?" *Transnational Lawyer* 7 (1994): 583.

72. For example, Abbott and Snidal, "Hard Law and Soft Law in International Governance."

73. Robert Keohane, *After Hegemony* (Princeton, N.J.: Princeton University Press, 1984).

74. Ibid.

75. Ken Abbott, "Trust but Verify: The Production of Information in Arms Control Agreements," *Cornell International Law Journal* 26 (1993): 1–58.

76. Richard B. Stewart, "Pyramids of Sacrifice? Problems of Federalism in Mandating State Implementation of National Environmental Policy," *Yale Law Journal* 86 (1977): 1196.

77. Ernst Haas, *The Uniting of Europe* (London: Stevens & Sons, 1958).

78. See Andrew Moravcsik, "Taking Preferences Seriously: A Liberal Theory of International Politics," *International Organization* 51, no. 4 (autumn 1997): 513–53. See also Jeffrey W. Legro and Andrew Moravcsik, "Is Anybody Still a Realist?" *International Security* 24, no. 2 (fall 1999): 5–55.

79. See Stephen D. Krasner, "Structural Causes and Regime Consequences: Regimes as Intervening Variables," in Stephen D. Krasner, ed., *International Regimes* (Ithaca, N.Y.: Cornell University Press, 1984).

80. See, for example, Moravcsik, "Taking Preferences Seriously."

81. This premise may be inferred from national positions in international negotiations and from rigorous studies by a host of scholars. See, for example, Gene M. Grossman and Alan B. Krueger, *Economic Growth and the Environment,* National Bureau of Economic Research Working Paper 4634, February 1994 (showing that air pollution levels are lower in richer countries than in poorer ones). See also Kramer, "The Single European Act and Environment Protection," esp. 680; Aaron Wildavsky, *Searching for Safety* (New Brunswick, N.J.: Transaction Books, 1988). That richer countries have more stringent environmental rules than poorer countries suggests that richer countries will produce less pollution per unit of output than poorer countries—not that richer countries produce less total pollution than poorer countries.

82. Several hypotheses for this exception may be offered. For example, perhaps Japanese policymakers consider Japan so vulnerable to claims about the relative closure of its market that they have decided to maintain a low profile at the WTO. Or perhaps the outcome of imperial Japan's experiences as a *demandeur* in international politics in the early and mid-twentieth century have created a diplomatic culture of reticence to act as a demandeur in international affairs.

83. Pure structural realist arguments deduce interests from power. See Kenneth Waltz, *Theory of International Politics* (Palo Alto, Calif.: Addison-Wesley, 1979). Consistent with such arguments, as suggested previously, a state's interest in trade-environment issues may be deduced partly, indirectly, and imperfectly from its power position: Power in the trade negotiating context correlates with level of development, which in turn is a good predictor of environment-friendliness in the trade context. Powerful states are rich states, so—consistent with the "richer is greener" thesis—rich, powerful states tend to be more supportive of green trade-environment positions than do weak, poor countries.

84. On the idea of integration "spillovers" generally, see Haas, *The Uniting of Europe,* and Ernst B. Haas, "Why Collaborate? Issue Linkage and International Regimes," *World Politics* 32 (1980): 357, and *Beyond the Nation-State* (Stanford, Calif.: Stanford University Press, 1964).

85. Several trade analysts have described "deep integration" as liberalization involving understandings on domestic as well as international topics. See, for example, Robert Lawrence, "Towards Globally Contestable Markets," in Organization for Economic Cooperation

and Development, *Market Access after the Uruguay Round: Investment, Competition and Technology Perspectives* (Washington, D.C.: OECD, 1996), 25.

86. Interests established by the operation of liberal political processes may be advanced by realist means since realism takes interests as determined exogenously. See, generally, Waltz, *Theory of International Politics* (Menlo Park: Addison-Wesley, 1979). There are several useful analyses that combine liberal state preferences, or liberal preference formation, with a realist model of politics at the international level. See, for example, Andrew Moravcsik, "Negotiating the Single European Act," *International Organization* 45 (1991): 19.

87. See also the discussion on pp. 127–28.

88. This approach to power in the trade context is similar to Albert Hirschman's. Albert Hirschman, *National Power and the Structure of Foreign Trade* (Berkeley and Los Angeles: University of California Press, 1945) (Nazi Germany developed national power over much of Eastern Europe in the 1930s through asymmetric trade opportunities and the fostering of dependence on Germany's large market).

89. For example, under the U.S. Marine Mammal Protection Act, the U.S. government may ban the importation of tuna caught by a means that kills more dolphins than the U.S. tuna fleet kills. Marine Mammal Protection Act, 16 U.S.C. §§1361–1407 (1994). Elizabeth DeSombre has identified several U.S. laws that attempt to limit imports on environmental grounds. See Elizabeth R. DeSombre, "Unilateral Action for Multilateral Goals: United States Environmental Sanctions" (draft paper presented at the annual meeting of the American Political Science Association, New York, September 1994) (on file with author). On coercive diplomacy generally, see Alexander George, David K. Hall, and William E. Simons, *The Limits of Coercive Diplomacy* (New York: Columbia University Press, 1971).

90. At times, richer, greener countries even pay cash to poorer, dirtier countries to induce improved environmental standards. See, for example, Ronald Herring, "Menaka Gandhi's Refrigerator Theory: India's Contingent Compliance with the Montreal Protocol" (conference draft presented at the annual meeting of the American Political Science Association, New York, September 6, 1994) (on file with author) (U.S. payment of $80 million compliance compensation package to China and India to induce them to accept Montreal Protocol); Raymond Clemencon, "Global Climate Change and the Trade System: Bridging the Culture Gap," *Journal of Environment and Development* 4 (1995): 29 (compensation packages are planned under the World Bank's Global Environment Facility). Professor Jody Freeman has pointed out that a debt-for-nature swap might also be considered "compensation" to a developing country for a specific environment-friendly action.

91. For example, a decision by the U.S. Trade Representative to launch an investigation under section 301 of the Trade Act of 1974, as amended, may be seen as signaling a threat to decrease market access. See Trade Act of 1974, §§301–10, Pub. Law 93–618, 88 Stat. 1978 (current version as amended at 19 U.S.C.A. §2411 [West Supp. 1996]). And a decision by a country to enter into negotiations that will create or deepen a free trade area is usually a clear signal of an offer to increase access to its market, provided that the increased access is reciprocated with trade-related promises.

92. TEEC, Articles 174 and 176; Kramer, "The Single European Act and Environment Protection," 678–82. See also Vandermeersch, "The Single European Act and the Environmental Policy of the European Economic Community," 417–19.

93. TEEC, Article 174(2). See Wilkinson, "Maastricht and the Environment," 221–39.

94. More specifically, at the end of the Uruguay Round, the United States and European

Union withdrew from the GATT 1947—which released them from the GATT 1947 MFN provision—and entered into the Agreement Establishing the World Trade Organization, which bound WTO members to the GATT 1994—which amounted to assuming a new MFN promise—along with environment-related agreements that the developing countries had threatened not to sign, such as the SPS and TBT Agreements. The GATT 1994 (combined with other Uruguay Round instruments) included new schedules of concessions offering lower tariffs than those found in the prior arrangements. See Richard H. Steinberg, "The Uruguay Round: A Legal Analysis of the Final Act," *International Quarterly* 6, no. 2 (April 1994): 62–63.

95. Robert Putnam has argued that trade negotiators must simultaneously play two "games," one at the international bargaining table and one with the legislative branch. Robert Putnam, "Diplomacy and Domestic Politics: The Logic of Two-Level Games," *International Organization* 42 (1988): 427. Negotiations on trade-environment issues may be seen as part of such a two-level game.

96. Richard H. Steinberg, "Trade-Environment Negotiations in the EU, NAFTA and GATT/WTO: State Power, Interests and the Structure of Regime Solutions," *BRIE Working Paper 75* (Berkeley, Calif.: Berkeley Roundtable on the International Economy, May 1995); Steinberg, "Trade-Environment Negotiations in the EU, NAFTA, and WTO."

97. Vogel, *Trading Up.*

98. Konrad von Moltke, "A European Perspective on Trade and the Environment," in Durwood Zaelke et al., eds., *Trade and the Environment: Law, Economics, and Policy* (Washington, D.C.: Island Press, 1993).

99. See, for example, Dimitris Stevis, "The Politics of Greek Environmental Policy," *Policy Studies Journal* 20 (1992): 695.

100. Now Article 94 of the TEEC.

101. See case 91/79, *Commission v. Italy,* 1980 E.C.R. 1099, 1106 (rejecting Italy's challenge to the Council directives on harmonization, which argued lack of competence, on the ground that "if there is no harmonization of national provisions [on the environment and health], competition may be appreciably distorted"); see also Kramer, "The Single European Act and Environment Protection," 661–62.

102. Now Article 95 of the TEEC.

103. Now Articles 174 to 176 of the TEEC.

104. See Kramer, "The Single European Act and Environment Protection"; see also Vandermeersch, "The Single European Act and the Environmental Policy of the European Economic Community."

105. Stephen Tindale, "European Environmental Policy," *DISSENT,* fall 1995, 455–56.

106. Wilkinson, "Maastricht and the Environment."

107. Article 95, para. 5, TEEC.

108. This is consistent with the neorealist argument that the world trading system is being regionalized. Stephen Krasner and Robert Gilpin, for example, have each argued that the world trading system is being regionalized as the structure of power in the system becomes more diffuse. See, for example, Krasner, "Structural Causes and Regime Consequences," and Robert Gilpin, *War and Change in World Politics* (Cambridge: Cambridge University Press, 1981).

109. Ibid.

110. The WTO's 1999 ministerial meeting in Seattle revealed deep splits between devel-

oped and developing countries and between the European Union and the United States over several issues, preventing the launch of a new round of multilateral trade negotiations. The number of protesters and the intensity of protests and riots in Seattle also suggest serious obstacles to rapid multilateral trade liberalization.

111. For a classic discussion of some of the limits of realist regime theory, see Stephen D. Krasner, "Regimes and the Limits of Realism: Regimes as Autonomous Variables," in Krasner, ed., *International Regimes.*

112. See discussion on pp. 290–92.

113. See Waltz, *Theory of International Politics.* See also Legro and Moravcsik, "Is Anybody Still a Realist?"

114. For the general point that realism does not account for feedbacks, see Krasner, "Regimes and the Limits of Realism."

115. For a definition of the term, see Krasner, "Structural Causes and Regime Consequences."

116. See, for example, Herman E. Daly, "From Adjustment to Sustainable Development: The Obstacle of Free Trade," *Loyola of Los Angeles International and Comparative Law Journal* 15 (1992): 33. See also Tindale, "European Environmental Policy," 455.

117. See discussion on pp. 292–94. See also Steinberg, "Trade-Environment Negotiations in the EU, NAFTA and GATT/WTO," *BRIE Working Paper 75;* Steinberg, "Trade-Environment Negotiations in the EU, NAFTA, and WTO"; and Vogel, *Trading Up.*

118. Daniel Esty, "GATTing the Greens—Not Just Greening the GATT," *Foreign Affairs,* November/December 1993, 32; C. Ford Runge, *Freer Trade, Protected Environment: Balancing Trade Liberalization and Environmental Interests* (New York: Council on Foreign Relations Press, 1994), 100–7.

119. See Andrea C. Durbun, "Trade and the Environment: The North-South Divide," *ENVIRONMENT,* September 1995, 16.

Index

About the Contributors

James Cameron is a founder and former director of the Trade/Environment Programme at the Foundation for International Environmental Law and Development (FIELD) at the University of London; a barrister; of counsel to Baker & McKenzie in London; a professor of law at the College of Europe in Bruges; and a director of the Global Environment and Trade Study (GETS). He also serves as special adviser to the British House of Commons Select Committee on Environment and as an adviser to the U.K. Foreign Secretary on global environmental policy. He launched the International Trade Law reports and coedited *Trade & the Environment: The Search for Balance* and *Dispute Settlement in the WTO* (with Karen Campbell, 1998).

Karen Campbell is staff counsel at West Coast Environmental Law in Vancouver, British Columbia, where she specializes in national and international environmental and trade law. From 1996 to 1998, she was a research fellow at the Foundation for International Environmental Law and Development at the University of London. She has published several articles on international environmental law and she is the coeditor of *Dispute Settlement in the WTO* (with James Cameron, 1998). She is a member of the Ontario and British Columbia bars. She has a B.A. from the University of Western Ontario; an LL.B. from Dalhousie University, Halifax; and an LL.M., with merit, from the University of London.

Sanford E. Gaines is professor of law at the University of Houston Law Center, where he teaches international environmental law and international trade regulation and serves as the codirector of the Mexican Legal Studies Program. An expert in the area of international and domestic environmental regulation, he has published several books and articles on these topics, including "Bridges to a Better Environment:

Building Cross-Border Institutions for Environmental Improvement in the U.S.-Mexico Border Area" (*Arizona Journal of International and Comparative Law,* vol. 12 [1995]); "Environmental Laws and Regulations after NAFTA" (*United States-Mexico Law Journal,* vol. 1 [1993]); and "The Polluter-Pays Principle: From Economic Equity to Environmental Ethos" (*Texas International Law Journal,* vol. 26 [1991]). He served as deputy assistant U.S. trade representative for environment and natural resources from 1992 to 1994. He served as executive director of the North American Institute in Santa Fe, New Mexico, from 1996 to 1999 and on the national advisory committee to the U.S. representative to the North American Commission on Environmental Cooperation from 1997 to 1999. He received a B.A., J.D., and M.A. in East Asian regional studies from Harvard University.

Damien Geradin is professor of law at the University of Liège Law School in Belgium, where he teaches EU economic law. He is also a director of the Regulation and Competitiveness Program at Yale University. He has been a visiting professor at the University of California, Los Angeles, School of Law, a visiting assistant professor at the Yale School of Forestry and Environmental Studies, and a visiting lecturer at Yale Law School. He is the author of many studies on trade, competition, and environmental protection published in law reviews, such as the *International and Comparative Law Quarterly,* the *Yearbook of European Law,* and the *Harvard Environmental Law Review.* His recent publications include *Trade and the Environment: A Comparative Study of EC and U.S. Law* (1997) and "Environmental Protection in Regional Trade Agreements" (with Daniel Esty), in *Regionalism and Multilateralism after the Uruguay Round* (P. Demaret et al., eds., 1997). Prior to beginning his academic career, he was a member of the Brussels bar and an associate at the international law firm of Coudert Brothers. He is a magna cum laude graduate of the University of Liège Law School and holds an LL.M from King's College London and a Ph.D. in law from Cambridge University, where he was a Humanitarian Trust Scholar in public international law.

Gustavo Grunbaum is associate counsel at Calpine Corporation in San Jose, California. Previously, he worked in the San Francisco office of the international law firm of Thelen Reid and Priest, where he specialized in international project finance and environmental law. Prior to joining private practice, he served as an intern with the Environmental Law Community Clinic, Natural Resources Defense Council, and the Office of General Counsel of the Environmental Protection Agency. He has a J.D. from Boalt Hall at the University of California, Berkeley, and a B.A. cum laude in economics/business and geography from the University of California, Los Angeles.

Naomi Roht-Arriaza is professor of law at the Hastings College of the Law. She has published a number of books and articles on the topics of human rights and environmental issues. Some of these titles include *Impunity and Human Rights in International Law and Practice* (1995), "The Need for Moral Reconstruction in the

Wake of Past Human Rights Violations: A Dialogue with Chilean Lawyer Jose Zala-quett" (*Human Rights in Political Transition: Gettysburg to Bosnia,* Robert Post and Carla Hess, eds., 1998), "The Committee on the Regions and the Role of Regional Governments in the European Union" (*Hastings International and Comparative Law Review,* vol. 20 [1997]), "Environmental Management Systems and Environmental Protection: Can ISO 14001 Be Useful within the Context of APEC?" (*Journal of Environment and Development* [1997]), and "Combating Impunity: Some Thoughts on the Way Forward" (*Law and Contemporary Problems,* vol. 59 [1997]). Professor Roht-Arriaza has also lectured extensively on the areas of trade and the environment and human rights. She received her J.D. from Boalt Hall at the University of California and an M.P.P. from the University of California, Berkeley. She is a member of the California bar and the American Society of International Law.

Gregory C. Shaffer is assistant professor of law at the University of Wisconsin Law School. He received his B.S. from Dartmouth College and his J.D. from Stanford Law School. Prior to joining the UW faculty, he worked as an international lawyer based in Paris for over seven years. His publications address such governance issues as linkages between domestic politics and international trade policy, the impact of disputes on domestic business practice in such areas as data privacy protection and genetically modified foods, the impact of trade liberalization on standards, and comparative institutional approaches to handling trade conflicts. These have been published in journals such as the *Yale Journal of International Law, Harvard Environmental Law Review, Fordham International Law Review, American Journal of International Law, European Law Journal,* and *Washington Quarterly.* He is co-editor of *Transatlantic Governance in the Global Economy* (Rowman & Littlefield 2001). He is a recipient of a U.S. National Science Foundation grant for his work on conflicts involving international trade and environmental policies within the World Trade Organization. He is a member of the steering committees of the UW Center on World Affairs and the Global Economy and UW's European Union Center.

Julie A. Soloway practices international trade and competition law with Davies Ward Phillips & Vineberg LLP in Toronto, Canada. She was formerly a research fellow at the Centre for International Studies, University of Toronto, where she specialized in the area of international trade law and completed her doctorate (S.J.D.) at the University of Toronto's Faculty of Law. She has published numerous journal articles on issues relating to trade dispute settlement, trade and the environment, and foreign investment. She has recently coauthored *Environmental Regulation and Corporate Strategy: A NAFTA Perspective* (Oxford University Press, 1999). She has also worked as a consultant to various trade associations, international organizations, and foreign governments on North American trade issues. In 1993, she graduated *cum laude* with an LL.M in international, European, and comparative law from the Vrije Universiteit Brussel.

Richard H. Steinberg is professor of law at the University of California, Los Angeles, and senior research fellow at the Berkeley Roundtable on the International Economy (BRIE) at the University of California, Berkeley. He has written over twenty articles and book chapters on international trade law and politics and recently coedited *Partners or Competitors? The Prospects for U.S.-EU Cooperation on Asian Trade* (Boulder, Colo.: Rowman & Littlefield, 1999). From 1989 to 1991, he was assistant general counsel to the U.S. trade representative. From 1991 to 1993, he practiced law at the international firm of Morrison & Foerster. He received a B.A. degree, magna cum laude, in economics and political science from Yale University (1982), a J.D. degree from Stanford Law School (1986), and a Ph.D. degree in political science from Stanford (1992). He was awarded a MacArthur Fellowship in International Security Studies in 1985 and a Ford Fellowship in Western Security and European Society for research at Harvard University in 1987–88. He is a member of the California bar, the American Society of International Law, and the Pacific Council on International Policy.

Lyuba Zarsky is founder of the Nautilus Institute for Security and Sustainable Development in Berkeley, California, and directs its Globalization and Governance Program. Her most recent publications are "The Asia-Pacific Economic Cooperation Forum and the Environment: Regional Environmental Governance in the Age of Economic Globalization" (*Colorado Journal of International Law and Policy* [1997]), "Havens, Halos, and Spaghetti: Untangling the Relationship between FDI and Environment" (in OECD, *Foreign Direct Investment and the Environment* [1999]), and "Civil Society and Urban-Industrial Environmental Governance in Asia" (*Asian Environmental Outlook* [2001]). She holds an M.A. in economics from the New School for Social Research. She has twice served on the U.S. delegation to meetings of APEC environment ministers and also serves on the Trade and Environment Policy Advisory Committee of the Office of the U.S. Trade Representative.